Quick Reference to MATERNITY NURSING

Beverly Raff, RN, PhD
Vice President-Professional Services
March of Dimes Birth Defects Foundation
White Plains, New York

Arlyne Friesner, RN, EdD
Consultant and Writer
Carle Place, New York

AN ASPEN PUBLICATION®
Aspen Publishers, Inc.

1989

Rockville, Maryland
Royal Tunbridge Wells

Library of Congress Cataloging-in-Publication Data

Raff, Beverly S.
Quick reference to maternity nursing/Beverly Raff, Arlyne Friesner.
p. cm.
"An Aspen publication."
Includes bibliographies and index.
ISBN: 0-8342-0051-1
1. Obstetrical nursing—Handbooks, manuals, etc. I. Friesner, Arlyne. II. Title.
[DNLM: 1. Obstetrical Nursing—handbooks. 2. Perinatology—handbooks.
3. Perinatology—nurses' instruction. WY 39 R136q]
RG951.R34   1989   610.73'678--dc19
DNLM/DLC
for Library of Congress
88-36801
CIP

Copyright © 1989 by Aspen Publishers, Inc.
All rights reserved.

Aspen Publishers, Inc., grants permission for photocopying for personal or internal use, or for the personal or internal use of specific clients registered with the Copyright Clearance Center (CCC). This consent is given on the condition that the copier pay a $1.00 fee plus $.12 per page for each photocopy through the CCC for photocopying beyond that permitted by the U.S. Copyright Law. The fee should be paid directly to the CCC, 21 Congress St., Salem, Massachusetts 01970.
0-8342-0051-1/89 $1.00 + .12.

This consent does not extend to other kinds of copying, such as copying for general distribution, for advertising or promotional purposes, for creating new collective works, or for resale. For information, address Aspen Publishers, Inc., 1600 Research Boulevard, Rockville, Maryland 20850.

> The authors have made every effort to ensure the accuracy of the information herein, particularly with regard to drug selection and dose. However, appropriate information sources should be consulted, especially for new or unfamiliar procedures. It is the responsibility of every practitioner to evaluate the appropriateness of a particular opinion in the context of actual clinical situations and with due consideration to new developments. Authors, editors, and the publisher cannot be held responsible for any typographical or other errors found in this book.

Editorial Services: Susan Bedford

Library of Congress Catalog Card Number: 88-36801
ISBN: 0-8342-0051-1

Printed in the United States of America

1 2 3 4 5

Table of Contents

Preface		ix
PART I—	HISTORY AND TRENDS IN MATERNAL CARE	1
Chapter 1—	Historical Background	3
Chapter 2—	Current Problems and Trends	11
	I. Modern Trends	11
	II. Current Problems	21
	III. What Remains To Be Done?	23
	IV. Changing Concepts in Maternity Care	23
PART II—	PRENATAL PERIOD	31
Chapter 3—	Reproductive System	33
	I. Male Anatomy and Physiology	33
	II. Female Anatomy	35
	III. Female Physiology	40
Chapter 4—	Family Planning	43
	I. Infertility	43
	II. Family Planning	51
	III. Nursing Process in Family Planning	67
Chapter 5—	Conception	69
	I. Fertilization	69
	II. Implantation	69
	III. After Implantation	70

Chapter 6— Fetal Development 71

    I. Fetal Physiology 76
    II. Fetal Development 76
    III. Factors Affecting Fetal Development 79

Chapter 7— Pregnancy 95

    I. Preparation for Parenthood 95
    II. Community Resources to Assist Preparation for
        Parenthood.. 96
    III. Prenatal Regimen.................................. 97
    IV. Nursing Care during the Prenatal Period
        Relating to Physical Needs 97
    V. Nursing Care during the Prenatal Period
        Relating to Psychological Needs 118
    VI. Nursing Care during the Prenatal Period
        Relating to Learning Needs....................... 121

Chapter 8— High-Risk Pregnancy 123

    I. Special Needs of High-Risk Mothers 123
    II. Factors That May Lead to a High-Risk Pregnancy 123

Chapter 9— Drugs Used during the Prenatal Period 161

PART III— THE INTRAPARTAL PERIOD...................... 177

Chapter 10—Stages of Labor and Nursing Implications.............. 179

    I. Position and Presentation 179
    II. Theoretical Courses of Labor 181
    III. Mechanisms of Labor in Vertex Presentation 182
    IV. Onset of Labor.................................... 183
    V. Stages of Labor 184
    VI. Management of Labor and Delivery Process 186

**Chapter 11—Drug and Anesthesia Administration in the
               Intrapartal Period** 211

    I. Relief of Discomfort during First Stage of Labor 211
    II. Mediating Factors Affecting Drug Use during
        Labor 211

    III. Drugs Used in the Intrapartal Period 212
    IV. Anesthesia Used during the Second and Third
        Stages of Labor 215
    V. Anesthesia for Cesarean Section 219
    VI. Nursing Intervention 220

Chapter 12—Prepared Childbirth 221

    I. Causes of Pain during Childbirth 221
    II. Exercise and Breathing Techniques 221
    III. Hypnosis 224
    IV. Nursing Intervention 224
    V. Advantages 225

Chapter 13—Complications of Labor and Delivery 227

    I. Deviations in Powers and Forces 227
    II. Passenger Abnormalities 230
    III. Placental Abnormalities 234
    IV. Abnormalities of Passage 234
    V. Operative Obstetrics 235
    VI. Induction and Augmentation of Labor 239
    VII. Accidents and Injuries in Labor and Delivery .. 249
    VIII. Nursing Care during Complications of Labor
         and Delivery 250

PART IV— THE POSTNATAL PERIOD 253

Chapter 14—Anatomy and Physiology of the Puerperium 255

    I. Definition of Puerperium 255
    II. Physiological and Anatomical Changes 255

Chapter 15—Psychology of the Puerperium 259

    I. Factors Influencing Adjustment to New Role 259
    II. Stages in Adjustment to New Role 259
    III. Postpartal Blues 262

Chapter 16—Nursing Care during Puerperium 263

    I. Nursing Goals 263
    II. Assessment and Intervention 263
    III. Drugs Used during Postpartal Period 275

Chapter 17—Breast Feeding 277

    I. Anatomy of the Breast 277
    II. Physiology 278
    III. Effect of Lactation on the Mother 278
    IV. Benefits of Breast Feeding to the Newborn 279
    V. Implications for Nursing Process 280
    VI. Contraindications to Breast Feeding 283
    VII. Breast Feeding and Drugs 283

Chapter 18—Complications of the Postpartum Period 285

    I. Postpartum Hemorrhage 285
    II. Puerperal Infection 288
    III. Noninfectious Thrombophlebitis 292
    IV. Breast Disorders 293
    V. Infections Common during Postpartum Period .. 294
    VI. Hematomas 295
    VII. Postpartum Eclampsia 296
    VIII. Postpartum Psychosis 296

PART V— NEWBORN 299

Chapter 19—Anatomy and Physiology of the Newborn 301

    I. Transition to Extrauterine Life 301
    II. Anatomy and Physiology of the Newborn 302
    III. Body Measurements 311

Chapter 20—Nursing Care of the Newborn 313

    I. Assessment 313
    II. Intervention 319

Chapter 21—High Risk Newborn 327

    I. Identification of Risk Factors 327
    II. Respiratory Problems 328
    III. Birth Injuries 335
    IV. Hemolytic Disease of Newborn 337
    V. Infections 339

Chapter 22—Birth Defects (Congenital Anomalies) and Other Complications   **347**

    I. Definition of Birth Defect...................... 347
    II. Classification 347
    III. Neural Tube Defects............................ 347
    IV. Neurological Disorders 348
    V. Congenital Heart Disease 349
    VI. Respiratory System 350
    VII. Gastrointestinal Malformations 351
    VIII. Genitourinary System........................... 352
    IX. Musculoskeletal System 353
    X. Inborn Errors of Metabolism 353
    XI. Chromosomal Aberrations 354
    XII. Baby of a Diabetic Mother...................... 355
    XIII. Postmaturity.................................... 356
    XIV. Parental Reaction to the Newborn with Complications.................................. 357

Chapter 23—Low Birthweight Infant................................ 359

    I. Definition 359
    II. Etiology of Preterm Labor and IUGR 359
    III. Prevention of Low Birthweight 361
    IV. Assessment..................................... 365
    V. Physical Characteristics of Preterm Infant....... 365
    VI. Problems of Preterm Infants 366
    VII. Problems of Small for Gestational Age (SGA) Babies 370
    VIII. Implications for Nursing Process................ 370
    IX. Parental Reaction.............................. 373

Appendix A—Laboratory Tests Used during Pregnancy...............377

Index 383

About the Authors

Preface

This compact yet comprehensive text covers the involvement of the maternity nurse at all levels of health care: preventive, curative, and rehabilitative. Written in outline format to facilitate rapid and selective retrieval of information, the book covers the physiological and psychological changes occurring in the maternity cycle and the implications of these changes.

Organized around the nursing process, the book provides essential data on assessment and interventive strategies for each period of the maternity cycle: antepartum care, intrapartum care, postpartum care, and care of the neonate. The management of high-risk pregnancies and preventive care are emphasized. All discussions are within the context of the authors' emphasis on such ethical issues as client rights and client advocacy.

In order to deliver comprehensive health care, the maternity nurse needs precise knowledge of the physiological and psychological changes occurring during the maternity cycle and an awareness of the influence of biophysical and psychosocial environmental factors on the health status and needs of the childbearing family.

The goal of this book is to provide essential knowledge needed by maternity nurses in a concise outline format. The outline format should prove helpful to student nurses who are preparing for State Board Examinations and College Proficiency Examinations. The text is also useful as a study guide to supplement a regular textbook for students who are enrolled in maternity nursing courses. The compact and accessible nature of the book makes it a useful reference manual for graduate practicing maternity nurses as well.

Part I

History and Trends in Maternal Care

Chapter 1

Historical Background

A. Early tribes of American Indians and African natives
   1. birth process relatively free of complications due to lack of disproportion between fetal head and maternal pelvis because intertribal marriages were rare
      a) major complications were abnormal presentations
   2. at time of birth, mother usually delivered child herself unless difficulty was encountered and she needed assistance of another woman
   3. over time, those women who had experience in assisting others gradually became known as midwives
      a) all knowledge of midwifery was based on experience
   4. if midwives were unable to deliver baby, medicine men and priests were called in to help through prayer
   5. childbirth associated with mystery and superstition
      a) usually celebrated with some kind of ceremony that gave thanks to the gods or warded off evil spirits
   6. most nomadic groups seemed to have less concern for the pregnant woman than did more settled groups
   7. period of recuperation varied
      a) some mothers returned to work immediately
      b) others spent days or weeks recuperating
   8. many groups practiced couvade where the father performs the act of childbearing; this ritual presumably drew away evil spirits that might harm mother and baby
B. Egyptian society (about 3,000 B.C.)
   1. highly organized society
   2. priesthood supervised abnormal deliveries
   3. majority of women delivered with assistance of midwives

4. obstetrical forceps used and cesarean sections were performed on dead mothers
5. in 1500 B.C., first recorded information about obstetrical practice found in Egyptian records
   a) descriptions of contraceptive methods found in ancient writings
   b) first pregnancy test described. Women would urinate over mixture of wheat and barley seeds mixed with dates and sand. If seeds sprouted the test was positive for pregnancy. This test may have had some success because of hormonal content of urine.

C. Greek and Roman cultures (beginning about 1000 B.C.)
   1. in early Grecian history, obstetrics was involved with religious practices, such as fertility rites
   2. Hippocratic period (460–377 B.C.)
      a) the beginning of the scientific study and practice of medicine
      b) normal deliveries assisted by midwives under supervision of physicians
      c) abnormal labor handled by physicians
      d) Hippocrates wrote about theory and practice of obstetrics
   3. obstare—Latin verb to protect or to stand by from which the word obstetrics is derived
      a) obstetrix—referred to birth attendant (midwife) who stood by the pregnant woman to give assistance
   4. Soranus of Ephesus was called the Father of Obstetrics because he was the first man to write about obstetrical theory and care
      a) wrote about podalic version
   5. Moschion practiced medicine in Rome
      a) wrote textbook for midwives
      b) improved upon Hippocrates' teachings

D. Hebrew culture
   1. although no medical assistance was given for difficult deliveries, cleanliness and good sanitation were practiced and emotional support was provided by family members

E. Eastern cultures
   1. Hindus practiced an organized system of medicine
      a) Susrata's contribution to the scientific knowledge of obstetrics included
         (1) knowledge of menstruation and gestation
         (2) establishment of prenatal and postnatal care
         (3) management of abnormal labor
         (4) use of forceps and cesarean section on dead mothers
         (5) practice of cleanliness and sanitation

F. Medieval period
   1. lack of progress in obstetrical science and practice
   2. loss of knowledge from previous cultures
   3. in Europe, a regression to mysticism in medical practice
   4. beginning of hospital and nursing services
      a) usually used only for the poor
G. Renaissance period
   1. establishment of Italian medical schools brought about increased knowledge in obstetrics
      a) Arantius described pregnant uterus and gestational development
      b) Vesalius accurately described pelvis
   2. William Harvey described circulation of the blood and physiology of pregnancy
   3. Ambrose Pare reintroduced the use of podalic version in obstetrics and helped establish first midwifery school in France. He also established obstetrical practice as part of medicine
   4. Handbook for midwives by Jakob Rueff widely used
   5. birthing chairs used for delivery
   6. Leonardo da Vinci depicted the true position of the fetus in utero
H. Seventeenth to nineteenth century
   1. 17th century
      a) Chamberlin family designed obstetrical forceps (circa 1580)
         (1) family kept information secret until 1813
      b) in 1618, Wittenberg performed first cesarean section on live mother
      c) Mauriceau referred to puerperal (childbirth) fever as an epidemic disease
   2. 18th century
      a) forceps modified by Smellie
      b) male physicians as obstetricians become fashionable
      c) obstetrical forceps presented to French Academy of Medicine by Palfyne
      d) Hunter contributed knowledge about placental anatomy
   3. colonial America
      a) used traditional English practices
         (1) deliveries attended by women
         (2) several weeks of confinement after delivery
         (3) average age at first birth was 22, with a subsequent pregnancy every 2–3 years
         (4) a child had only a 75–85% chance of surviving to age 21
            (a) in a family of seven or eight children, two or three were apt to die before the age of 10

b) many American physicians studied with Smellie and Hunter, who thereby greatly influenced American obstetrical practice
4. before 1800 less than 5% of births occurred in hospitals
5. Credé method named for and made famous by the Viennese obstetrician in 1881. At that time he used 2% $AgNO_3$ solution dropped from glass rod into eyes of newborn immediately after birth. This became routine in many countries and decreased the incidence of ophthalmia from 10% to 1%. Solution now used is 1% $AgNO_3$ (Ziegel & Cranley, 1984)

I. Twentieth century
  1. technological advances
     a) advances in anesthetics and analgesia
     b) discovery and use of antibiotics for infection control
     c) development and use of blood transfusion
     d) development and use of x-ray to determine cephalopelvic disproportion
     e) advances in general medical and surgical knowledge
     f) more accurate collection of vital statistics and improved methods of epidemiological research
     g) improved environmental sanitation and communicable disease control
     h) prenatal diagnosis and treatment
     i) fetal monitoring
     j) development of sonography and amniocentesis
     k) fetal surgery
  2. philosophical advances
     a) an important factor in improving the outcome of pregnancy during this century is the generally higher standard of living that prevails. Also, after World War II a change in focus from the person providing the care to the recipient of care brought about a change in terminology—from obstetrical care to maternity care. This broadened the scope of care to include prenatal and postnatal care, which promote the general health and wellbeing not only of the mother and child but that of the entire expanding family
     b) WHO definition of maternity care (WHO Report 1952): "The object of maternity care is to ensure that every expectant and nursing mother maintains good health, learns the art of child care, has a normal delivery, and bears healthy children. Maternity care in the narrower sense consists in the care of the pregnant woman, her safe delivery, her postnatal examination, the care of her newly born infant, and the maintenance of lactation. In

the wider sense, it begins much earlier in measures aimed to promote the health and wellbeing of the young people who are potential parents, and to help them develop the right approach to family life and to the place of the family in the community. It should also include guidance in parent-craft and in problems associated with infertility and family planning"
- c) consumerism, sparked by the interest in prepared childbirth during the 1960s, advocated for changes in obstetrical practice
    - (1) ASPO/Lamaze and International Childbirth Association formed from grassroots coalitions
    - (2) consumers advocated change through patient education and demanded family-centered care
    - (3) hospitals today actively seek patients by advertising birthing rooms, sibling visitations, and candlelight dinners for new parents
3. advances in research and knowledge
    - a) increased knowledge of the role of nutrition in the maternity cycle
    - b) increased number of hospital deliveries with excellent control of infection through improved medical and surgical asepsis and the establishment of hospital standards by accreditation agencies
    - c) increased safety in operative obstetrics
    - d) improved education to prepare professional practitioners
    - e) introduction of prepared childbirth and family-centered maternity care
    - f) increased research and progress in pharmacology
    - g) expanding knowledge in the field of genetics
    - h) treatment of the fetus in utero
    - i) improved education of health personnel in maternal and child care
        - (1) specialized training for physicians
        - (2) increased utilization of nurse-midwives for normal pregnancies and deliveries
        - (3) the advent of the clinical nurse specialist in maternal and child health
    - j) improvement of hospital standards
        - (1) accreditation has helped upgrade standards of building, maintenance, equipment, and hospital care
        - (2) infection control has reduced incidence of hospital-acquired infectious dieases
        - (3) qualifications of health care personnel employed in hospitals upgraded

       k) regionalized perinatal networks have been promoted by
          (1) federal "Improved Pregnancy Outcome Program"
          (2) Robert Wood Johnson Foundation
       l) high-risk pregnancies are detected early and referred to a specialized care facility in their region
4. governmental and voluntary programs
    a) 1900: Census Bureau established, which provided accurate statistics on population trends
    b) 1906: mortality statistics became reportable, which facilitated the development of control measures for maternal and infant morbidity and mortality
    c) 1907:
       (1) antepartal nursing care was established through the Association for Improving Living Conditions of the Poor
       (2) New York City milk supply improved through the dispensing of pasteurized milk
    d) 1909:
       (1) American Association for Study and Prevention of Infant Mortality was established to study and reduce the high infant mortality rates
       (2) first White House Conference on the "Dependent Child" resulted in
          (a) establishment of the Children's Bureau (1912), which conducted research and provided education to promote the health and welfare of children
          (b) establishment of child labor laws
    e) 1912: first child health station was started in New York City to deliver primary health care
    f) 1919: second White House Conference reorganized the Children's Bureau
    g) 1921: Sheppard-Towner Act: appropriated monies to improve health, welfare, and hygiene of mothers and children through the establishment of educational programs for health personnel and lay people
    h) 1923:
       (1) Margaret Sanger Research Bureau for planned parenthood and infertility research and assistance started
       (2) Frontier Nursing Service was established in Kentucky (utilized nurse-midwives)
    i) 1930: third White House Conference, which was devoted to all aspects of maternity and child care

j) 1935: Social Security Title V and Emergency Infant Care Act
    (1) administered by Children's Bureau
    (2) extended services to local areas through grants-in-aid
    (3) enabled states to perform the following services by providing funds for
        (a) establishment and operation of maternity clinics
        (b) operation of prenatal classes for parents
        (c) hospital maternity care for the indigent
        (d) premature care centers
        (e) public health nursing care for maternity patients
        (f) establishment and operation of well-baby clinics
k) 1940: fourth White House Conference, which was devoted to helping children grow into productive citizens in a democracy
l) 1945: United Nations World Health Organization (WHO): maternal child health given top priority in importance, along with tuberculosis and VD, as significant world health problems
    (1) UNICEF established: provided emergency food and medical supplies to mothers and children where necessary throughout the world
m) 1946: Hill-Burton Act provided funds for hospital expansion and set standards for accreditation
n) 1950: fifth White House Conference devoted to needs of children and youth
o) 1954: Manual of Standard for Hospital Care of Newborn Infants established: improved conditions in hospitals for prevention of infant morbidity and mortality
p) 1960: sixth White House Conference focused on problems of achieving full potential for youth
q) 1963: amendments to Social Security Act—"Maternal Child Health and Mental Retardation Amendments"
    (1) increased number of prenatal clinics
    (2) brought clinics to the neighborhoods where they were needed
    (3) established high-risk clinics for prenatal care
    (4) paid for hospital care, birth, prenatal care, and delivery for the needy
    (5) paid for hospital care of premature or injured babies
    (6) supported demonstration programs in comprehensive child health supervision for families that lacked motivation
r) 1970: seventh White House Conference focused on children and poverty

s) 1972: nurse practitioners functioning in extended roles
t) 1973: Child and Family Resource Program provided or made available prenatal and nutritional education
   (1) data demonstrated effectiveness of RhoGam in preventing Rh sensitivity in Rh-negative mother
u) 1975: National Advisory Council of Maternal, Infant, and Fetal Nutrition established.
   (1) WIC program: provides low-income families with supplemental food and nutrition education
   (2) Title XX: amendment to Social Security Act provides comprehensive services, which include family planning services
   (3) National Health Planning and Resources Act: provides for coordination of health care services and resources
v) 1979: designated as the Year of the Child by the United Nations to enhance care and well-being of children
w) 1983: Department of Health and Human Services published "Public Health Objectives for Pregnancy and Infant Health in the United States by the year 1990"

J. Development of maternity nursing
1. midwifery has its roots in ancient society
   a) formal training began in 18th century
   b) male physicians not involved in normal pregnancies, labor, and delivery
2. maternity nursing
   a) prior to the concept of family-centered maternity care, nursing care was based on meeting the immediate physical and technological needs of the pregnant woman
   b) today, a growing number of nurses are becoming involved with patient education throughout the maternity cycle
   c) nurses are becoming patient advocates and are assisting parents in their quest to participate fully in childbearing
3. scope of practice statements have been developed by national organizations to define general and specific nursing practice
4. specialization by nurses in the perinatal area
   a) nurse practitioner and clinical specialist roles are being incorporated into State Nurse Practice Acts

---

REFERENCE

Ziegel, E.E., & Cranley, M.S. (1984). *Obstetric nursing* (8th ed.). (p. 420). New York: MacMillan.

Chapter 2

Current Problems and Trends

I. MODERN TRENDS
A. Development of maternal-child care in U.S.: there has been a substantial improvement in the health and welfare of mothers and children over the past 50 years. This improvement is directly attributed to epidemiological research and the increased quantity and quality of health services offered. In order to understand the implications of past problems and future needs, it is essential to be familiar with statistical terms and trends in maternal and child health
  1. definitions of statistical terms—rates are for a calendar year
     a) birth rate: number of births per 1000 total population
     b) fertility rate: number of live births per 1000 population of women between the ages of 15 to 44 years
     c) neonatal mortality rate: number of deaths during first 4 weeks of life per 1000 live births
     d) fetal mortality rate or stillbirth: one in which any product of conception of 20 weeks or more gestational age dies in utero prior to birth; rate is number per 1000 live births
     e) perinatal mortality rate: number of deaths of fetuses and neonates from 20 weeks gestation to the 28th day of life per 1000 live births
     f) infant mortality rate: number of deaths of infants under 1 year of age per 1000 live births
     g) maternal mortality rate: number of maternal deaths per 100,000 live births
        (1) base was changed from 10,000 live births to 100,000 live births
  2. trends in birth rate (Figure 2-1)
     a) rates increased from 1930 to 1974 when the rate dropped to the lowest in U.S. history at 14.9 live births per 1000 population

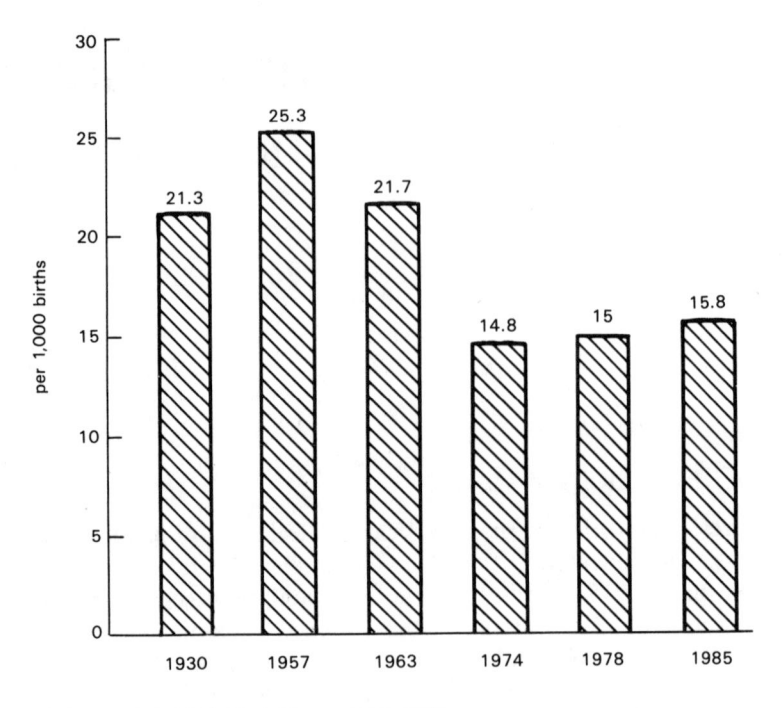

Figure 2-1 Trends in U.S. Birth Rates, 1930–1985

---

    b) 87 per 1000 women between ages 15 and 19 became pregnant in 1983, a decline of 1.6% from the 1980 rate.
    c) change in birth rate from 1984 to 1985 (Figures 2-2 and 2-3)
       (1) birth rate to teenagers increased .8%
       (2) the 35–39 year old age group had the greatest increase (4.8%) of all ages
       (3) approximately a 2% increase in the 20 to 29-year-old group
3. trends in fertility rates (Figure 2-4)
    a) the childbearing population comprises a smaller proportion of the total population, which reflects the aging population of the U.S. (Figure 2-5)
4. trends in maternal death rates (Figure 2-6)
    a) maternal death rates have steadily declined since the beginning of the century, reflecting improvements in technology, prenatal care, and living conditions
5. trends in infant death rates (Figures 2-7 and 2-8)
    a) the U.S. infant mortality ranking among 20 industrialized nations declined from sixth place in 1950–1955 to a tie for last place in 1980–1985 (*Science News*, 1986)

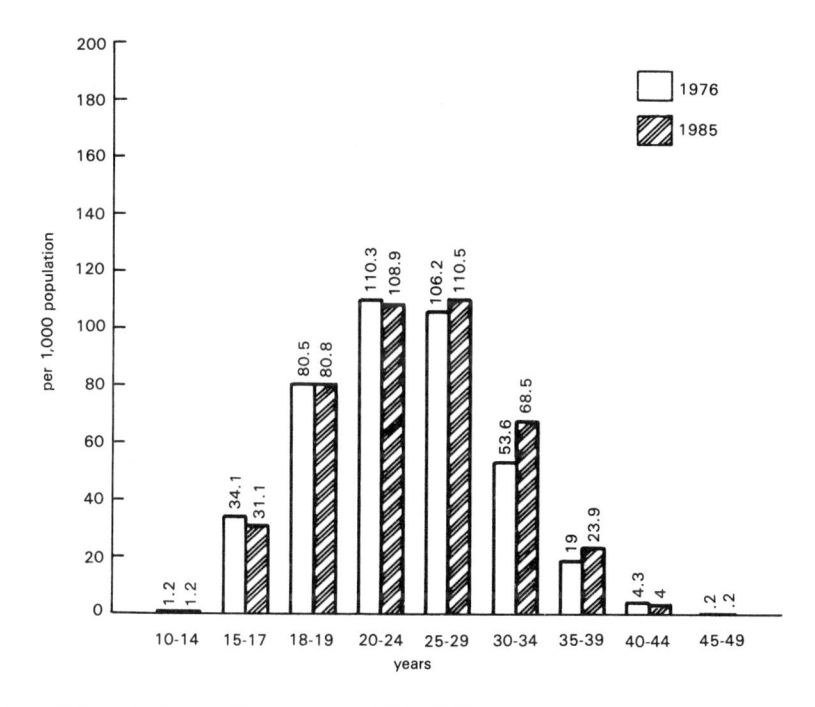

Figure 2-2 Birth Rate by Maternal Age, 1976–1985

---

    b) between 1983 and 1984 infant mortality increased in 6 of the U.S.' 22 largest cities (Hughes et al., 1987)
    c) in 1984 nearly 40,000 of the 3,669,141 children born in the U.S. died before their first birthday
    d) the Surgeon General has made it a national objective to reduce the national infant mortality rate to 9 per 1000 live births by 1990, with no racial or ethnic subgroups having a rate in excess of 12 deaths per 1000 live births
    e) from 1978 to 1984 infant mortality rates declined in approximately the same proportion for whites (22%) and blacks (20%); American Indians showed a larger decline of 31%
        (1) 1978—13.7%; 1984—9.5%
    f) the impact of AIDS on infant mortality cannot yet be accurately calculated
6. significance of statistical trends
    a) the overall statistical facts do not give an accurate picture of the differences in maternal and infant death rates for
        (1) high and low income groups
        (2) white and nonwhite groups (Figures 2-9 through 2-11)

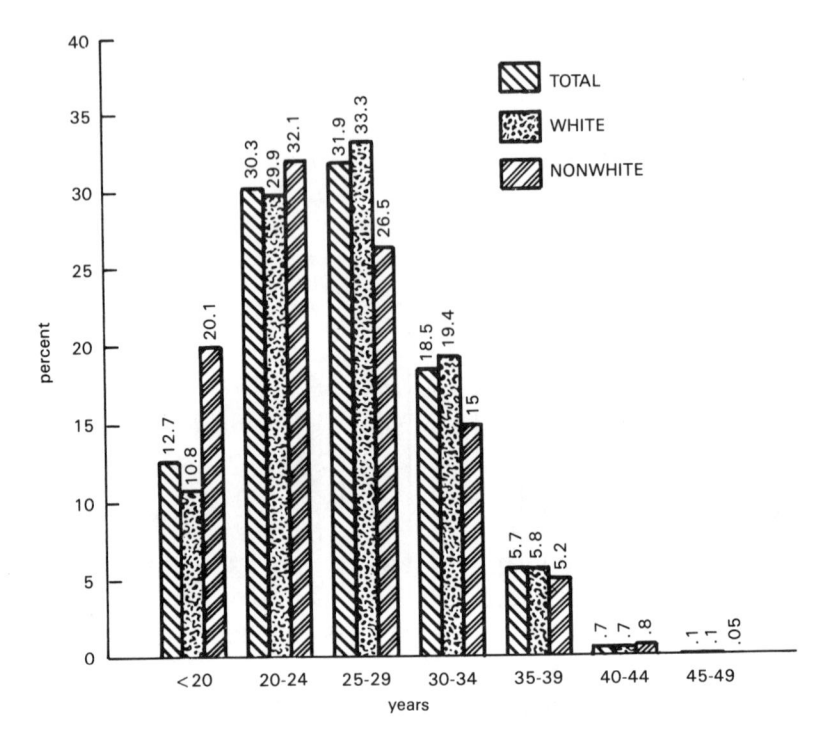

Figure 2-3 Total Births by Maternal Age and Race, 1985

---

    (3) urban and rural areas (Figures 2-12 and 2-13)
  b) low income groups, nonwhite groups, and those living in rural areas have a higher maternal and infant death rate than the national average
  c) provisional 1986 data indicate that Wyoming has the lowest infant mortality rate in the U.S. (6.9 per 1000) and Alabama the highest at 13.9 per 1000
    (1) Alabama's rate was exceeded by Washington, DC at 19.6 per 1000
 7. factors contributing to differences in infant and maternal mortality rates
  a) 6.4% of all births were of low birthweight in 1984
    (1) 5.6% of white infants and 12.4% of black infants were of low birthweights; the ratio of black to white low birthweight is over 2:1
  b) 1.19% of all births were of very low birthweight in 1984
    (1) .92% of white infants and 2.56% of black infants

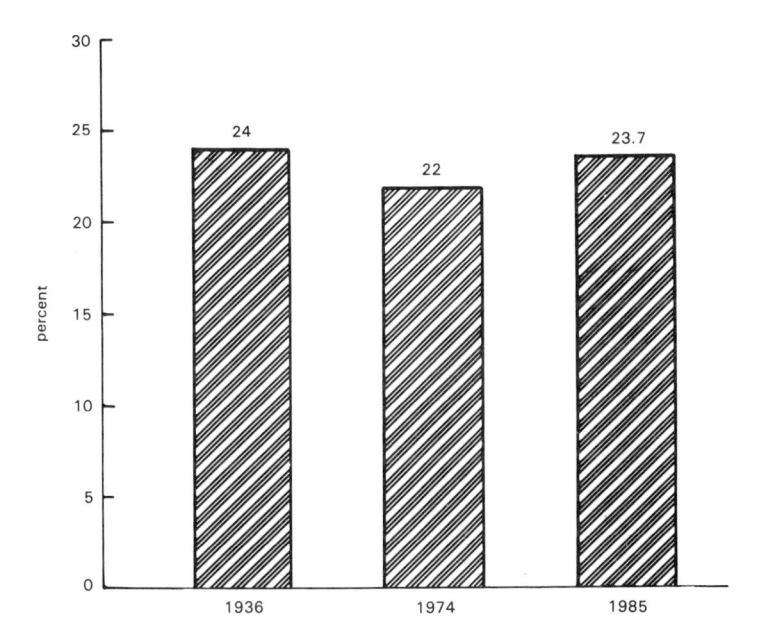

Figure 2-4 Trends in U.S. Fertility Rates, 1936–1985

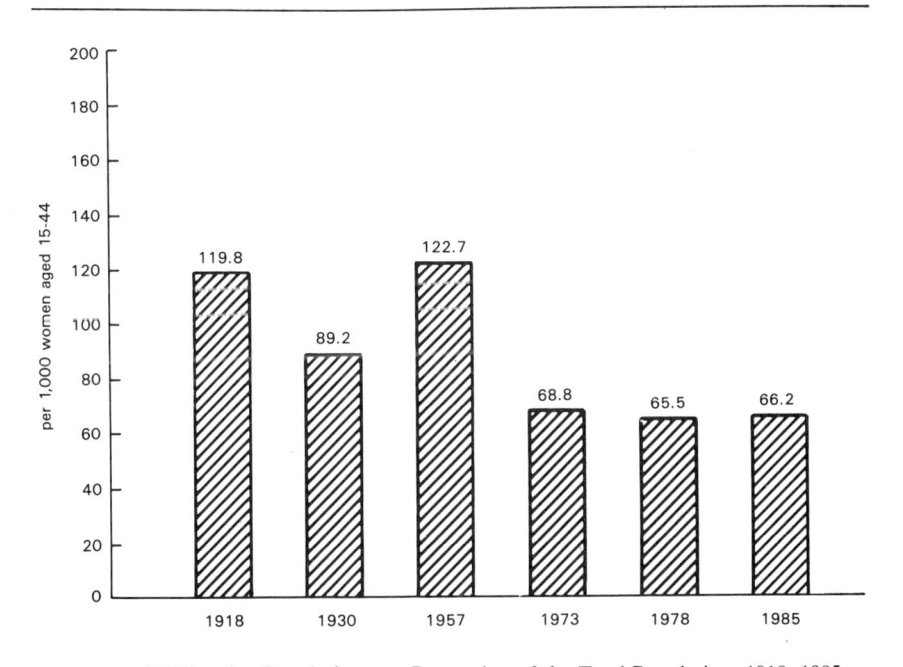

Figure 2-5 Childbearing Population as a Proportion of the Total Population, 1918–1985

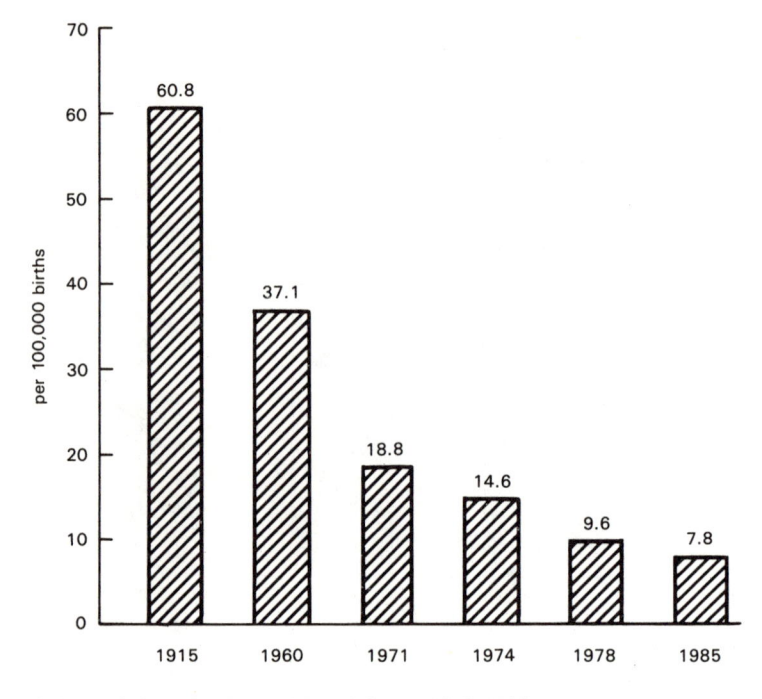

Figure 2-6 Trends in U.S. Maternal Death Rates, 1915–1985

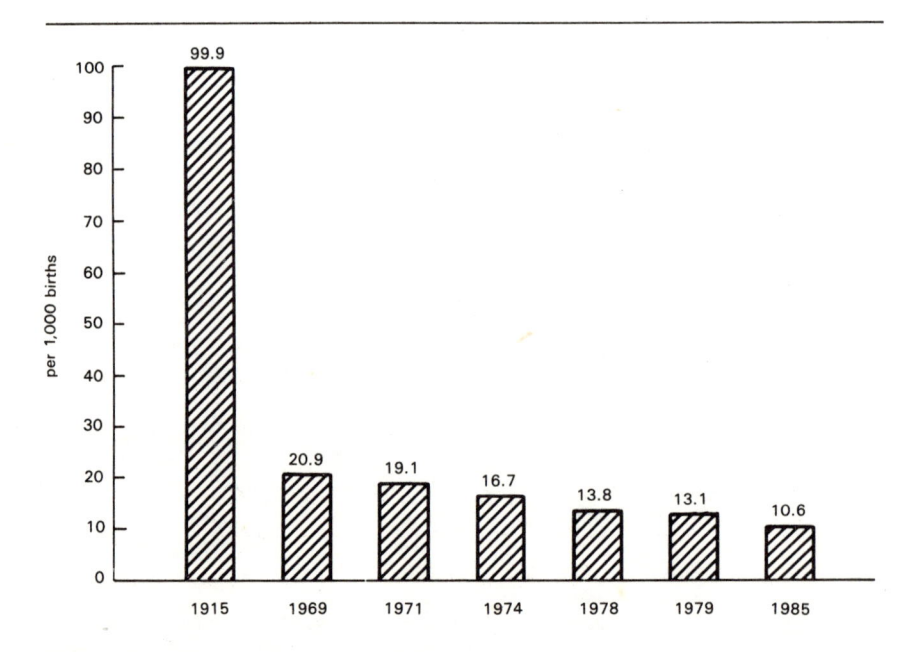

Figure 2-7 Trends in U.S. Infant Death Rates, 1915–1985

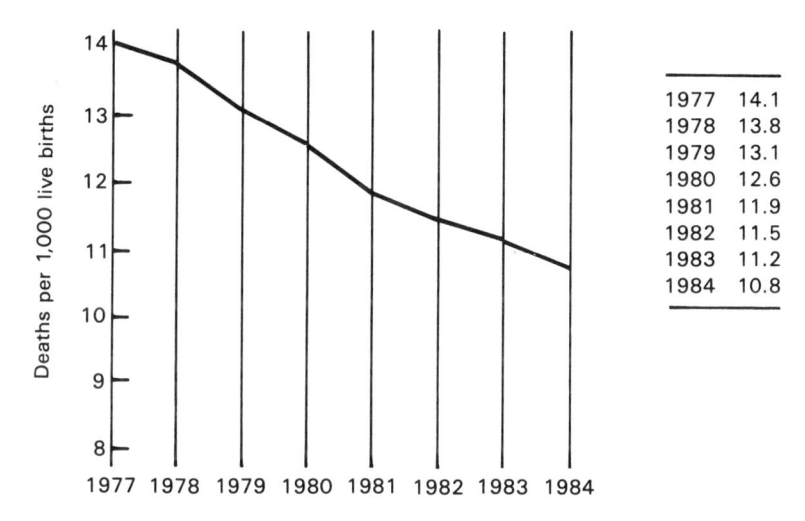

Figure 2-8 Infant Mortality Rates in the U.S., 1977–1984. *Source:* From National Center for Health Statistics, Division of Vital Statistics, National Vital Statistics System

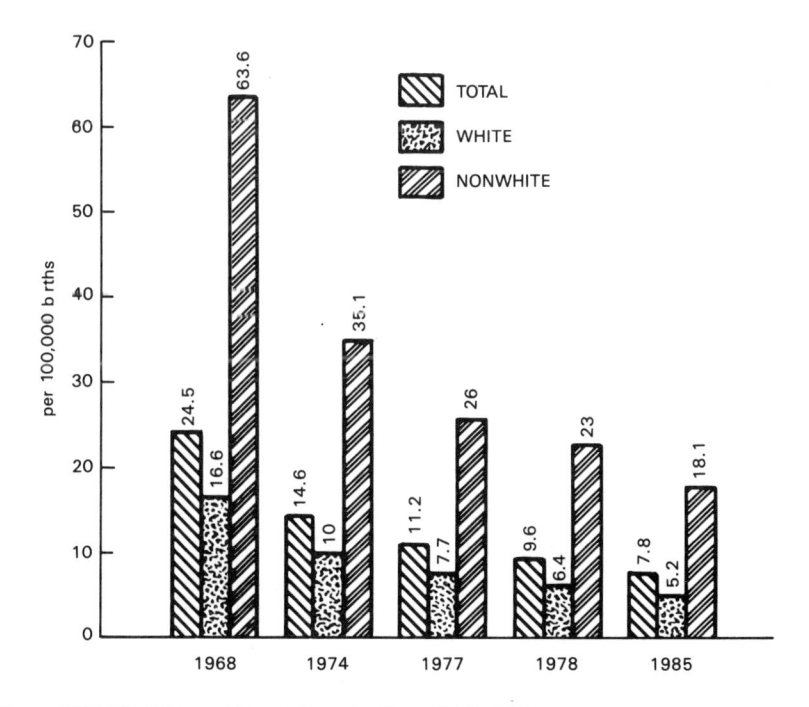

1977	14.1
1978	13.8
1979	13.1
1980	12.6
1981	11.9
1982	11.5
1983	11.2
1984	10.8

Figure 2-9 U.S. Maternal Death Rate by Race, 1968–1985

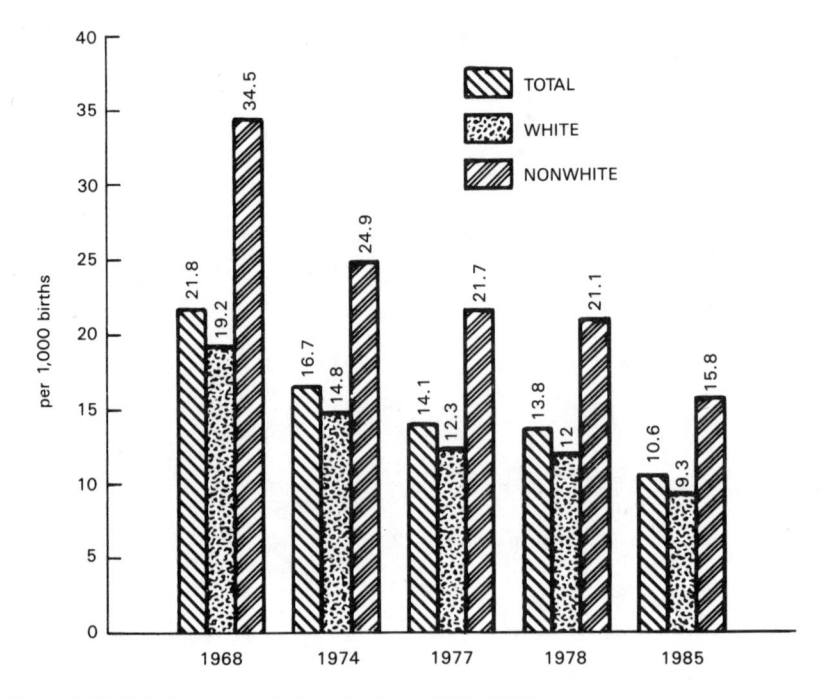

Figure 2-10 U.S. Infant Death Rate by Race, 1968–1985

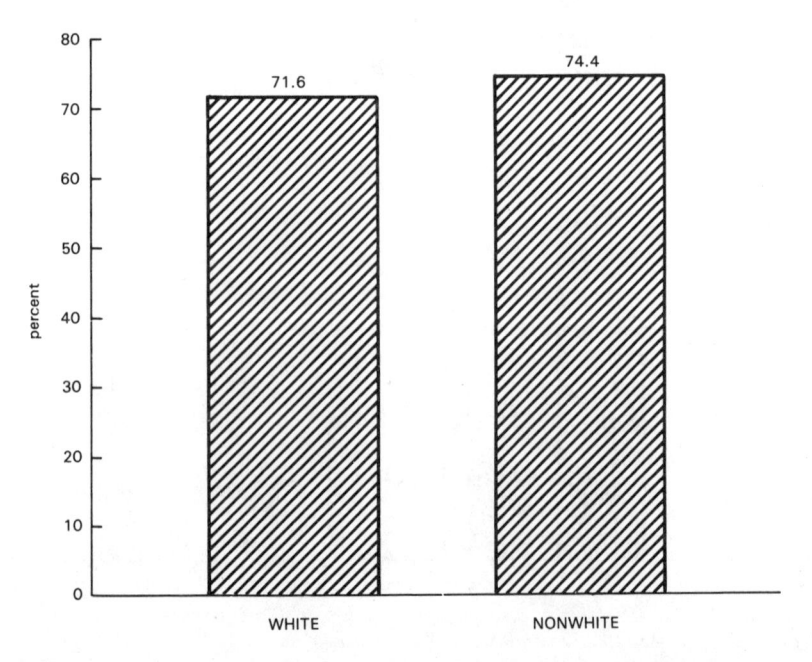

Figure 2-11 Percent Decrease in Neonatal Mortality Rate by Race, 1965–1985

Current Problems and Trends 19

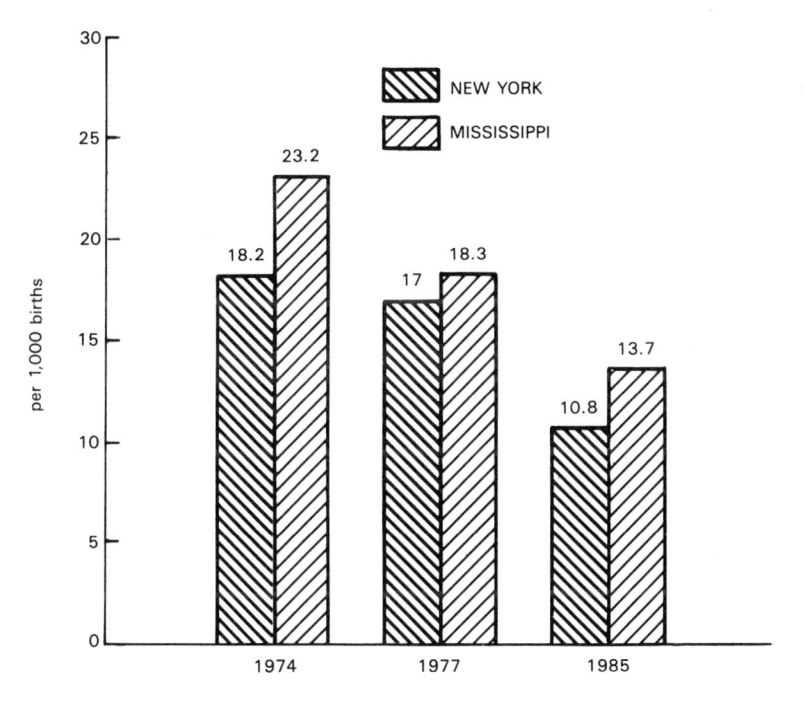

Figure 2-12 Infant Death Rate in New York and Mississippi, 1974–1985

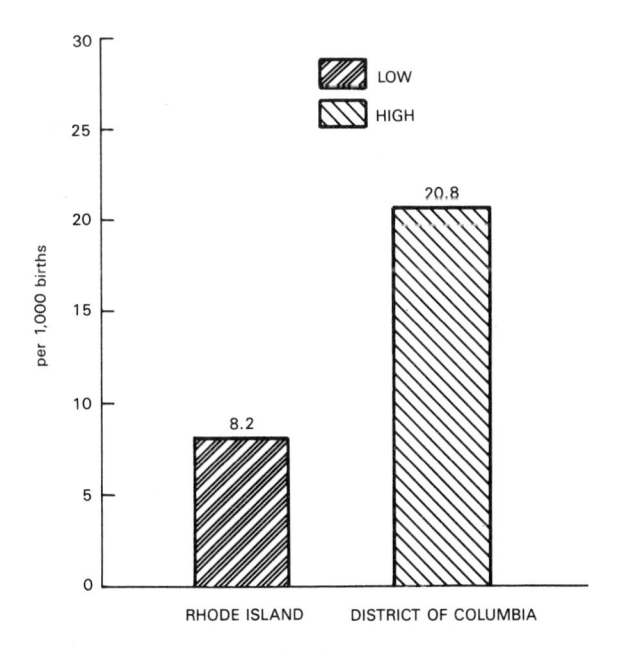

Figure 2-13 Range in U.S. Infant Mortality Rate by State, 1985

c) 79.6% of white women receive early prenatal care, whereas only 62.2% of black women enter prenatal care early (calculated by Children's Defense Fund)
d) 4.7% of white women and 9.6% of black women receive late or no prenatal care
e) 13.01% of babies were born to women under 20
   (1) 11.11% of white mothers and 23.64% of nonwhite mothers were under age 20
f) in many rural and nonwhite poverty areas, a low standard of living prevails
   (1) poor housing, sanitation, nutrition, and increased stress predispose mothers and infants to a higher incidence of morbidity and mortality
   (2) there is an increased incidence of pregnancies in adolescent mothers, leading to increased numbers of complications for mothers and infants
   (3) there is an increased incidence of out-of-wedlock pregnancies with concomitant problems
g) lack of knowledge about health in rural and poverty areas decreases motivation to seek out adequate preventive health care
h) maternal situational or economic deterrents
   (1) insufficient funds for transportation to clinics
   (2) ineligible for welfare and Medicaid
   (3) language difficulty
   (4) cultural traditions that do not include medical care
   (5) many illegal aliens are hesitant to register for care because they fear deportation
8. the Children's Defense Fund predicts that at the current rate of progress the nation will fail to meet nearly all of the Surgeon General's 1990 objectives for reducing infant mortality and low birthweight and for increasing the number of women receiving early prenatal care (Exhibit 2-1)

II. CURRENT PROBLEMS

A. Health care fails to meet the consumer's needs because it is
   1. fragmented
   2. uncoordinated

Exhibit 2-1 Public Health Objectives for Pregnancy and Infant Health in the United States by the Year 1990

Improved Health Status

1. By 1990, the national infant mortality rate (deaths for all babies up to 1 year of age) should be reduced to no more than 9 deaths per 1000 live births.
2. By 1990, the neonatal death rate (deaths for all infants up to 28 days old) should be reduced to no more than 6.5 deaths per 1000 live births.
3. By 1990, the perinatal death rate should be reduced to no more than 5.5 per 1000.
4. By 1990, no county and no racial or ethnic group of the population (*e.g.*, black, Hispanic, American Indian) should have an infant mortality rate in excess of 12 deaths per 1000 live births.
5. By 1990, the maternal mortality rate should not exceed 5 per 100,000 live births for any county or for any ethnic group (*e.g.*, black, Hispanic, American Indian).

Reduced Risk Factors

6. By 1990, low birth weight babies (less than 2500 g) should constitute no more than 5% of all live births.
7. By 1990, no county and no racial or ethnic group of the population (*e.g.*, black, Hispanic, American Indian) should have a rate of low birth weight infants (prematurely born and small-for-age infants weighing less than 2500 g) that exceeds 9% of all live births.
8. By 1990, the majority of infants should leave hospitals in car-safety carriers.

Increased Public-Professional Awareness

9. By 1990, 85% of women of childbearing age should be able to choose foods wisely (state special nutritional needs of pregnancy) and understand the hazards of smoking, alcohol, pharmaceutical products, and other drugs during pregnancy and lactation.

Improved Services-Protection

10. By 1990, virtually all women and infants should be served at levels appropriate to their need by a regionalized system of primary, secondary, and tertiary care for prenatal, maternal, and perinatal health services.
11. By 1990, the proportion of women in any county or racial or ethnic group (*e.g.*, black, Hispanic, American Indian) who obtain no prenatal care during the first trimester of pregnancy should not exceed 10 percent.
12. By 1990, virtually all newborns should be screened for metabolic disorders for which effective and efficient tests and treatments are available (*e.g.*, PKU and congenital hypothyroidism).
13. By 1990, virtually all infants should be able to participate in primary health care that includes well child care; growth development assessment; immunization; screening, diagnosis, and treatment for conditions requiring special services; appropriate counseling regarding nutrition, automobile safety, and prevention of other accidents such as poisonings.

Source: From *Promoting Health/Preventing Disease: Public Health Service Implementation for Attaining the Objectives for the Nation: Pregnancy and Infant Health,* Public Health Reports Supplement, September/October 1983: Department of Health and Human Services.

3. expensive
4. poorly distributed geographically and economically
5. impersonal and institutionally oriented
B. High maternal and infant mortality rates are found in nonwhite and rural populations
C. Maternal morbidity and mortality continue to be a problem
   1. major causes of maternal complications include
      a) hypertensive disorders of pregnancy
      b) hemorrhage
      c) infection
      d) heart disease
      e) diabetes
      f) amniotic fluid embolism
D. Infant mortality and morbidity remains a problem
   1. major causes of infant complications include
      a) prematurity
      b) congenital malformations
      c) infections
      d) respiratory complications and asphyxia
      e) blood incompatibilities
      f) sudden infant death syndrome
      g) birth injuries
E. Syndrome of poverty influences maternal and infant morbidity and mortality rates because it is associated with
   1. lack of education
   2. despair
   3. poor nutrition
   4. high birth rate
   5. lack of motivation to meet health needs
   6. poor housing and sanitation
F. Many of the legal/ethical issues facing professionals practicing in the area of maternal/infant health are not yet resolved
   1. liability associated with prenatal diagnosis, counseling, and treatment
   2. legal issues related to withholding or withdrawing treatment from newborns born very prematurely and/or with severe birth defects
   3. ethical issues relating to abortion, sterilization, prenatal surgery, as well as many other situations that have ethical implications
      a) it is a good policy for the staff to explore and clarify these issues with clergy representing different faiths
G. Number of childbearing age women who have no health coverage has increased to 9.5 million (*Health Care News,* 1987)

H. Cost cutting has reduced funding for maternal/child programs
   1. Maternal and Child Health Block program, family planning program, and migrant health center program operate at levels below that needed to maintain service at the 1981 level
I. Malpractice insurance for physicians, nurse-midwives, and nurse practitioners in obstetrics is increasingly expensive (*Hospitals,* 1986)
   1. 1983: ACOG Survey reported 9% of practitioners stopped obstetrical practice; in 1985 that number rose to 12%

III. WHAT REMAINS TO BE DONE?

A. Removal of socioeconomic factors as a barrier to adequate maternity and infant care
   1. treatment of the syndrome of poverty
B. New methodology to improve the delivery of maternal/infant health services
C. Provisions of increased education to consumers about important factors in the prevention of maternal/child disorders
D. Better utilization of health care personnel through expanded and changing roles and functions, such as nurse-midwives, nurse practitioners, and clinical nurse specialists
E. Increased numbers of health care workers in areas where shortages exist
F. Systematic planning for coordination and distribution of health facilities

IV. CHANGING CONCEPTS IN MATERNITY CARE

A. Family-centered maternity care began in the 1960s
   1. from conception until postnatal period the unit of nursing care is considered to be the family
   2. the rationale for the utilization of family-centered maternity care rather than obstetrical care is the impact that the pregnancy has on the family and the impact that the family has on the pregnancy
B. Changing nursing roles
   1. nurse-midwife: the role has evolved because of the need for increased comprehensive maternity care and the shortage of physicians qualified to give this care
      a) gives total family-centered maternity care to the family unit in normal maternity
         (1) responsible for
            (a) prenatal period supervision

                (b) management of labor and delivery
                (c) postnatal care
            b) receives special preparation
                (1) postgraduate education leading to certification varies in length
                (2) master's degree programs, which include certification
            c) practices in association with obstetricians
                (1) works in obstetricians' offices in private practice
                (2) employed by maternity centers, hospitals, and community health agencies
        2. clinical nurse specialist in maternity nursing
            a) prepared at the master's level
            b) acts as a role model and resource person for other nursing and technical personnel
            c) assists parents in coping with special problems arising during the maternity cycle
            d) functions in a teaching and leadership role
        3. maternity nurses
            a) there is an increasing emphasis on anticipatory guidance, counseling, and teaching throughout the maternity cycle in addition to the provision of safe, humanitarian care for parents and newborns
C. Standards developed
    1. Standards of Practice for Maternal-Child Health Nursing developed by the ANA (Exhibit 2-2)

Exhibit 2-2 Standards of Practice

The development of standards of practice is important in every profession. The following *Standards of Maternal-Child Health Nursing Practice* was developed by the Executive Committee and the Standards Committee of the Division on Maternal-Child Health Nursing Practice of the American Nurses' Association in 1973. These standards are process standards.

Maternal and Child Health Nursing Practice is based on the following premises:
1. Survival and the level of health of society are inextricably bound to Maternal and Child Health Nursing Practice.
2. Maternal and Child Health Nursing Practice respects the human dignity and rights of individuals.
3. Maternal and Child Health Nursing Practice is family-centered.
4. Maternal and Child Health Nursing Practice focuses on the childbearing, child-rearing phases of the life cycle which include the development of sexuality, family planning, interconceptual care and child health from conception through adolescence.

Exhibit 2-2 continued

5. Maternal and Child Health Nursing makes a significant difference to society in achieving its health goals.
6. Man is a total human being. His psychosocial and biophysical self are interrelated.
7. Human behavior shapes and is shaped by environmental forces and as such sets into motion a multitude of reciprocal responses.
8. Through his own process of self-regulation the human being attempts to maintain equilibrium amidst constant change.
9. All behavior has meaning and is influenced by past experiences, the individual's perception of those experiences, and forces impinging upon the present.
10. Growth and development is ordered and evolves in sequential stages.
11. Substantive knowledge of the principles of human growth and development, including normative data, is essential to effective Maternal and Child Health Nursing Practice.
12. Periods of developmental and traumatic crises during the life cycle pose internal and external stresses and may have a positive or negative effect.
13. Maternal and Child Health Nursing Practice provides for continuity of care and is not bound by artificial barriers and exclusive categories which tend to restrict and delimit practice.
14. *All* people have a right to receive the benefit of the delivery of optimal health services.

Maternal and Child Health Nursing Practice is aimed at:
1. Promoting and maintaining optimal health of each individual and the family unit.
2. Improving and/or supporting family solidarity.
3. Early identification and treatment of vulnerable families.
4. Preventing environmental conditions which block attainment of optimal health.
5. Prevention and early detection of deviations from health.
6. Reducing stresses which interfere with optimal functioning.
7. Assisting the family to understand and/or cope with the developmental and traumatic situations which occur during childbearing and childrearing.
8. Facilitating survival, recovery and growth when the individual is ill or needs health care.
9. Reducing reproductive wastage occurring at any point on the continuum.
10. Continuously improving the quality of care in Maternal and Child Health Nursing Practice.
11. Reducing inequalities in the delivery of health care services.

Standard I

Maternal and child health nursing practice is characterized by the continual questioning of the assumptions upon which practice is based, retaining those which are valid and searching for and using new knowledge.

Rationale: Since knowledge is not static, all assumptions are subject to change. Assumptions are derived from knowledge or findings of research which are subject to additional testing and revision. They are carefully selected and tested and reflect utilization of present and new knowledge. Effective utilization of these knowledges stimulates more astute observations and provides new insights into the effects of nursing upon the individual and family. To question assumptions implies that nursing practice

Exhibit 2-2 continued

is not based on stereotyped or ritualistic procedures or methods of intervention; rather, practice exemplifies an objective, systematic and logical investigation of a phenomenon or problem.

Standard II

Maternal and child health nursing practice is based upon knowledge of the biophysical and psychosocial development of individuals from conception through the childrearing phase of development and upon knowledge of the basic needs for optimum development.

Rationale: A knowledge and understanding of the principles and normal ranges in human growth, development and behavior are essential to Maternal and Child Health Nursing Practice. Concomitant with this knowledge is the recognition and consideration of the psychosocial, environmental, nutritional, spiritual and cognitive factors that enhance or deter the biophysical and psychological maturation of the individual and his family.

Standard III

The collection of data about the health status of the client/patient is systematic and continuous. The data are accessible, communicated and recorded.

Rationale: Comprehensive care requires complete and ongoing collection of data about the client/patient to determine the nursing care needs and other health care needs of the client/patient. All health status data about the client/patient must be available for all members of the health care team.

Standard IV

Nursing diagnoses are derived from data about the health status of the client/patient.

Rationale: The health status of the client/patient is the basis for determining the nursing care needs. The data are analyzed and compared to norms.

Standard V

Maternal and child health nursing practice recognizes deviations from expected patterns of physiologic activity and anatomic and psychosocial development.

Rationale: Early detection of deviations and therapeutic intervention are essential to the prevention of illness, to facilitating growth and developmental potential, and to the promotion of optimal health for the individual and the family.

Standard VI

The plan of nursing care includes goals derived from the nursing diagnoses.

Rationale: The determination of the desired results from nursing actions is an essential part of planning care.

Standard VII

The plan of nursing care includes priorities and the prescribed nursing approaches or measures to achieve the goals derived from the nursing diagnoses.

Rationale: Nursing actions are planned to promote, maintain and restore the client/patient's well-being.

Exhibit 2-2 continued

Standard VIII

Nursing actions provide for client/patient participation in health promotion, maintenance and restoration.

Rationale: The client/patient and family are provided the opportunity to participate in the nursing care. Such provision is made based upon theoretical and experiential evidence that participation of client/patient and family may foster growth.

Standard IX

Maternal and child health nursing practice provides for the use and coordination of all services that assist individuals to prepare for responsible sexual roles.

Rationale: People are prepared for sexual roles through a process of socialization that takes place from birth to adulthood. This process of socialization, to a large extent, is carried out within the family structure. Social control over child care increases in importance as humans become increasingly dependent on the culture rather than upon the family unit. The culture of any society is maintained by the transmission of its specific values, attitudes and behaviors from generation to generation. Attitudes and values concerning male and female roles develop as part of the socialization process. Attitudes toward self, the opposite sex and parents will influence the roles each individual assumes in adulthood and the responsibilities accepted.

Standard X

Nursing actions assist the client/patient to maximize his health capabilities.

Rationale: Nursing actions are designed to promote, maintain and restore health. A knowledge and understanding of the principles and normal ranges in human growth, development and behavior are essential to Maternal and Child Health Nursing Practice.

Standard XI

The client's/patient's progress or lack of progress toward goal achievement is determined by the client/patient and the nurse.

Rationale: The quality of nursing care depends upon comprehensive and intelligent determination of the impact of nursing upon the health status of the client/patient. The client/patient is an essential part of this determination.

Standard XII

The client's/patient's progress or lack of progress toward goal achievement directs reassessment, reordering of priorities, new goal setting and revision of the plan of nursing care.

Rationale: The nursing process remains the same, but the input of new information may dictate new or revised approaches.

Standard XIII

Maternal and child health nursing practice evidences active participation with others in evaluating the availability, accessibility and acceptability of services for parents and children and cooperating and/or taking leadership in extending and developing needed services in the community.

Exhibit 2-2 continued

> *Rationale:* Knowledge of services presently offered parents and children is the first step in determining the effectiveness of health care to all in the community. When it is recognized that needed services are not available, accessible or acceptable, the nurse takes leadership in working with consumers, other health disciplines, the community and governmental agencies in extending and/or developing these services. Services must be continually evaluated, expanded and changed if they are to improve the health and well-being of all parents and children within our society.
>
> *Source:* From *Standards of Maternal-Child Health Nursing Practice*, 1973, Kansas City, MO: American Nurses' Association. Copyright 1973 by American Nurses' Association. Reprinted by permission.

    2. standards for care have also been developed by NAACOG, the specialty organization for obstetrical, gynecological, and neonatal nursing, for
        a) obstetrical, gynecological, and neonatal nursing
        b) the obstetrical-gynecological nurse practitioner
        c) nurse providers of childbirth education
        d) these documents are available from NAACOG at 409 12th St., S.W., Washington, D.C., 20024
    3. many states have revised and expanded nurse practice acts to include provisions for nurse practitioners
        a) academic and credentialing parameters included
    4. ANA published in 1987 the Scope of Nursing practices, which reflects a consensus of the leading nursing organizations
        a) description of technical and professional roles

D. Team approach to maternity nursing
    1. many levels of personnel cooperate to deliver maternity care to families. Members of the team include professional and technical nurses, nurses aides, baby nurses, licensed practical nurses, physicians, physician assistants, nutritionists, social workers
    2. members of the team deliver the care for which their educational preparation has prepared them

E. An increasing dialogue between consumers and health care providers regarding the type and quality of maternity services being offered to the public
    1. consumers are increasingly demanding a real voice in the making of decisions regarding their care
    2. increasing dissatisfaction with the existing quality of care and the powerlessness of the consumer to effect change have led to an increase in the number of home deliveries, self-care, and health care by nonprofessionals

REFERENCES

The health lifeline: Out of reach of women and children. (1986). *Hospitals, 60* (2).

Hughes, D., Johnson, K., Rosenblum, S., Simons, J., & Butler, E. (1987). *The health of America's children: Maternal and child health data book.* Washington, D.C.: Children's Defense Fund.

Infant deaths and poverty. (1986). *Science News, 130,* 200.

National Health Care Campaign. (1987). *Health care news: Maternity patient dumping on the rise.* Washington, D.C.: National Health Care Campaign.

BIBLIOGRAPHY

American Nurses Association. (1980). *A social policy statement.* Kansas City, MO: American Nurses Association.

Committee on Perinatal Health. (1977). *Towards improving the outcome of pregnancy.* March of Dimes Birth Defects Foundation.

Cruikshank, B., & Larkin, J. (1986, November). Professional and employment characteristics of NPs with masters and non-masters preparation. *Nurse Practitioner,* pp. 45–49.

Department of Health & Human Services. (1980). *Promoting health/preventing disease: Objectives for the nation.* Washington, D.C.: U.S. Government Printing Office.

Facts you should know about teenage pregnancy. (1986). White Plains, NY: March of Dimes.

Hoff, G.A., & Schneiderman, L.J. (1985, December). Having babies at home: Is it safe? Is it ethical? *Hasting center report,* pp. 19–25.

Interprofessional Task Force on Health Care of Women and Children. (1978). Joint Position Statement: *The development of family-centered/maternity/newborn care in hospitals.*

Jensen, M., & Bobak, I. (1985). *Maternity and gynecological care* (3rd ed.). St. Louis: C.V. Mosby.

Klaus, Marshall, and Trause, Maryann. (1975). *Maternal attachment and mothering disorders.* Johnson & Johnson.

Lesser, A. (1985). The origin and development of maternal and child health programs in the United States. *American Journal of Public Health, 75* (6), 590–604.

Lyons, A., & Petrucelli, R.J. (1978). *Medicine: An illustrated history.* New York: Harry N. Abrams, Inc.

Maternal age & births in the 1980s. (1982, February). *Briefs,* pp. 1–2.

Miller, A. (1987). *Maternal health and infant survival.* Washington, D.C.: National Center for Clinical Infant Programs.

Moore, M. (1983). *Realities in childbearing* (2nd ed.). Philadelphia: W.B. Saunders.

National birthweight—specific infant mortality surveillance: Preliminary Analysis, 1980. (1986). *Morbidity and Mortality Weekly Report, 35* (17), 269–272.

Robert Wood Johnson Foundation. (1985). *The perinatal program: What has been learned, Special Report, Number Three.* Princeton, NJ: Author.

Sachs, B., et al. (1987). Maternal mortality in Massachusetts: Trends and prevention. *New England Journal of Medicine, 13* (11), 667–672.

The secret of maternal and child health. (1985). *American Journal of Public Health,* 75(6), 585–588.

Southern Regional Taskforce on Infant Mortality. (1985). *Final report.* Washington, D.C.: Southern Governors Association.

Part II
Prenatal Period

Chapter 3

Reproductive System

I. MALE ANATOMY AND PHYSIOLOGY (Figure 3-1)
  A. Urethra
     1. passageway for semen from vas deferens through the penis
     2. passageway for urine from bladder through the penis
     3. ends at the urinary meatus, which is the opening in the glans penis through which urine and semen are excreted
  B. Testes
     1. ovoid in shape
     2. two in number
     3. suspended in scrotum by spermatic cord
     4. sperm formed and stored in seminiferous tubules of testes
     5. testosterone is produced in testes
  C. Epididymis
     1. adjacent to testes in scrotum
     2. in addition to seminiferous tubules, acts as a storage reservoir for sperm
        a) sperm may remain alive for as long as a month in both epididymis and tubules
  D. Vas deferens
     1. conducts sperm from epididymis to urethra
  E. Seminal vesicles
     1. secrete mucoid material into upper end of vas deferens
     2. mucoid material helps keep sperm alive and motile
  F. Prostate gland
     1. secretes alkaline fluid to activate sperm
        a) fluid is secreted into vas deferens
        b) fluid is milky and opaque and forms part of the seminal discharge

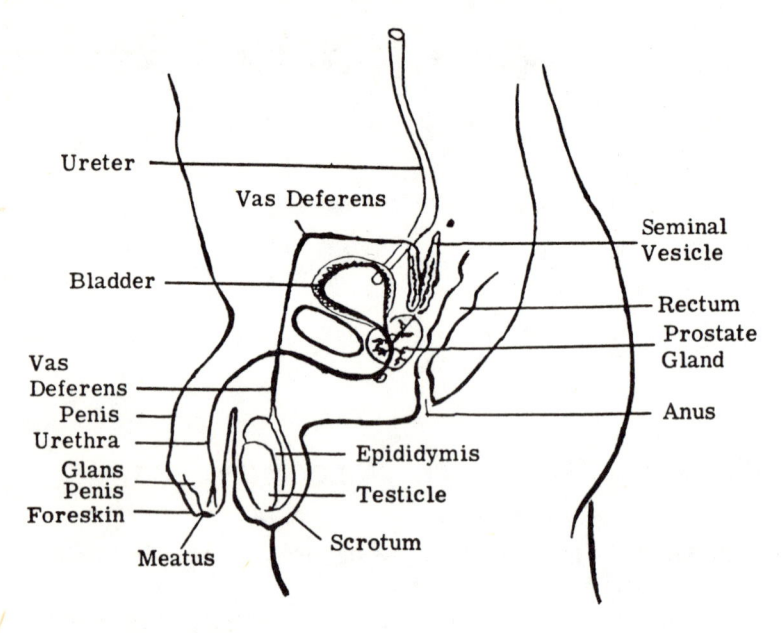

Figure 3-1 Male Reproductive System

G. Penis
   1. contains part of urethra
   2. organ of copulation
   3. divided into shaft and glans penis
      a) glans penis is most sensitive portion of penis
   4. erectile tissue lies around urethra and causes erection
   5. foreskin covers glans penis (removed by circumcision)
H. Bulbo-urethral glands (two)
   1. secrete mucus during the sexual act
   2. located on both sides of upper end of urethra
I. Sperm
   1. testes produce billions of spermatozoa throughout the life cycle
   2. contain head, neck, body, and tail
      a) the principal components are
         (1) head, which contains the genetic material of the male
         (2) tail, which provides motility through flagellar movement (back and forth)
   3. move at a velocity of approximately 1 to 4 mm/min through female genital tract to seek the ovum
   4. maturation of sperm cells (spermatogenesis)

    a) primary spermatocyte divides by meiosis to form secondary spermatocyte with haploid number of chromosomes (23)
    b) secondary spermatocyte matures into sperm cell
J. Hormonal influences on male reproductive system
  1. hormones are essential to the mechanism of reproduction and to the development and maintenance of secondary sex characteristics
    a) testes are dormant until puberty
      (1) anterior pituitary body secretes follicle-stimulating hormone (FSH) and luteinizing hormone (LH), which cause growth and function of testes at puberty
    b) secondary sex characteristics are generated by increased testosterone production at puberty
      (1) growth of testes and penis
      (2) growth of facial and body hair
      (3) deepening of voice and widening of musculature of chest and shoulders
    c) extraglandular estrogen production is present in small amounts
K. Physiology of ejaculation
  1. sexual stimulation causes increased amounts of blood to enter erectile tissue of penis, which thereby enlarges, causing an erection
  2. rhythmic peristalsis in genital ducts during orgasm causes semen to be propelled through epididymis, vas deferens, seminal ducts, and urethra
  3. semen
    a) consists of sperm and milky serous fluid from prostate and mucus from seminal vesicles
    b) normal range secreted at each ejaculation: 2.5–5 ml
    c) each milliliter contains 20–150 million sperm
    d) total ejaculate may contain up to half-billion sperm; minimum normal count is 125 million sperm per ejaculate
    e) contains fructose needed by sperm for nutrition
    f) prostate fluid highly alkaline, neutralizes acidic fluid from testes (sperm immobile in highly acid medium) and also neutralizes acidic vaginal mucosa

II. FEMALE ANATOMY

A. Pelvis (Figures 3-2 and 3-3)
  1. contains generative organs, bladder, and rectum
  2. forms part of birth canal
  3. shaped like a funnel with a wide mouth

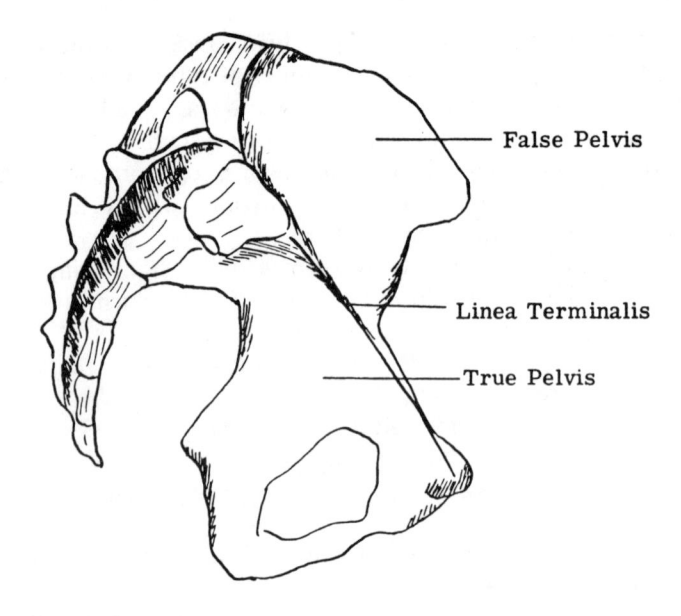

Figure 3-2 Female Pelvis

---

4. divided into false and true pelvis by the inlet or brim
    a) sacral promontory and ileo pectineal line are dividing points between true and false pelvis
5. bones of pelvis
    a) four bones joined together by
        (1) sacroiliac articulations
        (2) symphysis pubis
        (3) sacrococcygeal articulations
    b) bones of the pelvis
        (1) two innominate bones divided into three parts
            (a) ilium: flaring portion
            (b) ischium: lower part below hip joint
            (c) pubis: anterior portion
        (2) sacrum: posterior wall; pelvic portion of spinal column
        (3) coccyx: tail end of sacrum
6. inlet: heart-shaped entranceway into the true pelvis
    a) widest diameter: side to side
    b) narrowest diameter: anterior to posterior
    c) measurements of anterior-posterior diameter are important in determining the course of labor

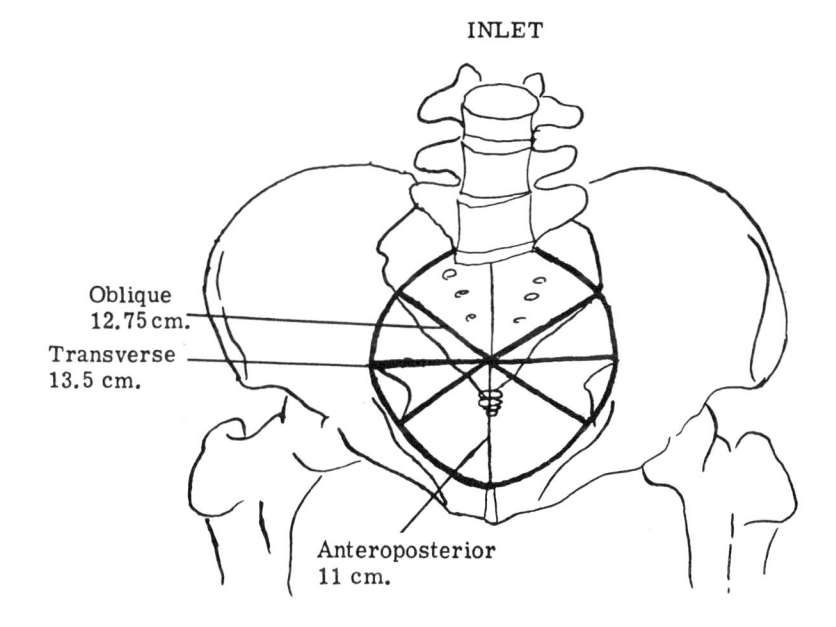

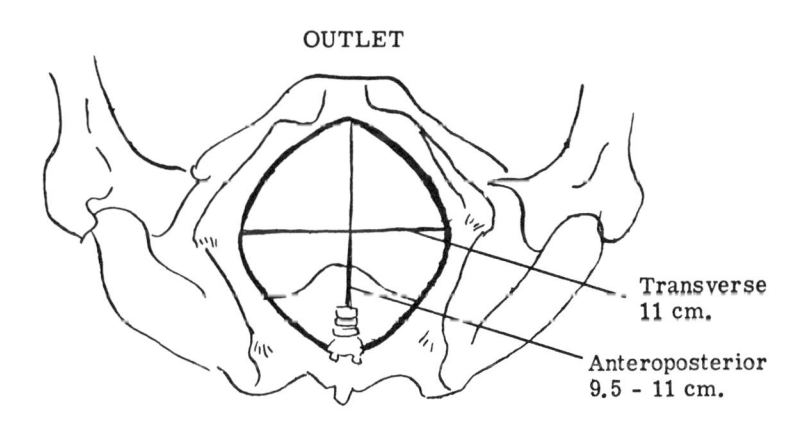

Figure 3-3 Normal Female Pelvic Measurements

7. outlet: entranceway to vaginal canal for delivery
    a) irregular in shape
    b) contains soft tissue
    c) boundaries are sacrum, coccyx, symphysis pubis, and tuberosities of ischia

d) largest diameter: anterior-posterior, necessitating rotation of baby's head after leaving inlet in order for delivery to take place
8. soft structures of pelvis: ligaments, muscles, vagina, and perineum
   a) form padding that protects the child
   b) form pelvic floor
      (1) retain pelvic organs in proper place
      (2) direct presenting part of child forward during labor
9. pelvic types
   a) classification is determined by shape and measurements
   b) the type of pelvis will influence the course of labor and delivery
   c) classification system
      (1) gynecoid: anterior and posterior of pelvic inlet are well rounded; sacrosciatic notch is curved, moderate in width and depth
      (2) anthropoid: deep anterior and posterior inlet; sacrosciatic notch is broad and shallow
      (3) android: wedge-shaped inlet, shallow posterior, pointed anterior; sacrosciatic notch is narrow, deep, and pointed
      (4) platypelloid: oval inlet, well rounded, with decreased anterior-posterior measurements; small sacrosciatic notch
   d) the closer the configuration of the pelvis is to the gynecoid shape, the more apt the labor and delivery will be normal

B. Ovaries (Figure 3-4)
   1. two glandular bodies shaped like almonds, on either side of the uterus

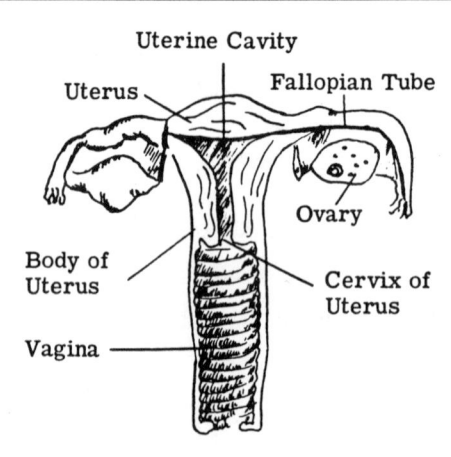

Figure 3-4 Female Reproductive System

2. attached by ligaments to pelvis
3. contain primordial egg cells
    a) about 400,000 ova are present at birth
    b) contained in follicles
4. surrounded by fatty tissue for protection

C. Fallopian tubes (oviducts)
1. attached to uterus on either side
2. widen at ovarian end to form finger-like projections (fimbriae)
3. act as a passageway for sperm and egg (conception most often occurs in upper third)

D. Uterus
1. located behind bladder and in front of rectum
2. nonpregnant state: hollow, pear-shaped organ weighing 50–60 g (2 oz)
3. divided into three parts
    a) fundus: uppermost portion
    b) corpus: body of uterus
    c) cervix: neck of uterus that opens into vaginal canal
        (1) internal os: opening from uterus to cervix
        (2) external os: opening from cervix to vaginal canal
4. uterine wall made up of three layers
    a) external: exometrium
        (1) continuation of pelvic peritoneum
    b) middle: myometrium
        (1) contains a large number of blood vessels, nerves, and lymph vessels
        (2) extremely muscular
    c) inner: endometrium
        (1) mucous membrane with rich supply of glands and blood
5. suspended in pelvic cavity by broad ligaments

E. Bartholin's glands
1. two small glands on either side of vaginal opening
2. secrete mucus

F. External genitalia
1. mons veneris: fatty cushion of connective tissue over symphysis pubis
2. labia
    a) majora: outer lips, protect inner vulva
    b) minora: inner lips, protect clitoris
3. clitoris: small projecting erectile organ
    a) well supplied with blood and nerves

        b) increases in size with sexual stimulation
        c) an organ of sexual excitement
    4. vestibule
        a) space under clitoris and labia
        b) contains openings of
            (1) vagina
            (2) urethra
            (3) glands of Skene's and Bartholin's
    5. vagina: organ of copulation
        a) muscular, membranous orifice 3–5 inches long
        b) excretory organ of uterus
        c) birth canal
        d) hymen: fold of elastic tissue partially occluding vagina before first coitus
    6. perineum: region from pubic arch of rectum
        a) forms external floor of pelvis
        b) provides muscular support for pelvic organs
    7. breasts
        a) complex structures that function to secrete and convey milk to the nipples
        b) milk secretion takes place in lobes of breasts
        c) a system of ducts leads milk to nipples
        d) areola surrounds nipples and contains Montgomery's tubercles
        e) immediately after puberty, estrogen and progesterone begin to prepare breasts for lactation
            (1) breasts enlarge and glandular elements begin to develop

III. FEMALE PHYSIOLOGY

A. Hormonal cycle (Figure 3-5)
    1. begins at puberty
    2. ends at menopause
    3. anterior pituitary secretes FSH (follicle-stimulating hormone), which activates primary graafian follicle, allowing ova to mature
    4. increased estrogen is produced by maturing follicle
    5. estrogen stimulates endometrium to become engorged with blood and prepare to receive fertilized ovum
    6. estrogen and FSH allow ova to complete maturation
        a) primary oocyte forms secondary oocyte, which becomes mature ovum with 23 chromosomes
    7. mature ovum is released through ruptured graafian follicle

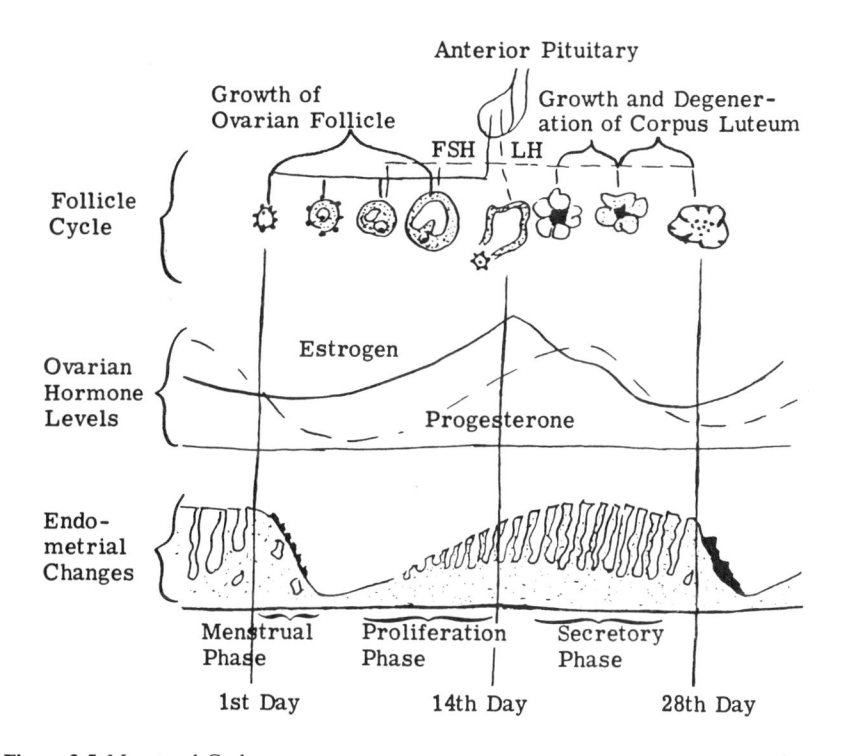

Figure 3-5 Menstrual Cycle

   8. high estrogen levels reduce pituitary FSH and increase LH (luteinizing hormone) production, thereby causing corpus luteum to secrete progesterone, which stimulates endometrium to increase blood supply and store glycogen
   9. hormone levels drop and endometrium and corpus luteum degenerate
      a) progesterone levels increase and cause LH to decrease
      b) menstruation begins
   10. usual range of menstrual cycle: 21–35 days
B. Current research is investigating the influence of various other substances on the ovarian cycle: folliculostatin, which regulates the secretion of FSH (also referred to as inhibin); gonadotropin-releasing hormone (GnRH) from the hypothalamus, which stimulates release of FSH and LH; cybernins; LH receptor-binding inhibitor; and others
C. Secondary sex characteristics develop in response to estrogen and progesterone secretion during puberty

1. growth of axillary and pubic hair
2. breast and genital enlargement
3. widening of hips
4. changes in vagina, cervix, fallopian tubes, and uterus

D. Estrogens produced at extra glandular sites are present in children and post-menopausal women; the level of this estrogen is too low to influence menstrual changes. Estrogen is a growth promoter

Chapter 4

Family Planning

I. INFERTILITY

A. Primary infertility: pregnancy not achieved after frequent, unprotected intercourse of 1 year
B. Secondary infertility: woman had one or more pregnancies and is unable to conceive subsequently under conditions of frequent, unprotected intercourse
C. Impaired fecundity: difficulty in conceiving or carrying a child to term
D. Fertility rates
   1. highest in temperate zone
   2. 10–15% of married couples have fertility problems. (33% of couples over age 35)
   3. fertility diminishes with age
      a) peak of female fertility at age 24 with a gradual decline to age 30 and a more rapid decline thereafter to age 50
         (1) pregnancy after 50 is rare
      b) peak of male fertility at age 24 with a gradual decline
         (1) male fertility may remain as late as 80–90 years of age
E. Causes of infertility
   1. genital tract abnormalities
      a) female
         (1) obstructions in genital tract from previous infection, injury, or congenital malformation of
            (a) cervix
            (b) vagina
            (c) fallopian tube
            (d) uterus
         (2) tumors and cysts
            (a) vaginal

(b) uterine
(c) ovarian
(3) allergic reaction to sperm cells
(4) abnormal pH of vagina
(5) endometriosis: accumulation of endometrial cells either in the uterus or at other sites
(6) endometritis: inflammation of the endometrium
(7) infections or inflammation of any of the organs of reproduction
    (a) mild infection with *T. mycoplasma*: associated with infertility. The organism causes a mild infection in either husband or wife. Symptoms may be so mild that they are not noticed
    (b) pelvic inflammatory disease (PID): presents a high threat to fertility; may be caused by a variety of organisms (gonorrhea and chlamydia are most common). Symptoms may include abdominal pain, pelvic tenderness, fever, and vaginal discharge
        1. use of plastic IUDs when a woman has multiple sexual partners increases the risk of PID
b) male
    (1) obstruction in genital tract from previous infection, injury, or congenital malformation of
        (a) vas deferens
        (b) seminal ducts
        (c) prostate
        (d) urethra
            1. hypospadias: urethral opening on underside of penis because of congenital malformation
            2. epispadias: urethral opening on upperside of penis because of congenital malformation
    (2) testicle injury
        (a) sperm production may be affected by
            1. radiation
            2. undescended testicles
            3. infection
                a. orchitis: infection and inflammation of testes
                b. venereal disease
                c. mumps with a secondary infection of testes
            4. trauma
            5. hyperthermia: excessive heat applied to testicles
            6. varicose vein in testicle

7. certain toxic agents: substances under investigation include pesticides, methylene chloride, ethylene bromide, ethylene oxide, and lead
8. such drugs as Tagamet can reduce sperm count; effect is reversible when drug is stopped
  2. endocrine abnormalities
    a) female
      (1) pituitary dysfunction
      (2) ovarian dysfunction
      (3) thyroid dysfunction
      (4) luteal phase defect: when ovulation occurs after the 14th day of the cycle there may be structural changes in the ovum (sometimes labeled "overripeness") that may cause embryonic defects and abortion. Signs of luteal phase defects include delayed ovulation, shortened secretory phase, and atypical temperature rise following ovulation
        (a) luteal phase defect may be a factor in infertility and habitual abortion
    b) male
      (1) testosterone dysfunction
      (2) pituitary dysfunction
      (3) thyroid dysfunction
      (4) FSH dysfunction
  3. systemic abnormalities in both male and female
    a) nutritional deficiency
    b) infection
    c) chronic disease
    d) fatigue
    e) emotional stress
  4. sexual malfunctioning in male and female
    a) male impotence and premature ejaculation
    b) female vaginismus
  5. chromosomal abnormality in male or female: Kleinfelter's or Turner's syndrome

F. Fertility workup
  1. both husband and wife should have a thorough history and physical
  2. female workup
    a) basal body temperature (BBT) graph to examine the ovulation cycle
    b) hormone assays for thyroid, luteinizing hormone, prolactin, testosterone, and progesterone level during the luteal phase

c) 24-hour urine collection done for 17-ketosteroids to determine adrenal function
d) timed endometrial biopsy to evaluate luteal phase of ovulation
e) anatomical problems are detected through
  (1) pelvic exam
  (2) tubal patency tested by
    (a) hysterosalpingogram (HSG): pelvic x-ray performed 2–6 days after end of menstruation. Dye is injected into uterus; fluoroscopy can show possible blockage of tubes or abnormal uterus
    (b) hydrotubation, which instills sterile saline instead of the dye used in HSG into the tubes. The procedure washes the tubes and widens them
    (c) CO_2 insufflation (Rubin's test)
  (3) laparoscopy to visualize the pelvic organs
  (4) cervical mucus examined for specific changes occurring during ovulation; mucus should show elasticity and ferning, and be clear and abundant
  (5) postcoital test (called the Sims-Huhner test) checks number of sperm, character of mucus, interaction of sperm with cervical mucus, and ability of sperm to swim in cervical mucus; immune incompatibility of sperm and cervical mucus is also checked

3. male workup
  a) semen analysis
    (1) man should abstain from ejaculation for 48–72 hours before test
    (2) semen is checked for volume, number of sperm, mobility, and morphology. Oligospermia: too few sperm; azoospermia: lack of viable sperm
    (3) if semen is abnormal then these steps are followed
      (a) hormonal assay for testosterone
      (b) FSH (follicle-stimulation hormone) is measured to determine if the seminiferous tubules are intact. Intact tubules secrete inhibin, which is a feedback regulator of FSH secretion. Irreversible sterility is the usual result of primary seminiferous tubule failure, but recovery from damage due to orchitis, drugs, or radiation may occur
      (c) urological workup for testicular injury or abnormality
      (d) history is checked for mumps, exposure to radiation, toxic substances, drugs, or increased scrotal temperature

Family Planning   47

    b) if semen is normal sexual disorders are examined
       (1) impotence
       (2) retrograde ejaculation: a rare disorder in which sperm are ejaculated into the bladder
    c) sperm is checked for autoimmunity, which causes sperm antibodies and inability to penetrate cervical mucus
G. Treatment
  1. genital tract abnormalities
    a) female
      (1) surgery
        (a) removal of obstruction, tumor, or cyst
        (b) correction of malformations
        (c) ovarian wedge resectioning for polycystic ovaries
      (2) tubal insufflation and hydrotubation for blocked fallopian tubes; tubal surgery to correct abnormality; catheter recanalization with balloon inflation of tube
      (3) desensitization methods for allergic reactions to sperm: condom used by male until antibody level of female drops
      (4) use of systemic and local drugs to alter abnormal acidic pH of vagina
      (5) treatment of inflammation and infection
        (a) *T. mycoplasma* infection is treated with doxycycline for 2–4 weeks; both husband and wife must be treated
        (b) PID is usually treated with penicillin or tetracycline or both, depending on the organism
      (6) endometriosis is treated by surgery or medical therapy with Danocrine; laser laparoscopy is a new method of treatment
    b) male
      (1) surgery for removal of obstruction, such as varicocele, and correction of abnormalities in the epididymis
  2. endocrine abnormalities
    a) female
      (1) disorders of ovulation include primary and secondary amenorrhea, anovulatory menstruation, and oligomenorrhea (menses occur irregularly at intervals of more than 6 weeks). Secondary amenorrhea may be caused by sudden weight loss or excessive physical activity, such as jogging
      (2) methods used to determine ovulation occurrence
        (a) basal body temperature (BBT) chart is kept for several months
          1. temperature must be taken rectally for 5 minutes before getting out of bed or before doing some

activity each morning (a specially calibrated thermometer is more accurate); a record is kept of daily readings. At the time of ovulation, there is a drop in temperature of from 0.5 to 1°F followed by a rise. There is a gradual return to preovulation temperature by the time menstruation occurs. Infections, severe stress, or illness may affect temperature readings
    a. intercourse should take place at time of maximum temperature drop if pregnancy is desired
    b. if there is no definite pattern of a temperature drop and rise during the cycle, ovulation may not be occurring
  (b) cervical mucus is examined for specific changes occurring during ovulation
  (c) an endometrial biopsy may be done to check for ovulation
(3) treatment of anovulation begins with administration of clomiphene (Clomid) to stimulate the pituitary to produce FSH and LH, which stimulate ovulation. If Clomid fails to produce ovulation, gonadotropin (Pergonal) is tried. Possible dangers of Pergonal use are ovarion hyperstimulation and multiple pregnancies; it requires careful monitoring of ovarian response through ultrasonic monitoring or estrogen measurements. Pulsatile gonadotropin-releasing hormone (GnRH) may be used instead of Pergonal because of its lower risk of multiple pregnancies, but it requires the wearing of a portable pulsatile infusion pump
(4) hyperthyroidism is treated by drugs, surgery, or radioactive iodine; hypothyroidism is treated with Synthroid
(5) poor cervical mucus may be treated with Premarin or cryosurgery
(6) hyperprolactinemia in patients with secondary amenorrhea can be treated by administration of bromocriptine
  b) male
    (1) gonadotropin deficiency is treated with gonadotropin (Pergonal) or Clomid. GnRH may be used
    (2) androgen deficiency is treated with testosterone therapy
    (3) bromocriptine has been used experimentally for men with elevated prolactin levels
3. sperm
  a) women who have allergies to their husband's sperm have been treated by the use of condoms for 6 months to reduce the level

Family Planning   49

of circulating antibodies. Failure of this method to work is followed by the administration of Medrol (methylprednisolone) for 4 to 5 months: antibody titers are used to check results of therapy. Good results have been obtained with the use of cyclosporine A for men
  b) an experimental method to increase motility is to incubate sperm in a high-protein mixture for 20 minutes
  c) new devices to be worn by men to induce testicular hypothermia are being tested
  d) if sperm count is low abstinence is advised for 1 week or longer to increase sperm count; first half of ejaculate contains the highest concentration of sperm
  e) artificial insemination by the husband (AIH) can be done using a split ejaculate that has a greater concentration of active sperm. If this method does not work donor insemination may be used (AID)
4. new methods of treating infertility
  a) in vitro fertilization: eggs are removed from a woman's ovary and fertilized in the laboratory with the father's sperm. The embryo is then inserted into the woman's uterus or fallopian tubes via catheter. Several eggs are usually fertilized to ensure success: embryos may be frozen until needed
    (1) in vitro fertilization is being investigated as a treatment for men who have mild to moderate semen disorders because fewer sperm are needed to fertilize an egg with this method
    (2) "Zona drilling" is a new method where a hole is made in the egg before fertilization to ensure that the sperm penetrates the egg
  b) ovum transfer: a woman may be implanted with a donor egg from another woman, which is fertilized with the husband's sperm. There are no regulations for this procedure, and many procedural and ethical questions remain to be explored
  c) gamete intra-fallopian tube transfer (GIFT) (Ullman, 1987)
    (1) program has resulted in a 35–40% pregnancy rate
    (2) helpful in such infertility problems as cervical mucus abnormalities, low sperm count and activity levels, endometriosis, and other unknown causes
    (3) women entered into the program must be under 40 years of age with a normal uterus, one functioning ovary, and one fallopian tube
    (4) on third day of menstrual cycle women receive daily Pergonal injections and oral Clomid. Blood estrogen levels are measured daily. On day six, daily ultrasound scans of

the ovaries are taken. When ultrasound shows at least two 18- to 20-mm eggs in each ovary the woman is given HCG to monitor ovulation; 34 hours after the HCG is given, the eggs are removed through a mini-laparotomy, placed in a buffered solution with the partner's sperm, and returned to the tube. After the procedure the woman is placed on progesterone therapy to aid in implantation and to support the endometrial tissues
    (5) there is a slight risk of ectopic pregnancy
5. surrogate motherhood: artificial insemination, by the father, of a woman who bears a child for a couple and then gives it up to them for adoption
6. systemic disorders: nutritional deficiencies are corrected, diseases and infections are treated, and emotional stress is treated by psychotherapy
7. sexual dysfunction
   a) female dysfunction is treated by specialists in sex therapy
   b) male impotence: psychological factors can be differentiated from physical factors by a test to monitor night-time tumescence or erections. Men normally have erections during the dream phases of sleep. If these erections are significantly lessened a physical cause is sought. Psychological impotence is treated by psychotherapy or sex therapy
      (1) physical causes
         (a) nerve signals needed to initiate an erection may be damaged by disease, injury, or radical prostate surgery
         (b) such drugs as beta-blockers and tranquilizers, alcohol, and smoking
         (c) hormonal imbalances
         (d) blood vessel and circulation disorders, such as leaky veins and clogged arteries in older men
      (2) treatment for physical causes
         (a) hormone treatments for hormonal imbalance
         (b) blood vessel artery bypass surgery to graft vessels into groin area to restore ample blood flow
         (c) tying off or removing veins to slow blood flow out of penis
         (d) injection into penile area of erection-producing drugs, such as papaverine and phentolamine: dosage must be carefully adjusted to prevent prolonged erections called priapism
         (e) internal prostheses can be implanted that can cause

erections at will. Several versions exist—the most natural type consists of a pump and fluid reservoir that can be inflated and deflated easily
H. Psychological problems of infertility
1. workups and treatment are expensive, lengthy, embarrassing, and sometimes painful
2. self image and self esteem are threatened
3. couple may romanticize pregnancy and be disappointed at the reality
4. infertile partner may feel guilty
5. pressure from friends and relatives may be painful
6. pressure to have sexual intercourse at specific times may lead to sexual dysfunction
7. surrogate pregnancies may lead to legal and emotional conflicts if the surrogate donor refuses to give up the child. Babies born with birth defects may not be accepted by the parties who have contracted with the surrogate mother
8. when children born of surrogate donors or artificial insemination from a donor grow up, the question of what to tell them about their origin arises. Children may have problems adjusting to their origin

II. FAMILY PLANNING

A. Rationale for family planning
1. overpopulation presents a threat to human survival
2. individual desire to control family size is influenced by economic, social, physical, psychological, and cultural factors
3. adequate spacing of pregnancies decreases the incidence of maternal and infant complications
B. Methods utilized by individuals for family planning
1. contraception
2. permanent male and female sterilization
3. abortion
   a) because of possible risk (0.5 deaths per 100,000 abortions and possibility of cervix becoming incompetent after several abortions) it is advisable not to utilize abortion as a method of primary contraception
C. Barriers to family planning
1. lack of knowledge about effective methods
2. misinformation about methods of family planning
3. lack of adequate family planning facilities and personnel

4. legal barriers to supplying services and equipment to minors
5. lack of money needed to secure services
6. religious and cultural attitudes toward family planning
D. Family planning services available
 1. there has been a great increase in the funding and development of family planning facilities by
    a) government agencies
    b) voluntary organizations, i.e., Planned Parenthood
 2. there has been a marked increase in research funding for effective family planning methods from government agencies
 3. Medicaid has enabled many indigent people to obtain family planning services
 4. the Commission of Population Growth and the American Future was created by Congress in 1970 to develop a national policy on population growth
 5. in 1970, Congress passed the Family Planning Services and Population Research Act, which authorizes funding for research and services in family planning throughout the country
 6. the Catholic Church has established clinics for research projects to instruct and improve the rhythm method of contraception
 7. throughout the country, many public and private schools are introducing sex education programs into the curricula that instruct teenagers in family planning
 8. changes in state abortion laws and the decision by the Supreme Court that most state abortion laws are unconstitutional have resulted in a drop in the birth rate and a decrease in out-of-wedlock births
E. What remains to be done?
 1. safer and more effective methods of contraception must be developed
    a) there has been a slowing of research and development of contraceptives in the U.S. by drug companies because an increasingly litigious climate has hindered the production and development of contraceptives by drug companies who wish to avoid being sued. Many types of IUDs that are available in other parts of the world have been taken off the market in the U.S. because of the many liability suits connected with the use of the IUD. Many promising new contraceptive methods are being denied to American women because of drug companies' reluctance to expose themselves to risk. In addition, federal funding for basic research has decreased over the past 6 years. To turn around

this situation, increased federal funding for basic research and low-cost insurance to protect drug companies against litigation must become available; drug companies must be held accountable for the safety of their products but they must also be free to experiment with new methods
   2. lack of knowledge and misinformation about family planning must be corrected by education in the schools and the community
   3. family planning services must be made available to all, regardless of financial status
   4. family planning services should be made available to minors who request them
   5. quantity and quality of family planning services must be increased
   6. maternal and child health nurses should develop the ability to counsel mothers in postpartum units and prenatal clinics about family planning
F. Methods of contraception: in choosing a method of contraception, a couple must consider effectiveness, compatibility, and safety
   1. coitus interruptus: oldest contraceptive procedure
      a) mode of action: male deposits semen outside of female genital tract by withdrawal of the penis before ejaculation
      b) acceptability
         (1) in the past widely used; currently it is decreasing in popular use throughout the world
         (2) requires no supplies or preparation and no cost
         (3) makes great demands on self-control of the male, may interfere with sexual satisfaction of both partners
      c) effectiveness: varies with technique—with well-motivated couples who are adequately informed, it compares in effectiveness with other mechanical methods
         (1) semen must be deposited completely away from vulva as sperm may enter vagina from external labia
         (2) pre-ejaculatory secretions may contain sperm in sufficient numbers to cause pregnancy
         (3) withdrawal must occur before ejaculation
      d) safety: no side effects have been proven, although many people believe mistakenly that this method can have physical or psychological effects
   2. breast feeding: many societies have used prolonged lactation periods to space their families
      a) mode of action: delays return of ovulation and menstruation
         (1) in order to prolong anovulation, major part of infant's diet must be breast milk

      b) effectiveness: prolongs anovulation for a certain period of time, but ovulation may return before menstruation reoccurs and pregnancy may result; not a reliable method
      c) safety: no side effects
  3. postcoital douche: widely used method in 18th and 19th centuries
      a) mode of action: plain water or vinegar douche used immediately after intercourse to mechanically remove semen from vagina; vinegar used for spermicidal effect
      b) acceptability: inconvenient and ineffective; still used in U.S. to some degree by poor and misinformed
      c) effectiveness: least effective method used; sperm may reach cervical mucus 90 seconds after ejaculation; douche may actually speed the movement of sperm toward the cervix
      d) safety: vinegar douche may change vaginal pH and secretions
  4. vaginal diaphragm: widely used before advent of pill and IUD; increased use currently because of its protective abilities against disease and fear of pill and IUDs
      a) mode of action: acts as mechanical barrier to the entry of sperm into cervical canal, blocking the cervical os; used with a spermicide cream for additional protection
      b) acceptability: decreased popularity in U.S. since development of the pill and IUD
        (1) must be fitted by a physician or health worker
        (2) must be inserted before intercourse. If intercourse does not occur within 1 hour additional spermicide should be inserted into vagina
        (3) many women dislike genital manipulation needed to insert diaphragm
        (4) may interfere with spontaneity of the sex act
        (5) must be left in place after intercourse for 6 hours
      c) effectiveness: high level of protection; failure rate averages 2–3 pregnancies per 100 women per year if used correctly; if used without proper instruction, rate is much higher
        (1) reasons for failure are
          (a) incorrect size
          (b) incorrect insertion
          (c) failure to use
          (d) tears or holes not detected in device
          (e) used without spermicide
      d) must be refitted after delivery, reproductive surgery, and weight change that is significant. To maintain effectiveness size of diaphragm should be checked periodically

Family Planning 55

    e) safety: no side effects; rarely a woman may have a reaction to rubber or cream used
5. condom: used widely before development of pill and IUD; increased use currently because of protection against AIDS and other sexually transmitted diseases
    a) mode of action: covers penis during intercourse and prevents deposit of semen in vagina. Sheath is made of rubber and other materials, such as sheep intestines
    b) acceptability: increased use because of protective capacities against disease
        (1) foreplay of sexual act must be interrupted to put on condom
        (2) may interfere with sexual sensation; non rubber condoms are less intrusive but may provide less protection against disease
        (3) may be purchased cheaply without a prescription
    c) effectiveness: highly effective when used with spermicides; failure rate averages 3 pregnancies per 100 women per year
        (1) FDA supervises standards of production and quality of condoms
        (2) high standard of quality exists in U.S.
        (3) failures due to tearing or slipping off
6. spermicides: infrequently used as a sole method of contraception in U.S.; usually utilized in conjunction with diaphragm or condom
    a) mode of action: jellies, creams, foams, suppositories, and tablets containing spermicides are inserted into vagina before intercourse where they diffuse over vagina and cervix and immobilize sperm on contact. The spermicides also act as a mechanical barrier through which sperm cannot swim
    b) acceptability: not widely used
        (1) simple to use, do not need examination or prescription
        (2) vaginal leakage may occur (messiness)
        (3) several minutes of waiting must occur for suppositories and tablets to melt
        (4) creams, foams, and jellies must be inserted with a tube applicator or sponge shortly before the sex act
        (5) effectiveness lasts on an average of 1 hour
    c) effectiveness: low rate of effectiveness; failure rate averages 30 pregnancies per 100 women
        (1) quality of spermicides varies; foam and vaginal contraceptive film are most effective forms
        (2) amount inserted may not be adequate

(3) uneven distribution of spermicide throughout the vagina
d) no side effects; a woman rarely reacts to the chemicals used
e) vaginal contraceptive film (VCF): thin film dissolves in vagina, releasing spermicide; effective up to 2 hours
7. vaginal sponge
    a) mode of action: barrier method works by preventing passage of sperm into reproductive tract; contains a spermicide
    b) acceptability: medium usage
        (1) widely available without a prescription
        (2) may be inserted up to 24 hours in advance
        (3) does not require additional spermicide
        (4) may protect against sexual diseases
        (5) in rare cases woman may have difficulty removing device
    c) safety: may cause reaction from spermicide
        (1) possible risk of toxic shock; should not be used during menstruation or by women who have cervical or vaginal infections; should not be used until 6 weeks after childbirth
    d) effectiveness: failure rate averages 11 pregnancies per 100 women; if used correctly, failure rate drops to 8.2 per 100 women
8. rhythm method: includes calendar rhythm and basal temperature rhythm; only method of contraception advocated by the Catholic Church
    a) mode of action: abstinence practiced for a period of time before, during, and after the estimated day of ovulation
        (1) in order to practice the rhythm method, the day of ovulation must be determined
        (2) day of ovulation may be determined by calendar method or basal body temperature chart (BBT)
            (a) calendar method depends on theory that the average ovulation occurs 14 days before first day of menstrual cycle
            (b) life of ovum is believed to be 12–24 hours after release from follicle
            (c) survival time for sperm is approximately 48 hours
            (d) considering all contingencies, such as a variation of ovulation, the life of sperm and of ovum, the unsafe period is considered to be 8 days
            (e) a log is kept for a period of time to determine the longest and shortest length of a woman's menstrual cycle
                1. the shortest cycle is used for calculation

2. 18 days are subtracted from last days of shortest cycle (14 days ovulation and 2 days variation in ovulation and 2 days life of sperm); this is first day of unsafe period: in a 28-day cycle, day 10 would be first day of abstinence
3. to determine last day of unsafe period, 11 days are subtracted from last day of longest cycle (14 days ovulation and 1 day life of ovum); in a 32-day cycle, day 21 would be last unsafe day
        (f) basal temperature chart, which is the more accurate method of the two, is described under section on infertility. The time of abstinence would be 2 days before ovulation and 72 hours after the drop and sustained temperature rise; the 72-hour span is used to be certain that ovulation has actually occurred. There are other small temperature fluctuations in the monthly cycle that are not related to ovulation. During ovulation the rise that follows the initial drop of 0.5 to 1° is sustained for at least 72 hours
    (3) BBT chart is usually combined with other methods to pinpoint ovulation more accurately
        (a) fern test examines cervical mucus for fern-like patterns that occur prior to ovulation
        (b) spinnbarkeit test examines cervical mucus for evidence of thin and watery consistency and extreme stretchability that occur prior to ovulation
        (c) Billings has developed a method of observation that can be utilized by women to determine when fertile mucus indicating ovulation is present
            1. during preovulatory period women are taught to check for appearance of increased mucoid secretion; at time of ovulation this secretion becomes clear, slippery, and profuse; abstinence should take place from the first appearance of cervical mucus until 3 days following the height of wetness
        (d) home detection kit is available to pinpoint ovulation; questions remain about the degree of accuracy of these kits
  b) acceptability: about one-third of practicing Catholics in this country use this method; a small percentage of women use this method for reasons other than religious ones
  c) effectiveness: BBT chart combined with mucus observation can

be highly effective if done correctly and conscientiously. Calendar method is very ineffective; failure rate averages 15 pregnancies per 100 women and is due to
- (1) irregularity of menstrual cycle
- (2) lack of correct instruction about method
- (3) infections and drugs affect temperature readings
- (4) couples may not always practice abstinence when indicated
- (5) a small minority of women do not show significant temperature changes even though they are ovulating

d) safety: no physical side effects; may cause anxiety

9. IUD (intrauterine device): widely used in U.S., Europe, and developing countries; use in U.S. is decreasing
    a) mode of action: a foreign body is placed permanently in the uterus where it exerts a contraceptive effect
        (1) exact method of action is unknown
        (2) theories as to mode of action are as follows
            (a) causes speedup of egg's movements through fallopian tube, enabling egg to reach endometrium before it has been completely prepared to accept it, thereby preventing implantation
            (b) endometrial tissues react to the foreign body by creating toxic substances that interfere with implantation
            (c) stimulates cellular exudates that affect sperm mobility
            (d) may prevent implantation because of a nonspecific inflammatory reaction within the uterine cavity
    b) types of IUDs
        (1) early accepted devices
            (a) Dalkon shield: removed from market in 1975
            (b) Lippes-Loop: polyethylene, double shape
            (c) Safe-t-coil: double-coil plastic
            (d) older models were designed to fit entire uterine cavity
            (e) newer models of Lippes-Loop and Safe-t-coil come in various sizes to conform to uterine condition
        (2) modern devices
            (a) constructed of polyethylene (inert plastic)
            (b) smaller in size than older devices
            (c) can be used by women who have not borne children
        (3) types of newer devices available in U.S.
            (a) Progestasert: T-shaped, hollow device that gradually releases progesterone for a period of 1 year. Exerts a localized effect; no increase in hormone level of the blood has been found

Family Planning 59

    (b) Copper T-33UA: T-shaped plastic device with copper coating; copper increases its effectiveness
- (4) women with the following conditions should not use an IUD
  - (a) fibroid tumors
  - (b) pregnancy
  - (c) pelvic inflammatory disease or a history of infection
  - (d) abnormal Pap smears
  - (e) cervical disease
  - (f) previous ectopic pregnancy
  - (g) anemia or leukemia
  - (h) allergies to copper
  - (i) vaginal bleeding
  - (j) multiple partners
  - (k) no previous pregnancies
- (5) IUD may be inserted by placing it in a straight thin tube called an inserter. The IUD is passed through the cervical os into the uterine cavity where the plastic resumes its original shape once inserter is removed. A thin thread remains in the vagina, which enables the woman to check the placement of the IUD

c) acceptability: would be an ideal contraceptive except for side effects and need for lower rate of failure; widely used throughout the world
- (1) removed from sexual act
- (2) inexpensive
- (3) requires little motivation or education on part of user
- (4) extensively used in national programs in countries with population problems and few financial resources

d) effectiveness: highly effective method. Less effective than the pill but more effective than other traditional methods. Failure rate averages 1.3–5.0 pregnancies per 100 women
- (1) failure is often due to expulsion of device
  - (a) expulsion rate highest during first menstruation and first 4 months after insertion
  - (b) expulsion rates are higher when device is inserted soon after a birth
  - (c) expulsion rates are higher in nulliparous women
- (2) women should be taught to check for expulsion
  - (a) checking vaginally for placement of string or beads
  - (b) after menstruation expulsion rates increase
- (3) pregnancy can occur with IUD in place

                (a) in order to decrease possibility of septic abortion, device is often removed when pregnancy is diagnosed
            (4) newer devices have lower expulsion rates
        e) safety
            (1) side effects include
                (a) excessive menstrual bleeding and bleeding between periods
                    1. newer devices decrease bleeding
                (b) uterine cramping
                    1. newer devices decrease cramping
                (c) depletion of iron from bleeding
                (d) increased incidence of ectopic pregnancy
            (2) voluntary removal rate is 34.8–36 per 100 users during first year
            (3) dangers include
                (a) perforation of uterus
                (b) women with previous histories of pelvic inflammatory disease may have recurrent flareups after insertion of IUD
                    1. warning signs include fever and pelvic pain, vaginal discharge
                (c) ectopic pregnancy
        f) the following factors affect failure, expulsion, and complication rates
            (1) size and type of device and inserter
            (2) timing of insertion
            (3) insertion technique
            (4) skill and experience of inserter
            (5) follow-up care
            (6) counseling and teaching of client
        g) recent legislation now allows IUD devices to be regulated by the FDA
    10. oral contraceptives: most effective and widely used contraceptives in developed countries
        a) mode of action: synthetic compounds similar to natural hormones occurring in the menstrual and pregnancy cycle are used in dosages that prevent ovulation
            (1) estrogen blood level is low following menstruation. In a normal cycle low estrogen levels stimulate the pituitary gland to secrete FSH, which causes an ovarian follicle to mature. The estrogen in the pill keeps the blood level high,

preventing the pituitary from secreting FSH and thereby preventing ovulation
- (a) progestin added to pills helps establish a menstrual cycle
- (2) when pills are discontinued, withdrawal bleeding or menstruation occurs
- (3) progestogen-only pills are known to alter cervical mucus and interfere with implantation

b) types of oral contraceptive pills
- (1) combined pills: estrogen and progestogen are combined and are taken every day for 20 or 21 days of each menstrual cycle, starting on day 5 of menstruation
- (2) triphasic pill: provides low doses of estrogen plus varying levels of progestogen. Total dosage is lower than the combination pill; may increase chances of irregular or absent periods
- (3) minipill contains progestogen only. Breakthrough or irregular bleeding may occur; has a higher risk of ectopic pregnancy than other pills
- (4) by 1989 all pills containing more than 50 mg of estrogen were removed from the market by FDA
- (5) there are many different forms of birth control pills on the market. Each one may have a different dosage of estrogen and progestogen, and each one must be prescribed by the physician according to the hormonal profile of the woman. When breakthrough bleeding occurs during the cycle, the pill or the dosage may have to be changed
  - (a) high-estrogen types of women should take progestogen-combinant pills that have an androgen reaction in the body
  - (b) high-androgen types of females should take estrogen-dominant pills that do not have an androgen reaction in the body
  - (c) high-estrogen pills include Enovid 2.5 mg, Ovulen, Ortho Novum 2 mg
  - (d) low-estrogen pills include Ovral, Provest, Ortho Novum 1 mg, Norinyl 1 +50, Brevicon
  - (e) high-progestogen pills include Ovulen and Demulen
  - (f) progestogen-only pills include Nor-Q.D. and Micronor
  - (g) some types of progestogen in pills may react as an androgen in the body

1. pills with androgen reaction include Ortho Novum 2 mg and Norinyl 2 mg
2. pills without an androgen reaction include Ovral and Provest

c) pills must be taken every day for 20–21 days in order to be effective
   (1) if pill is omitted patient is told to take two pills on following day but there is a risk of pregnancy
d) acceptability: highly popular in U.S., especially among younger women with better-than-average education. Women with limited education can also be taught to use them effectively. There has been a decrease in use in the past few years due to increased concerns about side effects
   (1) not connected with sex act
   (2) expensive compared to other methods. Government funding in U.S. has allowed distribution to low income women
   (3) simple to use, but does require motivation to take regularly
   (4) women who take pill need to be under regular medical supervision because of the possibility of side effects
e) effectiveness: most effective of all methods. Combined type has failure rate of 0.1 pregnancy per 100 women; failure usually due to omission of a pill. Failure rate for progestogen-only pill averages 2.2 pregnancies per 100 women. The pills with the highest dosage of estrogen have the highest rate of effectiveness
f) safety
   (1) side effects
      (a) nausea and vomiting, abdominal pains
      (b) breast engorgement
      (c) chloasma (brownish discoloration of skin)
      (d) spotting and bleeding between menses
      (e) fatigue
      (f) fluid retention and weight gain
      (g) amenorrhea
      (h) skin rash
      (i) loss of hair
      (j) vaginal discharge
      (k) headache
      (l) visual disturbance
      (m) acne
   (2) in attempting to eliminate side effects, it is important to be sure the patient is taking the pills correctly after a meal

at the same time each day. Other causes for symptoms must be ruled out. If symptoms persist, the pill type and dosage may need to be changed, e.g., from a high- to a low-estrogen pill for chloasma and breast engorgement and from low- to high-estrogen pill for acne
(3) dangers
   (a) an increased incidence of thromboembolic disorders and other vascular problems, such as myocardial infarction, stroke, and pulmonary embolism, has been shown to be associated with the use of the pill. Most complications occur in women over 35 who smoke. The number of cigarettes smoked per day and the dosage level of the pill are significant in determining risk. Death rates for smokers over 35 who took higher dose pills have averaged 84 per 100,000. Death rates in non smokers over 35 have averaged 23 per 100,000. Non smokers 15–24 years of age have a death rate of 0 to 0.6 per 100,000.
   (b) an association has been observed between the development of functional ovarian cysts and the use of biphasic and triphasic oral contraceptives
   (c) it has been determined that the lowest dose of estrogen in the pill is associated with the lowest occurrence of thromboembolic disease
   (d) blood pressure elevation of 1–4 mm Hg in 5% of women on oral contraceptive
   (e) increased incidence of gallbladder disease, urinary tract infections, eczema and sun sensitivity, coronary artery disease, and liver tumors has been found
   (f) new lower-dose pills have greatly decreased the incidence of side effects. Controversy remains as to whether the pill prevents the occurrence of certain cancers or is a risk factor. There are no definite findings at this time that the pill is a risk factor for breast or cervical cancer or other cancers
(4) beneficial effects
   (a) decrease in premenstrual tension
   (b) regular menstrual cycle
   (c) shorter and lighter menstrual periods, which may reduce the incidence of iron-deficiency anemia in women
   (d) decrease in menstrual cramping

(5) contraindications
  (a) breast cancer
  (b) severe varicosities
  (c) phlebitis or embolic disease
  (d) hepatitis within the past 2 years
  (e) liver damage
  (f) severe hypertension (uncontrolled)
(6) the following conditions may or may not be a contraindication and must be individually assessed
  (a) diseases of heart, lungs, or kidneys
  (b) diabetes
  (c) lupus erythematosus
  (d) arthritis (on steroid therapy)
  (e) sickle cell anemia
  (f) hyperthyroidism or tumors of thyroid
  (g) severe eye problems
11. male and female sterilization: a permanent method of birth control
  a) mode of action: cutting, ligation, or removal of portion of fallopian tubes in female, and vas deferens in male (vasectomy)
    (1) operation not usually reversible but some attempts at microsurgery have been successful
    (2) vasectomy may be performed under local anesthesia in physician's office; usually simple, uncomplicated procedure
    (3) tubal ligation traditionally performed under general anesthesia, using an abdominal or vaginal incision. Newer method is laparoscopy, which may be performed under local anesthesia by inserting a laparoscope into the abdomen and severing the fallopian tubes through the laparoscope. Only a tiny incision is necessary, and patient may return home that day
  b) acceptability: widely used in India and other overpopulated countries. Vasectomy gaining in popularity in U.S.; used mainly by older couples. In 1982 58.2% of couples 35–39 years of age were surgically sterile. This includes surgery for health reasons, as well as voluntary contraception
    (1) a problem that exists with this method is the slim chance of reversibility if the individual changes his or her mind
    (2) if successful, operation leaves person completely safe from pregnancy
  c) effectiveness: failure rate varies with method used and technique of surgeon. If operation is successful, there is complete

protection. In vasectomy there is a waiting period of approximately 2 to 6 weeks of active sexual activity for all sperm to be eliminated from the ejaculation as confirmed by laboratory test. It is advisable that other forms of contraception be used until a sperm-free specimen is obtained. In a small percentage of vasectomies, the cut ends of the vas may rejoin
  d) safety: as with any surgical procedure, there is a risk to life
    (1) male surgery safer than female, although risk to both sexes is very low
    (2) vasectomy: complications occur in 2–4% of cases and include
      (a) infection
      (b) hematoma
      (c) granuloma
      (d) epididymitis
      (e) no deaths have been recorded from vasectomy in the U.S.
    (3) tubal ligation: complications occur in 1–2% of cases and include
      (a) injury to bowel or uterus
      (b) excessive bleeding
      (c) mortality rate approximately 1 in 15–20 thousand cases and may be due to
        1. anesthesia reaction
        2. massive hemorrhage
        3. unrecognized infection of abdominal organs
  12. morning-after pill
    a) mode of action: large doses of estrogen 3–5 days after intercourse
    b) acceptability: used only as an emergency measure because of hazards of large estrogen doses
    c) almost completely effective in preventing pregnancy
G. Possible future methods of family planning
  1. female
    a) cervical cap: rubber thimble-shaped device that covers the cervix and is held in place by suction; acts as a barrier contraceptive and can be left in place for 3 days. Studies show it to be as effective as a diaphragm. Problems include limited range of sizes and an unpleasant odor when left in place. Newer version called Contracap is made with a special rubber that prevents odors and has a valve that allows for menstruation so it can stay in place for a year

b) long-acting injections of sythetic progestin: Depo-Provera and NET-EN given intramuscularly and injected every 2 or 3 months; act like the minipill; used in countries outside of the U.S. Concerns about this drug are cancer and possible birth defects if woman becomes pregnant while drug is still active
c) Norplant: tiny rods implanted in upper arm that deliver a steady low dose of synthetic progestin; lasts up to 5 years: inhibits ovulation; may cause irregular menstrual bleeding
d) electrical field method: insertion of a tiny sealed battery in cervix where it creates a low-voltage electrical field that immobilizes sperm. Battery lasts for a year; could be refined to deliver electricity only when needed
e) vaccine: stimulates the production of antibodies to prevent a fertilized egg from becoming implanted. Woman remains infertile for a full year
f) vaginal ring: rubber device inserted near cervix where it releases either progestin or a combination of estrogen/progestin to prevent ovulation; can be removed before intercourse
g) a long-acting progestin IUD similar to progestasert IUD that has a long-term (5–10 years) action
h) GnRH made in the form of a nasal spray (Nafarelin) taken once a day to prevent ovulation
i) a single oral dose of RU486, a progesterone antagonist, given late in the menstrual cycle to prevent pregnancy by preventing implantation; currently being tested for safety
j) improved methods to detect ovulation through detecting LH or progesterone in saliva, urine, or blood
2. male
a) subdermal implant to suppress sperm production: low-level androgen is constantly released from silicone rubber capsule
b) periodic injections of long-acting androgen
c) oral tablets of synthetic sperm production inhibitor: acts directly on testes to prevent the maturation of sperm
d) reversible vas deferens occlusion and ligation with insertion of removable silicon plugs
3. unisex
a) trials are presently being conducted on the use of a "super-agonist" for both men and women
(1) peptide hormones are variants of the brain hormone LHRH (luteinizing hormone-releasing hormone)
(2) prevent ovulation in women
(3) prevent sperm production in men

Family Planning 67

III. NURSING PROCESS IN FAMILY PLANNING

A. The emphasis for nursing as part of the total family planning team is to assist the family in planning and securing the desired family constellation
  1. nursing care in infertility
     a) assessment
        (1) period of time in which pregnancy has been actually sought
        (2) pattern of sexual activity
        (3) effect of infertility on interpersonal relationship of couple
        (4) effect of infertility on emotional health of each member of the family
        (5) external pressures from family and friends relating to infertility
        (6) coping patterns of couple for dealing with internal and external pressures
        (7) knowledge of process of conception and infertility
        (8) history of previous efforts directed toward treatment of infertility
        (9) ability of couple to understand the problem and explanations and instructions relating to the treatment of infertility
        (10) couple's level of motivation in following through on diagnostic procedures and treatments
        (11) additional data are gathered from physical and laboratory examinations that may reveal possible causes of infertility
     b) nursing diagnosis
        (1) problems identified may include
            (a) ineffective patterns of sexual activity, i.e., abstinence at time of ovulation
            (b) anatomical or physiological abnormalities
            (c) inadequate coping patterns for dealing with internal and external pressures related to infertility
            (d) inadequate understanding of prescribed treatments or instructions
     c) goal setting: both long- and short-term goals should be developed collaboratively with clients and other members of the health team
     d) nursing intervention
        (1) teaching and counseling
        (2) assisting couple with identifying and changing their interpersonal relationship patterns
            (a) referral to appropriate health personnel may be nec-

essary if problem goes beyond the scope of the nurse's competency
            (3) explanation of treatment and diagnostic procedures
            (4) assisting couple in exploring the implications and consequences of infertility on present and future life, i.e., adoption, artificial insemination, etc.
        e) evaluation
            (1) the nurse should evaluate nursing intervention and goal achievement on a continuous basis
    2. nursing care in contraception counseling
        a) assessment
            (1) client's knowledge of anatomy, physiology, or reproductive system
            (2) client's knowledge of contraceptive methods and possible consequences associated with use
            (3) client's attitudes toward each contraceptive method
            (4) economic considerations
            (5) client's ability to understand and carry out instructions
        b) nursing diagnosis: directed toward identifying potential barriers to successful use of contraceptive methods
        c) goal setting: the nurse and other members of the health team assist the client in determining which method of contraception is best suited for her needs
        d) nursing intervention: concerned with teaching and counseling the client in order for her to carry out the contraceptive method of her choice
        e) evaluation: return visits will allow the nurse to evaluate
            (1) client's understanding of how to use the contraceptive method
            (2) exploration of undesirable side effects or problems
            (3) client's satisfaction with contraceptive method

---

REFERENCE

Ullman, K. (1987, September). A gift for infertile couples. *American Journal of Nursing*, pp. 1130–1134.

Chapter 5
Conception

I. FERTILIZATION

A. Viability of sperm and ovum
   1. sperm remain alive for an average of 48 hours after ejaculation
   2. ovum remains viable for a period of 12–24 hours after ovulation
B. Fertile period is usually from 2 days before ovulation until 24 hours after ovulation occurs. For conception to take place sexual intercourse during this period is necessary
C. Fertilization
   1. may occur in abdominal cavity just before ovum enters fallopian tube
   2. usual place of fertilization is in the upper portion of fallopian tube
   3. enzyme secreted by sperm dissolves outer covering of ovum to allow penetration of sperm
   4. after one sperm enters ovum, the membrane surrounding it becomes impermeable
   5. two nuclei, each with 23 chromosomes, unite
   6. fertilized ovum now called a zygote

II. IMPLANTATION

A. Occurs approximately 7 days after fertilization
   1. during the period of the journey of the fertilized ovum, the endometrium, under the influence of progesterone, prepares for implantation
      a) becomes more vascular
      b) stores nutrients
   2. the fertilized ovum begins to undergo cleavage (rapid mitotic cell division) soon after fertilization
      a) zygote is now known as morula

3. morula takes an average of 3 days to travel through tube
   4. morula enters the uterus where it floats freely in uterine cavity for an average of 4 days, when it begins implantation
      a) morula becomes the blastocyst when it reaches uterine cavity
B. Blastocyst usually implants on the upper posterior wall of uterus
   1. outer portion of blastocyst made up of cells called trophoblasts
   2. trophoblasts penetrate into the uterine wall, digesting cells during their burrowing
      a) digested cells used for nutrition of the blastocyst
      b) the trophoblastic stage of fetal nutrition lasts until about the 12th week of pregnancy when placenta is fully formed and takes over

III. AFTER IMPLANTATION

A. Endometrium becomes known as the decidua
   1. becomes thick and vascular
   2. stores nutrients and vitamins
   3. divided into three parts
      a) decidua vera: lines main uterine cavity
      b) decidua capsularis: surrounds the ovum
      c) decidua basalis: lies under implantation site; forms maternal portion of placenta

Chapter 6

Fetal Development

I. FETAL PHYSIOLOGY

A. Placental development (Figure 6-1)
 1. chorionic villi: finger-like projections covered with membrane derived from trophoblastic layer of ovum
    a) penetrate uterine wall
    b) tap maternal blood supply, but membrane covering villi prevents fetal and maternal blood from mixing
    c) nutrients and waste products exchange by diffusion
    d) secrete chorionic gonadotropin
       (1) keeps corpus luteum from degenerating
       (2) enlarges corpus luteum, which secretes increased amounts of estrogen and progesterone until placenta is fully formed
       (3) excreted in urine of pregnant woman by eighth to tenth day after fertilization and is utilized in A–Z and Friedman Pregnancy tests
       (4) after full formation of placenta, chorionic gonadotropin production decreases, and placental secretions of estrogen and progesterone increase
 2. by the fourth month, maternal decidua basalis and fetal chorionic villi have formed placenta
B. Placental function
 1. placenta: temporary organ shared by mother and fetus
    a) allows exchange between maternal and fetal circulation
    b) blood of mother and fetus do not mix
       (1) exchange takes place by diffusion across fetal and maternal membranes
    c) organ of fetal nutrition, excretion, and respiration

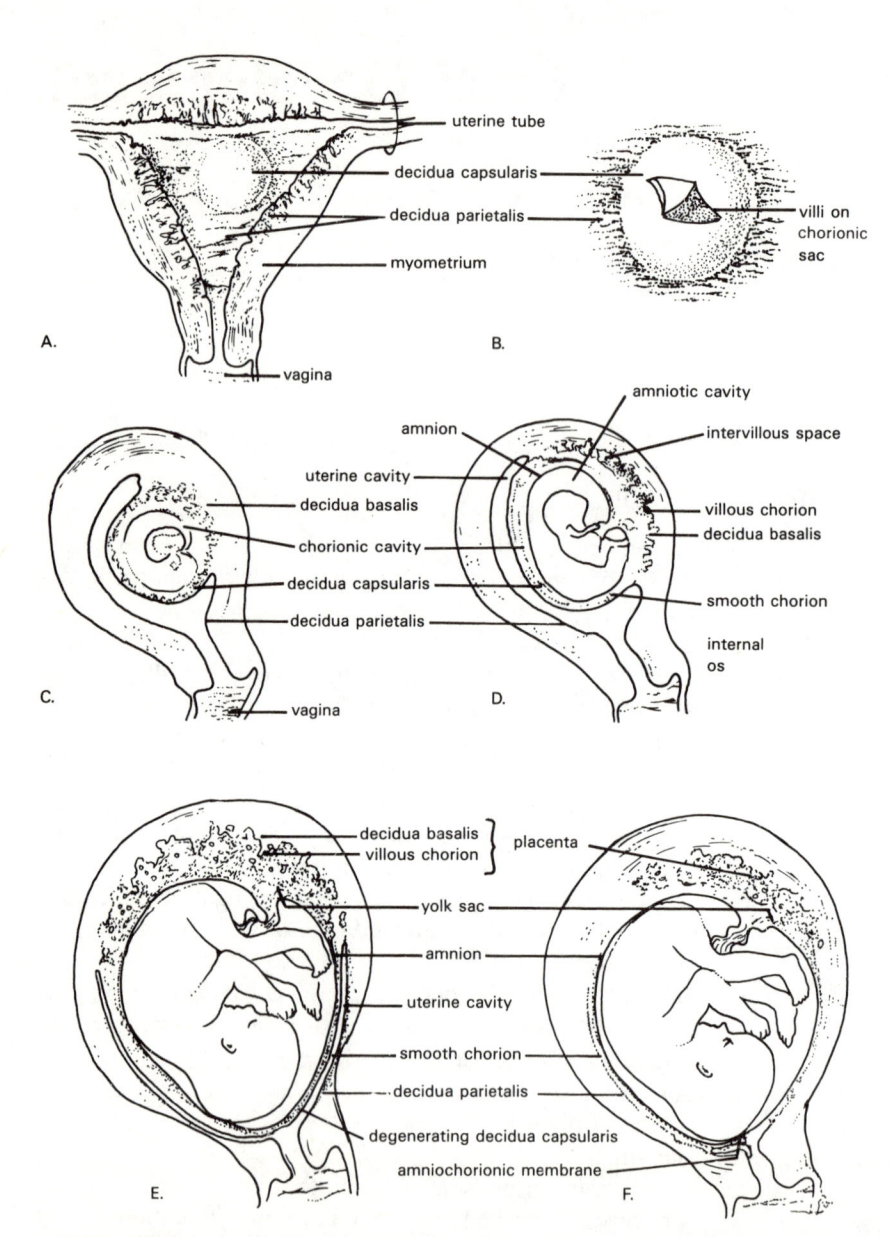

Figure 6-1 Support Systems for Fetal Development. (A) Drawing of a frontal section of the uterus showing the elevation of the decidua capsularis caused by the expanding chorionic sac of a 4-week embryo, implanted in the endometrium on the posterior wall. (B) Enlarged drawing of the implantation site. The chorionic villi have been exposed by cutting an opening in the decidua capsularis. (C–F) Drawings of sagittal sections of the gravid uterus from the 4th–22nd weeks, showing the changing relations of the fetal membranes to the decidua. In

2. offers fetus protection from some harmful substances
    a) new knowledge shows that many teratogenic substances pass the placental barrier.
3. immunity from some maternal antibodies is passively passed from mother to child
4. endocrine function
    a) human chorionic gonadotropin
        (1) maintains function of corpus luteum in early pregnancy
        (2) may regulate steroid production in fetus
        (3) used for pregnancy testing
            (a) negative results after 16–20 weeks
            (b) amount increases in multiple pregnancies
            (c) amount decreases in cases of threatened abortion
    b) human placental lactogen
        (1) acts in a manner similar to growth hormone
        (2) spares maternal glucose
            (a) increases availability of glucose to fetus
        (3) may affect incorporation of iron into erythrocytes
        (4) stimulates breast development
    c) estrogen
        (1) increases 1000 times during pregnancy
        (2) influences
            (a) growth of uterus by hypertrophy and proliferation of endometrium
            (b) breast development
            (c) relaxation of pelvic joints and muscles
            (d) gastric secretions
            (e) sodium and water retention
            (f) increase of blood fibrinogen
            (g) psychology
                1. emotional lability
                2. possible libido alteration
    d) progesterone
        (1) increases 10 times in pregnancy
            (a) produced in first 7 weeks by corpus luteum

(F), the amnion and chorion are fused with each other and the decidua parietalis, thereby obliterating the uterine cavity. Note that the villi persist only where the chorion is associated with the decidua basalis; here they form the villous chorion (fetal portion of the placenta).
Source: Modified from Moore, K.L.: *The Developing Human: Clinically Oriented Embryology,* 4th ed. Philadelphia: W.B. Saunders Co., 1988.

(2) influences
- (a) development of decidua cells of endometrium
- (b) decreased irritability of uterus
- (c) relaxation of smooth muscle
- (d) hypothalamus functioning
    1. changes the amount of fat stored
    2. stimulates respiratory center to decrease PCO_2; facilitates CO_2 transfer from fetal to maternal circulation
    3. increases basal temperature 0.5°F until midpregnancy

C. Fetal functioning
  1. respiratory
     a) some amniotic fluid components found in lungs of fetus
     b) most respiratory functioning occurs through placental circulation
  2. digestive
     a) digestive enzymes found in second trimester
     b) amniotic fluid swallowed after 12th week
     c) meconium in intestine during second half of pregnancy
     d) most digestive functions occur through placental circulation
  3. liver
     a) liver stores iron and carbohydrates from fourth month
  4. renal
     a) capable of functioning, but not utilized because of placental functioning
  5. fetal circulation (Figure 6-2)
     a) distinctive features
        (1) ductus venosus bypasses liver
        (2) foramen ovale from right atrium to left atrium bypasses right ventricle
        (3) ductus arteriosus shunt from pulmonary artery to aorta bypasses lungs
        (4) umbilical cord contains umbilical arteries and vein that connect placenta to fetus
        (5) hypogastric arteries return blood to umbilical arteries
     b) circulation pattern
        (1) from placental blood vessels through umbilical vein, passing through ductus venosus (small amount to liver for nourishment), into inferior vena cava, into right atrium through foramen ovale to left atrium, to left ventricle, through aorta to fetal circulation of head and upper extremities, to su-

Fetal Development   75

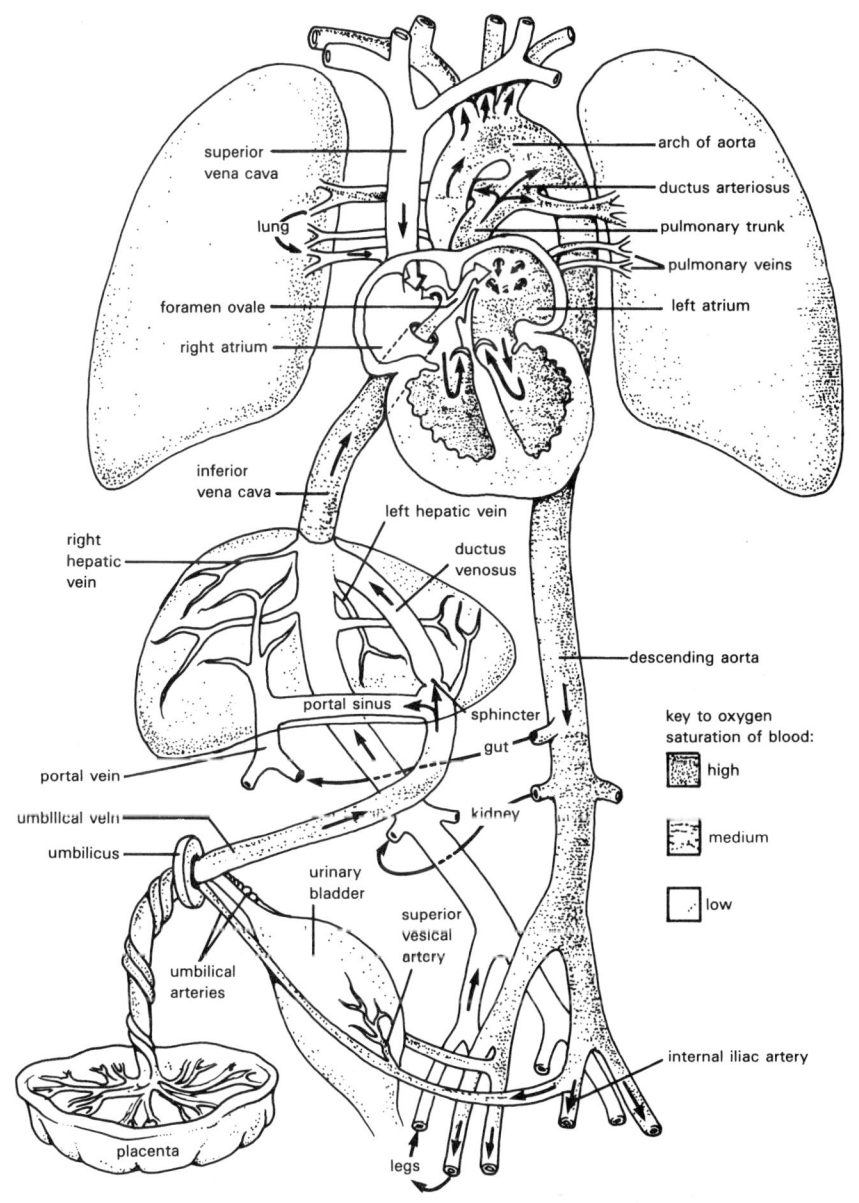

Figure 6-2 Fetal Circulation. The arrows show the course of the fetal circulation. The organs are not drawn to scale. *Source:* Modified from Moore, K.L.: *The Developing Human: Clinically Oriented Embryology,* 4th ed. Philadelphia: W.B. Saunders Co., 1988.

perior vena cava, to the right atrium (mixes with blood from inferior vena cava), some to the pulmonary artery to nourish lungs, most through ductus arteriosus to aorta, distributed to lower extremities, abdomen, and pelvis of fetus, to hypogastric arteries, to umbilical arteries to the placenta
            (2) exchange of gases and nutrients in the placenta is accomplished by the process of diffusion
                (a) when blood in maternal sinus has higher pressure of nutrients and oxygen than blood in chorionic villi, the nutrients and oxygen pass through membrane to fetal blood supply by diffusion
            (3) maternal blood and fetal blood remain separate and never mix, as they are separated by a membrane covering chorionic villi

II. FETAL DEVELOPMENT
  A. Development occurs by
      1. cell proliferation
          a) zygote (fertilized ovum) divides by mitosis; daughter cells continue to divide
      2. growth
      3. differentiation
          a) morphogenesis: organs and body take shape
          b) histogenesis: specificity of tissues occurs
      4. integration: coordination of organ system function
  B. Developmental principles
      1. direction of growth
          a) cephalocaudal: head to tail
          b) proximidistal: central to peripheral
      2. growth is regular, orderly, and predictable
      3. development occurs from the simple to the more complex
      4. growth does not occur in a linear way; there are periods of slow and rapid growth
  C. Anatomical development
      1. period of ovum: from fertilization to implantation, 5–7 days after conception
          a) 30 hours after fertilization
              (1) two-cell stage
              (2) floating free in fallopian tube
              (3) reaches uterine cavity at 12- to 16-cell stage, at which time it is called a morula

      b) 4 to 4.5 days: blastocyst forms
        (1) composed of
           (a) inner cell mass: embryo proper
           (b) outer cell mass (trophoblast): becomes fetal part of placenta
      c) 5–7 days
        (1) implantation begins
        (2) inner cell layer divides into
           (a) ectoderm: outer layer
              1. basis for development of
                 a. central nervous system (CNS)
                 b. skin
                 c. hair
                 d. nails
                 e. sweat and sebaceous glands
           (b) mesoderm: middle layer
              1. basis for development of
                 a. muscles
                 b. bones
                 c. kidneys
                 d. circulatory and reproductive systems
           (c) endoderm: inner layer
              1. basis for development of
                 a. liver
                 b. pancreas
                 c. digestive and respiratory systems
D. Fetal membranes
   1. Yolk sac: may play role in nutrient transfer
      a) partially incorporated into embryo to form foregut, midgut, and hindgut
      b) shrinks as pregnancy advances
   2. allantois: arises from hindgut of yolk sac
      a) later incorporated as umbilical vessels
   3. amnion: forms wall of amniotic cavity
      a) produces amniotic fluid
   4. chorion: outer lining of amniotic cavity
E. Amniotic fluid
   1. composition: 99% water with protein, glucose, and inorganic salts
   2. at term, fetus is immersed in 800 to 1200 cc
   3. functions
      a) protects fetus from injury
      b) provides thermal stability

c) allows for fetal movement
d) facilitates symmetrical fetal growth
e) is source of oral fluid
f) acts as collection system for excretions

F. Period of the embryo: from implantation to the completion of organogenesis (organ development) at 8 weeks gestation
  1. end of first lunar month
     a) 0.25 inches long
     b) bent over itself
     c) spine formed
     d) beginning formation of
        (1) eyes
        (2) ears
        (3) nose
        (4) heart
        (5) digestive tract
        (6) arm and leg buds

G. Period of the fetus: from completion of organogenesis to birth
  1. end of second lunar month
     a) head prominent, recognizable human face
     b) external genitalia present, but difficult to distinguish sex
     c) 1 inch from head to buttocks
     d) weighs 1/30th of an ounce
  2. end of third lunar month
     a) inches long; about 1 oz in weight
     b) sex can be determined
     c) bones begin to ossify
     d) baby teeth buds begin to form
     e) fingers and toes begin to form
     f) fetus moves but *not* felt by mother
  3. end of fourth lunar month
     a) 6.5 inches long; 4 oz in weight
     b) external genitals obvious
  4. end of fifth lunar month
     a) lanugo: fine downy hair over body surface
     b) 10 inches long, about 8 oz in weight
     c) quickening: mother can feel movement
     d) fetal heart heard
     e) will make effort to breathe outside of uterus but lungs insufficient to sustain life
  5. end of sixth lunar month
     a) 12 inches long; 1.5 lbs in weight
     b) considered viable but does not usually survive if delivered

            c) resembles miniature baby
            d) skin wrinkled: no fat pads
            e) vernix caseosa: cheesy substance to protect skin
         6. end of seventh lunar month
            a) 15 inches long; 2.5 lbs in weight
            b) better chance of survival if delivered
         7. end of eighth lunar month
            a) 16.5 inches long; 4 lbs in weight
            b) good chance of survival if delivered
         8. end of ninth lunar month
            a) 19 inches long; 6 lbs in weight
            b) well padded with subcutaneous fat
            c) survival same as term
         9. middle of tenth month
            a) 20 inches long; 7 lbs in weight
            b) skin white or pink
            c) lanugo mostly gone
            d) covered with vernix
            e) nails firm
NOTE: Length of full term varies from 240 to 300 days, usually 9.5 lunar months or 38 weeks

III. FACTORS AFFECTING FETAL DEVELOPMENT
   A. Causes of birth defects
      1. maternal metabolic disorders: 1–2%
      2. infection: 2–3%
      3. chromosomal aberrations: 3–5%
      4. radiation: 1%
      5. drugs and chemicals: 3%
      6. genetic transmission: 20%
      7. unknown: 69–73% (includes combinations and interactions among a variety of unknown factors):
   B. Sex determination
      1. female ovum carries only X gene
      2. male sperm carries either X or Y gene
      3. after fertilization
         a) if sperm contributes an X to zygote, sex will be female, XX
         b) if sperm contributes a Y to zygote, sex will be male, XY
   C. Abnormalities of fetal development
      1. a large percentage of abnormal fetuses are expelled by spontaneous abortion

2. infants who survive and are born with congenital malformations constitute approximately 3 to 5% of all live births
3. the developing fetus may be adversely affected by genetic factors or environmental factors
4. genetic factors
    a) 23 pairs of chromosomes exist in each cell
        (1) 22 pairs are called autosomes
        (2) one pair is called the sex chromosomes
    b) chromosomes contain the genes
    c) during meiotic or mitotic division, abnormalities may occur, producing a chromosomal defect
        (1) chromosomal defects may occur because of too much or too little chromosomal material in an autosome or sex chromosome pair
        (2) translocation and cross-over of chromosomes may occur
    d) autosomal defects
        (1) Down syndrome (mongolism): infant has 47 chromosomes as there is an extra chromosome at number 21 chromosome; this is called trisomy
            (a) trisomy 21 usually occurs in mothers over 35 and is not genetically transmitted
        (2) Down syndrome can also be caused by translocation of chromosomes
            (a) translocation Down syndrome is usually transmitted by a nonsymptomatic mother with a translocation, and subsequent pregnancies may be similarly affected
        (3) trisomy 13–15 and trisomy 17–18 also have occurred, causing severe abnormalities, and infants usually do not survive after birth
        (4) autosomal dominance
            (a) a dominant trait that causes disease is present in the heterozygous state (Dd)
                1. few congenital defects are transmitted through autosomal dominance
                2. conditions are usually milder than recessive traits
                3. there is usually a wide spectrum of variation in the disease manifestations
                4. condition may occur as a result of a mutation, rather than as an inherited gene
                5. autosomal dominant inherited conditions
                    a. cleft palate
                    b. polydactylia

c. cataracts
d. myopia
(5) autosomal recessive conditions
   (a) the individual with a congenital disease caused by a recessive gene inheritance is homozygous for gene (dd) (Figure 6-3)
      1. both parents must carry the recessive defective gene Dd + Dd
      2. 50% of the children will usually be Dd asymptomatic carriers
      3. 25% of children will usually be normal DD
      4. 25% of children will be exposed to risk of the disease because they have dd—two recessive genes
   (b) examples of diseases and defects caused by recessive autosomal inheritance
      1. inborn errors of metabolism
         a. protein disorders where defective or absent enzymes prevent metabolism of protein, resulting in eventual death or mental retardation if untreated
         b. some inborn errors of metabolism are dominantly inherited or sex linked but the majority are recessive autosomal defects
         c. phenylketonuria (PKU): a condition where the enzyme phenylalanine hydroxylase that is needed to convert the protein phenylalanine is missing

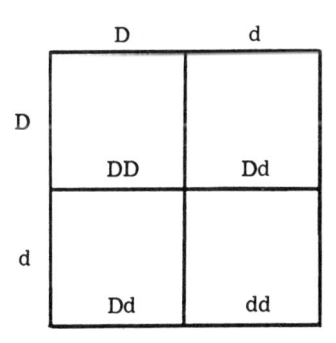

	D	d
D	DD	Dd
d	Dd	dd

DD - normal
Dd   carrier - no manifestations of disease
dd - disease

Figure 6-3 Genetic Transmission of Autosomal Recessive Conditions

d. maple syrup urine disease (MSUD) and galactosemia are two other examples of metabolic errors that have a much rarer incidence
2. other autosomal recessive diseases
   a. diabetes
   b. Tay-Sachs disease
   c. muscular dystrophy
   d. Cooley's anemia
   e. albinism
(6) sex chromosome abnormalities
   (a) one sex chromosome may be missing
      1. Turner's syndrome: one X missing, female appearance with few secondary sex characteristics
   (b) an extra X or Y may occur
      1. an extra Y or X chromosome does not necessarily result in abnormalities
      2. a male with XXY may develop Klinefelter's syndrome, which causes sterility and testicular atrophy
      3. some research shows an association between XYY in males and aggressive or criminal behavior; subsequent research has not supported this
   (c) sex-linked defects
      1. recessive gene is carried only on X chromosome
      2. male does not carry corresponding dominant gene on Y chromosome to neutralize effect of recessive gene on X chromosome
      3. trait causes disease in males, but they cannot transmit it
      4. females are carriers but do not develop the disease
      5. examples of sex-linked diseases
         a. hemophilia
         b. color-blindness
5. environmental factors
   a) teratology: study of the effect of environmental agents such as drugs, radiation, pollution, and viruses on the developing fetus which may possibly lead to abnormalities
      (1) teratogen may cause
         (a) mutation
         (b) chromosomal disruption
         (c) mitotic interference
         (d) alteration in nucleic acid integrity or function

(e) precursor or substrate deprivation
(f) alteration of energy source
(g) changed membrane characteristics
(h) alteration in osmolar balance
(i) enzyme inhibition
b) principles of teratogenesis
    (1) the effects of the teratogenic agent depend primarily on the timing and intensity of dosage
        (a) excessive dosage of a teratogenic agent may kill the fetus
        (b) a dosage strong enough to affect the developing embryo and cause damage must be introduced into the mother at the time of maximum sensitivity on the developing organ in order to have an adverse effect
        (c) certain teratogenic agents may be neutralized by the action of other substances
        (d) the greatest vulnerability of a developing organ is at time of greatest mitotic activity during organogenesis
        (e) when organogenesis is completed, a teratogenic agent cannot cause malformation in the organ
        (f) the health and genetic structure of the mother may affect the activity of the agent
c) types of teratogenic agents
    (1) components of normal body metabolism, such as vitamins and hormones
    (2) chemical agents, including drugs, gases, etc.
    (3) physical agents, such as radiation, decompression, hypothermia, hyperthermia, amniotic sac puncture, and noise
d) certain teratogens have been shown to be teratogenic in animals and have been strongly associated with fetal abnormalities in humans. Teratogens can also produce adverse effects on the neonate. Many additional substances are suspected of teratogenesis and continued research remains to be done in this area
    (1) to identify a teratogenic agent in humans the following conditions must be met
        (a) an abrupt increase in the incidence of a defect or syndrome
        (b) increase occurs with a known environmental change
        (c) documented exposure to environmental change early in pregnancy that produces a characteristic defect
        (d) absence of other facts that are common to all pregnancies and that produce an infant with that defect

(2) drugs
- (a) salicylates and acetaminophen: may affect kidney development and fetal bleeding
- (b) scopalomine: may cause early abortion
- (c) streptomycin: may cause deafness (eighth cranial nerve damage)
- (d) tetracyclines: may cause yellow teeth, slows bone growth
- (e) chloroquine: may cause deafness, damage to retina
- (f) anticonvulsants and barbiturates: may cause cleft lip and palate and other anomalies
- (g) thalidomide: may cause limb malformation (phocomelia)
- (h) meclizine: may cause cleft palate
- (i) anticancer agents: may cause cleft palate and other anomalies
- (j) amphetamines: may cause heart defects, cleft palate, and other anomalies
- (k) caffeine, theophylline: may cause fetal tachycardia, liver damage, deficient clotting mechanisms
- (l) androgens, estrogens, and DES: may cause masculinization of female infant or feminization of male infant, danger of cancer of vagina or cervix developing in women
- (m) corticosteroids: may cause cleft palate, club foot, and other anomalies
- (n) magnesium antacids: may cause magnesium toxicity
- (o) sodium bicarbonate: may cause metabolic alkalosis, edema, fluid overload
- (p) psychoactive drugs: may cause bone anomalies, chromosomal damage
- (q) antidepressants: may cause a variety of anomalies
- (r) vitamin D: may cause a variety of anomalies, including cardiopathies
- (s) narcotics: may cause still births and drug addiction
- (t) alcohol
    1. fetal alcohol syndrome
        a. growth deficiency: small at birth, smaller head circumference; remain shorter and thinner as they grow older
        b. facial deformities: short eye slits, flattened nasal

bridge, short nose and upper eyelid folds; there may be other anomalies
   c. CNS damage: slow development, lowered mental ability, may be hyperactive and irritable
   d. not all babies of alcoholic mothers develop FAS (fetal alcohol syndrome)
   e. factors to be considered include duration of drinking and amount of alcohol consumed each day
   f. at the present time the exact relationship between amount of alcohol consumed and development of FAS has not been determined
   g. moderate and social drinking may be related to spontaneous abortion and low birthweight
(u) a relationship has been established between fetal loss in nurses and exposure to antineoplastic drugs in Finland (Selevan, 1985)
(3) smoking: may cause prematurity, low birthweight, abortion, higher rates of perinatal mortality, fetal abnormalities, and placental abnormalities
(4) "TORCH" complex of infections: toxoplasmosis, rubella, herpes simplex virus, cytomegalovirus, and other viruses may be transmitted to the fetus and newborn and are capable of causing permanent damage
   (a) toxoplasmosis: protozoal infection transmitted through the placenta that may cause growth retardation, immune deficiencies, hearing and eye defects, and other anomalies
   (b) rubella viral infection: transmitted through the placenta can cause severe anomalies, such as deafness, eye defects, and other anomalies
   (c) cytomegalovirus (CMV): viral infection transmitted through placenta or through birth canal to neonate; may cause brain damage, liver disease, cerebral palsy, and other anomalies
   (d) herpes simplex (HSV): viral infection transmitted through placenta and through lesions in birth canal to newborn; may cause eye and CNS damage and other anomalies
   (e) hepatitis B: viral infection transmitted through placenta

and postnatally causes congenital hepatitis B in fetus and newborn
- (5) syphilis: bacterial infection can be transmitted through placenta or through lesions in birth canal; may cause congenital syphilis
- (6) x-rays: may cause congenital defects through radiation during organogenesis
- (7) heat: prolonged exposure to excessive heat may be harmful to the fetus; high maternal temperatures during illness or prolonged use of hot tubs may influence fetal development and prematurity
- (8) chemicals and gases: maternal exposure to lead, mercury, and anesthetic gases has been associated with fetal abnormalities; many chemicals are under study as possible reproductive hazards that may affect either the male or female
  - (a) vulnerability of male to toxic agents is manifested by
    1. changes in sperm production
    2. increase in spontaneous abortions in female partner
  - (b) exposure in male and actual birth defect not definitively established

6. multifactorial inheritance
   a) genetic susceptibility in combination with an environmental agent can produce a disease or structure defect; many genes may be involved
   b) no inheritance pattern can be identified but risk is higher in closely related individuals
   c) conditions caused by multifactorial inheritance
      (1) cleft lip and/or palate
      (2) congenital heart disease
      (3) neural tube defect (new research indicates that taking a simple vitamin pill with folic acid may prevent it)
      (4) hypertension

C. Nursing process in the prevention of birth defects; emphasis is on observation and evaluation
   1. assessment
      a) detailed family history to ascertain presence of inherited disorders
      b) history of possible teratogenic exposure of client
         (1) nutritional status and patterns
         (2) smoking
         (3) drug use
         (4) place of employment

(5) exposure to radiation
(6) infections and chronic illnesses
(7) place of residence
(8) occupational history of pregnant woman and spouse (Exhibit 6-1)

Exhibit 6-1 Occupational Health History

OCCUPATIONAL HEALTH HISTORY SCREENING QUESTIONNAIRE

Name:_____ Date:_____

Yourself

1. What is your current occupation?_____

2. When did you begin this work?
   Month_____ Year_____
   If you have held other kind of jobs please list them and indicate the time periods.

   _____ Month_____ Year_____

   _____ Month_____ Year_____

   _____ Month_____ Year_____

   _____ Month_____ Year_____

3. Have you ever been exposed to any of the following in your job (or in a hobby you pursue)? where? when?

		year began	year ended
a. industrial solvents	_____	_____	_____
b. chemical fume/dusts	_____	_____	_____
c. pesticides	_____	_____	_____
d. radiation, x-rays	_____	_____	_____
e. sterilizing agents (e.g., ethylene oxide)	_____	_____	_____
f. other (identify)	_____	_____	_____
_____	_____	_____	_____

Exhibit 6-1 continued

4. Have you ever developed a skin rash or allergy that you can relate to something you've worked with on your job?

         where?   year began year ended
         _____ _____ _____

5. Could anything on your job or hobbies cause lasting discomfort to your nose, throat, or chest?

         where?   year began year ended
         _____ _____ _____

6. Have you ever been injured on the job or filed a workers' compensation claim?

         where?   when? (year)
         _____ _____

7. Have you ever worked in a job that required you to wear protective equipment, such as a respirator, plastic gloves, or protective outerwear? Describe the condition requiring this use.

  Description   where?   year began year ended
  _____ _____ _____ _____

Your Spouse

1. What is his/her current occupation? _____

2. When did s/he begin this work?

         Month_____ Year_____

If s/he has held other kind of jobs please list them and indicate the time periods.

  _____ Month_____ Year_____

  _____ Month_____ Year_____

  _____ Month_____ Year_____

  _____ Month_____ Year_____

3. Has s/he ever been exposed to any of the following in his/her job (or in a hobby s/he pursues)? where?   when?

               year began year ended

  a. industrial solvents _____ _____ _____

  b. chemical fume/dusts _____ _____ _____

  c. pesticides _____ _____ _____

  d. radiation, x-rays _____ _____ _____

  e. sterilizing agents
    (e.g., ethylene oxide) _____ _____ _____

Exhibit 6-1 continued

                                            where?   year began   year ended
    f. other (identify)   _____ _____ _____

_____ _____ _____ _____

4. Has s/he ever developed a skin rash or allergy that s/he can relate to something you've worked with on your job?
                                    where?   year began   year ended
                                      _____ _____ _____

5. Could anything on his/her job or hobbies cause lasting discomfort to his/her nose, throat, or chest?
                                    where?   year began   year ended
                                      _____ _____ _____

6. Has s/he ever been injured on the job or filed a workers' compensation claim?
                                  where?   when? (year)
                                    _____ _____

7. Has s/he ever worked in a job that required s/he to wear protective equipment, such as a respirator, plastic gloves, or protective outerwear? Describe the condition requiring this use.
        Description   where?   year began   year ended
    _____ _____ _____ _____

Source: Adapted by permission from Women's Occupational Health Resource Center, Brooklyn, New York.

    2. nursing diagnosis: based on an evaluation of the assessment; possible problems identified
        a) low protein intake
        b) excessive smoking
        c) familial history of an inherited disease
        d) exposure to radiation
        e) exposure to environmental risk at work or at home

    3. goals
        a) change in behavior
            (1) smoking cessation
            (2) nutritional intake alteration
        b) occupational counseling
        c) support related to decision making if birth defect is found
            (1) referral to appropriate clergy is often helpful

    4. intervention: directed toward limiting exposure to teratogenic agents, prevention of transmission of inherited diseases, and assisting parents in coping with the possibility or actuality of malformations in offspring

a) providing information
   (1) drugs
      (a) client should be cautioned to avoid all nonessential drugs; risk factors in drug use should be explained
      (b) if drugs are necessary she should consult a physician
      (c) if she has used a drug the client should be advised to inform her physician
      (d) client should be advised to inform all health care providers of her pregnancy
   (2) x-rays
      (a) x-rays should be done immediately after menstrual cycle in all women of childbearing age
      (b) postponement of diagnostic x-rays unless essential until pregnancy is completed
   (3) infectious disease
      (a) avoid exposure
      (b) immunization to rubella before childbearing age
   (4) nutrition
      (a) caution about inappropriate or excessive vitamin and/or mineral use
      (b) counseling related to establishing and maintaining optimal nutrition
   (5) smoking cessation should be encouraged
      (a) referral to support group
b) providing counseling and support to assist parents when they have been informed that fetus has birth defect
   (1) information about options available
   (2) education about impact of defect on quality of life of unborn child
   (3) anticipatory grief counseling
c) genetic counseling referral if there has been exposure to teratogenic agent or there is concern about an inherited disorder
d) prenatal diagnosis: there are an increasing number of prenatal screening tests that can diagnose a birth defect by using
   (1) amniocentesis: withdrawal of fluid from the amniotic cavity by the insertion of needle through the abdominal wall into the uterus and amniotic cavity after the 14th week
      (a) ultrasound used to determine placement of needle
      (b) relatively low-risk procedure
   (2) fetoscopy: insertion of a cannula into abdominal wall through which a fetoscope (consists of light source and lens) is inserted

(a) direct observation in small segments possible
(b) fetal blood samples and tissue can be obtained
(c) increased risk of spontaneous abortion or preterm labor and delivery
(3) ultrasonography: high-frequency sound waves create echoes by the reflection off maternal and fetal organs, thereby enabling the fetus and placenta to be visualized
   (a) no adverse effects noted in humans
      1. long-term effects currently under investigation
   (b) can monitor fetal growth
   (c) can determine fetal size and volume of amniotic fluid
   (d) can uncover neural tube defects, skeletal deformities, fetal ascites, and hydrops fetalis
(4) chorionic villi sampling: a plastic catheter is inserted vaginally into the uterus. Using ultrasound as a guide the instrument is positioned so that a sample may be aspirated. Procedure can be done 8 to 10 weeks after last menstrual period
   (a) test results can be obtained rapidly because these cells divide quickly
   (b) risks to woman and her fetus are under investigation; one complication may be septic shock
   (c) neural tube defects cannot be determined by chorionic villi sampling
(5) prenatal diagnosis should be available to
   (a) women who are/or will be 35 at delivery
   (b) women who have had a child with a birth defect, chromosomal abnormality, or metabolic or structural disorder
   (c) couples with history of chromosomal abnormality or metabolic or structural disorder
   (d) suspected carriers of autosomal recessive trait or X-linked disorder
   (e) couples with family history of inherited disorder
   (f) couples with extreme anxiety or concern
(6) prenatal screening tests: approximately 200 conditions can presently be detected. The number of conditions for which testing is possible is increasing because of the new knowledge of gene mapping, chemical assays, and technology
   (a) alphafetoprotein (AFP): normal protein excreted early in pregnancy by the fetus into maternal bloodstream;

concentration rises until third trimester, then slowly decreases
1. high levels of AFP associated with neural tube defects during the second trimester
2. if high level is obtained a second test is performed. Final diagnosis is confirmed by other test procedures because other conditions (i.e., incorrect dating, multiple pregnancy) can raise level of AFP
3. about one in 700 live births (1 to 2 per 1000) in U.S. is affected with neural tube defect (NTD)
4. couples who have had a previously affected child have a 2–3% chance of recurrence
5. 90–95% of all cases occur without any familial history
6. vitamin supplementation is being studied as a possible prevention of NTD
 (b) heterozygote screening: can detect clinically normal carriers; usually offered to members of a high-risk ethnic group
1. Tay-Sachs disease: common among Eastern European Jews. Approximately 1 in 25 carry the mutant gene
2. sickle cell disease: common in people of black African descent. About 1 in 10 American blacks carry the gene and may have the sickle cell trait; 1 in 100 black couples have the risk of a child with the disease
3. beta thalessemia (Cooley's anemia): high incidence found in individuals of Mediterranean descent. Those of Greek and Italian ancestry have about a 1:25 chance of being a carrier of the gene

D. Prevention and treatment of birth defects
1. since end of World War II many technological advances have been used to treat birth defects and palliate abnormalities
2. fetal surgery has been used to place shunts to relieve obstructive uropathy and obstructive hydrocephalus
   a) a registry has been established
      (1) to provide updated information on cumulative results
      (2) to collect data that may provide guidance as to surgery's effectiveness and safety
3. intrauterine treatment of some metabolic disorders has begun
4. future efforts in prevention will probably be directed toward
   a) definition of causes

b) gene therapy
c) education about risks in the environment
d) increased efforts to control rubella, toxoplasmosis, and cytomegalia

REFERENCE

Selevan, S., et al. (1985, November 7). A study of occupational exposure to antineoplastic drug and fetal loss in nurses." *New England Journal of Medicine,* November 7, pp. 1173–1177.

Chapter 7

Pregnancy

I. PREPARATION FOR PARENTHOOD
A. Healthy sexuality is related to the ability to relate fully to the opposite sex and the capacity to trust and love
  1. infant finds pleasure through sense of touch
     a) if pleasurable feelings are not distorted, a positive attitude toward sexuality should develop
     b) healthy sexuality develops from a childhood in which developmental tasks were completed and basic human needs were met
        (1) ensures capacity of individuals to develop a trusting, open, caring relationship with others
  2. sex education
     a) accurate information that imparts a healthy acceptance of human sexuality should be given as soon as child shows readiness
  3. parental relationships set tone for future sexual relationships of children
     a) a loving, caring relationship of mutual respect between parents encourages the development of healthy heterosexual relationships

B. Attitude toward pregnancy depends on
  1. parents' childhood
  2. relationship of husband and wife
  3. socioeconomic factors
  4. cultural factors
  5. knowledge about pregnancy
  6. fear of pain, hospitalization, etc.
  7. desire for parenthood

C. Parental readiness for new role is related to their
  1. understanding of the parental role and a willingness to adapt to that role
  2. recognition of the uniqueness of children as individuals
  3. level of knowledge of basic stages of growth and development
  4. emotional maturity and family interpersonal and communication skills

II. COMMUNITY RESOURCES TO ASSIST PREPARATION FOR PARENTHOOD
  A. Maternity centers: provide counseling services, classes for expectant parents, prenatal and intrapartal services
    1. nurse-midwives often provide comprehensive care
  B. Prenatal clinics: provide physical assessment and care during pregnancy. Psychological and emotional support is also provided
  C. Classes for expectant parents are offered by
    1. hospitals
    2. community health agencies
    3. maternity centers
    4. Red Cross chapters
    5. trained personnel from ASPO (see below)
    6. course usually includes
      a) information about what to expect during pregnancy, labor and delivery, and the postpartal period and about the newborn
      b) encouragement of involvement of father
      c) verbalization of thoughts and feelings relating to parenting
      d) an attempt to reduce feelings of loneliness
      e) anticipatory guidance for parenthood
      f) preparation for labor and delivery
      g) preparation for new roles and new family developmental tasks
  D. La Leche League: an organization of nursing mothers that encourages and assists others who wish to breast feed their children
    1. chapters of La Leche League are organized in most major cities in the country
    2. literature relating to successful breast feeding is available from the organization
    3. regular meetings of mothers who are members of the organization are held in members' homes and are open to all
    4. nursing mothers are encouraged to call fellow members of the organization whenever they need assistance or advice

E. Community health nurses: maintain prenatal clinics and visit families throughout the maternity cycle for counseling, instruction, and assistance in solving problems
F. Private physicians: assist in the maintenance of physical and emotional health during maternity cycle
G. ASPO (American Society for Psychoprophylaxis in Obstetrics): classes given in Lamaze method of natural childbirth (for full explanation see Chapter 12)

III. PRENATAL REGIMEN
   A. Importance of early prenatal care
      1. early diagnosis of pregnancy decreases possibility of complications
         a) presumptive signs: cessation of menses, morning sickness, tenderness and fullness of breasts, frequent urination, Chadwick's sign, fatigue, fetal movement (quickening)
         b) probable signs: enlarged abdomen, Hegar's sign, ballottement, Goodell's sign, pregnancy tests based on chorionic gonadotropin in blood and urine
         c) positive signs: fetal heart beat and x-ray of fetal skeleton, sonogram, fetal movements felt by examiner
      2. regular frequent maternity supervision allows early diagnosis and treatment of complications
         a) decreases maternal and infant morbidity and mortality
   B. Prenatal health care delivery
      1. the prospective parents are part of a health team that may include one or more of the following personnel
         a) nurse-midwife
         b) physician
         c) nurse
         d) nutritionist
         e) social worker
      2. in many prenatal clinics the nurse functions as a coordinator of the health team
      3. each member of the health team delivers the health services that their education and experience prepare them to do. The nurse's role is carried out through utilization of the nursing process

IV. NURSING CARE DURING THE PRENATAL PERIOD RELATING TO PHYSICAL NEEDS
   A. History and general physical assessment will help determine if the pregnancy will proceed in an essentially normal pattern or if the client or fetus is at risk

1. initial prenatal visit
   a) physical exam
      (1) history and general physical
      (2) obstetrical exam determines general condition of reproductive organs
         (a) pelvis evaluated for shape and size
         (b) external measurements of pelvis determined
         (c) vaginal exam
            1. diagnostic tool to determine pregnancy
               a. Goodell's sign: softening of cervix
               b. Chadwick's sign: bluish hue of vaginal mucosa due to increased vascularity
            2. Pap smear
            3. internal pelvic measurements
      (3) breast exam
         (a) general condition
         (b) evaluation for lactation
      (4) lab tests
         (a) urine
         (b) VDRL
         (c) blood
            1. CBC
            2. type
            3. Rh
      (5) calculation for estimated date of confinement (EDC)
         (a) date of first day of last menstrual period; add 9 months and 7 days, or go back 3 months and add 7 days (Naegel's rule)
         (b) length of pregnancy varies, making calculation difficult
            1. average length of pregnancy: 266 days from time of conception or 280 days from first day of last menstrual period (10 lunar months or 40 weeks)
            2. range of duration of pregnancy: from 240 to 300 days considered within normal limit
      (6) possible problems identified during the initial visit
         (a) presence of acute or chronic disease or disability
            1. cardiovascular disease
            2. tuberculosis
            3. diabetes
            4. infectious disease
            5. venereal disease
            6. chronic debilitating disease

7. urological disease
8. anemia
   (b) blood incompatibilities
      1. Rh factor
      2. ABO
   (c) pelvic abnormalities or disproportions
   (d) previous Cesarean sections
   (e) history of previous difficulties during pregnancy
   (f) nutritional problems
   (g) history of previous premature births
   (h) adolescence
   (i) age over 35
   (j) high parity
   (k) socioeconomic status
   (l) emotional problems of parents
   (m) family interaction and role problems
   (n) exposure to teratogenic agents
2. continued monitoring of physical status will allow for detection of any change in status of client and fetus. Examinations during return visits include
   a) abdominal palpation and auscultation to determine
      (1) size of fetus
      (2) position of fetus
      (3) fetal heart rate
   b) fundal height is checked at every visit after the 13th week. Tape measure is used to measure from symphysis pubis to top of fundus
      (1) after 24th week, the approximate fundal height should equal the gestational age
      (2) if fundal height is less than it should be it may indicate intrauterine growth retardation (IUGR). If height is greater than it should be multiple gestation, hydramnios, or other conditions may be indicated
      (3) if measurements do not match gestational age, recalculate gestational age; possible use of ultrasound to assist in recalculation
      (4) if gestational age is correct check for possible problems
   c) fetal heart rate (FHR) may be heard by Doppler at 10 weeks and by fetoscope at 20 weeks. Allowing mother to hear tones assists in bonding
   d) Leopold's maneuvers are used to determine fetal lie and presentation after 30 weeks gestation

(1) palpate with fingers and palms
(2) palpate fundus for presence of head or breech position
(3) if head or breech position is felt fetus has a longitudinal lie. Check structure over inlet. If head or breech is palpated at sides of uterus, lie is transverse
(4) palpate position of fetal spine and small parts
(5) check for engagement of presenting part when time for delivery is near. Place both hands on presenting part and try to move from side to side. If presenting part is movable, part is not engaged.
- e) further testing of fetal status is described in Appendix A
- f) urine test to determine presence of
  (1) albumin
  (2) glucose
- g) weight determination
  (1) 25–28 lb desirable weight gain for entire gestational period to prevent low birthweight infants—some studies recommend as much as 32 lb
    (a) average weight gain during first trimester: 1.5 to 3 lb monthly
    (b) average gain per week during second and third trimester: 0.8 lb
    (c) sudden sharp gain of weight after 20th week of pregnancy may be danger signal of water retention and possible pre-eclampsia
    (d) approximate distribution of weight gain
      1. baby: 7.8 lb
      2. placenta: 2.0 lb
      3. amniotic fluid: 2.2 lb
      4. enlarged uterus: 2.4 lb
      5. enlarged breasts: 2.4 lb
      6. increased blood volume: 2.4 lb
      7. increased fluid in tissue: 5.8 lb
      8. total: 25 lb
    (e) studies have shown that a weight gain of less than 21 lb is a risk factor for low birthweight. There is a somewhat increased fetal death rate when the weight gain is over 35 lbs
- h) blood pressure reading
  (1) a sustained rise or fall of 15 mm Hg is significant
- i) breast examination to assess condition of nipples and breast tissue

Pregnancy 101

      j) vaginal examination in last trimester to determine
          (1) position
          (2) presentation
          (3) condition of cervix
  3. significant symptoms that may be an indication of a problem developing
      a) vaginal bleeding
      b) edema of face and fingers
      c) severe and continuous headache
      d) visual disturbances
      e) abdominal pain
      f) persistent vomiting
      g) chills and fever
      h) sudden escape of fluid from vagina
      i) a drop in hemoglobin or hematocrit
      j) presence of glucose or albumin in urine
      k) abnormal or absent fetal heart sounds
  4. nutritional assessment
      a) prepregnant weight patterns
      b) present weight
      c) color, skin turgor, signs of nutritional deficiencies
      d) presence of nausea and vomiting
      e) presence of any barriers to food ingestion (defective teeth, mouth infections)
      f) pre-existing conditions that will affect dietary needs, e.g., diabetes, anemia
      g) high risk factors relating to nutritional status
          (1) adolescents, especially those with out-of-wedlock pregnancies
          (2) women with low prepregnancy weight and those who do not gain enough during pregnancy
          (3) women with a history of frequent pregnancies
          (4) women with low socioeconomic status
          (5) women who lack knowledge of good nutrition
          (6) women with a history of children of low birthweight
          (7) women with diseases that influence nutritional status (TB, diabetes, alcoholism, drug addiction, etc.)
  5. sleep, rest, and exercise status assessment
      a) prepregnancy pattern of sleep, rest, and exercise
      b) present pattern of sleep, rest, and exercise
      c) complaints of fatigue
      d) opportunities for obtaining adequate sleep, rest, and exercise

e) barriers for obtaining adequate sleep, rest, and exercise
f) work conditions that mandate prolonged periods of sitting or standing
6. elimination pattern assessment
   a) prepregnant patterns of elimination, present patterns of elimination
   b) difficulties experienced with changing patterns of elimination
7. hygiene assessment
   a) prepregnant hygienic routines
   b) present hygienic routines
   c) presence of vaginal discharge
8. assessment of condition of breasts
   a) size, shape, and discomfort
   b) condition of nipples
   c) plans for breast feeding
   d) proper support of breasts
9. assessment of common conditions that may cause discomfort
   a) backache
   b) dyspnea
   c) varicosities
   d) leg cramps
   e) edema of lower extremities

B. The rationale for nursing intervention to meet the physical needs of the pregnant woman is primarily based on the bodily changes that occur during pregnancy and the changing needs of mother and child
   1. reproductive system changes
      a) uterus
         (1) increases in size from 2 oz to approximately 2 lbs
         (2) changes from solid organ that has capacity of 2 cc to a thin-walled muscular sac capable of holding full-term fetus (approximately 7 lbs)
            (a) accomplished by hypertrophy of existing muscle cells and formation of new ones
            (b) estrogen stimulates hypertrophy of muscle fibers
         (3) increases in contractile ability
            (a) rhythmic contractions throughout pregnancy: painless and irregular Braxton Hicks
         (4) rises out of pelvic cavity
            (a) third or fourth month: palpated above symphysis pubis
            (b) sixth month: at umbilicus
            (c) ninth month: at xiphoid process
            (d) tenth month: in first pregnancy (primipara) uterus drops down (lightening)

(5) as the uterus increases in size, the pressure on the abdominal wall causes the woman to walk with her shoulders thrown back and legs more apart to maintain body alignment
   (a) causes strain on muscles and ligaments of backs of thighs
   (b) muscular aches and cramps in late pregnancy
   (c) backache: caused by poor body alignment and relaxation of sacroiliac joints. Compensatory postural changes aggravate this condition
   (d) edema: common in lower extremities because of pressure of uterus on blood vessels
   (e) dyspnea: caused by pressure of growing uterus on diaphragm
   (f) varicose veins: caused by hereditary tendency and pressure in pelvis from enlarged uterus and on abdominal veins, causing stasis of blood in leg veins. The stasis in leg veins causes thinning and stretching of wall of veins
   (g) frequent urination: caused by
      1. the growing uterus putting pressure on bladder until third month
      2. after lightening, uterus again pushes against bladder in third trimester
b) cervix
   (1) softens in early pregnancy (Goodell's sign)
      (a) increased vascularization
      (b) proliferation of cervical glands that secrete mucus
         1. mucus plug expelled before labor
c) vagina
   (1) increase in vascularity
      (a) has purple hue (Chadwick's sign)
   (2) mucosa thickens
   (3) muscles hypertrophy
   (4) connective tissues loosen
   (5) increase in vaginal discharge
      (a) thick, white consistency
      (b) contains lactic acid; believed to help keep vagina free of pathogens
d) perineum
   (1) increased vascularity
   (2) hypertrophy of skin and muscles
   (3) loosening of connective tissues

2. breast changes
    a) enlargement
        (1) growth stimulated by estrogen and increased vascularity of tissue
        (2) progesterone changes tissue to secreting cells
        (3) growth of glandular (alveolar) tissue may cause pain and/or discomfort early in pregnancy
    b) nipples
        (1) deeply pigmented area surrounding nipple known as areola
        (2) erectile tissue
        (3) colostrum (precursor to milk)
            (a) thin, watery yellow substance
            (b) appears after third month
    c) Montgomery glands: embedded in areola's sebaceous glands
        (1) enlarge during pregnancy
3. gastrointestinal system changes
    a) distention of abdomen (mechanical)
        (1) striae gravidarum (reddish streaks) due to rupture and atrophy of connective tissue of skin due to stretching
            (a) after pregnancy grow lighter and silvery white, like scar tissue
            (b) may or may not occur
    b) decreased peristalsis and muscle tone
        (1) hormones of pregnancy (progesterone) increase muscle relaxation and decrease gastric motility. Reduced secretory activity and changes in carbohydrate metabolism contribute to nausea. By the beginning of the second trimester, estrogen level rises over progesterone and nausea usually decreases
            (a) constipation may occur if proper dietary habits are not practiced and if physical exercise is limited
    c) hemorrhoids: varicosities of rectum and anus that may cause pain, discomfort, and rectal bleeding
    d) hormonal and metabolic changes may lead to nausea and vomiting (morning sickness)
        (1) symptoms usually appear between 4th and 6th week and may last until the 15th week
        (2) emotional factors are believed to influence the severity and frequency of the symptoms
    e) heartburn: caused by reverse peristaltic waves causing backflow of stomach contents into esophagus
    f) flatulence: usually caused by bacterial action in the intestine

4. metabolic changes
    a) basal metabolism
        (1) decreases during first trimester
            (a) fatigue: common complaint
        (2) increases during third trimester
5. neurological changes
    a) altered because of homonal changes
    b) variations in sensations may occur
        (1) neuralgias
        (2) pruritus
        (3) tingling
6. cardiovascular system changes
    a) blood volume: increased about 30% (hydremia)
        (1) additional workload for heart: may lead to hypertrophy of heart muscle and poor circulation in extremities that can cause edema and varicosities
        (2) the highest level of cardiac output is reached during the 25th to 27th week (35% increase)
    b) blood pressure changes
        (1) there is a drop in blood pressure during the second trimester and then a rise in the third trimester
        (2) some women experience the "supine hypotensive syndrome" in the second half of pregnancy, which creates a drop in blood pressure when they lie on their backs due to compression of the inferior vena cava. This syndrome may cause faintness
7. respiratory system changes
    a) dyspnea may occur in last trimester
        (1) uterus pushes up diaphragm and chest cavity expands laterally
    b) vital capacity increased
8. urinary system changes
    a) kidneys: renal plasma flow increases approximately 20–25%, which increases the glomerular filtration rate by 50%, causing increased urinary output
    b) ureters: may dilate because of pressure; more evident in right ureter
    c) bladder: increased pressure because of enlarging uterus (first and third trimester), causing frequency
    d) urinary changes may predispose to urinary infection
9. skin changes
    a) striae gravidarum on abdomen, thighs, and breasts

b) linea nigra: brown or black line may form from mons to umbilicus
c) chloasma (mask of pregnancy): brown blotches on face that disappear after delivery
d) increased activity of sebaceous and sweat glands
10. endocrine system changes
    a) chorionic villi
        (1) secretes human chorionic gonadotropin (HCG) until development of placenta (fourth month)
        (2) maintains corpus luteum to aid in proliferation of uterine lining, which in turn secretes estrogen and progesterone; corpus luteum degenerates after fourth month
    b) placental trophoblasts produce human placental lactogen (hPL), which is involved with carbohydrate metabolism and possibly protein metabolism
    c) placenta secretes estrogen and progesterone, which balance each other in maintaining myometrial activity, tone, and circulation
    d) pituitary body
        (1) anterior lobe secretes lactogenic hormone after delivery
        (2) posterior lobe secretes oxytocic hormone that stimulates contraction of uterus prior to onset of labor
11. musculoskeletal system changes
    a) relaxation of ligaments and joints due to increase in relaxin
    b) leg cramps are caused by decrease of calcium or increase in phosphorus; may occur at any time but are more common in late pregnancy
    c) body alignment changes may cause a posture imbalance leading to the development of lordosis, backache, and varicosities

C. Nursing care related to physical changes
   1. intervention is based on assessment data
      a) nursing care related to gastrointestinal changes
         (1) assessment
             (a) degree of abdominal distention
             (b) elimination patterns
             (c) hemorrhoids
             (d) presence and degree of nausea
             (e) presence and degree of heartburn and flatulence
         (2) health teaching and counseling are directed toward alleviating present or potential problems
             (a) support garments may be required for pendulous abdomen

(b) constipation
  1. increase fluid intake if not contraindicated
  2. take warm liquids on rising and walk around the house for a few minutes after drinking the liquids
  3. increase dietary fiber
  4. walk and engage in mild exercise
  5. use stool softeners and bulk laxatives if above methods do not work. Avoid mineral oil and strong purgatives
(c) hemorrhoids
  1. avoid constipation, which aggravates condition
  2. lie in knee-chest position to alleviate discomfort
  3. use witch hazel compresses for reduction
  4. alternate ice packs with hot sitz baths for reduction and comfort
  5. reinsert the hemorrhoids into rectum along with Kegel exercises
  6. sleep with a pillow under hips
  7. use analgesic ointments
  8. use stool softeners
  9. at time of bowel movement place feet on stool 1 foot high, take a deep breath and push out with exhalation
(d) nausea (morning sickness)
  1. may occur at any time of day or night
  2. usually ceases after 14th week
  3. eat small frequent meals during day
  4. take dry crackers before getting out of bed in morning
  5. eating sweet liquids or food may help
  6. restrict fats
  7. eat solids separately from liquids
  8. avoid medication if possible
(e) heartburn
  1. restrict fat
  2. eat small frequent meals
  3. use antacids except sodium bicarbonate
  4. avoid foods that cause discomfort; keep food diary
  5. have good posture and do not recline after meals or bend over
  6. avoid very cold foods and limit beverages during meals

(f) flatulence
  1. avoid gas-forming foods, such as beans, cabbage, etc.
  2. daily elimination
  3. avoid fats and cold drinks
  4. exercise
b) nursing care related to breast changes
  (1) assessment
    (a) type of support worn
    (b) usual care of breasts
    (c) condition of nipple if mother plans to nurse
  (2) nursing intervention: health teaching and counseling
    (a) good support is necessary due to increased size and weight of breasts; wear bra 24 hours a day
    (b) cleansing of nipples without soap to prevent drying and caking of secretions
    (c) massage of breast with cream may be indicated to preserve skin softness and turgor
    (d) treatment of introverted nipples—check with physician before using these methods because they may stimulate labor; nipple stimulation can cause uterine contractions if it is prolonged
      1. thumbs are placed firmly on areola close to nipple
      2. thumbs stroke areola toward and away from nipple horizontally and vertically
      3. repeat four or five times in succession
    (e) ice packs or cold compresses will relieve tenderness in first and third trimester
c) nursing care related to reproductive system changes
  (1) assessment
    (a) posture and body mechanics
    (b) edema of lower extremities
    (c) dyspnea
    (d) varicosities
    (e) vaginal discharge
  (2) nursing intervention is directed toward client teaching and counseling for potential or present problems
    (a) for muscle strain and backache
      1. good body mechanics, posture, rest, and proper shoes assist in relieving backache
      2. pelvic tilt exercises are helpful
        a. stand 2 feet away from support (back of chair or sink)

b. bend forward at hip joints and place hands on edge of chair with arms straight
  c. raise hips and inhale
  d. round back, tuck buttocks under, and exhale; knees should be slightly flexed
  e. repeat above three times
  f. drop hands and stand erect by raising breast bone straight up. Shoulders should be relaxed, knees flexed, buttocks tucked underneath, weight evenly balanced on back of feet
 3. pelvic tilt exercises should be done 12 times a day
 4. squat instead of bending
 5. sleep on firm mattress for support
 6. wear maternity girdle for severe postural problems or obesity
 7. avoid stretching or bending that is awkward
 8. support upper leg with a pillow when sleeping in side-lying position
 9. use heat application for pain relief
(b) for edema
 1. rest and elevate feet to alleviate swelling
 2. prolonged sitting and standing aggravate condition; avoid tight clothing
 3. careful evaluation is necessary because edema may be sign of hypertensive disease of pregnancy
(c) for dyspnea
 1. sleeping in semi-Fowler's position will assist in relieving this symptom
 2. if heart disease is present, report any dyspnea to physician
 3. have good posture
 4. if caused by nasal congestion use saline nose drops and humidifier or vaporizer
 5. eat small frequent meals to avoid pressure on lungs from full stomach
(d) for varicosities
 1. elastic stockings are used to prevent pooling of blood in leg veins and to provide support. Put on before getting out of bed with legs elevated
 2. elevation of legs at frequent intervals assists return blood flow from extremities
 3. prolonged sitting or standing aggravates condition. Avoid constipation

4. varicosities may occur in vulva; discomfort may be relieved by assuming an elevated Sims position (hips raised on pillow) several times daily
5. anything that constricts circulation in legs should not be worn
     (e) for vaginal discharge
        1. douching prohibited. Wear cotton crotch panties and pantyhose
        2. personal hygiene important; perineal area should be cleansed from front to back
        3. discharge must be evaluated for possibility of presence of pathogens that must be treated
  d) nursing care related to urinary system changes
     (1) assessment
        (a) any symptoms of infection
        (b) knowledge of self-care
     (2) health teaching and counseling
        (a) adequate fluid intake is necessary to maintain bladder tone
        (b) immediate investigation of symptoms of infection
        (c) perineal area cleansing should be taught
  e) nursing care related to skin changes and general hygiene
     (1) assessment
        (a) skin status
        (b) changes in pigmentation
        (c) dental care practices
     (2) health teaching and counseling
        (a) moisturize and massage abdominal skin with cocoa butter
        (b) support abdomen
        (c) use bath oil to relieve dryness
        (d) use sunscreen on face
        (e) personal hygiene important to remove excess secretions
        (f) explanation of normal skin changes during pregnancy
        (g) regular dental hygiene should be maintained, including dental checkups. Bacterial growth in mouth may be increased. Dental x-rays should be avoided
  f) nursing care related to musculoskeletal system changes
     (1) assessment
        (a) leg cramps
        (b) postural imbalance

(2) health teaching and counseling
- (a) leg cramps: increase calcium intake and decrease phosphorus intake by decreasing milk intake and taking calcium lactate or gluconate pills
  1. relieve acute spasm by forcing toes upward and pressing down on knee
  2. elevate legs frequently during day
  3. engage in general exercise to improve muscle tone
- (b) good posture during pregnancy will prevent discomfort. To establish good posture the following principles should be stressed
  1. realignment of the pelvis: tilting it toward posterior allows uterus to be carried more directly on pelvic bones
  2. knees should be slightly flexed
  3. pelvic tilt exercise assists in realignment of pelvis
- (c) heavy lifting and stretching become a hazard when the body's natural alignment is altered

g) nursing care related to cardiovascular changes
  (1) assessment
   - (a) BP
   - (b) fatigue
   - (c) edema
   - (d) dizziness and faintness
  (2) health teaching and counseling
   - (a) avoid fatigue when exercising
   - (b) take rest periods during day; avoid prolonged standing or sitting
   - (c) elevate legs frequently
   - (d) avoid constricting garments
  (3) sustained changes in BP must be immediately checked by physician
  (4) for dizziness and faintness
   - (a) avoid hypoglycemia by eating frequent small snacks and avoiding caffeine
   - (b) avoid sudden movements
   - (c) avoid hyperventilation by taking slow deep breaths when lightheadedness occurs
   - (d) avoid "supine hypotension syndrome" by not using a flat supine lying position

h) nursing care related to neurological changes
  (1) assessment
   - (a) paresthesias: numbness and tingling of fingers and toes

(2) health teaching and counseling
    (a) prevent edema
    (b) avoid tight jewelry
    (c) correct posture (lordotic) that may put strain on brachial nerves
    (d) correct any vitamin or calcium deficiency
    (e) prevent hyperventilation that may cause symptoms
i) nursing care related to nutritional needs of mother and baby
    (1) the quality and quantity of nutrients consumed by the mother throughout her life will profoundly affect the course of her pregnancy and the health of her child
        (a) inadequate nutrition during childhood may interfere with the optimal development of pelvic structures in the mother
        (b) inadequate nutrition during childhood and adulthood may
            1. affect the mother's health and well-being
            2. affect hormonal production and menstrual cycle of the mother
            3. predispose the mother to maternal complications, such as toxemia
        (c) inadequate nutrition has a direct influence on the physical and mental growth and development of the fetus
            1. inadequate protein intake is associated with mental retardation
            2. inadequate vitamin and mineral intake has been associated with bone and teeth deformities
            3. inadequate nutritional intake has been associated with increased incidence of low birthweight babies
    (2) assessment
        (a) physical factors
            1. age
            2. weight and height
            3. type of body frame
            4. prepregnancy weight
            5. activity level
            6. nutritional status: color, nails, hair, skin turgor, etc.
            7. lab values: hemoglobin, hematocrit, serum folate
            8. nausea and vomiting
            9. lactose intolerance
            10. food allergies

(b) diseases or conditions that require special diets, such as heart disease or diabetes mellitus
   (c) sociocultural factors
      1. ethnic group
      2. economic status
      3. educational level
      4. food practices, i.e., vegetarianism
   (d) a diet history and daily log of food intake
(3) during adolescence the growth needs of the adolescent mother as well as the fetus must be considered and nutritional adjustments made accordingly. The 11- to 14-year-old teenager who is pregnant needs 2500 calories daily as compared to the 19- to 50-year-old woman who needs 2300 cal/day and the 15- to 18-year-old teenager who needs 2400 cal/day
(4) in counseling women about nutrition during pregnancy the following factors must be considered
   (a) cultural background
   (b) economic status
   (c) individual dietary habits
   (d) presence of symptoms that affect food intake
   (e) educational level
   (f) motivation of mother for changing food habits
(5) to implement a change in dietary habits it is necessary to
   (a) motivate individual to assume responsibility for participating actively in plans for change
   (b) respect and accept all individual factors influencing diet habits
   (c) educate individuals about nutrition using terminology and techniques appropriate for their level of understanding
(6) refer women who are financially distressed to such programs as WIC where they can receive nutritional assistance and supplementation
(7) recommended nutritional changes during pregnancy
   (a) caloric intake should be increased approximately 300 kcal daily in the second and third trimester
      1. adequate energy is required for the development and maintenance of new tissue related to the pregnancy
      2. adequate energy is needed for the increased activity

level of the pregnant woman's increasing heavier body as the pregnancy proceeds
3. basal metabolic rates increase about 20% in pregnancy
4. adequate weight gain is needed to meet total energy requirements of the pregnant woman and to ensure an adequate birthweight for the newborn
5. obese women should not diet during pregnancy but should maintain the required caloric intake to ensure fulfillment of energy requirements
6. diet should be regulated to avoid excessive weight gain

(b) minerals
1. calcium: increased by 0.4 g daily to a total daily intake of approximately 1.2 g in the last half of the pregnancy (adolescents, 1.6 g); essential for the fetus
    a. to ensure adequate development of bones and teeth
    b. to maintain normal muscle action
    c. to maintain normal blood clotting mechanisms and myocardial function
2. iron: requirements increase greatly during pregnancy. Supplements of 30–60 mg daily of ferrous sulfate or fumarate are recommended. Only 10% of ingested iron is absorbed. When iron is given in multivitamin and mineral supplements that contain calcium, magnesium, and other substances, very little iron is absorbed because these substances make the iron unavailable to the body. Iron should be given as a separate pill and should be taken several hours before or after meals. Vitamin C enhances iron absorption
    a. iron is needed for production of hemoglobin
    b. iron is stored by the fetus in the last trimester to ensure an adequate supply during early infancy when inadequate iron is taken in through the diet

(c) protein: increased by 30 g daily to a total daily intake of 74 g/day (adolescents, 82 g/day)
1. the rapid growth of the fetus, placenta, uterus, and

mammary glands and the increase in circulating blood volume account for the need for additional supplies of protein
(d) vitamins
    1. vitamin A: daily increase of 1000 IU is recommended to supply a daily intake of 6000 IU in the last half of the pregnancy (adolescents, same dose)
       a. vitamin A is necessary for
          (1.) cell growth and development
          (2.) tooth formation
          (3.) normal bone growth
          (4.) integrity of epithelial cells
       b. overdosages of vitamin A can produce abnormal bone and liver changes
    2. B-complex vitamins
       a. thiamine: increase of 0.1 mg to a total daily intake of 1.4 mg (adolescents, 1.5 mg)
          (1.) utilized in the metabolism of carbohydrates
       b. riboflavin: increase of 0.3 mg to a total daily intake of 1.5 mg (adolescents, 1.6 mg)
          (1.) essential for protein metabolism and energy metabolism
       c. niacin: increase to 15 mg (adolescents, 16 mg)
       d. vitamin B_6: increase of 5 mg
       e. vitamin B_{12}: increase of 1 mcg
       f. folic acid (folacin): increase to 800 mg/day (adolescents, same dose)
          (1.) needed for metabolic processes
          (2.) deficiency can lead to anemia
          (3.) under investigation for influence of deficiency on premature birth and neural tube defects
    3. vitamin C: increase of 5–10 mg to a total daily intake of 80 mg (adolescents, same dose)
       a. essential to develop connective and vascular systems of fetus
       b. facilitates absorption of iron
    4. vitamin D: during pregnancy 400 IU are recommended daily
       a. needed to facilitate calcium and phosphorous utilization

        b. overdosage of vitamin D intake should be avoided as it has been known to cause calcification of soft tissue, primarily of lung and kidney
    (e) all other nutrients should remain at nonpregnant levels. Guidelines for choosing foods should be the basic four groups. Women should be cautioned to read labels of vitamin supplements carefully to avoid overdosages
    (f) pica: an unusual compulsion for ingestion of nonfood items, such as dirt, clay, chalk, laundry starch, and ice. It is common but not limited to low-income black women living in southern rural areas of the U.S. Pica occurs in nonpregnant women also. The exact effect of pica on pregnancy is unknown, but it may contribute to malnutrition by displacing other foods in the diet and interfering with absorption of essential minerals
    (g) women who are strict vegetarians should be taught how to vary their diets so as to include all of the essential elements each day. Certain elements, such as vitamin B_{12}, will have to be received through supplements.
j) nursing care related to activity and rest needs of mother
  (1) assessment
    (a) present level of activity: exercise, work, sleep, and rest
    (b) prepregnant level of activity: exercise, work, sleep, and rest
    (c) signs of over- or underactivity, sleep, and rest
  (2) health teaching and counseling
    (a) exercising safely during pregnancy
      1. heart rate is increased during pregnancy, and vigorous exercise will increase it even further
      2. the hormone relaxin causes softening of connective tissues, which may make them more vulnerable to injury during vigorous exercise
      3. postural imbalance of pregnancy when the center of gravity shifts may make women at risk for injuries and falls
      4. vigorous exercise raises body temperature if prolonged and also may cause dehydration; effect on fetus is not known
      5. lying supine on back may lead to supine hypotension syndrome and faintness
      6. moderate exercise improves the mother's circulation and is not harmful to the fetus

Pregnancy 117

      7. walking, swimming, and moderate jogging if the woman is used to them and special pregnancy exercises, such as squatting and pelvic tilt, are beneficial. Avoid vigorous and prolonged exercise and sports with vigorous twisting and bending. Keep heart rate under 140 BPM. Avoid hot tubs, saunas, and steam rooms

(b) working during pregnancy
    1. the fetus may be exposed to physical, biological, or chemical hazards (see Chapter 6)
    2. hard physical work could possibly diminish blood flow to the fetus because of the need for increased blood flow to the working muscle tissues
    3. most important factor is the association between fatigue and the risk of preterm delivery. Excessive fatigue is related to posture, work at a machine, physical and mental load, and work environment. Long hours of work also predispose to fatigue. Work at a nonfatiguing job may not be harmful (Chamberlain, 1985)
    4. in counseling women about working during pregnancies the following advice may be given (*Contemporary OB/GYN*, 1984)
       a. take frequent breaks and rest periods. When fatigued, stop work and lie down if possible. Elevate legs frequently. Take walks and stretch legs and back gently. Wear support hose. For jobs that require standing or walking, cut down on activity or work part-time. Take rest periods. Empty bladder every 2 hours
       b. for jobs that require physical exertion or standing or walking, stop or reduce work 2–4 weeks before EDC
       c. avoid smoking areas, ladder climbing, heavy lifting, exhaustion, excessive stair climbing, running, overtime work, and in-flight airline work during final month
       d. women who have a history of premature births or fetal losses or who have serious high-risk complications of pregnancy or chronic illnesses should be carefully evaluated to determine when they should discontinue working

(c) sexual relationships during pregnancy
1. some women experience a decrease in libido during the first trimester due to nausea, fatigue, depression, and breast soreness. Libido may increase in second trimester due to decrease in physical discomforts. May decrease in third trimester due to enlargement of abdomen and fear of harming the baby
2. mood swings of pregnant woman influence libido
3. there are insufficient data available about the effect of intercourse on infection and premature labor. Current thinking is to recommend that women who are bleeding or who are prone to miscarriage or premature labor refrain from intercourse at the time of bleeding and at times of danger of labor precipitation, such as the last month of the pregnancy. Other methods of sexual satisfaction should be discussed. During the last month of pregnancy it is not known if sexual orgasm in the woman that causes uterine contractions may predispose to early labor. Intercourse should not take place when membranes have ruptured.

k) nursing care related to minor pain during pregnancy
  (1) best managed through the use of acupressure, acupuncture, biofeedback, or a noncontraindicated drug such as acetaminophen. If acupuncture is used, care should be taken that needles are sterile. The physician must recommend any of the above treatment modalities

V. NURSING CARE DURING THE PRENATAL PERIOD RELATING TO PSYCHOLOGICAL NEEDS
   A. Pregnancy usually occurs within the context of a family. The health and stability of the family will influence the course of the pregnancy, and the pregnancy will have a profound effect on all members of the family
   B. Assessment
      1. readiness of parents for their new role will depend on
         a) completion of developmental tasks of adolescence by both parents and assumption of the developmental tasks of the expectant family

b) desire for parenthood by both parents
    (1) not all pregnancies are wanted
    (2) in some planned pregnancies there are fears and lack of confidence in ability to handle parental role
    (3) unrealistic conception of what it is to be a parent may impede readiness to accept a new role
    (4) cultural influences on concepts of parenthood and preparation for parenthood within the family group
2. economic status of family may influence the family's acceptance of the pregnancy
    a) pregnancy may place a great financial burden on the family or may necessitate a change in the family's lifestyle
        (1) living quarters may become overcrowded
        (2) working woman may have to give up her job
        (3) expense of having and supporting a baby may drain family's resources
3. husband and wife's adjustment to marriage before pregnancy
    a) if either parent is unable to share the love and attention of the spouse, the pregnancy may become a threat to the stability of the marriage
    b) readiness of children in the family to accept a new baby
        (1) children who are insecure in their parents' love will be threatened by the arrival of a new baby
        (2) children between 18 months and 3 years of age may have particular difficulty in accepting a new baby because they are in the midst of resolving their own separation anxieties
        (3) children undergo a change in position and status within the family when a new baby is born
            (a) parental expectations of older children should not be radically altered because of the new baby's arrival
4. family relationships that are stress producing may affect the course of the pregnancy; pregnancy itself is a biological stress
    a) stress may be a causative factor in the development of
        (1) nausea and vomiting
        (2) hypertension
        (3) pre-eclampsia
        (4) postpartum psychosis
        (5) difficult labor
5. effect of pregnancy on the individual
    a) the mother's reaction to the pregnancy will be dependent on her individual
        (1) hormonal balance

(2) state of physical health
(3) emotional maturity
(4) mental health
(5) knowledge and understanding about pregnancy
  b) common emotional manifestations during pregnancy are
    (1) mood swings without relationship to external factors
    (2) increased irritability and sensitivity
    (3) changes in sexual drive (may increase or decrease)
    (4) introversion and passivity
    (5) narcissism (preoccupation with self and developing child as an extension of self)
    (6) disequilibrium between ego and id
      (a) ego control is diminished, allowing id to surface
      (b) increased fantasy life
      (c) old unresolved problems surface
    (7) ambivalence includes acceptance and rejection of pregnancy
    (8) reaction to altered body image
  c) the father's emotional reaction to the pregnancy will be dependent upon
    (1) emotional maturity
    (2) mental health
    (3) economic situation
    (4) cultural preparation for parenthood
    (5) behavioral changes in wife that directly affect the husband-wife relationship
    (6) knowledge and understanding of pregnancy
6. communication patterns within the family
7. coping patterns of the family
  a) family strengths and weaknesses
  b) outside support systems
    (1) extended family
    (2) social relationships
    (3) community agencies
8. cultural background
  a) meaning of childbearing
  b) practices related to pregnancy
9. effect of pregnancy on sexual pattern and relationship
10. how realistic are the parents' expectations and goals regarding parenthood

C. Intervention
  1. create an atmosphere in which the parents can verbalize freely about any possible or potential problem

a) nonjudgmental attitude
   b) respect for cultural values
 2. allow sufficient time for the development of a therapeutic nurse-client relationship
 3. provide assistance to the client in identifying problems and setting goals
 4. the severity of the problems identified will determine the scope of intervention; the nurse may
   a) provide information
   b) assist in exploration of family communication and coping patterns
   c) provide support through emphathetic and caring behaviors
   d) point out the strengths and support systems existing within the family and social circle
   e) provide sources and referrals for psychological counseling and therapy
   f) act as an advocate for the clients
     (1) educate them as to their rights and privileges within the health care system
   g) act as a liaison between agencies
 5. provide reassurance to the couple about the normality of such things as mood swings, introversion and passivity, decreased or increased libido, and ambivalence toward the pregnancy

VI. NURSING CARE DURING THE PRENATAL PERIOD RELATING TO LEARNING NEEDS

A. Assessment of parents
   1. accuracy and completeness of information regarding parenting
   2. misconceptions about the maternity cycle
   3. level of ability to understand information and instructions
   4. level of motivation to learn
   5. personal and cultural values that may influence acceptance of information and compliance with instructions
B. Intervention
   1. parents' classes may be recommended
   2. literature may be provided appropriate to the level of education and understanding of parents
   3. individual counseling and teaching by the nurse may be indicated
   4. teaching effectiveness is enhanced by
     a) choosing the time of optimum readiness for motivation to learn
       (1) information about labor and delivery process is meaningless in the first trimester of pregnancy

       b) limiting the amount of new information given at one time
       c) summarizing and writing down important points
       d) providing feedback mechanism to assess learning
          (1) asking clients to repeat information in their own words
          (2) asking clients at frequent intervals if they understand material presented
              (a) verify their understanding by nonverbal cues
       e) providing an atmosphere where questions can be asked freely
5. educational needs during the prenatal period may include
       a) anatomical and physiological changes of pregnancy
       b) labor and delivery process
       c) signs of labor
       d) nutrition
       e) signs of the development of possible or potential complications of pregnancy
       f) rationale for early and regular prenatal care
       g) safety precautions
       h) hospital admission and daily routine procedures
       i) hospital policies that affect mother-child-father interaction
       j) rights of consumers of health care
       k) planning and purchasing of layette and other infant items
       l) preparation for natural childbirth
       m) prenatal exercises
       n) hygienic care
       o) fetal development
       p) general health care of self, e.g., rest, posture, clothing, etc.
       q) care of the newborn

VII. NURSING PROCESS DURING THE ANTEPARTAL PERIOD INVOLVES THE ASSESSMENT OF PHYSIOLOGICAL, PSYCHOSOCIAL, AND LEARNING NEEDS IN TOTALITY, FOLLOWED BY PROBLEM IDENTIFICATION, GOAL SETTING, INTERVENTION, AND EVALUATION BY MUTUAL PARTICIPATION OF THE CLIENT AND THE HEALTH TEAM

REFERENCES

Chamberlain, G. (1985). "Effect of Work During Pregnancy." *Obstetrics and Gynecology* 65 (5):747–750. 1985.

Survey on work and pregnancy. (1984, April). *Contemporary OB/GYN*, p. 87.

Chapter 8

High-Risk Pregnancy

I. SPECIAL NEEDS OF HIGH-RISK MOTHERS

A. The term "high-risk" is used to identify those women who may encounter problems or have pre-existing conditions that may be detrimental to the outcome of the pregnancy. These women may need more intensive and frequent monitoring and care throughout the pregnancy
B. Must work through fears and doubts to accept the pregnancy
   1. fear of illness or death of self or baby
   2. fear of financial burdens
   3. fear of rejection by others if baby is abnormal
   4. fear of developing normal attachment feelings to child because child may die
C. Must comply with protocols of care in order to protect the pregnancy

II. FACTORS THAT MAY LEAD TO A HIGH-RISK PREGNANCY

A. Socioeconomic status
   1. low-income parents face problems relating to
      a) inadequate nutrition
      b) poor housing
      c) inadequate prenatal care
      d) sanitation
      e) untreated general health problems
      f) stress related to financial status
   2. implications for nursing process
      a) nurse may function as a consumer advocate advising about rights and making referrals where indicated
      b) nutritional counseling must reflect available resources
      c) nurse may facilitate utilization of prenatal facilities by recognizing possible and potential barriers caused by low-income status

B. Age
    1. under 16
        a) nutritional status of adolescent girls may be below par, increasing the risk factor
        b) adolescents are in a state of growth and development themselves, and pregnancy is an added physiological and psychological stressor to which the body must adapt
        c) higher incidence of hypertensive states of pregnancy and prematurity occurs in adolescents
        d) her schooling may be interrupted, and she faces the risk of losing friends at a time when peer acceptance is most important
        e) at a time when most adolescents are trying to establish their own autonomy, a pregnant teenager becomes physically, emotionally, and financially dependent
        f) implications for nursing process
            (1) assisting the adolescent in identifying and verbalizing her feelings about the pregnancy
            (2) assisting her to achieve the developmental tasks of adolescence
            (3) helping her plan for postpregnancy life
            (4) providing careful supervision and instruction about physical status during the maternity cycle to lessen danger of infant and maternal morbidity and mortality
            (5) making appropriate referral to social agencies whenever indicated
    2. over 35
        a) higher incidence of complications, including pre-eclampsia and fetal abnormalities
        b) increased rigidity of connective tissue
        c) hormonal levels may change
        d) childbearing at this age may cause emotional stress
        e) implications for nursing process
            (1) exploration of the meaning of the pregnancy to the family is important
            (2) careful monitoring of the pregnancy
            (3) amniocentesis is usually recommended by physician
C. Marital status
    1. out-of-wedlock pregnancy
        a) largest number of out-of-wedlock births occur in adolescents
        b) concealment of pregnancy may interfere with obtaining early prenatal care
        c) the adolescent father in an out-of-wedlock pregnancy often feels guilt and shame about the pregnancy

d) the out-of-wedlock mother may have to cope with feelings of guilt and shame about her pregnancy and in addition may be rejected by her family. However, changing attitudes toward premarital sex and out-of-wedlock pregnancy may significantly reduce feelings of guilt and shame
e) implications for nursing process
  (1) woman should be assisted in making her decision about the placement of her child, and support should be provided once her decision is made
  (2) if guilt feelings are present, assistance may be needed in coping with them
  (3) the needs of the family of the pregnant woman and the father should be assessed and met
  (4) school sex-education programs are an important preventive measure
D. Parity
  1. five or more pregnancies
  2. implications for nursing process
    a) counseling about the possibility of precipate birth
E. Previous history of difficult labor
F. Reproductive system disorders
G. Accidents
H. Previous or current history of mental or emotional disorders
  1. preventive psychosocial support or therapy may be needed
I. Disordered family relationships
  1. family therapy may be needed
J. Previous or current history of complications during pregnancy, including previous fetal loss
  1. hemorrhagic complications
    a) placental abnormalities
      (1) placenta previa
        (a) types
          1. total: cervical os completely covered by placenta
          2. partial: cervical os partially obliterated by placenta
          3. low or marginal implantation: placenta implanted at the opening of the os but does not cover it
        (b) etiology unknown but occurs more frequently in multiparous women who have had a rapid succession of pregnancies
        (c) symptoms
          1. painless bleeding usually in last trimester
          2. total placenta previa has earlier and more profuse bleeding

3. premature rupture of membranes
4. premature labor
5. abnormal presentation
6. delayed engagement
- (d) diagnosis is based on
    1. sonography: B-scan
    2. radiography: soft-tissue techniques, cystography techniques, amniography, IV placentography
    3. manual examination of the internal cervix is rarely done because of danger of hemorrhage. If it is done, a double set-up is used
- (e) treatment
    1. hospitalization
    2. bedrest with sedation
    3. very restricted activity as blood clotting provides hemostasis
    4. treatment of shock and replacement of blood
    5. immediate delivery if bleeding is severe
        a. deliver vaginally or by cesarean section, depending on placement of placenta
    6. constant observation
    7. if hemorrhage is controlled and pregnancy can be maintained, cesarean section is usually performed after the 37th week

(2) abruptio placentae
- (a) premature separation of the placenta before labor or delivery
- (b) etiology unknown: increased incidence occurs in
    1. hypertensive and pre-eclamptic patients
    2. violent labor
    3. uterine trauma
- (c) symptoms
    1. localized pain over uterus with or without hemorrhage
    2. uterus feels hard because of seepage of blood between uterine muscle fibers
    3. maternal shock
    4. absence of fetal heart sounds
    5. couvelaire uterus may develop
        a. bluish, ecchymotic discoloration of uterus caused by blood seepage into uterine walls
- (d) treatment
    1. hospitalization

      2. bedrest
      3. treatment for shock and replacement of blood loss
      4. concealed hemorrhage may lead to afibrogenemia
      5. deliver vaginally or cesarean section depending on symptoms
      6. constant observation
      7. hysterectomy may be indicated in couvelaire uterus
b) abortions
  (1) definition: expulsion of the products of conception before fetus is able to survive
    (a) classification of products of conception
      1. abortus: 500 g and under
      2. immature: 500–1000 g
      3. premature: 1000–2500 g
  (2) types
    (a) threatened: cervix closed, may be stopped
      1. painless vaginal bleeding before 28 weeks gestation
      2. occurs in approximately 16–25% of pregnancies
      3. if fetal life is confirmed by ultrasonogram 95–98% will usually progress to normal outcome
    (b) inevitable: cervix open, certain to occur
    (c) incomplete: all or part of conceptus retained, bleeding continues
    (d) complete: all of conceptus expelled, no further treatment
    (e) missed: fetus dies in utero, but not expelled until later months
    (f) habitual: three or more consecutive abortions
    (g) therapeutic
      1. medical indications, i.e., severe cardiac, mental illness, TB, etc.
      2. on demand
        a. statutes now permit abortion on demand
        b. Supreme Court decision in 1973 declared that statutes in states throughout the country that prohibited abortion were unconstitutional. Women and their doctors may not be prohibited from making decisions about having an abortion
        c. reasons for women choosing to have an abortion
          (1.) pregnancy unwanted due to social, cultural, economic, and psychological factors
          (2.) may be used as a form of contraception
          (3.) to abort a suspected deformed fetus

d. techniques
  (1.) early pregnancy to tenth week
    (a.) dilation and curettage (D&C): dilation of cervix with a scraping out of uterine linings with a curette; general anesthesia is usually used
    (b.) dilation and evacuation (suction method) (D&E): cervix is dilated and a suction tip is used to vacuum out contents of uterus; may be performed under general or local anesthesia
    (c.) a new experimental method for early abortion: use of RU 486, a progesterone antagonist during the first month of pregnancy. It causes uterine bleeding and uterine evacuation within 4 days of the first dose. A side effect of prolonged uterine bleeding may occur. When given alone, RU 486 is between 60–85% effective in producing complete abortion. A newer technique combining RU 486 with a vaginal pessary containing Gemeprost, a synthetic prostaglandin E analogue, is being used experimentally. This combination has been found to increase the percentage of complete abortions in early pregnancy and is a safe alternative to surgical evacuation
  (2.) after 14th week
    (a.) most common method currently is extra-amniotic infusion of prostaglandin E_2 in incremental doses (synthetic oxytocin is occasionally required additionally)
    (b.) experimental use of RU 486 as a pretreatment for prostaglandin E_2 infusion has been shown to reduce the induction-to-abortion interval and the total dose of prostaglandin needed
    (c.) saline induction: hypertonic saline solution injected into amniotic sac through abdominal wall. Labor usually follows 12 to 48 hours after injection. Patient must

be hospitalized. Performed under local anesthesia
   (d.) hysterotomy: used after 15th week; surgical incision into uterus with removal of uterine contents. Usually accompanied by tubal ligation. Performed in hospital under general anesthesia
3. dangers of abortion
   a. criminal abortions: abortions not performed by authorized health professionals. These abortions may lead to hemorrhage, lacerations, perforation of uterus, and infection and have a high morbidity and mortality rate
   b. complications of first trimester abortions
      (1.) perforation or cervical laceration
      (2.) bleeding
      (3.) complications of anesthesia
      (4.) incomplete evacuation
      (5.) infection
      (6.) Rh isoimmunization in Rh negative women
      (7.) cervical incompetence resulting in increased risk of spontaneous abortion and premature birth in subsequent pregnancies
   c. complications of second trimester abortions
      (1.) failure to abort
      (2.) birth of a live baby
      (3.) intravascular or intraperitoneal injection of hypertonic saline
      (4.) infection
      (5.) retained placenta
4. nursing implications of abortions
   a. careful observation after procedure for complications
   b. pre- and postabortion counseling is essential to explore with the woman her feelings toward pregnancy and procedure in order to resolve any guilt or remorse over action taken
   c. a nurse who works in an abortion facility should be nonjudgmental
   d. Rh-negative women should receive RhoGam after any type of abortion

(3) etiology of causation of spontaneous abortion cannot always be determined
   (a) embryonic defect—primary cause
   (b) improper implantation
   (c) incompetent cervix
   (d) endocrine disturbances
   (e) abnormalities of the placenta
   (f) diseases and infections of mother
   (g) defect in mother's immune system causes biochemical interference with the "blocking" response that prevents premature expulsion of the fetus; causes mother's body to reject the fetus

(4) symptoms
   (a) bleeding
   (b) pain of contractions

(5) treatment
   (a) bedrest
   (b) alcohol therapy
   (c) if bleeding continues, D&C is done
   (d) treatment for hemorrhage and shock if necessary
   (e) treatment of habitual abortions (three or more consecutive abortions)
      1. determination of etiology is essential
         a. most common causes are
            (1.) incompetent cervix
            (2.) hormonal dysfunction
            (3.) immune system defect
            (4.) abnormalities of uterus
            (5.) luteal phase defect
      2. luteal phase defect is treated by inducing ovulation with clomiphene and encouraging immediate fertilization. The pregnancy is then supported by progesterone administration until implantation takes place
      3. hormonal treatment, especially with synthetic estrogens, is strongly contraindicated because of highly increased incidence of vaginal carcinomas in female offspring
      4. treatment for incompetent cervix: inability of internal os to remain undilated
         a. cervix is sutured to prevent dilation; suture is removed 2 to 3 weeks before term
         b. bedrest

5. defects in the mother's immune system are being treated experimentally by a new treatment. Lymphotoxic antibody immunization is the innoculation of the mother with 0.2 oz of white blood cells from her husband just before or soon after conception. These foreign cells enhance the antibody production of the mother, which in turn stimulates the blocking responses of the fetus
  (6) emotional needs of women who have had a spontaneous abortion (miscarriage)
   (a) may become attached to the unborn child even before it moves and therefore will grieve after miscarriage
   (b) will experience physical and emotional pain during and after a miscarriage
   (c) may experience guilt (what did she do or not do to cause the miscarriage)
   (d) doubts about ability to ever have a viable child will surface
   (e) caring needs
    1. needs to be able to grieve by expressing her sadness and loss and having it acknowledged
    2. needs genuine concern and support for her grieving needs
    3. needs an understanding of the causes of spontaneous abortion and encouragement that she can be successful next time
 c) ectopic or extrauterine pregnancy
  (1) tubal
   (a) the rate of ectopic pregnancy increased from 4.5 per 1000 pregnancies in 1970 to 14.0 per 1000 in 1983. At the same time, the mortality rate decreased from 0.9 per 1000 ectopic pregnancies in 1980 to 0.5 per 1000 in 1983
   (b) the increased incidence thought to be due to improved diagnostic technology, increased use of IUDs, and increased incidence of pelvic inflammatory disease
   (c) caused by conditions that impair passage of the fertilized ovum through the fallopian tube and by abnormalities of the embryo's development. 95% of ectopic pregnancies occur within the fallopian tube, but they can also be found in other locations, including the ovary, cervix, and abdomen
   (d) may rupture or abort or may be propelled out into the abdominal cavity

(e) difficult to diagnose before rupture occurs as signs and symptoms vary with the gestational age of the pregnancy, and early symptoms may be confused with abdominal disorders. Early symptoms may or may not include nausea, breast tenderness, and amenorrhea. As the pregnancy progresses, pain and intermittent bleeding may occur. When tubal rupture occurs, pain may increase or decrease and patient may go into shock
(f) a careful history and the use of the following procedures help the physician establish a diagnosis: sensitive pregnancy testing (danger of false-negative test in early pregnancy), ultrasonography, culdocentesis, diagnostic peritoneal lavage, and laparoscopy
(g) treatment
 1. treatment of hemorrhage and shock
 2. surgery
 3. sometimes tube can be repaired
(2) abdominal pregnancy
 (a) rare: 1 in 15,000 pregnancies
 (b) may have symptoms of tubal or normal pregnancy
 (c) 20% carry to term; delivered by surgery
 (d) danger of hemorrhage and infection
 (e) on delivery, placenta left in place and absorbed
(3) interstitial and ovarian pregnancies are extremely rare
d) gestational trophoblastic disease
 (1) molar pregnancy: hydatidiform mole may be
  (a) invasive
  (b) noninvasive
 (2) associated with pathological conceptus in which the embryo is absent or dead prior to time of establishment of fetal circulation
 (3) trophoblastic proliferation occurs with edema of connective tissue stroma
 (4) in invasive mole there is a large amount of trophoblastic overgrowth and of penetration of the villi into the uterine wall
 (5) danger of developing into choriocarcinoma, which is an epithelial tumor of the embryonic chorion that is subject to early and widespread metastasis
 (6) prognosis
  (a) most hydatidiform moles have a benign course
  (b) a few become invasive moles
  (c) a very small number progress to choriocarcinoma

(7) etiology: unknown
    (a) more common in Far East (1:700); rate in U.S. is 1:2000
    (b) more prevalent in women over 40
(8) diagnosis
    (a) immunoassays to detect titer of
        1. human chorionic gonadotropin (HCG)
            a. in normal pregnancy, peak excretion is 10–12 weeks, then it drops. In molar pregnancies, usually HCG fails to drop or rises markedly
        2. human placental lactogen (hPL)
            a. is usually lower in molar pregnancy
    (b) sonography (beta-scan)
    (c) radiographic technique
(9) symptoms
    (a) excessive nausea and vomiting
    (b) rapid enlargement of uterus
    (c) amenorrhea followed by intermittent bleeding that is usually accompanied by grape-like vesicles
    (d) absence of fetal heart tones
(10) treatment
    (a) removal by D&C or vacuum aspiration
    (b) if excessive bleeding has occurred a blood transfusion may be needed
    (c) follow-up care
        1. pregnancy should be avoided for 1 year
        2. weekly tests for HCG titers
            a. negative titers should occur within 6 weeks after removal
            b. increased titers may indicate development of chorionic malignancy
        3. uterine bleeding, failure of uterus to contract, or signs of metastatic tumors may indicate chorionic malignancy (chest x-rays should be taken at 4 and 8 weeks post-D&C)
    (d) choriocarcinoma can be treated successfully with chemotherapy
e) nursing care in hemorrhagic complications
    (1) assessment
        (a) observation of vital signs
        (b) amount and character of bleeding
            1. amount
            2. color
            3. rate of flow

4. clots or tissue passed (save for examination by physician)
            (c) emotional reaction to condition
            (d) reaction to prescribed treatment
        (2) intervention
            (a) prevent infection
            (b) save expelled tissue
            (c) prevent shock
            (d) maintain fluid and electrolyte balance
            (e) provide support to patient throughout the experience
            (f) provide adequate and accurate information to patients
            (g) provide a climate for verbalization of feelings
2. hydramnios
    a) polyhydramnios: excessive quantity of amniotic fluid
        (1) normal volume: 1000 cc, over 2000 cc considered excessive
        (2) etiology unknown, associated with
            (a) multiple births
            (b) fetal malformation
            (c) hydrops fetalis
            (d) pre-eclampsia
            (e) may be related to inability of the fetus to swallow amniotic fluid
        (3) symptoms caused by the increased pressure exerted by the uterus on nearby organs
            (a) respiratory distress
            (b) edema of abdominal wall, vulva, and lower extremities
            (c) uterine pain
            (d) nausea and vomiting
        (4) diagnosis
            (a) excessive uterine enlargement
            (b) difficulty in hearing fetal heart tones and palpating fetus
            (c) ease of ballottement: testing for the rebound of fetus when pressure is applied to it through its fluid medium
            (d) increased fetal activity
            (e) sonography
            (f) radiography
        (5) management
            (a) amniocentesis: removal of amniotic fluid from uterus through insertion of needle through the abdomen into the amniotic sac
        (6) implications for nursing process
            (a) adequate information regarding the physiological basis for her symptoms

High-Risk Pregnancy   135

       (b) semi-Fowler position may relieve dyspnea
       (c) adequate abdominal support
       (d) adequate explanations of treatment regimen
   b) oligohydramnios: small amount of amniotic fluid
      (1) volume: less than 100 cc
      (2) in early pregnancy may cause amnion to come in contact with fetus and adhesion occurs
      (3) during labor first stage is prolonged because of decrease in hydrostatic pressure from amniotic fluid
3. hyperemesis gravidarum: pernicious vomiting
   a) etiology unknown but thought to be related to
      (1) hormonal changes; high levels of HCG
      (2) maladjustment of maternal metabolism
      (3) change in gastric motility
      (4) toxicity
      (5) psychic factors
   b) symptoms
      (1) pernicious vomiting
      (2) dehydration
      (3) marked weight loss
      (4) ketosis
      (5) rapid pulse (over 100 BPM)
      (6) hypertension
      (7) electrolyte imbalance
   c) treatment
      (1) adequate care of morning sickness may prevent condition
      (2) hospitalization
         (a) bedrest
         (b) sedation
         (c) IV or hyperalimentation therapy
            1. prevents dehydration and starvation
         (d) vitamin therapy (emphasis on B_6)
         (e) psychological counseling
         (f) careful observation of intake and output
   d) implications for nursing process
      (1) assess fluid and electrolyte needs
      (2) provide hygienic care after vomiting
      (3) provide opportunity for adequate rest
      (4) allow for verbalization of feelings regarding pregnancy
4. blood incompatibilities
   a) Rh factor
      (1) etiology: when Rh-negative mother conceives baby with Rh-positive father

(a) high incidence of Rh-positive babies because of dominance of Rh-positive factor gene
(b) sensitization of mother to Rh factor with production of antibodies occurs during labor and delivery of first baby or previous blood transfusions with Rh-positive blood
(c) during subsequent pregnancies, antibodies of mother pass through placenta to fetus, causing destruction of fetal red blood cells
    1. condition may be mild to severe, and results can range from anemia to hydrops fetalis in utero and kernicterus in the neonate
(2) management
    (a) prevention of antibody development in mother by RhoGam (Rh immune globulin), a vaccine that prevents sensitization
        1. should be given before 72 hours after delivery or abortion; may be given after 72 hours if necessary
        2. vaccine ineffective after sensitization of mother has occurred: usually 28 days after birth
    (b) if mother has been sensitized
        1. mother's antibody level is monitored
        2. if antibody level is increased, an intrauterine blood transfusion of fetus may be done
        3. a new experimental method of in utero exchange transfusion by direct intravascular injection of fetus is now in use
    (c) management of neonate
        1. frequent monitoring of bilirubin levels
        2. if bilirubin level rises above normal, exchange transfusion may be necessary
        3. light therapy may be used to reduce jaundice
b) ABO incompatibility
    (1) mother type O blood, father type A, B, or AB
    (2) fetus may have type A or B blood
    (3) blood cells of fetus hemolyze due to maternal antibodies present in mother's blood against A or B type blood
    (4) can occur in firstborn, does not increase in severity with subsequent pregnancies
    (5) disease varies in severity but is usually less severe than Rh factor
    (6) higher incidence in black infants
    (7) management

(a) every type A or B infant born to group O mother should have a Coombs test, hematocrit, blood smear, and bilirubin level before discharge from hospital
(b) light therapy may be used to reduce jaundice by breaking down bilirubin (infant's eyes must be protected)
(c) exchange transfusion may be necessary
c) implications for nursing process
(1) education of prospective parents to prevent sensitization
5. hypertensive states of pregnancy
a) classification
(1) pre-eclampsia and eclampsia
(2) hypertensive disease in pregnancy
(a) acute renal disease
(b) chronic hypertensive vascular disease
(c) superimposed pre-eclampsia or eclampsia
b) pre-eclampsia
(1) occurs only in pregnancy, usually after 20th week: 5–10% of all pregnancies
(a) may occur before the 20th week when trophoblasic disease is present
(2) higher incidence in
(a) primigravidas
(b) adolescents
(c) women over age 30
(d) low socioeconomic groups
(e) diabetic women
(f) women with chronic hypertension
(g) women with trophoblastic molar disease
(3) unknown etiology
(4) characteristics of the condition: hypertension, edema, and/or proteinuria
(5) mechanisms
(a) increased vascular reactivity resulting in widespread vasospasm and vasoconstriction
(b) blood supply to organs may be reduced
1. organs most seriously affected are brain, kidneys, liver, and placenta
(c) alteration in fluid and sodium retention
(d) leakage of plasma protein into the urine from the glomerular membranes of the kidney
(6) symptoms of mild pre-eclampsia
(a) a sudden onset of weight gain of 2 or more lb/week

- (b) a sustained rise in BP of 30 mm Hg or more systolic and 15 mm Hg or more diastolic over the prepregnancy or early pregnancy levels. BP in mild pre-eclampsia will remain below 160/110 mm Hg
- (c) urinary protein: less than 5 g/24 hr
- (d) edema may be absent or mild
- (7) symptoms of severe pre-eclampsia
    - (a) BP rises 60/30 mm Hg or more above early pregnancy or prepregnancy levels. BP will rise above 160/110
    - (b) urinary protein excretion will rise above 5 g/24 hr
    - (c) urinary output will decrease to 500 ml/24 hr or less: oliguria
    - (d) massive generalized or pulmonary edema may occur
    - (e) epigastric pain and cerebral or visual disturbances may be present: headache, blurring of vision, spots and double vision, hyperreflexia
- (8) effect on fetal development
    - (a) mild pre-eclampsia will usually not adversely affect the fetus
    - (b) as pre-eclampsia becomes more severe the decrease in placental perfusion of nutrients and oxygen may cause fetal hypoxia and an inadequate nutritional intake
    - (c) monitoring of fetal development
        1. measurement of fundal height and fetal heart rate (FHR)
        2. ultrasonic cephalometry
        3. urinary estriol levels
        4. stress and nonstress fetal heart monitoring
- (9) treatment
    - (a) the treatment of this condition has changed radically over the past few years and is still a subject of controversy. The goal of treatment is to prevent the occurrence of eclampsia and cerebrovascular and cardiovascular problems and to deliver an infant in good condition
    - (b) the former treatment of pre-eclampsia emphasized the use of diuretics and low salt diets. Recent research indicates that this type of therapy may lead to
        1. maternal electrolyte imbalance due to depletion of sodium and potassium
        2. hemorrhagic pancreatitis

3. electrolyte imbalance in the infant
4. reduced placental blood flow because of a decrease in the circulating blood volume
(10) current management of mild pre-eclampsia
 (a) management on an ambulatory basis
 (b) ample protein diet without restriction of salt or fluids: excessive salt intake should be avoided
 (c) frequent rest periods in lateral recumbent position
 (d) avoidance of fatigue
 (e) reduction of stress
  1. assist women through support and counseling to cope with stress factors
 (f) education regarding pregnancy in general and about the management of the present condition. Signs of change in the state of the condition must be carefully taught
 (g) frequent and comprehensive prenatal care and monitoring
 (h) the use of phenytoin is under investigation. Phenytoin has beneficial effects on hypertension, cerebral blood flow, cerebral edema, fluid balance, and peripheral edema. No significant side effects have been seen with this drug
(11) if condition progresses to severe pre-eclampsia, client must be hospitalized
 (a) complete bedrest in lateral recumbent position: increases glomerular filtration and promotes diuresis
 (b) diuretics may be prescribed for a short period of time with strict control of electrolytes if bedrest is not effective and if pulmonary edema occurs
 (c) the use of antihypertensive drugs (Apresoline, Nitropress, Hyperstat) is controversial but they are used if severe hypertension persists in order to prevent cerebrovascular accidents
 (d) termination of the pregnancy is the only really effective treatment for severe pre-eclampsia when the response to treatment is unsatisfactory or the pregnancy is near term. Induction of labor or cesarean section may be used
(12) implications for nursing process
 (a) assessment
  1. nutritional status and dietary pattern

                2. knowledge about what occurs during pregnancy
                3. activity and rest patterns
                4. frequent regular monitoring of vital signs, FHR, weight gain, presence of significant symptoms or changes
                5. possible family and environmental stressors
            (b) intervention
                1. educate client for self-management of own care, including current condition, course of pregnancy, nutrition, rest, etc.
                2. report any significant change to physician
                3. assist client to cope with identified stressors
                4. make referrals to other agencies when client needs further assistance
    c) eclampsia
        (1) symptoms
            (a) increase in severity of symptoms of pre-eclampsia
                1. blood pressure: 180/110 mm Hg
                2. albumin: 4+
                3. oliguria or anuria
                4. increased neurological involvement
                5. coma and convulsions
        (2) management
            (a) most eclampsia can be prevented by rigorous treatment of pre-eclampsia
            (b) hospitalization and bedrest
            (c) sedation
                1. barbiturates and tranquilizers are used
                2. phenytoin appears to be effective in preventing seizures without the dangerous sedative effects of other drugs on mother and fetus
            (d) magnesium sulfate blocks neuromuscular transmissions and depresses the CNS; may also cause peripheral vasodilation
                1. usually given as a 50% solution: 10 g administered in two 10-ml doses by deep IM injection as initial dose, followed by 5 g dose IM q 4 hr. As magnesium sulfate is painful, it should be given deep in the gluteal muscle by deep Z-track and the site massaged. Lidocaine 2% can be added to minimize pain
                2. has been given by IV slow infusion in 10–20% solution; IV can be combined with IM

3. excreted mainly by kidneys. Toxic levels may lead to cardiorespiratory arrest; may cause hypocalcemia in mother or fetus
4. blood levels should be monitored. Therapeutic level range of drug is 2.5–7.5 mEq/l. Toxic level is 12–14 mEq/l
5. signs of hypermagnesemia: may appear at 4 mEq/l
   a. thirst
   b. flushing and feelings of heat
   c. sweating
   d. depression of reflexes
   e. flaccidity
   f. extreme signs include circulatory collapse, CNS depression, and respiratory paralysis
      (1.) CNS depression signs include anxiety changing to drowsiness and coma
6. medication should be withheld and doctor notified if
   a. respirations drop below 12/min
   b. knee jerk reflex is absent
   c. urinary output drops below 30 ml/hr during IV infusions or 120 ml q 4 hr when IM dosage is administered
7. calcium gluconate is used as an antidote to magnesium sulfate in severe CNS depression
  (e) medications to promote vasodilation and to lower blood pressure may be used. If $MgSO_4$ is not effective in controlling seizures, thiopental sodium or amobarbital sodium may be used.
  (f) high-protein diet
  (g) intake and output recorded
  (h) parenteral fluid therapy: prevents acidosis
  (i) termination of pregnancy if not able to control progression of symptoms
(3) all symptoms usually disappear 2–4 weeks after delivery unless chronic hypertension or kidney damage occurs
(4) implications for nursing process
  (a) severe restriction of all stimuli
    1. restrict visitors
    2. ensure darkened quiet room
    3. plan nursing care to cause least amount of disturbance to patient
  (b) protection against injury during convulsions

1. Use side rails with padding to prevent injury
2. have padded tongue blade on hand to prevent injury to tongue. Do not force into clenched teeth
- (c) constant observation
    1. blood pressure, pulse, and respiration taken frequently
    2. neurological status constantly monitored
    3. kidney function checked by measuring urinary output and intake
- (d) client and family will need additional support and information to help them cope with the crisis as eclampsia is life threatening

d) a rare but severe complication of pregnancy-induced hypertension is the HELLP syndrome (*H*—hemolysis, *EL*—elevated liver enzymes, *LP*—low platelets)
  (1) assessment
   - (a) signs of hemolysis
       1. bleeding
       2. bruising
       3. petechiae
       4. abnormal lab values
   - (b) impaired liver function
       1. abnormal lab values
       2. signs of malaise
       3. anorexia
       4. nausea and vomiting
       5. jaundice
       6. pain
   - (c) low platelets
       1. bleeding
       2. abnormal lab values
  (2) management: preventive and symptomatic

6. diabetes
   a) during pregnancy, hormonal products are produced in the mother's body that act as antagonists to maternal insulin. Human placental lactogen is the most important of these hormones that decrease the amount of available maternal insulin. In response to this decrease the rate of maternal insulin secretion increases. The rate of insulin production also increases to meet the increased level of blood glucose needed to meet fetal energy requirements

High-Risk Pregnancy   143

b) if the maternal pancreas cannot secrete enough insulin, carbohydrate (CHO) intolerance and gestational diabetes may develop
c) classes of diabetes in pregnancy (White classification system)
  (1) class A (gestational): asymptomatic abnormal glucose tolerance test, normal fasting blood sugar, no insulin requirement. Glucose tolerance test usually returns to normal following delivery. A small percentage (25%) may develop diabetes within 5.5 years. May be managed on diet restrictions, or in rare cases with insulin
     (a) some newer studies (Tallarigo, 1986) indicate that even limited degrees of hyperglycemia that are currently considered within the normal range may be associated with neonatal complications
  (2) class B: diabetes with onset after age 20, duration less than 10 years; no sign of vascular disease
  (3) class C: onset of diabetes ages 10–19; duration 10–19 years; no signs of vascular disease
  (4) class D: onset of diabetes before age 10; duration 20 years or more; vascular lesion such as benign retinopathy, hypertension, calcified arteries in lower extremities
  (5) class E: pelvic arteries calcification
  (6) class F: diabetic nephropathy
  (7) class R: proliferative retinopathy
  (8) class G: frequent pregnancy failures
  (9) class H: cardiopathy
d) rate of occurrence
  (1) gestational diabetes: 2–3% of pregnancies
  (2) pregestational diabetes: 0.2–0.3% of pregnancies
e) women at risk
  (1) previous oversized babies: over 4000 g—9 lbs
  (2) previous unexplained perinatal deaths or congenital anomalies
  (3) habitual abortions
  (4) polyhydramnios
  (5) familial diabetes, particularly in siblings and parents
  (6) glycosuria (must differentiate between lactosuria and renal glycosuria)
  (7) obesity that is over 20% of ideal weight
  (8) history of pre-eclampsia
  (9) chronic vaginal moniliasis
  (10) retinopathy or neurosensory disorders

f) diagnosis
   (1) all women at risk should have a glucose tolerance test
   (2) some physicians recommend that all gravidas above age 25 should be screened with a 1-hour glucose tolerance test. If true blood glucose levels are 130 mg/100 dL or more, then a full glucose tolerance test should be performed
   (3) women with pregestational diabetes are given tests with fasting blood sugars
g) influence of diabetes on pregnancy
   (1) in women with poor metabolic control, perinatal morbidity and mortality rates are approximately three to five times higher than for infants of nondiabetic women
   (2) fetus may respond to increased and varying levels of blood glucose with fetal pancreatic beta-cell hyperplasia and fetal hyperinsulinism
   (3) elevated fetal insulin production may cause increased fetal body fat and organ weights (oversized infants)
   (4) synthesis of pulmonary surfactant may be delayed, increasing the risk of respiratory distress syndrome
   (5) after delivery the hypertrophied pancreas of the infant is still secreting increased amounts of insulin but the mother's blood glucose is no longer supplying glucose. This may cause severe neonatal hypoglycemia
   (6) episodes of hypoglycemia in utero may be a factor in causing an increased rate of stillbirths
   (7) increased incidence of hypocalcemia of neonate
   (8) increased incidence of pre-eclampsia
   (9) increased incidence of difficult labor and hydramnios
   (10) increased incidence of congenital malformations
   (11) increased rate of perinatal mortality
   (12) increased prematurity and RDS in neonates
h) influence of pregnancy on diabetes
   (1) first 20 weeks of gestation
      (a) output of insulin antagonist hormones is small
      (b) there may be a modest decrease in maternal insulin requirements
      (c) women maintained on their prepregnancy doses of insulin may experience hypoglycemic episodes
   (2) at 20 weeks gestation insulin requirements increase due to increased placental mass and increased secretion of insulin antagonists into maternal blood
      (a) danger of hyperglycemia and acidosis

High-Risk Pregnancy 145

(3) insulin needs decrease during labor. Fluids with glucose (IV) are given during labor
(4) immediately following delivery, diabetic mother becomes extremely insulin sensitive and must be carefully monitored. Insulin needs may drop dramatically during first 2 or 3 days following delivery. Normal insulin needs usually develop in 6 weeks postpartum
(5) long-term influence of pregnancy on diabetes is not clearly known. In clients with advanced classifications and the presence of advanced retinopathy or nephropathy some physicians may recommend abortion

i) management
  (1) gestational diabetes can usually be managed by dietary control
    (a) weight gain of 25 lb should be goal
    (b) sweets should be avoided
    (c) the obese diabetic should not diet during pregnancy
    (d) sufficient calories must be taken to prevent ketonemia and ketonuria: 1800–2200 cal/day diet
    (e) blood glucose level is monitored by regular fasting and 2-hour postprandial blood glucose levels. If fasting blood glucose rises over normal levels insulin may be needed
  (2) diabetic pregnancy
    (a) establishment of accurate EDC through menstrual history, fundal height, quickening, and ultrasonic measurement of crown-rump length or serial fetal biparietal diameter
    (b) dietary management: weight gain goal is 25 lbs; 30–35 cal/kg of ideal body weight per day including 100–125 g protein, 200–250 g CHO, 70–80 g fat; avoidance of concentrated sweets
    (c) careful evaluation of renal function and examination of fundi
    (d) baseline blood pressures are taken with frequent follow-up monitoring
    (e) insulin management
      1. goal: to keep blood glucose levels within normal range
        a. tight metabolic control should be established before conception takes place. If tight metabolic control has not been established at the beginning of the pregnancy, patient may have to be hospitalized to establish it. Maintaining maternal metabolism

as close to normal as possible is the major influencing factor on normal fetal growth and development
2. method to reach goal
   a. adherence to prescribed diet
   b. careful regulation of activity
   c. a glucose oxidase-impregnated finger stick can be used by the patient to determine blood levels. Fasting blood sugars are performed regularly by physician
      (1.) blood sugar levels are monitored before each meal and at bedtime. During one day per week the woman also monitors the levels 1 hour after each meal
      (2.) an optimum level of fasting plasma glucose concentration is 60 to 100 mg/dl, with emphasis on low end
      (3.) mean 24-hour plasma glucose values should approximate 80–110 mg/dl
      (4.) self-monitoring by patient of urine for ketones is done in the first morning urine specimen each day
      (5.) correlation between blood glucose level and urine glucose level is low
   d. careful monitoring of insulin dosage is essential throughout the pregnancy. Physician may prescribe split doses of combined intermediate and short-acting insulins
   e. mother usually seen weekly until 36th week, then twice a week
   f. renal function is regularly assessed. Periodic 24-hour urines are done for total protein and creatinine clearance
   g. fetal monitoring at 34 weeks becomes intensive
      (1.) stress and nonstress testing and fetal movement count: a significant drop in the number of fetal movements may necessitate immediate hospitalization
      (2.) oxytocin challenge test monitors fetal status
      (3.) urinary estriol can be monitored
      (4.) fetal maturity may be assessed by measuring

High-Risk Pregnancy 147

   amniotic fluid lecithin/sphingomyelin ratio (L/S)
 h. delivery is timed to prevent fetal injury; between 36–38 weeks is a risk point for the fetus. Careful monitoring of fetal maturity and fetal status enables the physician to determine the optimum time for delivery. Unless fetal jeopardy is indicated, labor is not induced before the 39th week of gestation and a Cesarean section is only performed if needed. During labor maternal blood sugar is measured every 1 or 2 hours and insulin is administered as necessary. During stage one of labor, insulin requirements may decrease to zero. IV fluid and glucose are administered during labor as ordered by physician
 i. postpartum insulin dosage is usually decreased following delivery
 j. diabetics may successfully breast feed their infants (caloric intake must be increased)
j) implications for nursing process
  (1) assess the level of understanding of the effect of the pregnancy on the diabetes and the diabetes on the pregnancy
  (2) assist woman in a more rigorous maintenance of balancing dietary activity and insulin requirements as infant outcome is related to maintaining appropriate insulin blood levels at all times
  (3) monitor the pregnancy closely and frequently
7. cardiac disease
 a) classification (established by New York Heart Association)
  (1) class I: heart disease with no limitation of activity and no abnormal symptoms
  (2) class II: heart disease with slight limitation of activity. Comfortable at rest; ordinary activity causes symptoms of fatigue, dyspnea, palpitations, pain
  (3) class III: heart disease with marked limitation of activity. Comfortable at rest; less than ordinary activity causes symptoms
  (4) class IV: heart disease with symptoms at rest; cannot perform any activity without discomfort
 b) classes I and II may deliver without too much danger. Mortality rate is 0.4 per 1000 births. Classes III and IV have higher mor-

tality rates (6.8 per 1000): abortion may be considered for these women because of the danger
c) there are normal physiological cardiovascular changes during pregnancy; it is important to differentiate from symptoms of heart disease
   (1) increase in maternal cardiac output
       (a) 20–24 weeks: resting cardiac output increases up to 40%; this increase remains until last 8 weeks of pregnancy when it begins to decrease. Some controversy exists about this decrease
       (b) in last trimester cardiac output is influenced by posture
           1. in supine position the enlarged uterus impedes venous return from lower extremities and decreases cardiac output
           2. lateral recumbent position decreases the impediment of venous return and helps maintain increased cardiac output
   (2) heart rate increases during pregnancy: may reach 15 beats above normal per minute at term
   (3) hyperventilation may occur: influenced by progesterone
       (a) may be incidents of paroxysmal tachycardia
   (4) a systolic murmur (grade 1–3) may develop
   (5) during labor, pain and uterine contractions increase the demands on the cardiovascular system
d) diagnosis of heart disease during pregnancy
   (1) physical signs of heart disease may be altered. With mitral and aortic stenosis there may be murmurs that are more easily heard, whereas mitral and aortic insufficiency murmurs may become less noticeable
   (2) diagnostic measures used during pregnancy should be noninvasive and nonionizing in order to prevent fetal damage. EKG, Holter monitoring, and echocardiography are useful
e) usual causes of maternal heart disease are congenital heart defects or damage caused by rheumatic fever
f) maternal risks: severe disability or mortality
   (1) pulmonary edema
   (2) heart failure
   (3) atrial fibrillation and embolization
   (4) bacterial endocarditis
g) fetal risks: depend on the severity of the maternal condition; cardiac failure may lead to perinatal mortality. Severe heart disease may lead to abortion or retardation of intrauterine growth

h) management stresses early detection, careful follow-up and aggressive management
   (1) class I and II
      (a) strict supervision
      (b) prevention of obesity: monitor salt intake, prevent anemia
      (c) physical activities restricted to avoid fatigue
      (d) adequate rest and sleep
      (e) stress and exposure to infections avoided
      (f) can usually carry to term with minimal problems
   (2) class III and IV
      (a) may need hospitalization
      (b) strict bedrest
      (c) sodium restriction
      (d) careful dietary monitoring: adequate but not excessive calories, iron and protein intake must be adequate
      (e) digitalis and thiazide diuretics
         1. can cross placental barrier
         2. careful supervision of fluid and electrolyte balance
         3. may need additional potassium
      (f) prevention of stress and infection
      (g) prophylactic antibiotics are sometimes prescribed for clients with rheumatic heart disease
   (3) labor and delivery must be carefully managed
      (a) prolonged labor avoided
      (b) cardiac monitor may be needed
      (c) danger of pulmonary edema or heart failure is present during labor, delivery, and immediately postpartum
      (d) analgesia must be carefully prescribed to prevent hypotension or respiratory depression in the newborn
      (e) IV fluids must be carefully monitored to prevent circulatory overload
i) implications for nursing process
   (1) assessment
      (a) client's understanding of her condition and the influence of pregnancy on same
      (b) client's ability and motivation to adhere to prescribed regime
      (c) frequent monitoring of vital signs and signs of discomfort during rest and activity
      (d) nutritional and activity and rest patterns

- (2) intervention
  - (a) assistance in maintaining prescribed regimen through teaching, counseling, and referrals
  - (b) teaching of client to recognize signs of significant change
  - (c) careful observation of any signs of change or danger throughout the pregnancy cycle
8. hypertension in pregnancy
   a) types
      (1) chronic hypertension present in the prepregnant state
      (2) hypertension only during pregnancy without proteinuria
      (3) in pre-eclampsia increase in BP usually occurs after 24th week. In hypertensive disease increase usually occurs earlier
         (a) may drop in first two trimesters and rise again during third
         (b) sustained BP of 140/90 mm Hg is usually a sign of condition (except in cases of hydatidiform mole)
         (c) hypertension superimposed by pre-eclampsia is very risky
   b) fetal outcome is related to amount of end-organ damage sustained before conception and the cause of the hypertension. Most women with uncomplicated essential hypertension have uncomplicated gestations
   c) risk factors: older women, family history, and obesity
   d) study of eye grounds, blood urine chemistry, and kidney function provide a more definitive diagnosis
      (1) creatinine and BUN levels are useful in determining prognosis of the pregnancy
   e) management
      (1) high-protein diet with adequate calories
      (2) frequent rest periods in left lateral position to improve uteroplacental and renal perfusion
      (3) clients on antihypertensive medication before pregnancy are maintained on the same medication. Dosage may need to be decreased during first and second trimester and increased in last trimester
      (4) medications are used only if necessary as they cross the placental barrier. Careful monitoring of client on medication is necessary
      (5) monitoring of fetal well-being
         (a) serial estriol levels
         (b) hPL determination
         (c) oxytocin challenge testing (OCT)

（d) if estriol and OCTs are normal, pregnancy is allowed to come to term. When L/S ratio indicates fetal maturity and cervix is ready, induction of labor is done
(e) if fetal distress becomes evident, induction is done even with an immature fetus
(6) implications for nursing process
   (a) assessment
      1. observation for changes in vital signs or other significant changes
      2. nutrition, activity and rest patterns
      3. stressors
   (b) intervention
      1. teaching and counseling regarding condition, management of treatment regimen, detection of significant change, nutrition, rest, and activity patterns
      2. assistance in identifying and coping with areas of present and potential stress

9. infections
   a) respiratory
     (1) may cause decrease of oxygen supply to fetus
     (2) tuberculosis (TB)
       (a) rate of new cases of TB has declined steadily in this country with the advent of chemotherapy. There are still, however, new cases reported each year, and the incidence in poor urban areas can be significant
       (b) inactive TB may become reactivated during pregnancy
       (c) diagnosis is based on
          1. history and physical
          2. tuberculin skin test
          3. chest x-ray for positive skin test
          4. bacteriological culture of sputum
       (d) the decision to have a chest x-ray must be carefully weighed because of its potential hazard to fetus of radiation exposure. A protective lead shield is used to protect the fetus during the x-ray
       (e) treatment: chemotherapy
          1. drug of choice: isoniazid in combination with a variety of other drugs in order to prevent drug resistance
          2. other antituberculosis drugs used with isoniazid: ethambutol, streptomycin, and rifampin
          3. most drugs are not dangerous to fetus, with exception of streptomycin, which may affect the acoustic nerve

4. hospitalization not required
5. client instructed to carry out isolation precautions until sputum is negative for tubercle bacillus
6. congenital tuberculosis is rare but can occur
    a. neonate born to a woman with acute untreated TB must be carefully screened
7. in active, sputum-positive cases of TB, infant must be separated from mother in order to prevent spread of disease to the baby. When sputum becomes negative many doctors recommend BCG vaccine for babies born to active, sputum-positive mothers
    a. mother should not breast feed in active cases
    b. infant should be followed up with regular tuberculin skin testing

(f) implications for nursing process
1. assessment
    a. client's understanding of condition and its effect on pregnancy and its communicability
    b. client nutrition, activity and rest patterns
    c. acceptance of condition by client and family
2. intervention
    a. teaching and counseling regarding self-management of treatment regime, diet, activity, and medical aseptic measures
    b. assist client to accept condition and to accept possible separation from infant if it is necessary

b) venereal diseases
(1) dangerous to the neonate
    (a) syphilis: screening by VDRL or RPR tests
        1. possibility of development of congenital syphilis if mother does not receive treatment during first trimester of pregnancy
    (b) gonorrhea: causes ophthalmia neonatorum if not treated; diagnosed by cultures
        1. instillation of prophylactic eye medication in neonate to prevent infection
(2) antibiotics are used in treating the condition
    (a) penicillin is the drug of choice
    (b) strains of syphilis and gonorrhea have arisen that are resistant to penicillin and must be treated by other appropriate antibiotics

c) herpes vaginalis
   (1) genital herpes is caused by herpes simplex viruses. There are two main kinds of herpes simplex viruses: type I (HSV-1) and type II (HSV-2). Either type may cause oral, genital, or anal herpes although genital herpes is most often caused by type II
   (2) primary genital herpes usually manifests as numerous genital lesions that are painful and with systemic symptoms, including headache, fever, and malaise. Nonprimary first episodes of genital herpes do not produce systemic symptoms with the genital lesions. Recurrent attacks may be asymptomatic, but there will be viral shedding that may spread the infection
   (3) pregnant women who are infected with genital herpes risk infecting their newborns with the disease. The infection in the newborn may be limited to skin, eyes, or mouth or can affect the CNS or internal organs. Death occurs in 15–50% of cases of brain and disseminated disease even with antiviral therapy. There may be permanent neurological impairment in children who do survive
      (a) women with primary genital herpes during pregnancy are at highest risk for transmitting the disease to their newborns. Current treatment is to monitor the viral shedding through cultures during the third trimester and delivering by Cesarean section if cultures are positive. There is currently disagreement among doctors about the administration of acyclovir, which is a specific medication for this condition, during the pregnancy. Some doctors are beginning to recommend the use of acyclovir for women who have primary genital herpes during pregnancy because of the great risk to the newborn
   (4) implications for nursing process
      (a) client must be educated as to the danger that the infection poses to the newborn
      (b) immediate reporting to physician if membranes rupture
      (c) client counseled to have frequent follow-up Pap smears
d) vaginal moniliasis: vaginal infection caused by *Candida albicans*
   (1) if infection is present at delivery, neonate may develop thrush: treated with Mycostatin and gentian violet
e) urinary infections
   (1) pyelonephritis of pregnancy is related to dilation of the ureters and urinary stasis. Early treatment of any urinary infec-

tion with appropriate antibiotic or urinary antiseptic is important in the prevention of the development of pyelonephritis
- (2) pyelonephritis is treated with hospitalization, bedrest in semi-Fowler's position, IV fluids, and ampicillin therapy
- (3) when other urinary infections such as cystitis are being treated sulfonamides should not be used in last few weeks of pregnancy because of the danger of hyperbilirubinemia in the newborn
- (4) prevention: all pregnant women should be screened for asymptomatic bacteriuria and taught preventive measures, such as good perineal hygiene, adequate fluid intake, frequent voiding, taking showers instead of baths, voiding during the night, and voiding immediately after intercourse

f) cytomegalovirus: found commonly in vagina during pregnancy
- (1) may be asymptomatic in mother
- (2) can cross placenta to infect fetus; may cause abortion, microcephaly, blindness, perceptual disorders, and other conditions associated with retardation of intrauterine growth; symptoms may develop later
- (3) may cause brain damage to newborn after delivery if infection is transmitted
- (4) diagnosis of disease
    - (a) tissue cultures from urine
    - (b) complement fixation antibody test
- (5) no available treatment
- (6) primary cases of the disease during the pregnancy present the most risk to the fetus. Primary cases may be asymptomatic or may have symptoms similar to mononucleosis. Recurrent episodes of disease present a much lower risk to fetus
- (7) children in day care centers have a high level of infection and may spread disease to pregnant women

g) toxoplasmosis: infection by a protozoan that is ingested as cysts in undercooked meat or is acquired through handling the excreta of an infected cat
- (1) usually mild in the adult; resembles infectious mononucleosis; may be asymptomatic
- (2) fetus has a 40% chance of developing the disease (death rate 10–15%)
    - (a) can cause chorioretinitis, a severe CNS syndrome with encephalitis, carditis, and other serious conditions

(3) diagnosis made by a positive Sabin-Feldman dye test that indicates a recent or active infection
(4) most cases of congenital toxoplasmosis occur when the mother acquires her infection during the pregnancy. Mothers who are seropositive before pregnancy usually do not present a risk to the fetus
(5) incidence of infection of neonate is highest when infection occurs during third trimester; severity of fetal illness is greater when infection occurs during first trimester
(6) if maternal infection is diagnosed, fetal blood testing is done to determine if fetus is infected
(7) new treatment includes treating mother with spiramycin throughout pregnancy if she is infected and adding pyrimethamine and sulfadoxine if the fetus is infected. This regime may reduce the severity of fetal manifestations
(8) abortion may be desired by parents because of high degree of probability of severe damage to fetus
(9) implications for nursing process
   (a) counsel pregnant women to cook meat till well done, wear gloves or avoid handling cat litter, and wash fruits and vegetables
h) rubella infection in the mother: carries a very severe danger to the fetus. Infection in the first 8 weeks carries greatest risk. In the third trimester there are no risks
   (1) causes abortions, growth retardation, blindness, deafness, mental retardation, and other serious problems
   (2) women who have not had the disease in childhood should be immunized before they become pregnant
   (3) a test for antibodies can indicate whether or not a woman has had the disease
   (4) implications for nursing process
      (a) education regarding importance of immunization against the disease in childhood
      (b) women who contract the disease when they are pregnant will need support if they contemplate an abortion
i) varicella: can pose a risk to mother and fetus during pregnancy
   (1) maternal risks
      (a) pneumonia
   (2) fetal risks
      (a) low rate of congenital malformation: controversy about the association

(b) clinical syndrome of hypoplasia of the extremities, cortical atrophy, cicatricial skin lesions, and ocular abnormalities has been identified, mainly in cases where infection occurred during the first 20 weeks of pregnancy
- (3) disease can be transmitted to the newborn at birth where there is a danger of mortality
- (4) implications for nursing process
    - (a) zoster immune globulin and zoster immune plasma are recommended for babies born to mothers who are infected at the time of delivery
    - (b) prevention of the infection by cautioning pregnant women to avoid contact with infected children
10. other disorders of pregnancy
    a) maternal PKU newborn screening and dietary treatment of children born with PKU has enabled many women with this disorder to escape mental retardation and to marry and have children
    - (1) intervention is necessary to prevent the children of these women from developing mental retardation, low birthweight, microcephaly, or congenital heart disease
    - (2) pregnant women with PKU who have discontinued their special diet during childhood must reinstate this diet before conception and during the pregnancy to prevent damage to the fetus
    - (3) all women should be asked about PKU during a history and physical so that they can be advised about their special needs during pregnancy
    - (4) in some areas a genetic registry of all PKU persons is kept and young women are recalled when they reach 12 years of age in order to give them this information
    - (5) implications for nursing process
        - (a) preventive health education with teenagers
        - (b) special diet counseling for pregnant women with PKU
    b) acute fatty liver of pregnancy: a rare disorder that occurs in 1 in 13,328 deliveries, mostly in primiparas carrying twins or males
    - (1) usually occurs after 35th week of pregnancy
    - (2) fetal and maternal mortality rates average 23% and 18% and would improve if early diagnosis and treatment were instituted
    - (3) symptoms
        - (a) headache
        - (b) fatigue
        - (c) malaise

(d) nausea and vomiting
(e) abdominal pain may be present
(f) back pain may signal pancreatitis
(g) mild hypertension and peripheral edema may occur
(4) if condition progresses, jaundice, bleeding from puncture sites, hematemesis, seizures, and coma may occur. There is usually no fever. Mild hypertension and peripheral edema may occur.
(5) treatment: immediate delivery by vaginal or cesarean section. As the condition occurs late in pregnancy the fetus usually survives. Maternal liver function usually improves rapidly after delivery.
c) puerperal pulmonary embolus: may occur during pregnancy but is most frequent after delivery (see Chapter 18)
11. psychosocial risk factors
a) battering during pregnancy (Helton, 1987)
(1) a major health problem in our society. It occurs across a wide spectrum of racial, religious, and economic backgrounds
(2) may include physical, sexual, psychological, and social abuse
(3) may begin or increase during pregnancy
(4) men who batter women may have low self-esteem and a desire to control others. Many were abused themselves as children
(5) may lead to miscarriage or alcohol or drug abuse. There is an increased risk of low birthweight infants.
(6) implications for nursing process
(a) assess possible battering in a private place away from male partner
(b) assist woman to verbalize her feelings and not to minimize the situation. Help her to understand that the problem is universal and widespread and that she is not to blame. Decrease her sense of hopelessness by providing referrals for assistance through community agencies and support groups
(c) assist woman in her ability to recognize signs of increased danger from the battering partner
(d) document all assessments and intervention on the health record
(e) if male partner requests help, refer him to appropriate agency

- b) court-ordered obstetrical procedures
    - (1) court-ordered obstetrical procedures in which women are forced to have surgical procedures against their will to benefit the fetus are a growing problem; they have been obtained for Cesarean sections and intrauterine transfusions that were performed on women against their will
    - (2) in most of the cases to date the women involved have been poor and on public assistance
    - (3) the problem of the rights of women and the rights of the fetus must be carefully examined so that the legal and civil rights of women are protected
    - (4) court-ordered procedures violate the principle of informed consent
    - (5) a recent appeals court ruling reversed a court-ordered Cesarean that was against the mother's will (Greenhouse, 1988)
- c) alcohol abuse
    - (1) alcohol abuse during pregnancy may lead to fetal alcohol syndrome (see Chapter 6)
    - (2) it is essential to obtain an accurate history of drinking patterns when counseling a pregnant woman who is abusing alcohol. The following questions should be asked.
        - (a) how often do you drink beer? wine? hard liquor?
        - (b) how much do you drink at each time?
        - (c) has your drinking changed in the past year?
        - (d) has your drinking changed since you became pregnant?
        - (e) have you made an effort to cut down on your drinking since you became pregnant?
        - (f) do you drink alone or in company?
        - (g) at what time of day do you drink?
    - (3) pregnant women are more receptive to alcohol counseling because of their concern for their child. It is important to explain clearly to the woman the effects of alcohol abuse on the fetus. If the woman is unable to stop drinking with supportive counseling from the nurse, a referral should be made to a treatment center for alcohol abuse
- d) drug abuse
    - (1) drug abuse may harm the fetus; heroin users may have AIDS
    - (2) an accurate history of drug use should be obtained
    - (3) addicted women usually have multiple health problems with a high incidence of infections and venereal disease. A care-

ful history and physical exam are needed to detect these conditions
(4) addicted women may be passive and unable to make decisions about their care
(5) addicted women usually have poor diets and are at risk for low birthweight babies, toxemia, miscarriage, placenta previa, and other conditions
(6) women addicted to heroin are usually enrolled in methadone maintenance programs. Total withdrawal may be dangerous to the fetus during the first and third trimesters. If withdrawal is requested it is usually tried during the 14th to 28th week and is done very slowly
(7) addicted women need intensive and supportive nursing care, as well as referral to appropriate treatment agencies
(8) it is most important for nurses caring for pregnant women who abuse substances or alcohol to maintain a nonjudgmental attitude when providing nursing care

e) women with psychosocial problems of noncompletion of developmental tasks of maturity, poor communication skills, poor interpersonal relations, inadequate support systems and/or history of child abuse. These women are potentially at risk and would benefit from intensive nursing intervention
(1) the following risk criteria are significant (Allen & Mantz, 1981)
   (a) negative feelings toward pregnancy after 20 weeks of gestation
   (b) denial of pregnancy and fetal growth
   (c) lack of interest in pregnancy, delivery, and baby
   (d) indulging in activities that may be harmful to baby
   (e) refusal to take part in any activity involved with preparation for childbirth and parenthood
   (f) unrealistic expectations of labor and delivery and parenthood
   (g) unwillingness to comply with important health care components, such as nutrition, rest, smoking cessation, etc.
   (h) insecurity about own mothering skills
   (i) no history of a positive parenting role model
   (j) a history of past or current psychiatric problems
(2) these women may be potential child abusers or may adversely affect fetal development or their own health during the pregnancy. If the nurse can develop a trusting relation-

ship with the woman, a careful history taking can elicit the potential problems and the potential resources available, including family, friends, and community agencies

(3) nursing care must include support and mothering for the mother

---

REFERENCES

Allen, E., & Mantz, M. (1981). Are normal patients at risk during pregnancy? *Journal of Obstetric, Gynecologic and Neonatal Nursing, 10,* 350–351.

Greenhouse, L. (1988, March 2). Appeals court vacates forced-Caesarean ruling. *New York Times,* p. A-17.

Helton, A. S. (1986). *Protocol of care for the battered woman: Prevention of battering during pregnancy.* White Plains, NY: March of Dimes.

Tallarigo, L., et al. (1986). Relation of glucose tolerance to complications of pregnancy in nondiabetic women. *New England Journal of Medicine, 315,* 989–992.

Chapter 9

Drugs Used During the Prenatal Period

A. All drugs used during pregnancy should be prescribed with extreme caution because of possible teratogenic effects (congenital malformations). Information about specific drugs should be obtained from the latest edition of *Physicians' Desk Reference* or from other reliable resources
   1. the nurse should counsel the patient about the possible effects of any drug prescribed and should caution her about the use of any over-the-counter drug or drugs that have not been prescribed
   2. since November 1980, a revised food and drug labeling program has been in effect: all prescription drugs that have a potential for harm to the fetus or are absorbed systemically must be categorized according to level of risk to fetus
      a) category A: controlled studies in women fail to demonstrate a risk to the fetus in the first trimester (and there is no evidence of a risk in later trimesters), and the possibility of fetal harm appears remote
      b) category B: either animal reproduction studies have not demonstrated a fetal risk but there are no controlled studies in pregnant women, or animal reproduction studies have shown adverse effect (other than a decrease in fertility) that was not confirmed in controlled studies in women in the first trimester (and there is no evidence of risk in later trimesters)
      c) category C: either studies in animals have revealed adverse effects on the fetus (teratogenic or embryocidal effects or other) and there are no controlled studies in women, or studies in women and animals are not available. Drugs should be given only if the potential benefit justifies the potential risk to the fetus
      d) category D: there is a positive evidence of human fetal risk, but the benefits from use in pregnant women may be acceptable

despite the risk, e.g., if the drug is needed in a life-threatening situation for a serious disease for which safer drugs cannot be used or are ineffective. There is an appropriate statement in "warnings" section of the labeling
      e) category E: studies in animals or human beings have demonstrated fetal abnormalities or there is evidence of fetal risk based on human experience, or both, and the risk of the use of the drug in pregnant women clearly outweighs any possible benefit. The drug is contraindicated in women who are or may become pregnant. There is an appropriate statement in the "contraindications" section of the labeling
      f) also included in the new labeling requirements are a drug's known effects on reproduction and any nonteratogenic adverse effects, such as narcotic withdrawal symptoms in the newborn or hypoglycemia in the fetus attributed to the mother's use of the drug
   3. a nurse should check all literature on the drug before administering it. If any question arises as to the safety of the drug, more information should be obtained
B. Changes in maternal physiology that affect drug action
   1. drug absorption is believed to be similar to the nonpregnant state
   2. serum albumin has lower concentration levels because of increase in volume of plasma, thus decreasing albumin-binding capacity of the drug and resulting in more "free" drug for placental transfer
   3. increase in amounts of circulating steroid hormones influences the metabolism of drugs in the liver
      a) hepatic blood flow is not increased
      b) some bile stasis may occur as pregnancy advances; this may delay degradation of drugs
   4. increased renal perfusion and glomerular filtration may increase the speed of drug excretion
C. Role of the placenta
   1. drugs are transferred across the placenta primarily by simple diffusion
   2. drug transfer is greater during late pregnancy
   3. any drug in sufficient concentration will eventually cross the placenta (Rayburn & Zuspan, 1980)
   4. some drugs may act on fetoplacental unit and reduce placental blood flow or interfere with the active transport of nutrients and wastes or other nutritive functions of the placenta
D. Drug effects on the fetus
   1. some drugs crossing the placental barrier usually reach fetal levels that correspond to 50–100% of maternal serum concentrations

2. total drug exposure of the fetus is more important than rate of placental transfer
3. chronic exposure to a drug may influence fetal cell growth
4. some drugs have higher affinity for specific target areas, for example
   a) heart: digoxin
   b) skeleton: tetracycline, warfarin
   c) red blood cells: sulfonamides
   d) otic nerve: streptomycin
   e) platelets: aspirin
5. pharmodynamic effects of drugs may be more pronounced in the fetus than the mother because the activity and concentration of some liver enzymes and rate of some enzymatic reactions are probably lower in the fetus
6. excretion of most drugs is slower in the fetus
   a) excretion takes place by
      (1) simple diffusion through placenta
      (2) fetal kidneys into amniotic fluid
         (a) amniotic fluid can be swallowed by fetus
7. drug treatment of the fetus
   a) the drug treatment of various fetal complications is being investigated. The risks and benefits of such treatment are unclear
   b) drug administration takes place by
      (1) passive transplacental route
      (2) direct intra-amniotic instillation

E. Self-medication
   1. should include prohibition of tobacco, alcohol, and/or stimulants
      a) infants of smokers
         (1) are more likely to be of low birthweight
         (2) may have greater risk of congenital heart defects
         (3) have higher incidence of respiratory system infection in first year of life
         (4) are at increased risk of adult cancers
      b) coffee, tea, cocoa, and cola contain naturally occurring stimulants; the effect of these stimulants on the fetus is controversial

F. Street drugs
   1. maternal heroin, cocaine, or barbiturate use results in withdrawal symptoms in the newborn
      a) new research on cocaine use in pregnancy reveals that cocaine use by the mother may cause prematurity, very small size at birth, stiff limbs, higher risk of crib death, and, rarely, malformed genital and urinary organs, absent small intestines, and stroke; even a single dose by the mother may cause defects

2. the woman should be assessed for use of these drugs and referred for treatment
G. Drug dependence (Chasnoff, 1986)
    1. number of women between ages 18–34 using drugs continues to increase
    2. identification of drug-dependent women
        a) physical appearance
            (1) not well oriented
            (2) overly fatigued
            (3) pupils: dilated or constricted
            (4) uterine size not congruent with stated gestational age
            (5) track marks, abscesses, edema in extremities
        b) medical history
            (1) positive for hepatitis, cirrhosis, or other illnesses associated with drug use
        c) obstetrical history
            (1) positive for spontaneous abortion, premature labor, or fetal death: may indicate possible drug use
            (2) positive signs indicative of possible drug use during present pregnancy
                (a) poor weight gain
                (b) spotting or bleeding
                (c) inactive or hyperactive fetus
                (d) premature contractions
        d) past history of drug abuse
    3. intervention
        a) confrontation by skilled counselor
        b) education
        c) referral to clinical dependence treatment center
        d) referral for high-risk obstetrical care
    4. obstetrical aspects of maternal addiction
        a) social environment that is not conducive to positive pregnancy outcome
            (1) poor nutrition
            (2) lack of or intermittent prenatal care
            (3) drugs may be adulterated with agents, such as quinine, chalk, or sugar
            (4) drugs may vary in potency
        b) medical complications
            (1) anemia
            (2) vaginitis

(3) sexually transmitted diseases (STD)
(4) pyelonephritis
c) obstetrical complications
(1) abortion
(2) ectopic pregnancy
(3) low birthweight
(4) premature rupture of membranes
(5) hypertensive disease of pregnancy
(6) abruptio placenta or placenta previa
(7) malpresentation
(8) puerperal morbidity
(9) stillbirth
5. approaches to management
a) prenatal care and support with no attempt to alter addiction
(1) associated with high risks for both mother and fetus
b) acute detoxification
(1) almost never advised during pregnancy because it may lead to fetal death
c) slow detoxification with methadone substitution and subsequent withdrawal
(1) may be harmful to fetus
(2) physical aspects of drug dependence should be complemented by psychosocial counseling
d) methadone maintenance
(1) may affect fetus and newborn
e) low-dose methadone maintenance with psychosocial counseling
(1) maintenance dose: keep as low as possible to possibly avoid effect on fetus and newborn
f) drug-free communities
(1) if part of acute detoxification program, precautions as above need to be taken
H. Drugs used in normal pregnancy (Table 9-1)
1. before drugs are used, nonpharmacological measures should be attempted to relieve discomforts. The woman should be warned against using over-the-counter drugs. Before administering a prescribed drug, the nurse should check the dosage, adverse effects, and the possibility of a teratogenic effect on the fetus and not administer if any adverse effects on mother or fetus are suspected
2. antacids
a) should be avoided during first trimester when possible
b) during late pregnancy because of slight relaxation of the cardiac

sphincter and pressure of enlarging uterus there may be some regurgitation of stomach acid into the esophagus causing heartburn. An antacid may be prescribed by the physician
- (1) the patient should be warned about taking extra doses
    - (a) large quantities of calcium carbonate may cause an increase in the secretion of stomach acid
    - (b) sodium bicarbonates should be avoided during pregnancy
        1. high sodium content
        2. systemic absorption
        3. produce gaseous CO_2 in the stomach
    - (c) large doses of magnesium trisilicate may damage fetal kidneys
    - (d) magnesium hydroxide may damage fetal neurological and neuromuscular systems
3. antiemetics
    - a) nausea and vomiting is a common complaint during the first trimester. All medication must be by prescription and should be used cautiously
4. laxatives
    - a) constipation may occur during pregnancy. The physician may order a laxative or stool softener
    - b) the following should NOT be used during pregnancy
        - (1) liquid petroleum; for example, mineral oil: blocks absorption of fat-soluble vitamins
        - (2) danthron: absorbed systemically
        - (3) castor oil: too severe for pregnancy
        - (4) Clysodrast: may be hepatotoxic
5. analgesics
    - a) pain may be experienced during pregnancy. It is usually the result of low back pain, sciatica, headache, or muscle cramps
    - b) should be used sparingly and only after consultation with physician. All analgesics should be avoided during organogenesis; may have teratogenic effect
    - c) acetaminophen is the drug of choice during pregnancy: a retrospective study (Collins, 1981) showed no evidence of teratogenicity
    - d) indomethacin and other anti-inflammatory drugs should be avoided during pregnancy
        - (1) pulmonary hypertension and disturbed cardiopulmonary adaption in the neonate have been reported

e) codeine: can cause addiction and neonate can have withdrawal symptoms
6. sedatives
   a) restlessness and difficulty in sleeping may occur in the last trimester
   b) the woman should be warned to avoid nonprescription drugs
   c) barbiturates taken near delivery may have adverse effects on neonate, and analgesics or anesthetics given during delivery may be potentiated by sedatives
7. vitamins and minerals
   a) poor nutrition increases the risk during pregnancy
   b) vitamins and minerals may be given routinely. The woman should be cautioned against supplementing the prescribed vitamin therapy
   c) high doses of vitamins A and D have been associated with fetal anomalies
   d) iron: difficult to obtain necessary iron from diet. Therefore a supplement is usually prescribed
      (1) may cause gastric irritation, diarrhea, or constipation
      (2) causes dark stools
      (3) ferrous gluconate may enhance teratogenic effect of aspirin

I. Drugs used in high-risk pregnancies
   1. infections
      a) a variety of antibiotic agents may be prescribed
      b) each drug should be checked for possible teratogenic effects as well as maternal effects and to make sure they are not contraindicated during pregnancy
   2. thromboembolic problems
      a) heparin: appears to be safe during pregnancy
         (1) dosage varies according to patient status and laboratory findings
         (2) may be given IV or subcutaneously
         (3) clotting time should be checked before administering
         (4) patient should be checked for signs of bleeding
         (5) patient should be warned about taking over-the-counter drugs, especially those containing aspirin
      b) coumarin derivatives: have teratogenic and long-lasting effects but have been used without adverse effects from 14–36 weeks of gestation (Merrill & VerBurg, 1986)
         (1) coumarin derivatives interact with many other drugs

(2) dosage must be carefully and individually prescribed because the major adverse effect is overdose
   (a) patient should be followed with frequent test of prothrombin time
   (b) prothrombin time should be checked before administering
3. cardiovascular problems
  a) cardiac glycosides (i.e., digoxin and digitoxin) increase force of myocardial contractions
    (1) drug used and dosage are individually prescribed
    (2) close observation is essential
    (3) lab experiments indicate these drugs cross the placental barrier; however, usually no adverse effects are noted in the human infant
      (a) it is important to monitor the newborn for signs of toxicity
  b) hypertensive conditions sometimes require medication to control
    (1) antihypertensives
      (a) Aldomet: safety in pregnancy not established but no specific fetal effects are known
        1. may cause sedation, depression, sodium retention, dizziness, and weakness
        2. tolerance may occur in 2 to 3 weeks. Report to physician
      (b) Apresoline: reserved for treatment in severe cases when patient is hospitalized
        1. may cause palpitations, tachycardia, flushing, hypotension
        2. no known adverse fetal effects
      (c) propranolol (Inderal)
        1. may lead to small placenta and growth retardation
        2. may cause postnatal bradycardia and hypoglycemia in infant
        3. may reduce contractibility of uterus
        4. since an increased rate of stillbirths has been noted, use during pregnancy is not recommended unless the potential benefits outweigh the risk of the fetus (PDR, 1985)
      (d) reserpine: has many trade names
        1. may cause postural hypotension, bradycardia, fatigue, sedation, depression, lethargy, headache, and dizziness

Drugs Used During the Prenatal Period 169

2. anesthetics and stress of labor may potentiate hypotensive effect
3. nasal congestion in the neonate is also a side effect. Therefore, it has been advised that medication be changed during pregnancy because neonate is obligate nasal breather. If not discontinued, nursery personnel should be advised

   (e) hydralazine: vasodilator
   1. may cause headache, tachycardia, palpitations, and angina
   2. other effects include sodium retention and GI disturbance
   3. if given abruptly may cause a precipitous drop in FHR

(2) diuretics: not used to treat pregnancy-induced hypertension; however, are still used to treat hypertension not related to pregnancy. Beneficial risks must be weighed when prescribing drugs
   (a) thiazides and furosemide are drugs of choice during pregnancy
   (b) thiazides include such drugs as Diuril, Esidrix, and Hydro DIURIL, among others
   1. dose varies according to drug given and individual status
   2. may cause electrolyte imbalance
   3. may have adverse effects of neonatal fluid balance
   4. thrombocytopenia and elevated bilirubin levels have been observed in newborns
   (c) furosemide (Lasix) has caused fetal abnormalities when taken during organogenesis; used only in hypertensive crisis or pulmonary edema for short period only
   1. contraindicated if patient is allergic to sulfonamides
   2. may cause electrolyte imbalance
   3. potentiates antihypertensive drugs

(3) anticonvulsants
   (a) Valium: mild sedative and CNS depressant; should be discontinued several days before delivery. If given within 24 hours of delivery, monitor fetus for signs of depression. Report changes immediately to physician. Effects on fetus include
   1. fetal tachycardia
   2. fetal heart rate variability

            3. newborn lethargy, hypotonia, respiratory depression
            4. failure to suck
        c) magnesium sulfate
            (1) used as a sedative and anticonvulsant
                (a) causes vasodilation and therefore lowers blood pressure
            (2) cannot be given to a woman who is digitalized
            (3) should not be given in repeated doses unless reflexes and respiratory rate are checked
                (a) depresses reflexes and respiration
            (4) antidote is calcium; when administering magnesium sulfate an ampule of calcium gluconate should be readily available
            (5) signs of intoxication include hot feeling, flushing, thirst, sweating, depressed reflexes, hypotension, and flaccidity
            (6) may lead to CNS depression, respiratory depression, and circulatory collapse
        d) sedatives
            (1) phenobarbital: raises the threshold for seizures
                (a) tolerance may develop
                (b) may cause rashes and/or ataxia
            (2) sodium amytal: used in eclampsia when convulsions persist
    4. preterm labor: tocolytic agents
        a) most effective if used early in labor
            (1) used if contractions occur more than 2 times in 15 minutes
            (2) used if there is any sign of cervical change
        b) if possible delivery should be delayed at least 24–48 hours after administration
            (1) delay allows time to administer glucocorticoids to mother to enhance maturation of fetal lungs
        c) progestational agents
            (1) effectiveness in humans not well established
            (2) if taken early in pregnancy may cause masculinization of female fetus
        d) ethanol
            (1) believed to block release of oxytocin and may have direct depressant action on myometrium
            (2) use has been discontinued because of adverse effect on mother and fetus
        e) magnesium sulfate
            (1) can alter myometrial contractility
            (2) thought to be a calcium antagonist
            (3) careful monitoring; can be toxic
            (4) not approved by FDA as tocolytic agent

f) beta-adrenergic receptor stimulants
   (1) Ritodrine, Isoxsuprine, Terbutaline, Salbutomol, Fenoterel
   (2) maternal side effects
       (a) maternal tachycardia
       (b) maternal hypotension
       (c) chest tightness or pain
       (d) S-T segment depression
       (e) pulmonary edema
       (f) hyperglycemia
       (g) some fatalities
   (3) fetal side effects
       (a) tachycardia
       (b) hypoglycemia
   (4) should not be used in women with history of
       (a) cardiopulmonary or vascular disease including
           1. migraine headache
           2. asymptomatic arrythmias
       (b) intrauterine infection
       (c) diabetes
       (c) active bleeding from any site
           1. women considered for treatment should have a pretocolytic ECG
           2. careful monitoring for adverse effects should be continued throughout treatment
g) antiprostaglandins
   (1) may inhibit synthesis of prostaglandins or block their action on target organs
   (2) may cause cardiovascular changes in fetus, including premature closure of ductus arteriosus

Table 9-1 Reported Effects from Drug Exposure on the Fetus

Drugs	First Trimester Effects	Second and Third Trimester Effects
1. Analgesics		
Acetaminophen	None known	None known
Narcotics	None known	Depression, withdrawal
Salicylates	Frequent reports—none proven	Prolonged pregnancy and labor, hemorrhage
2. Anesthetics		
General	↑ Anomalies, abortion	Depression
Local	None known	Bradycardia, seizures
3. Anorexics		
Amphetamines	↑ Anomalies	Irritable, poor feeding
Phenmetrazine	Skeletal anomalies	Unknown
4. Anti-Infection Agents		
Aminoglycosides	Skeletal anomalies	Nephrotoxic, ototoxic
Cephalosporins	None known	↓ Positive cultures
Chloramphenicol	None known	"Gray baby" syndrome (?)
Clindamycin	None known	Unknown
Erythromycin	None known	None known
Ethambutol	None known	None known
Ethionamide	↑ Anomalies	None known
Isoniazid	None known	None known
Metronidazole	?Mutagenesis/carcinogenesis	None known
Penicillins	None known	↓ Positive cultures
Rifampin	None known	None known
Sulfonamides	None known	Hemolytic anemia, thrombocytopenia, hyperbilirubinemia
Tetracyclines	Impaired bone growth	Bone growth, stained teeth (enamel hypoplasia)
5. Anticoagulants		
Coumadin	Nasal hypoplasia, ophthalmogic abnormalities, epiphyseal stippling	Hemorrhage, stillbirth
Heparin	None known	Hemorrhage at placental site with possible stillbirth
6. Anticonvulsants		
Barbiturates	Anomalies (?)	Bleeding, withdrawal
Carbamazepine	↑ Anomalies	Bleeding, withdrawal
Clonazepam	Facial cleft	Withdrawal, depression
Ethosuximide	None known	None known
Phenytoin	IUGR, craniofacial abnormalities, mental retardation, hypoplasia of phalanges	Hemorrhage ⎫ Depletion of vitamin K-dependent clotting factor
Primidone	Same as barbiturates	Hemorrhage
Trimethadione	IUGR, mental retardation, facial dysmorphogenesis	Hemorrhage
Valproic Acid	Unknown	Unknown ⎭
7. Antiemetics		
Bendectin	None known	None known
Phenothiazines	None known	None known

Table 9-1 continued

Drugs	First Trimester Effects	Second and Third Trimester Effects
8. Cancer Chemotherapy		
Alkylating agents	Abortion, anomalies	Hypoplastic gonads, growth delay
Antimetabolites		
folic acid analogs	Ab, IUGR cranial anomalies	Hypoplastic gonads, growth delay
pyrimidine analogs		
arabinoside	Ab	Hypoplastic gonads, growth delay
purine analogs (cytosine, 5-FU)	Ab	Hypoplastic gonads, growth delay
Antibiotics (Actinomycin)	Ab	Hypoplastic gonads, growth delay
Vinca Alkyloids	Ab	Hypoplastic gonads, growth delay
Hormones	(See #13)	Hypoplastic gonads, growth delay
9. Cardiovascular Drugs		
Antihypertensives		
alpha-methyldopa	None known	Hemolytic anemia, ileus
guanethidine	None known	None known
hydralazine	None known	Tachycardia
propranolol	None known	Bradycardia, hypoglycemia, IUGR with chronic use
reserpine	None known	Lethargy
Beta-sympathomimetics	None known	Tachycardia
Digitalis preparations	None known	Bradycardia
10. Cold and Cough Preparations		
Antihistamines	None known	None known
Cough Suppressants	None known	None known
Decongestants	None known	None known
Expectorants	Fetal goiter	None known
11. Diuretics		
Furosemide	None known	Death from sudden hypoperfusion
Thiazides	None known	Thrombocytopenia, hypokalemia, hyperbilirubinemia, hyponatremia
12. Fertility Drugs		
Clomiphene	Chromosomal anomalies (?)	Unknown
13. Hormones		
Androgens	Masculinization-female fetus	Adrenal suppression (?)
Corticosteroids	Cleft in animals, not in humans	Growth delay
Estrogens	CV anomalies	None known
Progestins	Limb and cardiovascular anomalies, VACTERL syndrome	None known

continues

Table 9-1 continued

Drugs	First Trimester Effects	Second and Third Trimester Effects
14. Hypoglycemics		
Insulin	None known	Hypoglycemia (unlikely)
Sulfonylureas	Anomalies	Suppressed insulin secretion
15. Lazatives		
Bisacodyl	None known	None known
Dioctyl Sodium Sulfosuccinate	None known	None known
Mineral Oil	↓ Vitamin absorption	None known
Milk of Magnesia	None known	None known
16. Psychoactive Drugs		
Antidepressants: Tricyclics	CNS (?)/limb defects	None known
Benzodiazepines	Facial clefts and cardiac	Depression
Hydroxyzine	None known	None known
Meprobamate	Facial clefts	None known
Phenothiazines	None known	None known
Sedatives	None known	Depression
Thalidomide	Phocomelia	None known
17. Thyroid Drugs		
Anti-Thyroid		
^{131}I	Goiter, abortion, anomalies	Goiter, airway obstruction, hypothyroid, mental retardation
PTU	None known	Same
Tapazole	Aplasia cutis	Same, aplasia cutis
Thyroid USP	Does not cross	None known
18. Tocolytics		
Alcohol	Fetal alcohol syndrome	Intoxication, hypotonia, lethargy
Magnesium Sulfate	None known	Hypermagnesemia, respiratory depression
Beta-Sympathomimetics	None known	Tachycardia, hypothermia, hypocalcemia, hypo-hyperglycemia
19. Vaginal Preparations		
Antifungal Agents	None known	None known
Podophyllin	Mutagenesis (?)	Laryngeal polyps (?), CNS effects (?)
20. Vitamins (high doses)		
A	Renal anomalies	None known
B	None known	None known
C	None known	Scurvy after delivery
D	Mental retardation	None known
E	None known	None known
K	None known	Hemorrhage if deficiency

Source: From "Drugs during Pregnancy: Part II, Drug Effects on the Fetus" by W.F. Rayburn and J.D. Iams, 1980, *Perinatal Press, 4* (9). Copyright 1980 by Perinatal Press, Inc. Reprinted by permission.

REFERENCES

Chasnoff, I. (1986). *Drug use in pregnancy*. Lancaster: MTP Press Ltd.

Collins, E. (1981, November). Maternal and fetal effects of acetaminophen salicylates. *Obstetrics and Gynecology*, pp. 575–625.

Merrill, L.K., & VerBurg, D.J. (1986, June). The choice of long-term anti-coagulants for the pregnant patient. *Obstetrics and Gynecology*, pp. 711–714.

Rayburn, W.J., & Zuspan, F.P. (1980). Drug use during pregnancy: Part I, Principles of perinatal pharmacology. *Perinatal Press* 4 (8).

BIBLIOGRAPHY

Acres, L. (1987, April). The foetal alcohol syndrome. *Nursing RSA Verpleging*, pp. 41–43.

Bower, B. (1987, May 2). Lead in utero: Low-level danger. *Science News*, p. 277.

Brooten, D., and Miller, M. *The Childbearing Family: A Nursing Perspective*, 2nd ed., Boston: Little, Brown & Co. 1983.

Brown, Z.A., et al. (1987, November 12). Effects on infants of a first episode of genital herpes during pregnancy. *New England Journal of Medicine*, pp. 1246–49.

Chervenak, F.A., et al. (1986, July 31). Advances in the diagnosis of fetal defect. *New England Journal of Medicine*, pp. 305–307.

Council on Scientific Affairs: Effects of Physical Forces on the Reproductive Cycle. *Journal of the American Medical Association*, pp. 247–250.

Council on Scientific Affairs. (1985, June 21). Effects of toxic chemicals on the reproductive system. *Journal of the American Medical Association*, pp. 3431–3437.

Everson, R.B. (1980). Individuals transplacentally exposed to maternal smoking may be at increased cancer risk in adult life. *Lancet, 2*, 123–127.

Few, B. (1987, September/October). Nifedipine for the treatment of premature labor, *Maternal Child Nursing*, p. 309.

Gantes, M., Kirchhoff, K. & Work, B. (1985). Breast massage to obtain contraction stress test. *Nursing Research, 34* (6), 338–341.

Gillespie, S.A., et al. (1981). A reference for clinicians: Discomforts of pregnancy, issues in health care of women, *3*, 375–396.

Grannum, P.A., et al. (1986, May 29). In utero exchange transfusion by direct intravascular injection in severe erythroblastosis fetalis. *New England Journal of Medicine*, pp. 1431–1434.

Horan, M. (1984). Discomfort and pain during pregnancy. *Maternal Child Nursing, 9*, 267–269.

Jensen, M., & Bobak, I. (1985). *Maternity and gynecologic care* (3rd ed.). St. Louis: C.V. Mosby.

Kaplan, M.M. (1985, August 8). Acute fatty liver of pregnancy. *New England Journal of Medicine*, pp. 367–370.

Kalter, H., & Warkany, J. (1983). Congenital malformations. *New England Journal of Medicine*, Part I, February 24, pp. 424–428; Part II, March 3, pp. 491–496.

Lieber, M. (1980, September/October). Nonstress antepartal monitoring. *Maternal Child Nursing*, pp. 335–339.

Lindheimer, M.D., & Katz, A.I. (1985, September 12). Hypertension in pregnancy. *New England Journal of Medicine,* pp. 675–679.

Lipman, A. (1984, May). Drug use in pregnancy: Here are the new labeling categories. *Modern Medicine,* p. 211.

Maternal serum AFP: Educating physicians and the public. (1985, December). *American Journal of Public Health,* pp. 1374–1375.

Mayberry, L., & Inturrisi-Levy, M. (1987, March/April). Use of breast stimulation for contraction stress tests, *Journal of Obstetric and Gynecologic Nursing,* pp. 121–124.

Menning B.E. (1982). *Modern trends in infertility and conception control.* Philadelphia: Harper and Row.

Moore, Dianne, et al. (1981, May/June). Nursing care of the pregnant woman with diabetes mellitus. *Journal of Obstetric and Gynecologic Nursing,* pp. 188–194.

Moore, K.L. (1982). *The developing human.* Philadelphia: W.B. Saunders.

Moore, M.L. (1983). *Realities in childbearing.* Philadelphia: W.B. Saunders.

Neonatal screening for inherited disease. (1985, July 4). *New England Journal of Medicine,* pp. 43–44.

Nieman, J.K., et al. (1987, January 22). The progesterone antagonist RU 486. *New England Journal of Medicine,* pp. 187–190.

Nurses Drug Alert. (1983, July). *American Journal of Nursing,* p. 1063.

Olds, S. London, M., & Ladewig, P. (1987). *Maternal newborn nursing* (3rd ed.). Los Angeles: Addison-Wesley.

Orne, R., & Hawkins, J.W. (1985). Reexamining the oral contraceptive issues. *Journal of Obstetric and Gynecologic Nursing, 14,* 30–36.

Rubin, P. Prescribing in pregnancy. *Obstetrical and Gynecological Survey 42* (7), 428–429.

Shannon, D.M. (1987, November/December). HELLP syndrome: A severe consequence of pregnancy induced hypertension. *Journal of Obstetric and Gynecologic Nursing,* pp. 395–402.

Smith, J. (1988, May/June). The dangers of prenatal cocaine use. *Maternal Child Nursing,* pp. 174–179.

Sullivan, J.M., & Ramanathan, K.B. (1985, August 11). Management of medical problems in pregnancy—Severe cardiac disease. *New England Journal of Medicine,* pp. 304–309.

Whitley, N. (1985). A manual of clinical obstetrics. Philadelphia: J.B. Lippincott.

Part III

The Intrapartal Period

The following terminology will be useful in the understanding of this unit:

Gravida: pregnant woman
Primigravida: first pregnancy
Primipara: a woman who has had one delivery beyond 20 weeks
Multipara: a woman who has delivered two or more children
Gravida: refers to a pregnancy of any duration
Para: refers to previous pregnancies that have reached the period of viability; for example

Gravida I Para O (GIPO)—first pregnancy

She becomes a primipara after delivery of a viable fetus whether it is alive or dead at birth.

Gravida III Para O (GIIIPO) is in her third pregnancy after two abortions—when she delivers a viable child, her status will be Gravida III Para I (GIIIPI).

Past obstetrical history may be recorded as 7-2-3-6. The first digit refers to the number of full-term infants that a woman has delivered. The second digit refers to the number of prematures. The third digit refers to the number of abortions. The fourth digit refers to the number of living children.

Chapter 10

Stages of Labor and Nursing Implications

Labor can be considered a contest between the forces of expulsion and the forces of resistance.

I. POSITION AND PRESENTATION (Figure 10-1)
A. Attitude of fetus: customary position that baby assumes in utero
   1. relationship of one part of the fetus to another
      a) arms, legs, and head usually flexed
      b) fetus ovoid: conforming to uterus shape
B. Lie
   1. relationship of long axis of fetus to the long axis of mother can be
      a) longitudinal
      b) transverse
C. Presentation
   1. presenting part is that part of fetus that engages at inlet and can be felt through the cervix
D. Position
   1. determined by some arbitrarily determined point on the fetus to right or left side and front or back of mother's pelvis
      a) position may affect the length and difficulty of the labor process
      b) the pelvis is divided into four regions to assist in describing the position of the presenting part of the fetus; the regions are
         (1) left anterior
         (2) left posterior
         (3) right anterior
         (4) right posterior
   2. longitudinal lie: long axis of fetus parallel to long axis of mother
      a) cephalic positions

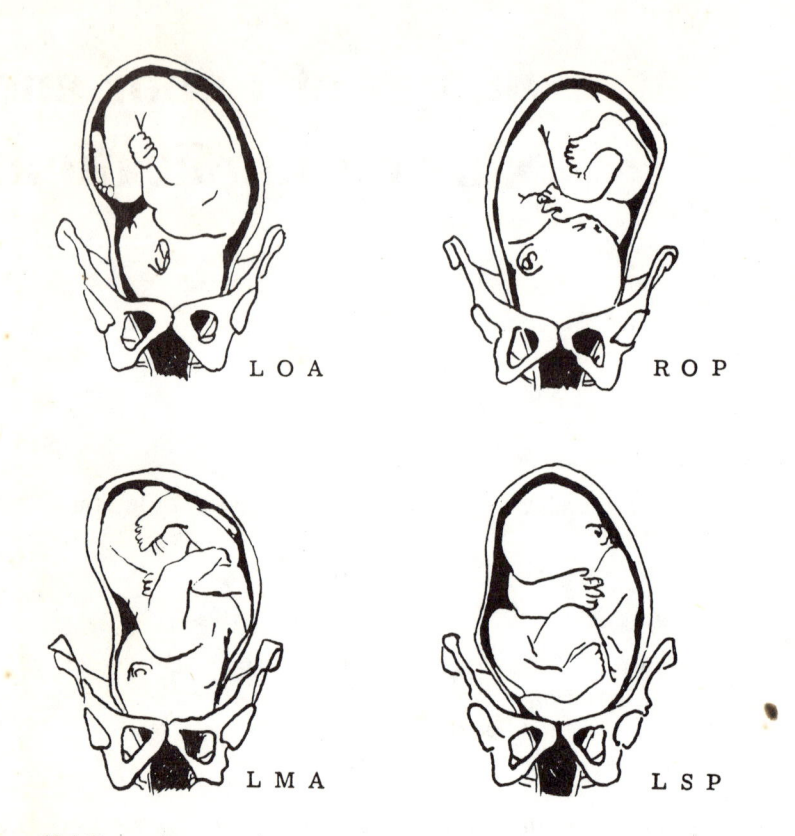

Figure 10-1 Types of presentations

---

   (1) vertex: head sharply flexed so that vertex presents
      (a) occiput is the point to determine this position, e.g., right occiput anterior (ROA) means that the occiput faces the right front of the mother's pelvis
   (2) face: neck extended, face presents, chin (mentum) is point for position, e.g., left mentum anterior (LMA) chin faces left front of mother's pelvis
   (3) brow: sinciput is point for position; neck partially extended and brow presents
      (a) rare and difficult to deliver
      (b) frequently converts spontaneously or by version to vertex or face
  b) breech positions: sacrum used as point of position
   (1) frank breech: buttocks presenting part, thighs flexed, and legs extended

Stages of Labor and Nursing Implications 181

       (2) full breech: buttocks present, thighs flexed on abdomen, and legs flexed on thighs
       (3) footling breech: one or both feet present
       (4) right sacroposterior (RSP): sacrum faces right posterior portion of mother's pelvis
   3. transverse lie: long axis of fetus horizontal to long axis of mother
     a) shoulder presentation: scapula is the point used for determining position in a transverse lie
       (1) very rare and must be delivered by Cesarean section

II. THEORETICAL CAUSES OF LABOR
A. The precise physiological mechanisms that bring about labor are unknown. The mechanisms are complex, and probably labor begins because of an interaction of factors that originate within the maternal, placental, and fetal systems
   1. hormonal factors
     a) progesterone
       (1) produced jointly by the maternal-placental-fetal unit
       (2) blocks uterine contractions during the pregnancy
       (3) although no decline in peripheral plasma progesterone levels has been demonstrated before labor begins, it is thought that a possible decrease in local progesterone at the site of the placenta may play a role in increasing the contractility of the uterus. This effect is thought to be precipitated by the production of prostaglandins by the uterine decidua and fetal membranes
     b) oxytocin
       (1) produced by posterior lobe of pituitary
       (2) uterine sensitivity to oxytocin increases as pregnancy progresses
       (3) uterine muscle sensitivity to oxytocin is enhanced by estrogen and inhibited by progesterone
       (4) oxytocin alone will not cause labor to begin, but its presence in combination with other substances plays a role in the labor process
     c) prostaglandins
       (1) the administration of prostaglandin E_2 or F_2 will initiate myometrial contractions at any stage of gestation
       (2) prostaglandins are used to induce labor or to induce abortions

(3) there is increasing myometrial sensitivity to prostaglandins as pregnancy advances
(4) prostaglandins are increased in the amniotic fluid and peripheral blood circulation of the mother just before and during labor
(5) it is thought that increasing uterine volume in late pregnancy may cause an increase in the production of prostaglandins, which in turn may stimulate the onset of labor
2. aging of placenta
   a) degeneration of trophoblasts
   b) decrease in placental function
      (1) causes decrease in uterine blood flow
      (2) reduced uterine blood flow causes increased uterine activity
3. uterine distention
   a) full organ tends to contract and empty itself when stretched
      (1) postulated to be a factor in premature labor with multiple pregnancies and polyhydramnios
   b) pressure on nerve endings and increased irritability of muscles may stimulate contractions

III. MECHANISMS OF LABOR IN VERTEX PRESENTATION

A. In order for area of least diameter of fetal head to pass through birth canal certain movements are necessary
   1. engagement: when largest transverse diameter of the head has passed through the pelvic inlet
   2. descent: gradual progressive movement throughout labor
      a) progress measured by station: relationship of vertex to ischial spines
         (1) station +4: head floating, freely movable
         (2) station −3 −2 −1: progression toward ischial spines
         (3) station 0: vertex at ischial spines—engagement
         (4) station +1 +2 +3: progression toward pelvic floor
         (5) station +4: vertex at perineum
   3. flexion: chin flexed, head tipped forward; presents smallest head diameter to birth canal allowing further descent
   4. internal rotation: head is turned to side on the diagonal so that it can pass under the symphysis pubis
      a) longest diameter of fetal head aligned with largest diameter of pelvis
   5. extension: head is pushed forward through vulva V outlet because it offers least resistance

6. restitution: immediately after head is born, occiput rotates back to original position
7. external rotation: shoulders change from transverse to anterior-posterior position
8. expulsion: delivery

B. Powers of labor include
   1. uterine contractions: the effectiveness of which are measured by their
      a) frequency
      b) intensity
   2. voluntary abdominal muscular contractions during second stage of labor
   3. fetal head, which acts as a battering ram to dilate cervix and birth canal
   4. amniotic fluid within fetal membrane, which applies hydrostatic pressure to cervix and aids in dilation

IV. ONSET OF LABOR

A. Premonitory signs
   1. lightening (engagement): settling of head into true pelvis
      a) usually occurs 10–14 days before labor in primigravida
      b) may not occur until labor begins in multipara
      c) increased pressure caused by descent of baby's head may result in
         (1) shooting pains in legs
         (2) increased vaginal discharge
         (3) frequency in urination
   2. pink show
      a) discharge of mucus plug
      b) small capillaries rupture and blood mixes with mucus
   3. rupture of membranes: amniotic sac (membranes) breaks causing a gush or leakage of amniotic fluid
      a) may occur prior to onset of labor or at any stage in labor process
         (1) physician should be notified because of danger of
            (a) prolapsed cord
            (b) infection
      b) labor usually begins within 24 hours after rupture
   4. early contractions may be experienced as low back pains
   5. abdominal cramps
   6. diarrhea

7. cervix begins to become soft and effaced and moves to an anterior position. This process is called ripening
B. Differentiation between true and false labor
   1. false labor: Braxton-Hicks contractions
      a) contractions are irregular
      b) contractions do not increase in intensity, duration, or frequency
      c) usually confined to lower segment of abdomen and groin
      d) there is no further softening or effacement of cervix
      e) no further descent of head occurs
   2. true labor
      a) contractions occur at regular intervals
      b) intervals between contractions shorten
      c) duration and intensity of contractions increase
      d) contractions usually are felt in the back and radiate to the abdomen
      e) increased cervical dilation and effacement occur
      f) further descent of presenting part occurs

V. STAGES OF LABOR
A. First stage: starts with first true contraction and lasts until full dilation (at 10 cm) and effacement of cervix occurs
   1. duration in
      a) primigravida: usually 6–18 hours
         (1) labor is considered prolonged if first stage exceeds 20 hours
      b) multipara: usually 2–10 hours
         (1) labor is considered prolonged if first stage exceeds 14 hours
   2. characteristics
      a) at onset of labor, contractions usually occur every 20 to 30 minutes and are of short duration and mild intensity
         (1) each contraction has three phases
            (a) increment: increasing intensity of the contraction
            (b) acme: height of intensity of contraction
            (c) decrement: decreasing intensity of contraction
      b) intact fetal membranes increase efficiency of contraction through the mechanism of hydrostatic pressure of the fluid against the cervix
      c) contractions increase in intensity and frequency until transition stage is reached (8 cm) at which time
         (1) contractions become stronger and closer together. Sometimes they appear to be almost continuous (1 to 2 minutes apart, lasting 45 seconds)

(2) mother may perspire profusely
(3) mother may be nauseous and vomit
(4) she may have a period of violent shaking and teeth chattering
(5) there is an increase in bloody show
(6) there may be difficulty in relaxing between contractions
d) contractions are totally involuntary
(1) dilation of cervix cannot be hastened by bearing down on the part of the mother
B. Second stage: from full dilation of cervix to birth of baby
1. duration in
a) primigravida: 30 minutes to 3 hours
b) multipara: 5–30 minutes
2. characteristics
a) bloody show increased
b) pressure on rectum causes patient to feel a desire to defecate
c) bearing-down reflex appears spontaneously
d) voluntary abdominal musculature should be utilized to assist in bearing down
e) perineal bulging is observed
f) crowning: head becomes visible on perineal floor during contraction
g) caput: head visible on perineal floor at all times
C. Third stage: after birth of baby to birth of placenta
1. duration: 5 10 minutes
2. characteristics
a) separation of placenta
(1) gush of vaginal blood
(2) umbilical cord descends
(3) fundus rises in abdomen
(4) uterus becomes firm and globular
b) expulsion of placenta
(1) bearing down by mother assists expulsion
(2) Schultze mechanism: fetal side detached and expelled first
(3) Duncan mechanism: maternal side detaches and is expelled first
D. Fourth stage: first hour after delivery
1. characteristics
a) recovery from anesthesia
b) stabilization of vital signs, bleeding, and fundal muscle tone
(1) may be most critical time of intrapartal period because of increased danger of maternal hemorrhage

c) mother may have intense emotional reactions, such as crying to relieve tension
d) mother usually exhausted and wants to sleep
e) sudden severe chill may occur that is believed to be related to sudden change of intra-abdominal pressure or a nervous reaction to the childbirth experience

VI. MANAGEMENT OF LABOR AND DELIVERY PROCESS

A. The management of the labor and delivery process has profound immediate and long-range implications for the physical and emotional well-being of the family unit. Technological advances have depersonalized the meaning of childbirth in our society and have also diminished the influence that parents can exert over the birthing process. Parents should have an opportunity to explore the implications of various childbirth management regimes and should be allowed to make educated decisions as to the manner in which their labor and delivery will be conducted
   1. areas in which decisions need to be made
      a) the place where delivery will occur
         (1) there are an increasing number of alternate birthing centers across the country. These centers are home-like, but usually are located in or near a hospital.
         (2) many more women choose to deliver at home. Caution should be advised because emergencies do arise unexpectedly
      b) who will be in attendance at the delivery
         (1) an increasing number of institutions allow not only husbands but also siblings, family members, and/or friends to be present with the woman during labor and delivery
      c) when the patient is in a traditional hospital setting, other factors need to be considered
         (1) elective induction or stimulation of labor for convenience is contraindicated
         (2) shaving of the pubic areas
            (a) many studies indicate that shaving of the pubic area does not influence the incidence of infection
            (b) many institutions have abandoned the use of the pubic prep or have substituted a mini-prep of the perineal area
         (3) the routine use of enemas during early labor is being re-evaluated

- (4) use of analgesics and anesthesia
  - (a) the mother should be informed of possible risks involved in the use of large doses of analgesia and anesthesia. Studies show possible risks to be
    1. respiratory initiation and early respiration rhythms of the newborn may be affected
    2. sucking reflex may be diminished
    3. depression of CNS of newborn may occur
    4. regional anesthesia may prevent mother from assisting in the expulsion phase, necessitating the use of forceps
    5. regional anesthesia may cause hypotension, resulting in a decrease in the oxygen supply to the fetus
- (5) position during labor
  - (a) mothers are sometimes encouraged to lie on their backs
    1. causes compression of the major blood vessels by the uterus
    2. may impede progress of labor
    3. may diminish oxygen supply to fetus
  - (b) sitting, walking or assuming a side position in bed are preferable positions during labor
- (6) isolation of the woman in labor
  - (a) increases fear and anxiety
  - (b) depersonalizes and dehumanizes the birth experience
  - (c) denies the woman the opportunity to have support from people who are important to her
  - (d) there is no scientific indication that the presence of someone other than health personnel during labor and delivery will adversely affect the process
- (7) management of delivery
  - (a) the use of lithotomy position for birth may
    1. affect blood pressure, cardiac return, and pulmonary ventilation
    2. impede bearing-down efforts
    3. impede placental expulsion
    4. necessitate use of episiotomy
  - (b) positions that are preferable include
    1. squatting
    2. semisitting position with soles of feet firmly placed on bed
- (8) immediate separation of mother and child after delivery

may interfere with mother-child bonding and the successful establishment of lactation
(9) the belief that all deliveries should take place in a hospital with a physician in attendance is open to question
   (a) nurse-midwives have been shown to manage a normal labor and delivery effectively
   (b) alternative facilities for normal deliveries are being developed by groups, such as the Maternity Center of New York
(10) alternatives to the traditional labor and delivery room
   (a) birthing rooms provide a warm, comfortable environment where the woman who will not be receiving an inhalant anesthesia may labor and deliver her baby in the same room. Birthing rooms are located in hospitals and in alternative free-standing birth centers that have hospital backup. Although protocols vary in each institution most birthing rooms provide the following options
     1. woman may wear own gown and robe
     2. support person may remain through the entire process
     3. routine use of enemas is discouraged
     4. perineal shaving is not performed
     5. fluid intake is encouraged; IV fluids are not given unless needed
     6. ambulation is encouraged until fetal membranes rupture. In some places ambulation may be permitted if fetal head is engaged. If woman desires to be in bed, position is changed frequently
     7. a labor/birthing bed is used with or without stirrups
     8. fetal monitoring is not used unless fetus is at risk
     9. urination is encouraged frequently
     10. if episiotomy is not desired the integrity of the perineum may be maintained by stretching the vaginal outlet, perineal massage with oil, or hot soaks to perineum
     11. a gentle birth will be provided. If the woman has requested a LeBoyer birth and the institution allows it, this will be permitted. Birth in a darkened room with a temperature of 72°F, minimal noise

in the room, cord cut after pulsation stops, baby placed on mother's abdomen where she cuddles and wraps in warm blanket, support person places baby in a warm bath; baby is dried, rewrapped, and placed in mother's arms to nurse
12. use of Pitocin is not routine; baby is offered to mother to nurse after the birth if she so desires
13. if baby and mother are to be discharged that day, they may both remain in the room until the time of discharge
14. delivery may be by nurse-midwife or physician
15. birthing rooms are available only for low-risk women who will be having a normal vaginal birth. If the following symptoms develop, the woman will usually be transferred to a traditional labor room:
    a. temperature: 100.4°F
    b. hemoglobin: 9.5 gm/100 ml
    c. significant rise or fall of maternal blood pressure
    d. significant vaginal bleeding
    e. problems in the progress of the labor or fetal problems

(11) use of electronic fetal monitoring
   (a) electronic fetal monitoring records the fetal heart rate (FHR), either externally by an ultrasound device that picks up the heartbeat through the mother's abdomen or internally by the use of a fluid-filled catheter inserted into the uterus. This catheter senses contractions, and electrodes attached to the fetal scalp record the FHR. Fetal scalp blood is also sampled either intermittently for pH or continuously by continuous monitoring of scalp tissue pH, a noninvasive procedure
   (b) there is much controversy about the use of this procedure for low-risk pregnancies as studies show that the results of fetal electronic monitoring for all women leads to a rise in cesarean births, many of which are thought to be unnecessary. Risks of fetal monitoring include injury and infection of the baby's scalp, fetal hemorrhage, and damage to the mother
   (c) abnormal FHR patterns detected on fetal monitoring do not always mean that the fetus is in distress. Often

a decision to do a cesarean section is based on an abnormal FHR pattern without further lab checks, such as fetal scalp blood pH, to determine if there is fetal acidosis
- (d) there is currently an increasing opinion among physicians that fetal monitoring should be used only for high-risk labors, such as oxytocin stimulation of labor, dysfunctional labor, abnormal FHR, or meconium-stained amniotic fluid

(12) informed consent
- (a) women in labor may be asked to participate in perinatal research. A woman in labor is considered to be a special or captive subject because of the vulnerability of her situation and the possibility that she may perceive a negative threat if she refuses to participate. The need for personal support during labor may influence the woman's decision to participate in the study
- (b) in informing pregnant women in labor about a research project for which their informed consent is needed it is important to be sensitive to the special needs of the woman and to avoid undue influence. The usual guidelines for informing subjects about informed consent should be followed with special care and sensitivity

B. Nursing care during the first stage of labor
1. admission of patient
    a) assessment
      (1) identification
      (2) vital signs (TPR, BP, FH) are monitored with increasing frequency as labor progresses
      (3) history and physical examination
          (a) history includes information essential for the management of labor and delivery
            1. obstetrical status determined, i.e., primigravida or multipara and EDC
            2. history of symptoms of patient in this labor, i.e., presence of show, rupture of membranes, and character and duration of contractions
            3. any allergies that are present
            4. presence of any current or recent illness in herself or family
            5. time of ingestion of last meal

Stages of Labor and Nursing Implications

6. plans for breast or bottle feeding
7. when she last slept and whether she is fatigued
8. whether or not patient feels any discomfort
9. any special physical problems or disabilities
10. any blood incompatibilities
11. serological test reports
    - (b) physical examination includes general and obstetrical status
        1. obstetrical examination will determine stage and progress of labor
- (4) mother's knowledge and attitudes toward labor and delivery
    - (a) desires regarding management of labor and delivery
    - (b) preparation for childbirth
    - (c) fears and concerns
- (5) family relationships
    - (a) marital status
    - (b) desires regarding presence of family member or friend during labor and delivery
    - (c) arrangements or concerns about children at home
- b) intervention is based on the rationale that fear and anxiety increase muscular tension and lead to an increase in the perception of pain
    - (1) orient to hospital
        - (a) explanation of routines
        - (b) introduction of staff
    - (2) provide information regarding
        - (a) status of labor
        - (b) what to expect as labor progresses
        - (c) mechanisms to reduce pain
    - (3) give medications as ordered and desired
    - (4) establish a patient record
    - (5) provide for draping and screening to ensure client privacy
    - (6) report immediately any deviations from the normal in observation of the client's general or obstetrical status
2. remainder of first stage of labor: assessment of safety, physical status, and psychosocial status will determine nursing intervention
    - a) level of consciousness
        - (1) assessment
            - (a) orientation to time and place
            - (b) level of wakefulness
            - (c) arousability

(d) reaction to pain
(e) level of concentration
(f) time and dose of analgesia administration
(2) intervention
(a) protect from injury
(b) use side rails if necessary
(c) assist in and out of bed to prevent falls
b) environmental hazards
(1) assessment
(a) aseptic techniques
(b) condition of electrical equipment
(c) temperature and air circulation of labor room
(2) intervention
(a) asepsis: measures must be taken to prevent the introduction of pathogens into the vaginal canal, i.e., precautions used during vaginal examination include use of sterile gloves and antiseptic preparation to cleanse perineal area
c) physical status of mother and fetus
(1) fetal heart
(a) assessment
1. throughout labor the monitoring of the FHR is vital because it is an indicator of any changes in fetal condition
2. normal rate: between 120–160 BPM with regular rhythm
a. rate slows at height of contraction of uterus
b. rate increases at the end of uterine contractions
3. rate of fetal heart below 100 or above 160 with uterus at rest may indicate fetal distress
4. auscultation of fetal heart
a. must differentiate between fetal heart and other sounds
(1.) funic souffle: blood rushing through umbilical arteries is synchronous with fetal heart
(2.) uterine souffle: blood going through large uterine blood vessels is synchronous with mother's pulse
b. impediments to auscultation of fetal heart
(1.) maternal obesity
(2.) pendulous abdomen
(3.) polyhydramnios

Stages of Labor and Nursing Implications 193

        (4.) posterior occiput presentation
        (5.) taking of FHR at height of contraction
        (6.) loud maternal souffle
     c. locations of fetal heart
        (1.) cephalic presentations
           (a.) loudest below umbilicus
           (b.) anterior positions: FH will be heard clearly in either right or left quadrant
     d. posterior presentations: best heard at point of mother's side closest to fetal back
        (1.) breech presentation
           (a.) loudest above umbilicus
        (2.) with descent and rotation of fetus, fetal heart position changes
     e. methods for determining FHR
        (1.) fetal stethoscope: nurse may have difficulty in hearing and counting; lack of a continuous pattern available for determining baseline norm; can usually detect deviations from the norm if the nurse is skilled
        (2.) ultrasonic monitoring device (Doptone/ Doppler): a battery-operated unit that provides continuous auscultation over a limited period of time. There is no printed record, and there is difficulty in hearing during strong contractions. If FHR is very fast every beat may not be detected. If FHR is very slow the movement of both fetal heart valves may be picked up and the rate may be doubled
        (3.) electronic monitoring: the most accurate method but is the subject of much controversy regarding its use
        (4.) FHR in low-risk pregnancy should be checked every
           (a.) 9-30 min in first stage of labor
           (b.) 9-15 min in second stage of labor
           (c.) 9-10 min when prepared for delivery
 (b) intervention
    1. any change in FHR or rhythm that may indicate fetal distress should be reported immediately

a. patient should be turned on side
b. oxygen may be administered
(2) contractions
  (a) assessment
    1. frequency, intensity, and duration must be determined
    2. can be measured manually by placing both hands over the uterus where the tightening and relaxing of the uterus during the contraction can be felt
    3. most accurate measurements of uterine contractions are made by electronic monitoring, which is not considered necessary for normal births of low-risk mothers
    4. interval is considered to be from the increment of one contraction to the increment of the next
    5. normal frequency during active labor: every 2.5–5 minutes
    6. contractions occurring less than every 2 minutes: tachysystole
    7. sustained contractions that are continuous and lasting longer than 90 seconds: tetonic contractions; may be due to oxytocin administration
    8. resting tone of uterus is pressure between contractions and can only be measured by electronic monitoring. Hypertonus, which is a resting pressure above 30, may cause fetal anoxia
    9. hyperactive labor: contractions with pressure above 50 may cause fetal anoxia
    10. hypoactive labor: contractions with pressure less than 30 may cause prolonged labor
  (b) intervention
    1. contractions less than 2 minutes apart or more than 90 seconds in length should be reported. Hypoactive labor should be reported
    2. the nurse should assist the woman to participate in her own care through decision making and goal setting and helping her conserve energy
    3. the nurse can assist the client in coping with discomfort by
      a. his or her presence: laying on of hands
      b. informing her of the progress of labor and the meaning of the contractions

c. teaching breathing and relaxation techniques
d. giving medication as indicated and prescribed
e. providing reassurance to reduce fear and anxiety
f. applying cool cloth to forehead
g. allowing verbalization of feelings regarding pain, discomfort, and fear
h. supporting attempts to follow prepared childbirth technique
i. providing encouragement

(3) electronic monitoring of fetal heart and contractions
  (a) used for continuous monitoring of the frequency, intensity, and duration of contractions and for continuous monitoring and recording of FHR patterns so that the FHR can be evaluated under the stress of a uterine contraction, as well as during relaxation period
  (b) the significant factor in monitoring is the relationship between the FHR and the uterine contractions. Monitoring assists in detecting fetal distress that may be caused by maternal hypo- or hypertension, anemia, bleeding, fetal cord compression, head compression, placental separation, and other complications
  (c) external monitoring: one or more sensing devices attached to woman's abdomen by straps during labor Tocotransducer records contractions
    1. information recorded on graph paper; a continuous wave pattern is formed and represents the frequency, intensity, and duration of the contraction
    2. the FHR pattern is also recorded by an ultrasound transducer; when plotted against the labor pattern, significant changes in fetal heart rate can be more accurately determined
    3. if the patient attempts to breathe abdominally for relief she may have difficulty using the proper technique due to presence of equipment
    4. not used as often as internal monitoring because it is less accurate and more restrictive
    5. straps should fit correctly; if they are too loose, sensors will not pick up sounds
    6. if patient moves around, the sensors may become dislodged, or the readings may reflect the change in position

7. if the fetus changes position, the sensors may need to be repositioned
8. it is recommended that the woman remain in the supine position. This may cause
    a. maternal hypotension: careful monitoring of maternal blood pressure is necessary
    b. back discomfort
    c. pressure on abdominal blood vessels
9. the nurse can assist the patient and her family by
    a. careful explanation of the equipment and the rationale for its use
    b. giving back rubs for discomfort
    c. changing position frequently
    d. removing straps every 2 hours to powder abdomen

(d) internal monitoring: sensing devices are introduced directly into the uterus through the cervix
  1. contraction sensor: a fluid-filled catheter that transmits changes in pressure to the monitor. It is placed in the amniotic fluid. Correct placement is important; the strain gauge must be at height of catheter tip
  2. fetal sensor: a spiral scalp electrode that is placed on fetal scalp or on the presenting part. In vertex presentations it is placed on scalp with care taken to avoid the fontanels and the face. In a breech presentation care must be taken to avoid the external genitals
  3. sterile technique must be used for insertion
  4. in order to use internal monitoring, cervix must be dilated, membranes ruptured, and presenting part must be accessible
  5. women are more comfortable than with external monitoring but they may be restricted in ambulation
  6. provides more accurate information but its use in normal, low-risk labor is not recommended by current research. It presents risks to mother and baby and is believed to be responsible for an increasing and unnecessary cesarean section rate
  7. risks include fetal scalp abscess and lacerations,

bleeding and maternal infection, uterine perforation, and perforation of placenta
8. candidates for monitoring: women at risk including labor induction, women with pre-eclampsia, diabetes, heart disease, Rh sensitization, vaginal bleeding, polyhydramnios, premature labor, meconium-stained fluid in a vertex presentation, abnormal FHR, and other complications
(e) implications for nursing process
1. careful and complete explanation of procedure to mother and to any members of the family present
2. all questions should be answered
3. readjustment of sensors whenever they become displaced
4. observation of recordings at appropriate intervals
5. give reassurance about progress of labor, as well as emotional support
6. safety precautions to prevent accident from use of electric equipment should be practiced
   a. check cords and plugs for fraying
   b. if a tingling sensation is felt by woman during use of monitor, discontinue at once
7. provide for comfort with changes of position and use of extra pillows
(f) interpretation of fetal monitoring data
1. measures the FHR and the strength of the uterine contraction (IUP)
2. baseline data
   a. measures FHR and uterine tone in the absence of contractions; measures short- and long-term variability of FHR
   b. FHR evaluated for 10 minutes
   c. deviations in baseline data
      (1.) normal FHR: 120–160 BPM
      (2.) bradycardia: below 120 BPM. A FHR below 100 may indicate a congenital heart defect, fetal hypoxia, or a reaction to drugs, especially local anesthesia. It may also be normal if variability is normal and decelerations are absent
      (3.) tachycardia: over 160 BPM. May indicate

reduced fetal oxygen, fetal arrythmia, maternal fever, or a reaction to drugs. It may also be caused by maternal anxiety or fetal infection. If decelerations are absent, may not be dangerous
    (a.) moderate tachycardia: 160–180 BPM
    (b.) marked tachycardia: 180 BPM and over
3. periodic data
   a. measures changes in the FHR in relationship to uterine contraction
   b. any change from baseline data is termed a fluctuation
   c. a significant fluctuation is more than 15 BPM
   d. an increase in FHR during a contraction: acceleration
   e. a decrease in FHR during a contraction: deceleration
      (1.) early deceleration: a response to compression of the fetal head; it does not indicate pathology. It has an early onset in relationship to the contraction
      (2.) late deceleration: begins after the contraction is established. When persistent or it reoccurs it usually indicates fetal anoxia when there is a decrease in baseline variability
         (a.) observation for the occurrence of bradycardia must take place
      (3.) variable deceleration: may occur at any time during the contraction without any uniform pattern
         (a.) may be related to partial brief cord compression
         (b.) associated with neonatal depression when severe or prolonged
(g) significance of data
   1. persistent bradycardia is an ominous sign, especially if it follows a contraction
     a. may indicate cord compression or separation of placenta
     b. if turning the patient on her other side and administration of O_2 do not improve FHR pat-

tern, emergency delivery, usually Cesarean section, is indicated if other diagnostic factors agree
2. tachycardia when persistent or accompanied by late deceleration is an indication of fetal distress if confirmed by other measures
3. loss of beat-to-beat variation (not induced by drugs, such as diazepam or atropine) is a serious development and often is the prelude to fetal death
4. normal FHR patterns have a positive correlation to high Apgar score and low neonatal morbidity. An abnormal pattern, although related to a low Apgar score and a high neonatal morbidity, does not occur in all cases. More data and research need to be done in order to assess more accurately the findings of fetal monitoring
5. variability: baseline
   a. long-term variability: the wave-like fluctuation of the fetal heart rate over several seconds or minutes. Normal long-term variability is 6–25 BPM
   b. short-term variability: measures beat-to-beat variability and is the measure that is usually referred to as "variability." Normal range is 6–25 BPM
   c. variability: the normal response of the fetus to changes in fetal activity and responses to drugs. A nonvariable FHR may indicate potential problems, a response to drugs, or prematurity. If decelerations are present they may indicate a serious problem
6. electronic monitoring is subject to errors of interpretation and is influenced by the correct placement of the catheter. In addition to data from electronic monitoring it is essential that doctors consider such factors as fetal scalp pH, maternal vital signs, drugs and treatment given to mother, maternal position, and station of the presenting part before making a decision that the fetus is at severe risk
   a. factors that may cause changes in FHR
      (1.) compression of vertex
      (2.) uteroplacental insufficiency
      (3.) compression or occlusion of umbilical cord

                (4.) maternal hypotension or hypoxia
                (5.) contractions of unusual frequency, duration, or strength
                (6.) improper administration of oxytocics
                (7.) maternal position
            b. if abnormal tracings occur, the immediate nursing intervention is to
                (1.) change patient's position from supine to side or from one side to another or ELB/ATE
                (2.) administer O_2 by mask (6–7 L/min)
                (3.) stop oxytocin administration
                (4.) notify physician
                (5.) prepare for cesarean section if pattern persists
    (4) fetal blood sampling
        (a) a blood sample is obtained by the physician from the fetal scalp after the membranes rupture
            1. scalp is swabbed with a disinfectant before puncture
        (b) fetal acidosis follows fetal hypoxia
            1. authorities believe that fetal distress can only be confirmed when FHR changes are correlated to fetal blood acidosis
        (c) most infants with blood samples that read pH 7.15 or less have low Apgar scores
        (d) consecutive readings of pH below 7.20 that show a continuing decrease indicate the need to assess for prompt delivery
        (e) fetal acidosis may be caused by maternal respiratory alkalosis and subsequent decrease in cardiac output, which is the result of hyperventilation. Hyperventilation is usually self-limiting in the conscious adult and can be controlled by having the patient breathe into a paper bag. This probably does not have adverse effects on the fetus
        (f) a new method of continuous assessment of fetal pH by a pH scalp electrode and monitor that assess tissue pH is under investigation. Although technical problems still remain to be worked out, the method has shown that a continuous monitoring of fetal scalp pH can provide effective information about fetal acidosis without the trauma of obtaining fetal scalp blood. This method may help in decreasing cesarean section rates

as the stable fetal scalp pH can assist in diagnosing fetal risk when FHR rates show deviations from normal patterns
(5) vital signs
  (a) assessment
    1. if TPR and BP are normal they should be monitored at systematic intervals
    2. if deviations occur, more frequent monitoring should be carried out
    3. baseline pulse, temperature, and BP should be established
    4. BP and pulse may rise slightly during active labor
    5. deviations in pulse and BP should be evaluated in relation to baseline values for each client
  (b) intervention
    1. a rise in TPR may indicate dehydration or infection and should be reported immediately
    2. a sustained rise or fall of 15 mm Hg or more in systolic or diastolic should be reported
      a. a rise in BP may indicate toxemia
      b. a fall in BP may indicate hemorrhage, shock, or reaction to drugs
        (1.) an increase in pulse rate may be the first sign of hemorrhage
(6) vaginal discharge
  (a) assessment
    1. type, amount, and character of bleeding
    2. time of occurrence, amount, and character of amniotic fluid discharge
  (b) intervention
    1. differentiate between bloody show and hemorrhage
    2. if hemorrhage is suspected, save all linen to evaluate blood loss and monitor vital signs
    3. bloody show increases in amount as labor progresses
    4. suspected hemorrhage should be reported immediately
    5. if head is not engaged when membranes rupture careful supervision and bedrest are indicated because of danger of prolapse of the cord

6. after rupture of membranes fetal heart should be checked and fluid inspected for signs of meconium
7. meconium-stained fluid in vertex presentation should be reported immediately as it presents a hazard to the fetus
8. perineal care should be given frequently as indicated
9. perineal pads should not be used; padding should be placed on bed
10. aseptic technique should be utilized during all examinations

(7) contour and size of abdomen
   (a) assessment
     1. abnormal bulges or ridges
     2. bladder distention
   (b) intervention
     1. shape of uterus indicates fetal position and changes during the process of labor
     2. abnormal bulge or ridge may indicate Bandl's ring
     3. a full bladder may impede labor
       a. encourage voiding
       b. catheterization may be necessary

(8) comfort
   (a) assessment
     1. objective and subjective signs of client discomfort
   (b) intervention
     1. change position frequently, assisting mother to find those positions that are most comfortable
     2. if possible, ambulate until membranes rupture
     3. attend to personal hygiene
       a. frequent mouth care if fluids are restricted
       b. perineal hygiene as necessary, including fresh linen on bed
     4. relieve pain
       a. provide support, reassurance, and assistance with breathing and relaxation measures
       b. information to counteract myths and fears of labor
       c. keep informed of progress of labor
       d. relieve back pain by massage, pressure, cold applications to sacral area, and a change in position

                e. offer medication when desired, indicated, and ordered
        (9) nutrition
            (a) assessment
                1. dehydration
                2. edema
                3. nausea or vomiting
                4. time of last meal
            (b) intervention
                1. fluids and solids as ordered by physician
                2. peristaltic action slows at onset of labor, interfering with digestive process
                3. careful monitoring of IV fluids if administered
        (10) psychosocial status
            (a) assessment
                1. feelings and fears about labor
                2. knowledge and preparation for labor
                3. desire for a member of the family or close friend to be present during the labor process
                4. cultural attitude toward pain
                5. expectations of labor management, including use of medications or natural childbirth
            (b) intervention
                1. encouragement of verbalization of fears and expectations about labor
                2. reassurance and explanation of labor process when indicated
                3. never leaving the patient alone for other than short periods of time
                4. nonjudgmental reactions to patient's behavior during labor
                5. allowing the patient to have the person of her choice remain with her throughout labor
                6. assisting the lay person who remains with patient to provide comfort and support for patient
                7. establishing a sincere and caring relationship with the patient so that trust is established
                8. touching the patient often provides a nonverbal means of comfort and reassurance
                9. use of breathing and relaxation techniques that reduce pain and tension should be introduced to patient whenever indicated

10. reassurance and encouragement that labor is progressing normally are helpful when patient becomes discouraged at length of time involved in labor process
11. respecting patient's desire for privacy and avoiding unnecessary exposure
12. keeping the patient's family informed of her progress
13. during transition period the client's psychosocial needs become intensified
    a. contractions become stronger, longer, and more frequent
    b. bearing-down sensations appear
    c. client may become irritable and frightened
    d. trembling of legs may occur
    e. nausea and vomiting may occur
14. the nurse may assist the client during the transition period by
    a. reassuring her that she is entering the final stage of labor and that transition is not a long period of time
    b. helping her refrain from bearing down until full dilation occurs
        (1.) use panting-type breathing
    c. explaining the meaning of all her symptoms

C. Nursing care during the second stage of labor
1. assessment
    a) progress of labor
        (1) perineal bulging, crowning, and caput
        (2) bearing-down effort of mother
    b) continued monitoring of all vital signs, including contractions and fetal heart
    c) mother's response to the change in status of labor
2. intervention
    a) avoid precipitate delivery: patient should be brought to delivery room at proper time
    b) use surgical asepsis in delivery room to prevent infection
    c) avoid injury by proper transportation to and positioning in delivery room
        (1) traditional delivery position is lithotomy; trend to other positions is occurring; lithotomy is not the position of choice
            (a) lithotomy position if used for a prolonged period may

cause increased stasis of blood in leg veins and predispose to thrombophlebitis
- (b) if lithotomy is used, care should be taken that pressure is not exerted on the popliteal vein. Padding should be used to prevent pressure
- (2) preferred positions are squatting and sitting
- d) if leg muscle cramps occur straighten the leg and have the ankle dorsiflexed, keeping knee rigid
- e) assist mother in effective use of bearing-down impulse
  - (1) pushing efforts should be concentrated in abdomen; pushing out should be in the vaginal area, not the rectum
  - (2) pushing should occur when the cervix is fully dilated
  - (3) spontaneous pushing is usually shorter than controlled pushing, which is usually done with the controlled exhalation of a breath and a bearing-down effort
  - (4) vulva is usually cleansed with an antiseptic solution and the area is draped
- f) prevent perineal lacerations
  - (1) the most popular technique has been an episiotomy: the cutting and repairing of the perineum by the birth attendant
    - (a) this technique is increasingly being questioned by women who are asking their birth attendants not to use it
    - (b) studies do not show that an episiotomy prevents lacerations or preserves the integrity of the pelvic floor
  - (2) lacerations include
    - (a) first-degree tears of vaginal mucosa, fourchette, and/or skin of the perineum
    - (b) second-degree tears of vaginal mucosa, fourchette, and/or skin of the perineum, and muscles of the perineal body not including the anal sphincter
    - (c) third-degree tears of the superficial tissues, the muscles of the perineal body, and anal sphincter but not the rectal mucosa
    - (d) fourth-degree complete tears involving tears of the rectal mucosa
  - (3) third- and fourth-degree lacerations are related to
    - (a) low parity
    - (b) young age
    - (c) forceps deliveries with episiotomies
    - (d) weight gain over 30 lbs
    - (e) anemia

                (f) lengthy second stage of labor
                (g) epidural and pudendal anesthesia
            (4) first- and second-degree lacerations are associated with
                (a) greater age
                (b) multiparity
                (c) prepregnant obesity
                (d) low weight gain
                (e) short second stage of labor
                (f) no anesthesia, forceps, or episiotomy
                (g) large infant (Fischer, 1979)
            (5) measures to prevent lacerations include prenatal stretching, pelvic floor exercises, perineal massage, slow delivery of head, warm compresses, and delivery position (use of birthing chair prevents tension on perineum)
        g) provide continued encouragement and support to the woman and any support person in the delivery room during the delivery. Pressures of delivery should not interfere with relations and communications previously established

D. Nursing care during the third stage of labor
    1. separation of the placenta usually occurs 1 to 5 minutes after birth of the baby
        a) signs of separation include protrusion of umbilical cord from the vagina; change in uterus to become more globular and firmer in consistency, and position becomes higher in abdomen; and a sudden gush of blood
        b) mother is urged to push to expel the placenta
        c) if mother is unable to push because of anesthesia, downward pressure may be placed on the fundus. Be sure the uterus is firm before exerting pressure or it may become inverted
        d) after placenta is expelled the fundus is massaged to aid in contraction and prevent excessive blood loss
        e) placenta must be examined to be sure that it is intact as remaining fragments may cause hemorrhage. If placenta is not expelled it must be removed manually.
        f) baby may be put to the breast to stimulate uterine contractions
        g) administration of oxytocic as ordered by physician
            (1) Syntocinon, Pitocin, and ergotamine are commonly used; may be administered IV or IM
                (a) may be ordered first after delivery of baby and again after delivery of placenta

E. Immediate care of the newborn
   1. establish and maintain patent airway
      a) remove mucus from nose and mouth by wiping and gentle suctioning with bulb syringe
      b) if respiration fails to begin
         (1) stimulate crying by gentle stroking
         (2) administer oxygen
         (3) resuscitate infant
            (a) mouth to mouth
            (b) positive pressure
      c) position baby on side to prevent aspiration
   2. keep baby warm and safe
      a) baby is wrapped
      b) may be placed in a warmer or incubator
   3. identification
      a) baby's footprints and mother's fingerprints are taken in delivery room and kept on baby's chart
   4. care of cord
      a) after clamping, inspect for bleeding and abnormalities
         (1) three vessels should be present
      b) no dressing needed on cord stump
   5. care of eyes
      a) prophylactic treatment for ophthalmia neonatorum required by law
      b) silver nitrate 1% instilled. Latest research indicates that irrigation with normal saline or sterile water does not diminish conjunctivitis reaction to the silver nitrate. Sodium chloride may precipitate the silver nitrate (silver chloride precipitate). American Academy of Pediatrics does not recommend rinsing (Lum et al., 1980)
      c) tetracycline ointment is an effective treatment without toxicity
   6. observation
      a) do Apgar scoring at 1 and 5 minutes after birth
         (1) heart rate, respiratory effort, muscle tone, reflex irritability, and color rated from 0–2
         (2) 10 is considered a perfect score
         (3) any baby with an Apgar below 7 after 5 minutes must be observed for abnormalities
      b) observe and inspect newborn for any abnormalities
   7. administration of vitamin K
      a) to prevent hypothrombinemia as normal flora in intestine needed

for synthesis of vitamin K are not present in newborn for approximately 1 week
   8. baptism
      a) if there is any danger of death of the newborn many Christian parents wish to have baby baptized
         (1) notify clergy
         (2) if unavailable, nurse or doctor should baptize child
F. Nursing care during fourth stage of labor
   1. assessment
      a) observe type, amount, and character of bleeding
      b) palpate for the height and firmness of fundus
      c) monitor vital signs frequently
      d) observe perineal area for hematomas or edema
      e) note reaction to and recovery from anesthesia
      f) observe for nausea and vomiting
      g) with conscious patients ascertain subjective symptoms of
         (1) pain
         (2) dizziness
         (3) headache
      h) observe mother-child-father interaction
      i) measure urinary output and bladder distention
   2. intervention
      a) palpate uterus frequently; should remain firm and at umbilicus
         (1) if fundus relaxes or becomes boggy, gently massage until firm; express any clots
         (2) if massage fails to maintain fundal tone, notify physician immediately
      b) maintain airway position and patency until recovery from anesthesia
      c) protect from injury
         (1) check body alignment of anesthesized patients
         (2) put side rails in place
      d) if bladder becomes distended
         (1) assist in voiding
         (2) catheterize if necessary
      e) give analgesia if ordered or necessary
      f) give mouth and personal hygiene
      g) offer emotional support
         (1) allow her to sleep by reducing disturbances
         (2) allow full expression of feelings with empathy shown by nurse

(3) allow mother to see and touch baby as soon as she is ready, to facilitate bonding
    (a) report deviations from normal mother-child interaction to the postpartal nursing staff for follow-up care

REFERENCES

Fischer, S. (1979). Factors associated with the occurrence of perinatal lacerations. *Journal of Nurse-Midwifery, 24* (1), 18–22.

Lum, B., Batzel, R., & Barnett, E. (1980, September). Reappraising newborn eye care. *American Journal of Nursing,* pp. 1602–1603.

Chapter 11

Drug and Anesthesia Administration in the Intrapartal Period

I. RELIEF OF DISCOMFORT DURING FIRST STAGE OF LABOR
A. Pain arises from the contractions of the uterus. Contractions are necessary for labor to progress and for delivery of the infant
   1. pharmacological relief of pain should not interfere with the pattern of uterine activity
   2. prenatal preparation may reduce the need for medication during labor
B. Pharmacological agents to relieve pain should be selected on an individual basis according to the needs of the woman and to ensure the welfare of the fetus
   1. need for drugs varies with each individual
      a) emotional status
      b) pain threshold
      c) prior experience
      d) cultural expectations
      e) physical status
C. Pharmacological agents have effects on both the mother and fetus. The drug used should
   1. not affect the efficiency of uterine contractions
   2. allow for the woman's participation in her labor

II. MEDIATING FACTORS AFFECTING DRUG USE DURING LABOR
A. Placental transfer is influenced by
   1. drug properties
      a) fat-soluble drugs cross placenta easily

        b) molecular weight
           (1) under 600: cross placenta easily
           (2) over 1000: placental transfer is relatively little
        c) drugs bound to proteins cross poorly
    2. uteroplacental blood flow
    3. relative pH of maternal/fetal blood
    4. surface area of the placenta
    5. thickness of placental membranes
  B. Maternal health
    1. hypo- or hypertension
    2. cardiac or respiratory depression
  C. Fetal health
    1. antidepressants may produce newborn depression in a compromised fetus
    2. preterm fetus more easily depressed than full-term fetus

III. DRUGS USED IN THE INTRAPARTAL PERIOD

  A. Sedatives
    1. barbiturates are classified as hypnotics and are used to produce sleep and mild tranquilization and sedation
        a) most commonly used barbiturates
           (1) Nembutal
           (2) Seconal
           (3) phenobarbital
        b) useful early in labor, especially in tense and anxious women
        c) method of administration is usually PO but may be given IM or IV
        d) relatively safe for both mother and child in early labor; may cause slowing of contractions in mother if dosage is excessive for the individual. Potentiates action of narcotics and tranquilizers. If given late in labor or in combination with narcotics, may depress newborn's respirations
           (1) the infant may be depressed and drowsy for up to 48 hours
               (a) effect on maternal-infant interaction needs to be considered
           (2) may cause CNS depression and apnea
        e) implications for nursing process
           (1) careful and continuous observation of patient is necessary as excessive doses may cause respiratory and/or circulatory depression in the mother and child
           (2) side rails must be utilized in patients receiving barbiturates

(3) effect of medication should be explained to mother and those with her
(4) once medication is given, room should be kept darkened and as quiet as possible
(5) maternal side effects can include vertigo, decreased perception of sensory stimuli, nausea and vomiting, and hypotension
   (a) may cause restlessness when used alone
(6) may slow labor
(7) must be used with caution when cardiac, hepatic, or respiratory conditions are present
(8) heavily sedated patients are unable to communicate the progress of labor to the nurse, increasing the possibility of precipitate delivery

B. Analgesics are used for relief of pain usually in combination with drugs that potentiate their effect
1. commonly used narcotics
   a) meperidine (Demerol): frequently used narcotic
      (1) pain relief usually within 10 minutes after IM administration
      (2) small IV doses preferred by some physicians because of more rapid effect
      (3) prolonged effects can include decreased attentiveness and social responsiveness and increased lability of emotional state
         (a) effects may last up to 6 weeks
   b) synthetic narcotic agonist-antagonist analgesics
      (1) butorphanol (Stadol) (Blum, in press)
         (a) crosses placenta; can cause respiratory depression
      (2) nalbuphine (Nubain) (PDR, 1985)
         (a) crosses placenta and can cause respiratory depression
         (b) use cautiously if premature delivery is expected
      (3) both drugs must be utilized with caution in drug-addicted women because they are narcotic antagonists and can induce acute withdrawal symptoms in mother and fetus if mother is addicted to heroin
   c) implications for nursing process
      (1) careful and continuous monitoring of maternal respirations and FHR
      (2) safety precautions include side rails and observation for possible nausea and vomiting that may be a side effect of drug
2. inhalation analgesia
   a) usually self-administered from mask strapped to wrist
      (1) concentration determined by physician

(2) mother inhales during contractions
b) if properly used there is good pain relief without loss of consciousness
c) implications for nursing process
(1) monitor vital signs closely
(a) check for cardiac arrythmias
(2) check
(a) FHR
(b) state of consciousness
(3) stay with patient; overdose possible if administered by anyone other than patient
(4) notify physician if
(a) FHR is abnormal
(b) mother loses consciousness
(c) cardiac arrythmias occur
C. Narcotic antagonists
1. naloxone (Narcan), levallorphan (Lorfan), and nalorphine (Nalline)
a) can reverse the effect of narcotic depression on mother and/or infant
b) does not reverse action of any other drug
c) Narcan: reverses pain relief instantly
d) Lorfan: not to be used in absence of narcotic
e) implications for nursing process
(1) inform other personnel of use of drug so that mother and infant can be observed
D. Tranquilizers
1. used to relieve apprehension and restlessness
2. may be used to augment action of analgesic or barbiturate
a) dosage of narcotic or barbiturate must be decreased
3. diazepam (Valium) and hydroxyzine hydrochloride (Vistaril) commonly used
4. used early in labor
5. cross the placenta
6. should not be used in preterm labor
7. may cause maternal hypotension
8. may delay onset of neonatal respiration
9. implications for nursing process
a) same precautions to be used as in narcotic or barbiturate use
E. Amnesiacs
1. hyoscine (Scopolamine) formerly used; rarely used today
a) may cause excessive dryness of respiratory passages, extreme restlessness and agitation, and flushing of skin

b) safety precautions, such as side rails and careful observation, must be carried out
c) acts as a CNS depressant
d) high concentrations may impede oxygenation
e) used primarily in operative obstetrics

IV. ANESTHESIA USED DURING THE SECOND AND THIRD STAGES OF LABOR
A. General anesthesia: not in common use today
   1. inhalation
      a) contraindications
         (1) fetal
            (a) prematurity
            (b) distress
         (2) maternal
            (a) upper respiratory infection
            (b) when patient has eaten prior to administration
            (c) multiple births
      b) types
         (1) nitrous oxide with oxygen
            (a) given with contractions; mother does not lose consciousness
            (b) anesthesia level may be deepened after delivery
         (2) cyclopropane with oxygen
            (a) highly explosive
            (b) most potent of all agents
            (c) when given with oxytocin or vasopressors, may cause cardiac irregularity
         (3) methoxyflurane (Penthane)
            (a) high-potency, volatile, nonflammable ether
            (b) not irritating to respiratory tract
            (c) contraindicated with history of liver disease
            (d) associated with renal failure
      c) disadvantages
         (1) prevents mother's participation in birth and interactions with baby after birth
         (2) stops the bearing-down reflex
         (3) causes neonatal depression
         (4) predisposes woman to pulmonary aspiration
            (a) very often woman in labor has eaten
            (b) gravid uterus may impair function of gastroesophageal junction as a result of changes in gastric position

           (c) gravid uterus and lithotomy position increase intragastric pressure
        d) implications for nursing process
           (1) constant observation of FHR, maternal vital signs, and uterine bleeding is necessary
           (2) anesthesia may cause fetal and/or maternal respiratory distress
           (3) may slow down uterine contractions
           (4) may relax perineal musculature, causing rapid expulsion of baby

B. Regional anesthesia: blocks transmission of painful stimuli from uterus, cervix, vagina, and perineum to thalamic pain centers in brain
   1. pudendal block
      a) local anesthetic agent blocks pudendal nerve, causing perineal analgesia
         (1) used for
            (a) spontaneous delivery
            (b) low forceps delivery
            (c) episiotomy
            (d) perineal repair
      b) does not alter maternal respiration or other body functions
      c) does not affect uterine contractions but may affect bearing-down reflex
      d) does not affect fetal respirations
   2. paracervical block
      a) rapid, complete relief of uterine pain
      b) minimal maternal side effects
         (1) no change in vaginal and perineal sensations
            (a) does not interfere with bearing-down reflex
      c) has been associated with
         (1) fetal bradycardia and acidosis
         (2) fetal deaths have been reported
      d) should be avoided in preterm labors or with a fetus at high risk
      e) electronic fetal monitoring is indicated with the use of paracervical block
   3. peridural (epidural) anesthesia
      a) injection of anesthesia into extradural space; does not penetrate the dura or spinal cord
      b) may be administered into
         (1) caudal space within sacrum
         (2) epidural space at second, third, or fourth lumbar interspace

c) may be given by a single injection or by continuous injection over a period of hours
d) vasodilation of legs (mother reports warm feeling) is usually sign that block is working
e) if given too early may slow labor
f) major disadvantage is severe maternal hypotension and therefore decrease in placenta blood flow
g) mother does not feel the desire to bear down in second stage
    (1) second stage may be lengthened
    (2) forceps may be required for delivery
h) may interfere with the woman's ability to void
    (1) observe for bladder distention
    (2) woman may need to be catherized
i) may cause infection. If there is any evidence of infection at injection site, peridural anesthesia is not used
j) implications for nursing process
    (1) explain that legs may feel weak and may shake
    (2) monitor fluids
    (3) hypotension needs immediate attention. Turn mother to left side, hydrate, and provide oxygen
    (4) monitor postdelivery for
        (a) uterine and bladder tone
        (b) return of sensation
4. continuous caudal block
    a) peridural analgesia produced by injection of a local anesthetic into the sacral canal with an epidural catheter in intermittent doses. Woman is placed in either Sims or modified knee-chest position for insertion of needle
    b) maternal effects are minimal
        (1) may cause hypotension
    c) criteria for use
        (1) patient in active labor; contractions every 3 minutes of 40-second duration
        (2) engagement
        (3) dilation
            (a) primigravida: 5–6 cm
            (b) multipara: 4–5 cm
    d) may impede progress of labor
    e) may cause CNS depression of fetus if large doses are administered
    f) advantages
        (1) complete absence of pain and decreased anxiety

g) disadvantages
    (1) may cause maternal hypotension
    (2) may prolong labor
    (3) increased incidence of forceps delivery
    (4) larger doses required than with subarachnoid block
h) contraindications
    (1) fetal
        (a) prematurity
        (b) postmaturity
        (c) fetal distress
        (d) breech
    (2) maternal
        (a) infection at local site
        (b) CNS disease
        (c) hypotension
        (d) hypovolemia
        (e) fear of procedure

C. Spinal anesthesia (subarachnoid)
  1. mid-subarachnoid block
     a) most frequently used
     b) if successful, provides complete relief from perineal pain in all patients and relief of uterine pain in 90–95% of patients
     c) has no effect on maternal or fetal respirations
     d) may cause temporary drop in blood pressure or may cause severe hypotension
        (1) if blood pressure drops below 100 mm Hg systolic, treatment to prevent shock should be initiated
  2. usually given once when head is on the perineum
     a) woman is seated near edge of delivery table with support for feet
        (1) back is arched
        (2) after injection, patient remains seated for 20–30 seconds, then is placed in supine position with head on pillow and pelvis on wedge to relieve pressure
  3. spinal block at any level eliminates the bearing-down reflex
     a) proper preparation of patient will allow spontaneous delivery
     b) forceps easily applied because of perineal relaxation
  4. advantages of spinal block
     a) simplicity
     b) rapidity of action
     c) high success rate
     d) low incidence of maternal and fetal side effects when properly performed

Drug and Anesthesia Administration in the Intrapartal Period

   5. disadvantages
      a) maternal hypotension
      b) bearing-down reflex abolished
      c) early relaxation of perineum
      d) postspinal maternal headache
   6. contraindications
      a) infection of local site
      b) CNS disease
      c) cephalopelvic disproportion
      d) hypovolemia: lack of sufficient fluid in blood
      e) fear of procedure
      f) deviations in normal blood pressure
   7. after delivery
      a) encourage fluids
      b) keep head flat for 8–12 hours
      c) monitor for
         (1) spinal headache
         (2) urine output
         (3) uterine relaxation

V. ANESTHESIA FOR CESAREAN SECTION
A. May be subarachnoid or epidural block or general anesthesia
   1. local infiltration is no longer justified unless a skilled anesthetist is unavailable (Reeder et al., 1980)
   2. spinal anesthesia may
      a) provide inadequate analgesia
      b) may cause maternal hypotension
      c) time required may delay surgery
      d) contraindicated in some maternal conditions
   3. general anesthesia
      a) few contraindications
      b) method of choice when there is maternal
         (1) hypovolemia
         (2) shock
         (3) abnormal blood coagulation
         (4) septicemia
         (5) fear or refusal of spinal anesthesia
      c) disadvantages
         (1) associated with neonatal depression
         (2) eliminates maternal/infant contact after delivery
         (3) places the mother at risk for pulmonary aspiration

VI. NURSING INTERVENTION

A. Nursing role extends beyond administration of drugs
   1. provide pertinent information regarding various methods of pain relief
   2. provide support and encouragement for woman in labor
   3. encourage woman's participation in decision-making process
   4. provide nonpharmacological nursing support for relief of pain
B. The client who receives any type of analgesic or anesthetic must have continuous monitoring of
   1. vital signs
   2. fetal status
   3. level of consciousness
C. The nurse must have knowledge of
   1. types and dosage of medications used
   2. complications that may occur
   3. early signs and symptoms of complications
   4. actions to initiate until the arrival of appropriate medical personnel when an untoward reaction occurs

---

REFERENCES

Blum, M. (in press). *Selected drugs used during labor and delivery: Effects on the fetus and the neonate* (2nd ed.). White Plains, NY: March of Dimes.

Reeder, S., et al. (1980). *Maternity nursing.* Philadelphia: J. B. Lippincott.

Chapter 12
Prepared Childbirth

I. CAUSES OF PAIN DURING CHILDBIRTH
A. First stage of labor
 1. dilation of cervix
  a) distention, stretching, and possible tearing
 2. uterine contractions
 3. stretching of the lower uterine segment
 4. contractions felt
  a) in lower back at beginning of labor
  b) with progress during labor they encircle lower torso, both back and abdomen
 5. descriptions of discomfort vary, and intensity of pain perceived is highly individualized
B. Second stage of labor
 1. stretching and distention of the birth canal and perineum
  a) produces severest pain
  b) cause stretching, tearing, hemorrhage within the fascia, skin, and subcutaneous tissues
C. Delivery
 1. decrease in pain reported at time of delivery
 2. sensations usually described include pressure, stretching, splitting, or on occasion burning
 3. pressure of presenting part causes degree of numbness in the perineum

II. EXERCISE AND BREATHING TECHNIQUES
A. Dr. Read, an English obstetrician, began the movement encouraging natural childbirth

1. the Read method of natural childbirth assumes that a normal birth is a physiological process that should not lead to extreme pain
    a) fear and anxiety about labor that are influenced by cultural conditioning are responsible for pain during labor and delivery by inducing muscular tension
    b) the fear-tension-pain syndrome could be alleviated through education and that proper use of the body could facilitate labor
2. the Read method consists of
    a) education about pregnancy and childbirth to dispel fears and misapprehensions
    b) exercises to strengthen and increase flexibility of muscles used in labor
        (1) pelvic rocking
        (2) tailor sitting
        (3) squatting and kneeling
    c) methods of completely relaxing body musculature
    d) breathing used throughout labor
        (1) slow abdominal breathing during the first stage. Abdomen is raised during contractions to allow the uterus to rise without pressure
        (2) during second stage of labor diaphragmatic breathing is used to assist in expulsion
        (3) moderate panting is used during delivery of head
    e) proper use of abdominal and perineal muscles during bearing-down phase of labor
B. Psychoprophylactic method of childbirth: Lamaze method
    1. Dr. Lamaze was a French obstetrician who became interested in the Russian use of Pavlov's stimulus response theory to decondition women in labor to the fear-tension-pain syndrome
    2. Dr. Lamaze modified the Russian method and introduced it to the Western world
    3. the Lamaze method consists of
        a) education for childbirth to dispel fears and misapprehensions
        b) methods for achieving relaxation of body musculature
        c) conditioning for labor and delivery through development of consciously controlled activity that displaces pain sensations of contractions in the brain
            (1) controlled variations of breathing techniques or patterns for each stage of labor
            (2) massage and counterpressure
    4. positioning is used to assist in increasing maternal comfort
    5. exercises similar to Read method to strengthen pelvic musculature

6. major emphasis on physical fitness, posture, comfort, and controlled relaxation
C. Eclectic approaches
   1. increasingly, prepared childbirth educators have been departing from the rigidity involved in using a particular method. Approaches to prepared childbirth are eclectic in nature and draw from various theoretical frameworks
   2. the management of the labor is the responsibility of the laboring woman and the coach. They will select from the available techniques those measures that provide the most comfort and assistance
      a) objectives of the techniques used are to reduce perception of painful stimuli and discomfort and to assist the birth process through active participation, relaxation of the body musculature, and the correct use of the muscles of expulsion
      b) most of the techniques used are thought to activate paingating mechanisms and to increase production of brain opiates (endorphins)
   3. techniques used in prepared childbirth
      a) breathing techniques: increase cortical stimulation
         (1) cleansing breath: used before and after contractions
         (2) slow chest breathing: inhale through nose and exhale through mouth; diaphragmatic breathing used mostly in first stage of labor
         (3) abdominal breathing: abdomen is raised and breath is held during the contraction and exhaled when peak of contraction is passed; used mostly in first stage of labor (Read method)
         (4) as labor intensifies and slow chest breathing or abdominal breathing no longer brings relief, the slow chest breathing is combined with shallow effortless breathing at a moderate pace high in the chest. Panting was formerly used for this stage but it has been replaced by the shallow breathing in order to prevent hyperventilation. During transition, variations of shallow breathing, such as shallow breathing with mouth open and then blowing out through pursed lips, and varying the pace of the breathing are helpful. This type of breathing is also helpful during the slow delivery of the head
      b) back labor is helped by positioning in either the side-lying position or tailor sitting. Firm pressure to the sacrococcygeal area or application of heat or cold to this area is helpful. Particular attention should be paid to relaxing the back, buttock, and leg muscles during a contraction

c) it is extremely important for the nurse to assist the woman in maintaining control and not giving in to panic or hysteria. Maintaining eye contact with coach or using the eyes to focus on a particular object reduces panic and aids in reducing pain stimuli
d) each stage of labor should use whatever combination of techniques brings the greatest relief of discomfort. Deep chest or abdominal breathing plus relaxation will usually be successful in the first stage of labor. It is during transition period that the woman needs the greatest amount of support and assistance and the greatest amount of controlled activity to reduce discomfort and avoid panic
e) massage: increases cortical stimulation; effleurage: light stroking by woman of abdomen and thighs
f) a variety of positions should be used during labor to increase comfort, including walking, standing, side-lying, or pelvic rocking position
g) when the cervix is fully dilated woman should squat or recline in a semisitting position with knees elevated. After taking a cleansing breath the woman breathes in deeply at start of contraction, holds breath for 5 seconds to fix thoracic and abdominal muscles, and slowly releases the breath as she pushes down with abdominal muscles while relaxing the perineal muscles. She may need to take several breaths during one contraction

III. HYPNOSIS
A. Success depends on client's susceptibility to suggestion
B. Requires personnel prepared and trained in hypnotic techniques

IV. NURSING INTERVENTION
A. Assess pain
1. signs of acute pain include
a) moaning or crying
b) muscle tension
c) perspiration
2. there may be minimal expression of even acute pain in some clients
B. Use a variety of methods to relieve pain
1. allow the woman to choose the position in which she is most comfortable
a) in early labor she may be most comfortable ambulating

b) during the second stage the woman may be most comfortable sitting at a 35–45° angle
   c) lying flat on the back may cause pressure on major blood vessels
2. explain to the client what she should expect
   a) knowledge reduces anxiety
3. teach muscle relaxing exercises
4. use distraction techniques
   a) as labor intensifies it becomes increasingly difficult to distract client
   b) focusing on object, breathing, and relaxation are methods used to distract a client
5. encourage relaxation by cutaneous stimulation
   a) back rubs
   b) Lamaze-type abdominal massage

V. ADVANTAGES

A. Allows for a decreased use of analgesics and anesthesia during labor, which decreases probabilities of side effects of these drugs to mother and baby
   1. prepared childbirth does not preclude the judicious use of medication when necessary
B. Intensifies maternal-paternal-child relationships by allowing both parents full participation in birth process
C. Knowledge and understanding of childbirth reduces fear, anxiety and pain and make this experience one of joy

Chapter 13

Complications of Labor and Delivery

A difficult labor is called dystocia.

I. DEVIATIONS IN POWERS AND FORCES

A. Uterine dysfunction: labor that lasts longer than 24 hours is considered prolonged
   1. hypertonic uterine dysfunction, formerly known as primary uterine inertia, usually occurs during the latent phase of labor before active cervical dilation begins
      a) contractions are weak, ineffectual, and uncoordinated
      b) the force of the contraction is distorted due to incomplete relaxation of uterine muscles
      c) contractions are painful but do not allow labor to progress
         (1) strength of contraction may be determined by resistance at the abdominal wall to pressure of a finger at the acme of contraction. With a stronger contraction there will not be any indentation of abdominal wall
      d) causes
         (1) muscle weakness and/or nerve defects
         (2) overdistention of uterus (multiple births, hydramnios)
         (3) emotional factors
      e) management
         (1) rest and analgesia
         (2) oxytocics after a period of rest
         (3) instillation of prostaglandin gel after rest
         (4) enema after rest period
         (5) use of intrauterine pressure monitor
   2. hypotonic uterine dysfunction, formerly known as secondary uterine inertia, occurs during active phase of labor, causing ineffectual contractions; labor does not progress

a) contractions are usually short, irregular, and infrequent and do not cause much discomfort
b) causes
   (1) overdistention of uterus
   (2) bladder or bowel distention
   (3) weak abdominal muscles
   (4) emotional factors
   (5) cervical rigidity
   (6) too early use of analgesia
   (7) fatigue
   (8) maternal age and parity
   (9) pelvic disproportion or fetal malposition
c) management
   (1) evaluate for disproportion and/or malposition; cesarean section may be indicated if above conditions are implicated
   (2) if no abnormality is present, oxytocins may be given, or local prostaglandin gel instilled into uterus
   (3) amniotomy (artificial rupture of membranes) may be done
   (4) IV fluids are usually ordered to prevent dehydration
   (5) continuous emotional support and encouragement
   (6) provide for patient comfort and rest
   (7) use of intrauterine pressure monitor

3. dangers to fetus in conditions of uterine dysfunction
  a) anoxia
  b) injury to brain from constant prolonged pressure on head
4. dangers to mother in conditions of uterine dysfunction
  a) exhaustion
  b) dehydration
  c) infection
  d) hemorrhage
  e) mental strain

B. Pathological retraction ring (Bandl's ring) is an extreme thinning of lower uterine segment with a concomitant thickening of upper segment marked by a ridge (Bandl's ring)
  1. danger of rupture of uterus
  2. cesarean section is usually indicated

C. Precipitate delivery
  1. minimum resistance of soft parts leading to a rapid delivery
  2. maternal dangers
    a) lacerations
    b) hemorrhage
    c) infection

Complications of Labor and Delivery

3. fetal dangers
   a) anoxia
   b) injuries
   c) infections
4. prevention
   a) those with previous history of rapid labor or high multiparity should be admitted to the hospital early in labor and transferred to the delivery room before full dilation occurs

D. Premature rupture of membranes (PROM)
   1. affects 2–5% of deliveries: four main categories
      a) clearly term: 37–40 weeks
      b) borderline maturity: 35–37 weeks
      c) premature: 25–35 weeks
      d) immature: less than 25 weeks
   2. management
      a) clearly term: expectant management for 12–24 hours and delivery; bedrest and fetal monitoring are used
      b) borderline maturity: assess fetal pulmonary maturity and use electronic fetal monitoring until delivery. If there is no fetal distress or maternal infection, short-term therapy to prevent contractions with magnesium sulfate or terbutaline is sometimes used
      c) premature: same treatment as above; under 25 weeks outcome is poor
   3. major danger is premature labor and maternal infection. Antibiotics are sometimes given to prevent infection. Maternal infection may lead to fetal infection. Fetus may also develop fetal lung hypoplasia from prolonged PROM

E. Meconium aspiration syndrome
   1. serious problem that occurs in 1 in 400 births
   2. the risk of poor fetal outcome with meconium-stained amniotic fluid with a nonbreech presentation is increased with associated fetal distress (late deceleration, fetal scalp pH less than 7.25), low Apgar score, thick meconium, intrauterine growth retardation, and postterm pregnancy
   3. prevention
      a) identify high-risk patient (intrauterine growth retardation and postterm pregnancy)
      b) do antepartum tests to detect chronic fetal distress
      c) do continuous FHR monitoring and frequent scalp sampling
      d) place mother in lateral recumbent position

e) use sedation and analgesia to reduce fetal respiratory movement
f) prompt delivery if fetal hypoxia occurs
g) suction nasopharynx before delivery of thorax
h) if meconium is seen in larynx after delivery, intubate and suction trachea to remove meconium. Administer oxygen
i) this treatment greatly lowers incidence and severity

II. PASSENGER ABNORMALITIES
A. Abnormal presentations
1. may cause prolonged or difficult labor and trauma to mother and baby
2. fetal rotation is achieved by spontaneous rotation, artificial rotation, or maternal posturing
3. artificial rotation either manually or with forceps may cause laceration of vagina and cervix, rupture of uterus, injury to bladder or rectum, or hemorrhage. Fetal damage may include intracranial hemorrhage, skull fracture, facial paralysis, cephalohematoma, bruising, cord compression, or brain damage
4. postural rotation either before or during labor may assist a posterior or transverse presentation to rotate to anterior. Mother assumes a hands and knees posture, which may be combined with a pelvic rock and a stroking motion on the abdomen from front to back on the side of the fetal small parts
5. Cesarean section may be necessary if above methods fail
B. Types of abnormal positions
1. occiput posterior
a) head must rotate in an arc of 135° instead of normal 45° arc
b) signs
(1) contractions felt primarily in the back
(2) almost continuous back pain
(3) membranes rupture early in labor
(4) frequent and irregular contractions
(5) presenting part remains high until late in labor
c) most posterior presentations rotate spontaneously
(1) if spontaneous rotation does not occur, persistent posterior may require intervention
(2) posterior presentation may rotate halfway and become a transverse and require intervention
d) management
(1) manual rotation may be necessary

Complications of Labor and Delivery 231

            (2) deep mediolaterial episiotomy
            (3) forceps may be indicated
            (4) back massage and positioning to aid in relief of discomfort
        e) excessive molding of fetal head may occur
    2. face-brow
        a) usually caused by any condition that interferes with flexion, i.e., prematurity, short cord, platypelloid pelvis
        b) baby's face or brow is distorted after delivery by edema and cyanosis
        c) baby may have hoarseness because of laryngeal edema
        d) danger of maternal hemorrhage following version or high forceps; usually corrects spontaneously or cesarean section is done
    3. shoulder: transverse lie
        a) may rotate spontaneously
        b) podalic version may be done but is dangerous as uterus may rupture
        c) cesarean section usually performed
        d) clinical signs
            (1) abdomen broader than it is long
            (2) head or buttocks may be palpated at pelvic brim
            (3) fundus is empty
        e) prognosis depends upon early diagnosis
            (1) if labor is allowed to continue, danger of ruptured uterus or prolapsed cord
            (2) danger of maternal hemorrhage after version or high forceps
    4. prolapsed cord
        a) if presenting part does not fit closely and fill inlet of pelvis, danger of prolapse exists
        b) predisposing factors
            (1) breech presentation
            (2) transverse lie
            (3) premature rupture of membranes with floating head
            (4) hydramnios
            (5) pelvic deformity
            (6) multiparity
            (7) premature labor
            (8) long cord
            (9) low-lying placenta
        c) prognosis
            (1) labor is not affected
            (2) maternal: no danger

(3) fetal anoxia
    (a) dependent upon time lapse between prolapse and delivery and amount of cord compression
d) management
   (1) prevention
      (a) bedrest after membranes rupture
      (b) membranes should not be ruptured artificially unless head is engaged
   (2) treatment
      (a) if baby is not viable condition is not treated
      (b) if cervix is fully dilated patient is delivered immediately vaginally
      (c) measures for decreasing cord compression and its effects
        1. knee-chest position for mother
        2. Trendelenburg position may be preferred
        3. presenting part pushed up vaginally away from cord to prevent cord compression
        4. oxygen by mask to mother
        5. frequent monitoring of fetal heart
        6. patient is told not to bear down
        7. cord is not handled
          a. no attempt should be made to replace cord
      (d) if cervix is not completely dilated, immediate cesarean section is done
5. breech presentation: 3–4% of pregnancies
  a) types
    (1) frank breech: buttocks presenting part, with thighs flexed and legs extended (most common)
    (2) complete breech: buttocks presenting part, with thighs and knees flexed
    (3) footling: one or both feet present, extension of thighs and knees
    (4) kneeling: knee presents, thighs extended, and knees flexed
  b) etiology
    (1) overdistended uterus
      (a) multiple births
      (b) hydramnios
      (c) hydrocephalus
      (d) large baby

    (e) pelvic abnormality that interferes with the enlargement of the head
   (2) premature baby
   (3) placenta previa
  c) clinical manifestations
   (1) head is at fundus
   (2) fetal heart at or above umbilicus
   (3) engagement usually does not occur
   (4) membranes rupture early
   (5) meconium-stained amniotic fluid
  d) prognosis
   (1) maternal: no significantly greater mortality
    (a) may have prolonged labor
    (b) if delivery is spontaneous no increase in trauma to perineal area
    (c) increased incidence of forceps delivery, which may cause trauma to perineal area
   (2) baby: fetal loss three times higher than in vertex presentation
    (a) asphyxia
    (b) brain injury due to rapid delivery of head
    (c) skeletal injury
    (d) premature separation of placenta
  e) management of breech
   (1) reduce incidence of complications by x-ray pelvimetry or sonogram
   (2) constant monitoring of FHR and maternal status
   (3) cesarean section performed if
    (a) fetus is larger than 8.5 lbs
    (b) there is fetopelvic disproportion
    (c) labor does not progress
    (d) fetal distress occurs
   (4) external version may be done
C. Fetal abnormalities may lead to necessity for cesarean section
  1. hydrocephalus: enlargement of the cranium due to excessive accumulation of cerebrospinal fluid (CSF)
  2. anencephaly: abnormally small cranium due to the absence of cranial bones and/or portions of the brain
  3. oversized baby
  4. postmaturity (bones do not mold easily)
  5. edema of fetus (hydrops fetalis)

6. short umbilical cord
   a) less than 20 inches is abnormal
   b) may be twisted rather than short
   c) fetus cannot descend
   d) may cause anoxia
D. Multiple pregnancy may cause
   1. overdistention of uterus
   2. postpartal hemorrhage
   3. premature births have an increased incidence
   4. general anesthesia to be contraindicated

III. PLACENTAL ABNORMALITIES
A. Retained placenta
   1. placenta separates but is held by contracted cervix
   2. management
      a) manual removal
B. Adherent placenta
   1. placenta does not separate, needs manual separation and removal
C. Placenta accreta: extremely rare
   1. villi of placenta invade muscles of uterus
   2. no blood loss unless manual removal is attempted
   3. persistent attempt at removal may lead to
      a) hemorrhage
      b) perforation or rupture of uterus
      c) shock
   4. management
      a) conservative
         (1) left alone to absorb
         (2) antibiotic therapy
         (3) oxytocin administered
      b) radical
         (1) if bleeding is uncontrollable, hysterectomy is performed

IV. ABNORMALITIES OF PASSAGE
A. Uterus
   1. developmental
      a) double uterus (bicornate): full-term pregnancy extremely rare with this condition
   2. displacement
      a) ventrofixation: cervix is displaced in region of sacral promontory

             (1) if cervix cannot be repositioned, cesarean section is necessary
        3. tumors (fibroids and neoplasms)
             a) block pelvis
             b) cause malpresentations
             c) do not allow for adequate contractions
             d) may necessitate cesarean section
B. Cervix
    1. may be rigid or resistant due to
        a) scar tissue
        b) chronic inflammation
        c) rigid tissue (elderly primipara over 35)
        d) if dilation does not progress, cesarean section may be necessary
C. Vagina
    1. congenital malformations
    2. acquired obstruction
        a) cystocele and rectocele
    3. may impede delivery
D. Vulva
    1. edema
        a) irritation from antiseptics
        b) may cause extreme discomfort to patient
E. Bony pelvis
    1. may be contracted or deformed
    2. clinical manifestations depend on
        a) degree of contraction
        b) size of fetus
    3. management
        a) trial labor
        b) cesarean section if indicated

V   OPERATIVE OBSTETRICS

A. Cesarean section: child is delivered through an incision in the abdominal and uterine walls
    1. incidence of cesarean sections increasing because of
        a) increased use of fetal monitoring and misdiagnosing of fetal distress
        b) changing philosophy of management of labor
             (1) minimize fetal trauma in breech presentation
             (2) prolonged labor will increase stress to mother and fetus

(3) prevent sepsis when there is premature rupture of membranes
(4) pregnancies in which there is an unfavorable uterine environment will be terminated because of the advances in newborn intensive care
(5) advances in anesthesia, blood replacement, and antibiotics make cesarean section delivery method of choice in some complications of pregnancy
2. controversy surrounds the increased incidence, and efforts to control overuse are currently being investigated
3. indications
    a) any condition that precludes vaginal delivery
    b) repeat sections are left to the discretion of the physician and are not mandatory
        (1) vaginal delivery may be considered after a previous Cesarean delivery
    c) placenta previa
    d) premature separation of placenta
    e) toxemia if severe
    f) fetal distress
4. management
    a) preoperative care
        (1) insertion of Foley catheter to prevent accidental injury to bladder
        (2) abdominal and pubic prep
        (3) preoperative medication as ordered
            (a) atropine is usually ordered
            (b) narcotic drugs are avoided because they are CNS depressants
        (4) preparation of back because spinal anesthesia is anesthesia best suited to procedure
        (5) type and x-match of blood
        (6) routine lab studies
        (7) general physical exam
        (8) consent form signed
        (9) explanation of rationale for section and what to expect during the procedure to the client and her family
        (10) continued observation of FHR and maternal vital signs
    b) immediate postoperative care
        (1) maintain airway if general anesthesia is used
        (2) monitor vital signs

(3) monitor intake and output
   (a) check patency of Foley catheter
   (b) check IVs for rate of infiltration
(4) relieve pain
(5) provide hygienic care
(6) maintain body alignment if spinal anesthesia is used
(7) encourage deep breathing
(8) if spinal anesthesia is used, head should remain flat for 8–12 hours
(9) observe for hemorrhage and shock
(10) massage of fundus is contraindicated
(11) administer oxytocics as ordered

5. psychosocial impact on patient
   a) may be relieved that labor is over, but may feel failure or defeat
   b) may undergo a grieving process
      (1) loss of vaginal delivery
      (2) loss of active participation in labor process
   c) increased anxiety about her welfare and that of her child
   d) increase in fatigue and pain
   e) may need more time to meet her own dependency needs
   f) support of spouse and significant others facilitates recovery
   g) may have influence on future childbearing

B. Forceps
   1. indications
      a) prolonged labor, weakened fetal or maternal condition
      b) prolapsed cord
      c) fetal distress
   2. criteria
      a) no cephalopelvic disproportion
      b) cervix should be completely dilated
      c) membranes must be ruptured
      d) fetal head must be engaged
      e) bladder must be emptied
      f) if any of these conditions are not met, forceps should not be used
   3. types of forceps
      a) outlet or low forceps
         (1) head is on the pelvic floor and is crowning
            (a) some of the benefits are believed to be
               1. more controlled delivery

2. less exposure of head to pressure against the perineum
            3. minimization of trauma to maternal tissues
         b) mid-forceps
            (1) head is engaged
            (2) some manipulation necessary
               (a) usually rotation of head
            (3) dangers associated with forceps delivery depend upon
               (a) position and level of presenting part
               (b) skill of the obstetrician
         c) high- forceps: head not engaged
            (1) this procedure is no longer justified, Cesarean section is safer
      4. dangers of forceps
         a) maternal
            (1) lacerations to vagina and cervix
            (2) rupture of uterus
            (3) injury to bladder or rectum
            (4) hemorrhage
         b) fetal
            (1) brain damage
            (2) intracranial hemorrhage
            (3) skull fracture
            (4) facial paralysis
            (5) cephalohematoma
            (6) bruising
            (7) cord compression
         c) because of the dangers, forceps are used only when absolutely necessary
C. Vacuum extraction: popular in Europe
   1. a vacuum cup that uses an electric pump to build up negative pressure is attached to head of fetus. Traction on the fetal head is exerted by a steady pull on cup
   2. used in cases of failure to rotate, fetal distress, delay in second stage of labor, cephalopelvic disproportion, and serious disease in the mother where strenuous efforts need to be reduced by the mother in the second stage of labor. It is considered by some to be a better alternative to forceps
   3. danger of fetal scalp or brain damage if used by unskilled operators
   4. must have a vertex presentation, ruptured membranes, and no serious cephalopelvic disproportions. There should be complete

dilation and head should be engaged. Vacuum is sometimes used when cervix is not fully dilated when there is fetal distress. Should not be used before 36 weeks
    5. local anesthesia is usually used
    6. cup should not remain on head longer than 40 minutes
    7. forceps should never follow an unsuccessful extraction. A Cesarean section is usually performed
    8. scalp of baby is usually edematous after extraction and may be bruised; the chignon (head swelling) usually disappears in a few days
    9. baby should be observed for signs of cerebral irritation, such as poor sucking, listlessness, vomiting, high-pitched cry, spine rigidity, jaundice, or infection (Galvan et al., 1987)
D. Episiotomy
    1. indications
        a) to prevent perineal lacerations
    2. types
        a) midline
        b) right or left mediolateral
    3. the routine use of episiotomy to prevent laceration has been questioned because in many cases careful management of delivery can prevent lacerations

VI INDUCTION AND AUGMENTATION OF LABOR
A. Use of agent to bring about labor to increase the speed and intensity of labor
B. Indications
    1. postmaturity
        a) prolonged gestation is associated with increased perinatal mortality, intrauterine asphyxia, and convulsions
        b) there is controversy as to whether the prolonged gestation causes the increased risk or whether babies at risk tend to be overdue
        c) doctors may choose prophylactic induction at 42 weeks or selective induction based on fetal monitoring to identify a fetus at risk
    2. maternal diabetes or pre-eclampsia
    3. uterine inertia
    4. ruptured membranes for more than 24 hours in full term fetus
    5. management of incomplete, inevitable, or missed abortion

C. Contraindications
1. high parity
2. previous cesarean section
3. multiple births
4. first baby
5. cephalopelvic disproportion
6. abnormal presentation
7. overdistention of uterus
8. fetal distress
9. unfavorable fetal presentation
10. hypersensitivity to drug
11. should never be used for convenience

D. Amniotomy
1. allows presenting part to become a more effective dilating wedge
2. use of amniotomy as a means of induction is being seriously reconsidered
    a) if there is a long period of time elapsed between amniotomy and delivery, there is danger of infection
    b) there is a danger that labor will not follow rupture of membranes
3. management
    a) prepare client for vaginal examination
    b) maintain sterile technique
    c) immediately after procedure check
        (1) amniotic fluid for meconium
        (2) fetal heart

E. Drugs used for induction
1. synthetic preparations of oxytocin
    a) various trade names include Pitocin and Syntocinon
    b) given by IV drip
        (1) when 1 IU of oxytocin is added to 1000 ml of IV fluid, each ml contains 1 mU of oxytocin. 1 IU = 1000 milliunits (mU)
        (2) IV bottle should be clearly labeled with
            (a) name of drug
            (b) amount of drug
            (c) time drug added
    c) piggyback set-up should be used so that oxytocin administration can be immediately halted and there is an open vein for emergency
        (1) the IV should be administered very slowly and response closely monitored

(2) any contractions lasting more than 1 minute or occurring less than 2 minutes apart necessitate immediate adjustment of medication administration
(3) careful observation of patient reaction to drug, FHR, and vital signs
(4) constant physician supervision of drug administration is necessary
(5) IV discontinued immediately if any untoward signs occur
(a) contraction lasting over 90 seconds
(b) abnormalities in FHR
d) in order to smooth the transition from the preparatory phase of labor to the active phase during induction, the dose is increased every 45 to 60 minutes. The dosage is regulated by an infusion pump. The beginning dosage is low and is gradually increased. There may be variations in the interval between increases of the drug depending on the protocol of the physician. Drug is increased until there are contractions every 2–3 minutes. When active phase of labor is achieved oxytocin may be reduced or stopped
e) danger of severe and prolonged contraction exists
(1) may cause uterine tetany (tetanic contraction—no relaxation)
(a) rupture of uterus
(b) premature placental separation
(c) fetal hypoxia
2. a newer drug that is under investigation for bringing about cervical ripening is prostaglandin E_2 gel. The gel may either lead to spontaneous labor or may facilitate a successful oxytocin induction. The gel does not usually have side effects that are common with oral or parenteral prostaglandin. It is instilled into the uterus through the vagina

F. Preterm labor
1. definition: spontaneous onset of regular uterine contractions less than 10 minutes apart between the 20th and 37th week of gestation resulting in cervical effacement and dilation
2. causes: exact mechanism is unknown but theories include
a) spontaneous rupture of membranes
b) cervical incompetency
c) such conditions as uterine anomalies, polyhydramnios, and multiple births that cause increased uterine distention and increased contractility
d) fetal anomaly

- e) placenta abruptio or previa
- f) fetal death
- g) previous preterm delivery or late abortion
- h) systemic disease in the mother
- i) hormonal changes
    - (1) a rise in prostaglandin levels: prostaglandin secretion increases when the level of free fatty acids, especially arachidonic acid, is increased
    - (2) arachidonic acid becomes elevated from stress, fasting, trauma, viral and bacterial infections, especially of the urinary tract, and hemorrhage, as in placenta previa
- j) personal lifestyle, including smoking, fatigue from lack of rest and overwork, and poor nutrition
- k) cervical manipulation that is traumatic can release prostaglandins. Sexual intercourse that is unusually aggressive may cause an increase in fatty acid levels
- l) DES exposure

3. implications for nursing process with women at risk
    - a) reduce stress-related biochemical changes through counseling, development of support systems, avoidance of stressful situations, and the use of relaxation techniques
    - b) screen pregnant women to identify those at risk and institute a prevention and follow-up program
    - c) teach women to recognize the signs of preterm labor, which may be very subtle, and how to palpate and time uterine contractions
        - (1) uterine contractions that occur regularly every 10 minutes or less with or without
            - (a) low dull backache
            - (b) constant or intermittent menstrual-like cramps in the lower abdomen
            - (c) intermittent pelvic pressure
            - (d) abdominal cramping with or without diarrhea
            - (e) any change or increase in vaginal discharge, especially if it becomes mucus-like, watery, and blood-tinged
        - (2) if contractions occur, woman is advised to lie down immediately for at least an hour on her side (not supine). If contractions continue, she should notify physician or nurse-midwife immediately
    - d) increase daily rest periods to decrease pressure on uterus and increase blood flow to fetus. For women at risk, lying one

Complications of Labor and Delivery 243

       hour three times a day in a left-lateral position is recommended
- e) report any signs of urinary infection immediately
- f) maintain a balanced diet and avoid dieting or fasting
- g) do not stimulate nipples as a preparation for breast feeding
- h) intercourse should be gentle or may have to abstain
- i) decrease strenuous activities, such as heavy lifting, cleaning, sports, or outside work
- j) an ambulatory tocodynamometer may be worn to transmit recordings of uterine contractions to physician
- k) for women at high risk, weekly follow-up that includes close monitoring of cervical change may be instituted. Care must be taken not to irritate or traumatize the cervix during the examination

4. management
   a) three categories of care for women with signs of preterm labor
      (1) category 1: uterine contractions that stop with bedrest and cause no cervical change
         (a) woman is placed on bedrest, on left side in Trendelenburg position, which may reduce cervical pressure of fetal presenting part. Woman is carefully monitored with an external electronic monitor
         (b) it is important to evaluate level of stress and anxiety and to use nursing measures to alleviate these if present
         (c) a gentle baseline cervical exam is done
         (d) if no cervical change, woman is sent home and careful follow-up care is instituted. Modified bedrest is advised
      (2) category 2: uterine contractions that do not stop with bedrest but cause no cervical change
         (a) woman is placed on bedrest as in category 1
         (b) a gentle baseline cervical exam is done
         (c) uterine activity is monitored carefully and cervix is rechecked
         (d) if no cervical change, woman is sent home on modified bedrest and careful follow-up care is instituted
      (3) category 3: persistent uterine activity with cervical change
         (a) bedrest as above
         (b) baseline cervical exam and repeat exams every 12 hours
         (c) continuous electronic external monitoring
         (d) drug therapy begun

                (e) if uterine contractions are suppressed and there is no further cervical change, woman is sent home on modified bedrest
            (4) women who present with uterine contractions and cervical effacement greater than 80% and dilation greater than 3 cm are usually treated for short-term prevention of labor, which may be effective for a few days; bedrest and drug therapy are used. Women are usually transferred to a tertiary care center where the premature infant can receive appropriate care
        b) drug therapy
            (1) should not be used in the following conditions
                (a) placenta previa or placenta abruptio
                (b) placental insufficiency and fetal compromise
                (c) severe pre-eclampsia
                (d) fetal anomalies
                (e) intrauterine infection
            (2) IV ethanol (not usually used currently)
                (a) suppresses oxytocin and vasopressin from maternal posterior pituitary
                (b) crosses the placenta
                    1. fetal blood level of alcohol equals that of the mother within 2 hours
                (c) side effects
                    1. intoxication of mother
                    2. nausea, vomiting
                    3. headache
                    4. restlessness
                    5. hypoglycemia and lactic acidemia
                    6. may cause respiratory distress in newborn if labor is not arrested
                (d) contraindications
                    1. liver disease
                    2. reformed alcoholics
                    3. extreme caution in women with epilepsy and diabetes
                    4. reservations have arisen about the use of ethanol therapy because of the danger of fetal alcohol syndrome; research is needed to answer questions about the association between therapy and F A S
                (e) implications for nursing process
                    1. prevent aspiration if woman becomes nauseous

2. give antacids to prevent stomach irritation
3. maintain fluid intake to prevent dehydration
4. prepare patient and family carefully to minimize anxiety and embarassment because of behavior related to intoxication
5. maintain careful supervision to prevent injury
- (3) magnesium sulfate
  - (a) inhibits smooth muscle contractibility
  - (b) crosses the placenta
    1. concentration in fetal plasma rapidly reaches that of the mother
  - (c) side effects
    1. warmth, flushing
    2. headache
    3. pulmonary edema
    4. perspiration
    5. respiratory depression
    6. neonatal depression
  - (d) contraindications
    1. impaired renal function
    2. reduced urinary output
    3. woman who is digitalized
  - (e) IV calcium can help prevent the neuromuscular blocking properties of magnesium in mother and newborn
  - (f) if given within 2 hours of delivery may cause neuromuscular or respiratory depression in newborn
  - (g) magnesium sulfate toxicity may develop: antidote is calcium gluconate, 10% solution
  - (h) implications for nursing process
    1. careful monitoring of woman including reflexes, respiratory rate, and urinary output is necessary
    2. woman should not be left alone during therapy
- (4) ritrodrine
  - (a) beta-adrenergic stimulant
  - (b) inhibits smooth muscle contractibility
  - (c) side effects
    1. nervousness, restlessness, anxiety
    2. chest pain, hypotension
    3. hyperventilation
    4. pulmonary edema
    5. increase in FHR
    6. fetal hypocalcemia

7. fetal hypoglycemia
(d) contraindications
1. maternal hemorrhage
2. eclampsia and severe pre-eclampsia
3. chorioamnionitis
4. intrauterine fetal death
5. maternal cardiac disease, pulmonary hypertension, hyperthyroidism, and uncontrolled diabetes
6. sensitivity to drug
7. maternal conditions that would be adversely affected
(e) administered in IV via infusion pump. Initial dose is usually 0.1 mg/min; increased by 0.05 mg/min q 10 minutes until contractions cease or until maximum dose of 0.35 mg/min is reached. After 12 hours of therapy, dose is decreased by 0.05 mg/min q 30 min until 0.10 mg/min is reached. A PO dose is usually given 30 minutes before stopping IV. Woman will be continued on PO dose as long as needed
(f) implications for nursing process
1. careful monitoring of vital signs, uterine contractions, and FHR
2. strict bedrest in correct position (left lateral position during infusion)
3. strict intake and output and weigh daily
4. watch for overhydration, pulmonary edema, and respiratory distress syndrome (RDS)
(5) prostaglandin inhibitors are not recommended at this time because of side effects
(6) terbutaline sulfate
(a) beta-adrenergic stimulant
(b) not used as frequently as ritodrine
(c) maternal effects
1. tachycardia
2. palpitations
3. sweating
4. headache
5. nervousness, restlessness, and anxiety
6. tremors
7. pulmonary edema
8. lethargy
9. drowsiness

          10. tinnitus
          11. dizziness
          12. nausea and vomiting
       (d) fetal side effects
          1. tachycardia
          2. hypoglycemia
       (e) administered via IV and followed by PO maintenance dose
       (f) implications for nursing process: same as for ritodrine
   5. prevention of preterm labor necessitates the identification of pregnancies at risk. The following test (Exhibit 13-1) developed by the state of Florida is one method that can be used to identify mothers at risk

Exhibit 13-1 Preterm Labor: The Healthy Baby Test

Babies born too soon or weighing below five-and-a-half pounds are more likely to have serious health problems. This is the leading cause of death and disabilities for Florida's babies.

This simple test will help you decide whether you may need special care during your pregnancy so *you* can have a healthy baby.

Here's how to take the healthy baby test. Answer each question 'yes' or 'no' by putting a check in the box. The test is in two parts. In *Part I* answer the questions if you are *NOW PREGNANT* or if you are *PLANNING A PREGNANCY*. In *Part II* answer the questions only if you are *NOW PREGNANT*. Then add up the score from your answers in Part I and Part II.

Part I. Answer the questions below if you are *NOW PREGNANT* or if you are *PLANNING A PREGNANCY*.

	YES	NO
Have you ever given birth to a small baby (5½ pounds or less)?	(10)	(0)
Do you have sickle cell disease?	(10)	(0)
Have you had an operation on the mouth of your womb (cervix)?	(5)	(0)
Have you had an abortion or miscarriage after three months of pregnancy?	(5)	(0)
Have you ever had a kidney infection?	(5)	(0)
Are you younger than 17 years of age?	(5)	(0)
Do you drink beer, wine or alcohol every day?	(5)	(0)
Have you had two or more abortions or miscarriages in a row?	(5)	(0)
Do you have fibroid tumors in your uterus?	(5)	(0)
Have you had serious long-term heart or kidney trouble?	(3)	(0)

Exhibit 13-1 continued

What is your education?		
less than ten years of school	(2)	
ten-twelve years of school	(1)	
over twelve years of school	(0)	
Are you on your feet for five hours or more per day (example: waitress, beautician, store clerk)?	(3)	(0)
Are you in a high stress job (example: nurse, doctor, secretary, manager, teacher)?	(3)	(0)
Are you in a physically demanding job (example: construction or police work)?	(3)	(0)
Do you travel more than 1½ hours round-trip each day for your employment?	(3)	(0)

TOTAL PART I _____

Part II. Answer the following questions only if you are *NOW PREGNANT*.

	YES	NO
Are you pregnant with twins or triplets?	(10)	(0)
Have you had surgery on your abdomen during this pregnancy?	(10)	(0)
Has your doctor told you that you have placenta previa (afterbirth coming ahead of the baby)?	(10)	(0)
Have you used any street drugs during this pregnancy (example: cocaine, crack, heroin, smack)?	(10)	(0)
Have you been told that the mouth of your womb (cervix) is starting to thin out (efface) or open up (dilate)?	(6)	(0)
Have you had bleeding after 12 weeks (3 months) of this pregnancy?	(5)	(0)
Were you told that you were underweight for your height at the start of this pregnancy?	(5)	(0)
Have you had a bladder infection during this pregnancy?	(5)	(0)
Have you been told that you haven't gained as much weight as you should in this pregnancy?	(3)	(0)
After 32 weeks of pregnancy, have you been told that your baby is breech (rear end first)?	(3)	(0)
Do you have high blood pressure?	(2)	(0)
Did your prenatal care begin after your fourth month?	(3)	(0)

TOTAL PART II _____

Now add up your score for each part and enter the scores below:

RESULTS:

10 or more points: Your chances of having a baby born too soon and too small to be healthy are *much higher* than normal.

5–9 points: Your chances of having a baby born too soon and too small to be healthy are *slightly higher* than normal.

0–5 points: Your chances of having a baby born too soon and too small to be healthy are *no higher* than normal.

Exhibit 13-1 continued

If you are concerned about your score on this test, be sure to talk with your health care provider. Your local March of Dimes can give you more information about low birth weight babies and preterm labor. If you are having trouble obtaining prenatal health care contact your local county public health unit for assistance.
Remember: to have a healthy baby
1. See your doctor early and often
2. Don't drink, smoke or use drugs
3. Eat well balanced meals

Source: Reprinted by permission of the State of Florida Department of Health and Rehabilitative Services, Maternal and Child Health Office, State Health Office, Tallahassee, Florida.

VII ACCIDENTS AND INJURIES IN LABOR AND DELIVERY
A. Lacerations
   1. cervical: sulcus tear extends to cervix from perineum
      a) increased possibility of hemorrhage if not adequately repaired
      b) surgical repair and vaginal packing are used
   2. perineal
      a) first degree: perineal skin, fourchette, and mucous membrane
      b) second degree: muscles of perineal body
      c) third degree: includes rectal sphincter
      d) surgical repair at time of delivery
B. Rupture of uterus
   1. causes
      a) contracted pelvis
      b) Bandl's ring
      c) previous Cesarean section
      d) improper use of instruments
      e) improper use of oxytocin
   2. symptoms of impending rupture
      a) continuous contractions
      b) restlessness
      c) bladder appears full but patient cannot void; not relieved by catheterization
      d) tender uterus
   3. symptoms of acute rupture
      a) sharp tearing pain in lower abdomen (feeling of something tearing)
      b) pain ceases
      c) hemorrhage and shock quickly follow

    4. should not be allowed to occur; careful observation can prevent rupture
    5. if it occurs hysterectomy may be done
C. Inversion of uterus (turned inside out)
    1. etiology
        a) usually trauma, i.e., pulling on cord or fundal pressure
        b) may be spontaneous
    2. dangers
        a) shock
        b) hemorrhage
        c) infection
        d) high mortality rate
    3. management
        a) replacement of uterus
        b) blood replacement
D. Sudden death in labor
    1. causes
        a) anesthesia
        b) aspiration
        c) amniotic fluid embolism
        d) transfusion reaction
        e) cerebrovascular accident

VIII. NURSING CARE DURING COMPLICATIONS OF LABOR AND DELIVERY
  A. Assessment
    1. directed toward detecting early signs and symptoms of possible problems
        a) contractions
            (1) frequency
            (2) duration
            (3) intensity
        b) vaginal discharge
            (1) color
            (2) amount
            (3) character
        c) vital signs
        d) stress and anxiety level
        e) abdominal contour
        f) fetal heart rate

        g) fatigue and exhaustion
        h) abnormal pain
B.   Intervention
    1. intervention is based on an understanding and interpretation of the assessment
    2. immediate reporting of any deviation from normal
    3. explanation of status to the client and her family
    4. realistic reassurance as to outcome of labor and delivery
    5. explanation of procedures
    6. encouragement as to progress
    7. creation of an atmosphere where client and family can freely verbalize their fears and concerns

REFERENCE

Galvan, B., & Broekhuizen, F. (1987, July/August). Obstetric vacuum extraction. *Journal of Obstetric and Gynecologic Nursing*, pp. 242–247.

BIBLIOGRAPHY

Anderson, G., & Lomas, J. (1984). Determinants of the increasing Cesarean birth rate, *New England Journal of Medicine, 311* (14), 887–892.

Andrews, C. (1981). Nursing intervention to change a malpositioned fetus. *Advances in Nursing Science*, pp. 53–66.

Banta, H. D., & Thacker, S. B. (1979). Policies toward medical technology: The cases of electronic fetal monitoring. *American Journal of Public Health, 69* (9), 931–934.

Belsey, E. M., Rosenblatt, D. B., Lieberman, B. A., Redshaw, M., Caldwell, J., Norarianni, L., Smith, R. L., & Beard, R. W. (1981). The influence of maternal analgesia on neonatal behavior: I. Pethidine. *British Journal of Obstetrics and Gynaecology, 88*, 398–406.

Brengman, S., and Burns, M. (1988, March). Hypertensive crisis in L & D. *American Journal of Nursing*, pp. 325–328.

Chilton, C., and Wade, J. (1986). *Intrapartum fetal monitoring and newborn resuscitation: A workbook for nurses*. White Plains, NY: March of Dimes.

Couzinet, B., et al. (1986, December 18). Termination of early pregnancy by the progesterone antagonist RU 486. *New England Journal of Medicine*, pp. 1565–69.

Formato, L. S. (1985). Routine prophylactic episiotomy: Is it always necessary? *Journal of Nurse-Midwifery, 30* (3), 144–148.

Gorvine, B., et al. (1982). *Health Care of Women: Labor and Delivery*. Monterey, CA: Wadsworth Health Sciences Division.

Grimes, D. A., and Schulz, K. F. (1985). Morbidity and mortality from second-trimester abortions. *Journal of Reproductive Medicine, 30* (7).

International Childbirth Education Association. (1988). Position Paper: *Epidural anesthesia for labor*. Des Moines, IA: Author.

Karmel, M. (1959). *Thank you, Dr. Lamaze*. Philadelphia, J. B. Lippincott.

Keller, C., & Copeland, P. (1972, January). Counseling the abortion patient is more than talk. *American Journal of Nursing*, pp. 25–27.

Kintz, D. L. (1987, March/April). Nursing support in labor. *Journal of Obstetric and Gynecologic Nursing*, pp. 126–130.

Laga, M., et al. (1988). Prophylaxis of gonococcal and chlamydial opthalmia neonatorum. *New England Journal of Medicine, 318* (11), pp. 653–657.

Leboyer, F. (1975). *Birth without violence.* New York: Alfred A. Knopf.

McKay, S., & Roberts, J. (1985). Second stage labor: What is normal? *Journal of Obstetric and Gynecologic Nursing, 14* (2), 101–106.

Neeson, J. D., & May, K. A. (1986). *Comprehensive maternity nursing.* Philadelphia: J. B. Lippincott.

Ogburn, M. D. (1986, Summer). The mystery of preterm labor. *Childbirth Educator*, pp. 20–27.

Pritchard, J. A., et al. (1985). *Williams obstetrics* (17th ed.). Norwalk, CT: Appleton-Century-Crofts.

Rayburn, W. F., & Iams, J. D. (1980). Drug use during pregnancy: Part II, Drug effects on the fetus. *Perinatal Press, 4* (9), 131–136.

Snydal, S. H. (1988). Methods of fetal heart rate monitoring during labor. *Journal of Nurse-Midwifery, 33* (1), 4–14.

Wagner, P. G. (1981). Continuous fetal tissue pH monitoring. *Journal of Obstetric and Gynecologic Nursing, 10* (3), 164–169.

Wetzel, S. K. (1982, July/August). Are we ignoring the needs of the woman with a spontaneous abortion? *Maternal Child Nursing*, pp. 258–59.

Part IV

The Postnatal Period

Chapter 14

Anatomy and Physiology of the Puerperium

I. DEFINITION OF PUERPERIUM: 6- to 12-week period from the end of labor to the complete involution of uterus and healing of pelvic structures

II. PHYSIOLOGICAL AND ANATOMICAL CHANGES
   A. Uterus
      1. size and position after delivery
         a) fundus: hard, globular, and contracted, usually felt at umbilicus if bladder not distended
         b) usual weight: 100 g
      2. after delivery the uterus descends into pelvic cavity approximately 1 cm/day. By the tenth day, fundus usually cannot be palpated
      3. at the end of puerperium weight of uterus is 40–60 g
      4. process of involution is accomplished by
         a) autolysis of protein of uterine lining. Waste products are excreted in urine, causing albuminuria
         b) two layers of decidua are involved in involution
            (1) one is cast off as lochia
            (2) underlying layer becomes endometrial lining
               (a) entire endometrium restored by third week
         c) placental site: completely regenerated within 6 weeks
         d) large uterine blood vessels become smaller
         e) well-contracted uterus clamps down on maternal blood vessels and controls hemorrhage
         f) uterus is a very tactile organ immediately after delivery and responds to massage by contracting

g) involution occurs more rapidly in primipara or breast-feeding mother because of increased muscle tone in primipara and release of oxytocin during breast feeding
h) factors delaying involution
(1) multiparity
(2) conditions causing overdistention of uterus
(a) hydramnios
(b) large-sized baby
(3) infection
(4) retained placenta or membranes
(5) hormonal deficiencies
i) subinvolution occurs when uterus fails to return to normal size
B. Cervix
1. immediately after delivery cervix is soft, flabby, and partly open
2. after 1 week muscle begins to regenerate and finger cannot be introduced
3. small lacerations may heal spontaneously or need cauterization
4. external os remains somewhat wider than in the nonparous woman
C. Lochia: contains blood from placental site, decidua, cervical secretions, epithelial cells, and bacteria
1. Lochia rubra: 1–4 days; bright red
a) if persists longer than 2 weeks, may indicate retained placenta or membranes
2. Lochia serosa: 4–10 days; pinkish brown in color
3. Lochia alba: 10–14 days; whitish discharge due to increase in leukocytes
4. should not be excessive, scant (during rubra), or foul smelling
5. blood clots may be passed immediately after delivery
D. Perineum
1. vaginal distention decreases, but muscle tone never returns to preparous state
2. lacerations, tears, sutures, swellings gradually heal
E. Abdominal wall
1. soft and flabby for some time
2. striae fade to silvery white, but always remain
3. diastasis of the recti muscle (separation of abdominal muscle) may occur due to loss of muscle tone
F. Urinary tract
1. ureteral dilation disappears in 2 weeks
2. increased output (diuresis) second to fifth day due to excretion of extracellular fluid

3. urine may contain increased amounts of acetone (CHO breakdown), nitrogen, albumin (protein autolysis of uterus), and lactose from production of mammary glands
4. urethra and ureters become slightly dilated and edematous

G. Breasts
1. soft immediately after delivery
2. high levels of estrogen and progesterone secreted by placenta inhibit anterior pituitary secretion
3. after delivery of placenta, inhibition is removed and lactogenic hormone (prolactin) is secreted, which stimulates production of milk
    a) synthetic estrogen and androgens given intramuscularly immediately after delivery suppress lactogenic hormones in patients who do not wish to breast feed
4. engorgement of breasts may occur 2 days postpartum
    a) caused by venous and lymphatic secretion stasis
    b) various degrees of engorgement occur
    c) in most severe type, breasts are swollen, hard, red, and painful

H. Blood
1. decrease in volume following blood loss in delivery
2. hemodilution of blood (hydremia) is decreased in first week postpartum through excretion by kidneys and from skin
3. moderate anemia may occur due to blood loss
4. leukocytosis occurs during labor and immediately afterwards
5. fibrinogen levels are elevated
6. immediately after delivery, pulse rate slows

I. Weight loss
1. usually 10–12 lb immediately after delivery; 13 lb more are gradually lost after the initial loss
2. loss of weight due to
    a) delivery of baby and placenta
    b) hydremia reduction
    c) excretion of retained fluid
    d) uterine involution
3. although back to normal weight, patient may appear obese because of poor abdominal muscle tone

J. Skin
1. mask of pregnancy gradually fades
2. linea nigra fades but never disappears
3. striae fade but remain silvery white
4. primary areola may never resume original color
5. secondary areola fades in 3 months

K. Hormonal
   1. nonlactating woman
      a) ovulation within 3–6 weeks
      b) menstruation within 5–8 weeks
   2. lactating woman
      a) return of menstrual cycle varies; may be delayed until weaning
      b) because of variation, breast feeding is not a reliable form of contraception

Chapter 15

Psychology of the Puerperium

I. FACTORS INFLUENCING ADJUSTMENT TO NEW ROLE
A. Change in metabolism
   1. tremendous drop in hormonal levels of estrogen and progesterone
B. New sense of responsibility may be influenced by
   1. maturity of new parents
   2. fear of failure to measure up to ideal parental role
   3. lack of knowledge of newborn
   4. financial worries
   5. marital relationships
C. Attention diverted from mother to baby
D. Development of maternal instinct and bonding may be delayed
   1. analgesia and anesthesia that preclude experiencing the birth process and immediate separation of mother and child may be a factor in this delay
E. In out-of-wedlock mother, guilt, shame, and feelings of hostility toward child may be present and may influence the maternal-child relationship

II. STAGES IN ADJUSTMENT TO NEW ROLE
A. Immediately after delivery there is a need for sleep that, if interrupted, causes patient to experience sleep hunger
   1. after natural childbirth, patient may be so exhilarated, she may not be aware of her own exhaustion
B. Classification of phase of puerperal restoration according to Rubin (1961)
   1. taking-in phase
      a) lasts 2–3 days

b) mother passive and dependent
    (1) expresses own needs rather than baby's
        (a) in order for mother to meet baby's needs, her own needs must be met
        (b) needs physical care and attention to her emotional needs
    (2) verbalizes reactions to delivery so that experience can be integrated
c) symbiotic relationship ends and child should begin to be recognized as an individual
2. taking-hold phase
    a) third to tenth day
    b) mother strives for independence and autonomy; she wants to care for herself and her child
        (1) initiates action
        (2) strong anxiety element
            (a) unsure of mothering role
            (b) unsure of ability to physically care for child
        (3) develops maternal responsibilities and feelings
        (4) may experience rapid and frequent mood swings
            (a) may have ambivalent feelings about the baby
        (5) curious and interested in care of baby
    c) stage of maximum readiness for new learning
3. letting-go phase
    a) from 2 weeks postdelivery to several months
    b) infant is perceived as an individual separate from the mother
    c) both parents adjust to their new parental role
    d) ambivalent feelings about parenthood and about their readiness for their new role will be present
    e) parents attempt to adjust to changes in their lifestyle that parenting brings
C. Establishment of new role
    1. the birth of a baby may be viewed as a developmental crisis
        a) roles are reassigned
        b) new responsibilities added
        c) values reoriented
        d) needs are met in new ways
    2. LeMasters' study revealed that new parents have not been adequately prepared for new role and may have difficulties in adjustment (LeMasters, 1965)
        a) mother's relationship to partner changes
        b) father may feel isolation, economic pressure, dissatisfaction with paternal role

c) mother may feel fatigued and may have decrease in satisfaction due to confinement in home, loss of social contacts, burden of additional household duties, and guilt about not being a "better mother"
D. Maternal-child interaction
   1. immediately after delivery the mother may not have grasped the reality of the birth
   2. the mother will react to the infant according to her perceptions of its needs. This perception will be based on the child's
      a) sex
      b) activity level
      c) appearance
      d) size
   3. the first interaction between mother and infant is one of exploration and examination
      a) a primipara will usually explore with hand and fingers
      b) a multipara will usually enfold the infant using her arms as extensions of her body
   4. initial behavior is usually concerned with ability to function in mothering role
      a) a primipara in her first contact may show signs of tension
         (1) flushed face
         (2) excessive perspiration
         (3) body rigid
         (4) may be anxious for baby to be taken away
   5. maternal cues that indicate acceptance and claiming of infant as her own
      a) assigns cultural values regarding sex
      b) identifies resemblance of baby to family members
      c) calls baby by name
      d) touching and fondling child
      e) assumes en face position with baby
   6. an important factor in maternal-infant bonding and paternal-infant bonding is the match between the expectations and the temperament of the parents and the behavior, temperament, and responses of the infant. When babies do not respond to the attempts of their parents to soothe, comfort, or play with them the parents may become anxious or may draw back from the relationship and bonding may be weakened. Reciprocity and synchronization of maternal-infant behavior are crucial factors
E. Paternal-child interaction
   1. may exhibit fear and anxiety about handling baby
   2. may show positive reactions similar to mother

III. POSTPARTAL BLUES

A. Incidence may be decreasing due to
   1. better obstetrical care
   2. better preparation for new role
   3. allowance for verbalization of feelings
B. Timing and severity of symptoms vary with the individual
   1. usually comes on within 2 weeks of childbirth and ends within 3 months
C. Manifestations
   1. loss of energy
   2. crying
   3. anxiety, fear, and confusion
   4. insomnia (may indicate more serious emotional upset)
   5. concern about her body
   6. misinterpretation of actions and words of others, primarily her partner
   7. extreme control
      a) mother insists everything is okay
D. Theories of etiology
   1. stress of labor and birth
   2. hormonal changes
      a) placental secretion ceases
      b) lactation begins
      c) new research shows an association between postpartal blues and high levels of estrogen, low levels of progesterone, and abnormal levels of other hormones postpartally
   3. immaturity
   4. family, social, and economic problems
   5. need for rest ignored
      a) overstimulation leads to lack of sleep and exhaustion that may bring about feelings of depression
E. Mother may verbalize
   1. a sensation of feeling unprotected
   2. a feeling of emptiness
      a) removal of baby may be compared to amputation

REFERENCES

LeMasters, E.E. (1965). Parenthood as a crisis. In H.J. Parad (Ed.), *Crisis intervention: Selected readings* (pp. 200–205). New York: Family Association of America.

Rubin, R. (1961, November). "Basic Maternal Behavior." *Nursing Outlook*, pp. 683–685.

Chapter 16

Nursing Care During Puerperium

I. NURSING GOALS

A. The major goals of nursing during the puerperium are to
   1. assist in maternal restoration of physiological and psychological status
   2. assist parents in adjusting to and accepting new roles
   3. assist in parent-child bonding so that an adequate parent-child relationship can be formed

II. ASSESSMENT AND INTERVENTION

A. Assessment and intervention are based on the physiological and psychological changes occurring during the puerperium
   1. new practices in maternity that allow for early discharge after 24 hours influence the type of care needed by maternity patients
   2. in most cases the observations and assessment by the nurse of postpartum regeneration and recovery must be taken over by the new mother. Teaching the new mother to take over this responsibility must be accomplished during the short period of time that the mother is in the hospital. This task is further complicated by the fact that the mother is in the taking-in phase at this time and may not be maximally receptive to the teaching
   3. in cases where the nurse feels that further nursing support is needed in an early discharge mother, a referral to a home health care agency should be made

B. Assessment and intervention for restoration of physiological status
   1. uterine involution
      a) assessment

(1) check fundus daily for position and tone; mild tenderness is felt during palpation
   (a) instruct mother to relax abdominal muscles during palpation of the fundus to reduce possible discomfort during the procedure
   (b) palpate the uterus by placing the side of one hand on top of and cupped slightly behind the top of the fundus, and placing the other hand on the bottom of the uterus suprapubically with very slight pressure to provide support
   (c) before palpating the fundus, observe to see if there is a full bladder (bladder bulge over the symphysis pubis). Bladder should be emptied before palpation or massage of fundus
   (d) when assessing fundal tone and position, consider the influence of infant size, length of labor, hydramnios, and multiple births. Fundus of a multipara will usually be larger and higher than a primipara
   (e) first day postpartum fundus should be at or below the umbilicus at midline of abdomen
   (f) fundus continues to descend each day until it can no longer be palpated (usually by the tenth day); there should be no tenderness
      1. involution will be slower in multiparas
      2. uterus usually descends about 1 cm/day; at 2–3 days postpartum it is about 2–3 finger breadths below umbilicus
   (g) fundus should remain firm and well contracted at all times
   (h) bladder distention will inhibit involution and may push fundus to the side of the abdomen
(2) check color, amount, and odor of lochia
   (a) should proceed from bright red to white discharge
(3) afterpains primarily in multiparas or may occur in primiparas if blood clots form
   (a) decreased uterine muscle tone makes it difficult to maintain a state of tonic contraction. When uterus relaxes slightly at intervals, strong contractions occur to return uterus to well-contracted state
   (b) usually subside within 48 hours
   (c) the uterus contracts when the mother sees or hears her infant and after oxytocic drugs are administered

b) nursing intervention
  (1) if relaxation occurs, massage is done to return uterus to well-contracted state
    (a) massage should be gentle and should express any blood clots
      1. to express blood clots, apply pressure with one hand to fundus with equal pressure applied to bottom of uterus above symphysis pubis; apply pressure for a few seconds with periods of rest between intervals until blood clot has been expressed
      2. if fundus is boggy, massage gently with a circular motion on top and slightly in back of top of uterus until fundus contracts firmly. Always support bottom of uterus with one hand during massage
    (b) overstimulation of uterus through massage should be avoided as it may lead to muscle fatigue and relaxation of the uterus
    (c) if massage is ineffective, physician should be notified
  (2) oxytocics are given to assist involution
  (3) breast feeding assists involution
  (4) medication to relieve pain is given when necessary for afterpains
    (a) abdominal breathing exercises may be beneficial
    (b) explanation of causes of pain and reassurance as to transient nature of pain are helpful
  (5) in early discharge mother is taught how to palpate fundus and how to recognize signs of abnormal involution that must be reported to physician
  (6) mother is taught to recognize the normal progression of lochia
    (a) lochia rubra: dark red containing placental debris and clots; from 1–24 hours postpartum; moderate with no abnormal odor. Rubra occurs for 2 to 3 days in diminishing amounts. Foul odor, excessive amount, or bright red color are abnormal signs
    (b) lochia serosa: pinkish-brown, lasts 4–10 days. If it returns to bright red lochia in a heavy flow after this time then it may signal postpartum hemorrhage, possibly from retained placenta. Most common between days 5–15. If minimal amount of bleeding, may be delayed healing of site from too little rest. Should be reported to physician.

(c) lochia alba: yellowish-white at day 10; may last 6 weeks. If it returns to lochia rubra, treat as above.
2. post partum chill
    a) may occur immediately after delivery
    b) not followed by fever
    c) theories of etiology
        (1) nervous reaction combined with exhaustion following birth
        (2) disequilibrium between internal and external temperatures caused by
            (a) perspiration during labor
            (b) loss of body fluids
            (c) change of intra-abdominal pressure
    d) nursing intervention
        (1) keep patient warm
        (2) reassure
3. sleep
    a) immediately postpartum, the new mother needs deep, long, uninterrupted sleep
        (1) patient should be placed in a quiet, darkened room
        (2) patient should be disturbed as little as possible
    b) subsequent sleep and rest patterns should be monitored through the assessment of
        (1) mother's statements
        (2) nurses' observations
    c) hindrances to sleep
        (1) perineal soreness
        (2) hemorrhoids
        (3) afterpains
        (4) anxiety
    d) nursing intervention
        (1) relieve any discomforts
        (2) allow mother to verbalize anxieties
        (3) reduce environmental noise during night
        (4) plan nursing care to allow for daytime rest period and early morning sleep
        (5) may provide analgesia and sedatives when other comfort measures fail
4. perineal healing
    a) etiology of trauma
        (1) lacerations
        (2) suturing
        (3) hemorrhoids

(4) hematomas
b) assessment of the perineal area is done daily by visual inspection; check for
    (1) degree of inflammation and signs of infection
    (2) swelling
    (3) discoloration
    (4) discharge around area of trauma
    (5) abnormal odors
    (6) patient's subjective feelings of discomfort
    (7) healing process
c) nursing intervention
    (1) sitz bath (only with physician's orders)
    (2) infrared lamp (only with physician's orders)
    (3) if there is a hematoma, ice pack offers some relief; if applied early may prevent hematoma
    (4) witch hazel compresses
    (5) stool softeners to aid in preventing discomfort from bowel movement
    (6) elevate pelvis on pillow to reduce vasocongestion in varicosities of vulva or hemorrhoids
    (7) suppositories to relieve discomforts of hemorrhoids (only with physician's orders)
    (8) rubber ring to relieve pressure on perineal area
    (9) exercise to increase blood circulation to perineal area and increase muscle tone
        (a) Kegel contractions: contract and relax muscles alternately as if starting and stopping urinary flow; can be done in any position and should be repeated frequently
    (10) personal hygiene
        (a) mother is usually bathed and given perineal care soon after delivery
        (b) perineal care is done by nurse and is taught to patient when she is capable of assuming responsibility
            1. purpose is to prevent infection, cleanse area, and provide soothing warmth
            2. cleansing during perineal care should be based on principles of asepsis
5. re-establishment of bladder function
   a) assessment
       (1) distended bladder is recognized by bulge under uterus and displacement of uterus upward and laterally

            (2) measure first voiding to rule out retention with overflow (over 100 cc)
            (3) continuous observation of intake and output
            (4) check for signs of infection
                (a) pain or burning on voiding
            (5) check concentration of urinary output by assessing color, quantity, and odor
        b) nursing intervention
            (1) inability to void is a common problem
                (a) etiology
                    1. long labor and/or traumatic delivery
                    2. swelling of perineal area around urethra
                    3. poor bladder tone due to pressure
                    4. reflex spasm of bladder sphincter due to pain
                    5. fatigue
                    6. diminished sensitivity due to drugs and anesthesia
                    7. emotional factors (fear of letting go)
            (2) encourage patient to void by usual methods frequently
            (3) maintain adequate fluid intake
            (4) catheterize if indicated as ordered
                (a) with extreme bladder distention (over 1000 cc), do not completely empty bladder to prevent possibility of shock
            (5) record amount of first voiding
    6. re-establishment of bowel function
        a) assessment
            (1) may be constipated
                (a) caused by decreased intra-abdominal pressure and relaxation of abdominal muscles
                (b) mother may be afraid to have bowel movement because of
                    1. pain from soreness of perineal area
                    2. fear of rupturing sutures
        b) nursing intervention
            (1) encourage mother to take the time to have first bowel movement
            (2) support perineal area with pad while bearing down
            (3) encourage fluid and high fiber intake
            (4) use cathartics and enemas as necessary
    7. breasts
        a) assessment
            (1) whether mother will breast feed
            (2) engorgement

Nursing Care During Puerperium 269

-
  -
    - (3) nipple inversion or cracking
    - (4) presence of colostrum
    - (5) signs of inflammation
      - (a) heat
      - (b) redness
      - (c) pain
  - b) nursing intervention
    - (1) ice packs to relieve engorgement
    - (2) soothing ointments to prevent nipple cracking
    - (3) breasts should be supported with well-fitting bra
      - (a) nipple at midline
      - (b) no downward or upward pressure on breasts
      - (c) if engorgement is so severe that baby cannot feed, milk should be manually expressed
    - (4) nipples should be cleansed without soap
    - (5) any sign of infection or inflammation should be reported to physician
8. abdomen
   - a) assessment
     - (1) mother should raise her head and shoulders while lying flat in bed with legs extended
     - (2) nurse can then assess the width of the diastasis recti (separation of muscles at middle of abdomen)
   - b) nursing intervention
     - (1) chin-raising postpartum exercise will help strengthen abdominal muscles
       - (a) woman lies on back and slowly raises head and tries to put chin on her chest. Head is raised to a count of four and lowered to count of four. Both head and shoulders may be raised as progress is made in the exercise
9. vital signs
   - a) assessment
     - (1) temperature: may rise slightly after delivery due to dehydration
       - (a) any temperature of 100.4°F for 2 successive days after the first postpartum day may be an untoward symptom. Early discharge mother should continue to monitor temperature
     - (2) pulse
       - (a) bradycardia may occur, usually between 60 and 70
         1. caused by decreased cardiac output

2. hydremia
            (b) tachycardia
                1. may be caused by difficult labor
                2. may indicate hemorrhage, shock, or illness
        (3) blood pressure
            (a) should remain normal
            (b) hypotension may occur after saddle block
            (c) if elevated, may be sign of complications
            (d) hypertension may be a sign of pre-eclampsia
            (e) moderate elevation of blood pressure may occur from use of ergotrate or excitement
    b) nursing intervention
        (1) frequent monitoring of all vital signs immediately after delivery
        (2) routine observation during subsequent period
        (3) careful observation will help prevent or detect complications
10. nutrition
    a) assessment
        (1) weight loss after delivery
        (2) intake of nutrients
            (a) increased need for protein and vitamins
                1. aid in repair of tissue and healing process
            (b) increased iron intake
                1. aid in restoring blood to its normal state
        (3) postanesthesia nausea and vomiting
        (4) nutritional status
            (a) skin color and turgor
            (b) overweight or underweight
            (c) excessive fatigue
            (d) signs of vitamin deficiencies
            (e) hemoglobin and hematocrit lab reports
        (5) cultural dietary patterns
        (6) knowledge of nutrition
        (7) usual eating habits
        (8) economic resources to meet nutritional needs
    b) nursing intervention
        (1) immediately after delivery
            (a) if nausea occurs
                1. prevent aspiration
                2. limit fluid intake
                3. provide medications as ordered

            4. do mouth care
            5. provide ice chips to relieve thirst
         (b) monitor parenteral fluid intake
      (2) provide a diet that is nutritionally adequate and meets the cultural patterns and eating habits of the client
      (3) teach nutrition as indicated by assessment
      (4) assist in budgetary planning to meet nutritional needs
      (5) if anemia is present
         (a) conserve patient energy
         (b) provide food high in iron
         (c) iron and vitamin supplements may be ordered
      (6) do nutritional counseling for obesity or underweight
   11. ambulation is now permitted within an hour after delivery
      a) observe for signs of weakness or fainting
C. Assessment and intervention relating to mothering role
   1. assessment
      a) reaction to labor and delivery
         (1) excitement or depression
         (2) anger and hostility
         (3) fears
         (4) change in partners' relationship
         (5) mother-child interaction
      b) puerperal restoration
         (1) dependency needs
         (2) learning needs
            (a) knowledge of infant and child care
            (b) cultural values relating to childrearing
               1. father's role
            (c) economic factors
            (d) community resources
            (e) parents' level of ability to understand and assimilate instruction
         (3) initiative
         (4) assumption of mothering role
         (5) readiness for discharge
            (a) available assistance in the home for new mother and child
            (b) plans for child care
         (6) parental adjustment to new role
            (a) identify maladjustment cues
               1. is unhappy with sex or appearance of baby
               2. does not talk about baby

3. does not touch or look at baby
4. calls baby "it"
2. intervention
   a) taking-in process: 2–3 days
      (1) allow patient to be dependent
      (2) do not rush mother into taking over responsibility for own care and care of baby
      (3) encourage verbalization of delivery experience and of fears and anxieties
      (4) if early discharge, encourage parents to get help for a few days so that mother may meet her own needs
   b) taking-hold phase: 4–14 days
      (1) constant reassurance and encouragement in mothering role
      (2) avoid fatigue in care of baby
      (3) mother assumes initiative in care of self and baby
      (4) optimum time for instruction by home care agency nurse
   c) going home
      (1) instruction given for care of self
         (a) postpartal examination
         (b) personal hygiene
         (c) sexual activity
         (d) information regarding re-establishment of menstrual cycle and fertility
         (e) importance of avoiding fatigue and muscle strain
      (2) instruction relating to child care
         (a) importance of continuing health care and supervision
         (b) physical care of infant
         (c) information regarding normal growth and development
         (d) safety precautions
         (e) feeding techniques
   d) parental-child bonding
      (1) parental feelings may take time to develop after the birth of the first child
      (2) the work of Klaus and Kennell (1976) on maternal-infant bonding emphasizes the importance of providing opportunities immediately after birth for the development of bonding or attachment behaviors between parents and baby
      (3) early and prolonged contact between parents and baby has a positive effect on parent-infant bonding
      (4) being present at the birth of their baby increases attachment behavior

(5) parents have common ways of responding to their new babies
  (a) mothers usually touch and fondle their infants in the en face position, making eye contact with them and talking to them
  (b) the response of the infant with body or eye movements to the mother's attachment behavior strengthens the bonding process
  (c) fathers who handle their infants with close eye and skin contact soon after the birth also strengthen parental attachment behaviors
  (d) parents who are responding to the recent loss of another child or loved person may have difficulty with early bonding
  (e) parents who have a high level of anxiety over their infants right after birth may continue to be anxious as the child grows and develops
  (f) some parents take longer to develop bonding behaviors than others, even with early contact
  (g) a high state of alertness in mother and infant increases attachment behaviors immediately after birth
(6) early parental bonding may be a factor in the prevention of child abuse
(7) new parents should be informed of the normality of lack of immediate strong feelings toward the child
(8) facilitation of parental bonding can be accomplished by
  (a) allow mother to examine and touch her undressed child
  (b) following delivery encourage parents to spend time in close contact with the newborn; immediate breast feeding is encouraged
    1. if mother has been anesthesized, safety precautions must be observed
  (c) allow mother to verbalize her concerns and questions
  (d) point out positive factors about baby's adjustment and progress
  (e) provide positive reinforcement of mother's mothering activities
  (f) primiparas need detailed and repetitive instruction about child care activities. All mothers need support and encouragement
  (g) rooming-in provides an optimum situation for bonding

   (h) stay with mother during feeding time if anxiety is present
   (i) provide father with an opportunity to verbalize feelings about child and assist him in carrying out child care activities. Give positive reinforcement
   (j) discuss with parents the theories of reciprocity and help them become aware of the baby's temperament and needs. Help them avoid over- and understimulation of child and show them various methods of responding to a child's cry
 e) parents should be counseled about the possibility of postpartal blues occurring after discharge from hospital
  (1) the transitory nature of phenomenon should be explained
  (2) knowledge of the possibility of having ambivalent feelings about the baby should be explained to parents to prevent guilt feelings from occurring
  (3) husband and family should be aware of the importance of providing assistance to the mother to prevent feelings of helplessness and overwhelming responsibility
  (4) support system should be developed: friends, relatives, babysitter
  (5) mother should get plenty of rest and sleep
  (6) recovery from childbirth should not be rushed
  (7) start an exercise program such as walking
 f) it is important for new mothers to resolve and integrate some of the disappointments or unexpected events of the delivery experience in order to move forward in their new role
  (1) women who failed to have a natural childbirth or who had to have a cesarean may feel that they have failed to live up to their own and their friends' expectations
  (2) women must reconcile the real attributes of their babies in terms of appearance, sex, temperament, and health with their fantasies
  (3) women must come to terms with the real state of their body image and the imagined state of returning to their prepregnant state
  (4) women who are unskilled and fearful of handling the baby must face up to this reality and reach out for help
  (5) the nurse can greatly assist in these tasks by allowing free verbalization of all of the above problems and by helping women to work through these feelings. They must be re-

assured that most women experience many of these feelings (Mercer, 1981)
- g) sexuality counseling
  - (1) some women experience sexual pleasure during birthing and during breast feeding. They may be disturbed by these feelings and think that they are abnormal. It is important for the nurse to assure them that these are common experiences
  - (2) following delivery sexual activity may decrease because of fatigue, overinvolvement with the infant, fear of pain, poor vaginal lubrication, and fear of pregnancy. The father may feel that his wife has withdrawn from him and transferred her interest to the infant. It is important for the nurse to advise parents that open communication and sharing of fears and needs are important in maintaining a good sexual relationship following delivery

III. DRUGS USED DURING POSTPARTAL PERIOD

A. Oxytocic drugs are usually given immediately after delivery by injection or IV and for several days postpartum. They are given orally to assist in involution by stimulating uterine contractions
  1. ergonovine maleate (Ergotrate): 1/320 g
  2. methylergonovine maleate (Methergine): a synthetic form of Ergotrate; dosage is usually 1/320 g
  3. drugs may increase intensity of afterpains and also may elevate blood pressure

B. Lactation suppressants inhibit pituitary from secreting prolactin by raising estrogen blood level. All antilactogenic drugs should be given as soon as possible after delivery
  1. Deladumone is a long-acting estrogen-androgen combination that is given immediately after delivery by injection; only one dose is needed
  2. stilbestrol and diethylstilbestrol are examples of synthetic estrogens that are administered by mouth as soon after delivery as possible. The usual dosage is 5 mg. Headache, vomiting, and dizziness are rare side effects

C. Analgesics are used as necessary to ease the discomfort of afterpains or perineal soreness. Darvon is most commonly used and is usually given in 32- or 65-mg doses and administered orally

D. Many sedative preparations have been used to assist the patient in

sleeping. Sedatives should be avoided because of their adverse effect on the sleep cycle
E. Antibiotics may be prescribed to control any infection that may occur. Dosage and preparation used vary with organism responsible for infection
F. In breast-feeding mothers, medications should be used with extreme caution as they enter the milk supply

REFERENCES

Klaus, M.H., & Kennel, J.H. (1976). *Maternal-infant bonding.* St. Louis: C.V. Mosby.

Mercer, R. (1981, September/October). The nurse and maternal tasks of early postpartum. *Maternal Child Nursing,* pp. 341–345.

Chapter 17

Breast Feeding

I. ANATOMY OF THE BREAST
   A. Composition
      1. internal
         a) glandular tissue
         b) fat
         c) each breast contains 15–20 lobes connected by fibrous tissues and fatty walls
            (1) lobes subdivided into lobules
            (2) lobules contain acini cells
               (a) milk secretion originates in acini cells
               (b) capillaries in acini cells filter essential elements needed for milk production from blood by osmosis
         d) duct structure
            (1) duct network carries milk from lobule to lobe to nipple
            (2) lactiferous sinuses and ducts form reservoirs for milk storage
               (a) located near nipple
      2. external
         a) covered by skin
         b) areola
            (1) surrounds nipple
            (2) color varies with skin tone
               (a) darkens with pregnancy
            (3) contains Montgomery glands: sebaceous glands that enlarge during pregnancy
   B. Nipple
      1. erectile tissue
      2. contains milk duct openings
   C. Size of breast does not affect lactation ability

II. PHYSIOLOGY

A. During pregnancy
1. rapid development of glandular tissue
   a) because of estrogen levels
2. glandular tissue becomes secreting cells
   a) because of progesterone levels
3. lactogenic hormone (prolactin) inhibited by estrogen and progesterone until after birth, thereby preventing milk production
4. colostrum production begins during second trimester of pregnancy

B. Establishment of lactation
1. decreased levels of estrogen and progesterone after delivery cause pituitary to secrete lactogenic hormone
2. colostrum secretion increases and provides adequate nourishment until milk production on the third day
   a) milk production may be preceded by engorgement lasting 24–48 hours

C. Mechanisms of breast feeding
1. sucking activates nerve impulses from nipple to spinal cord to pituitary gland
   a) anterior pituitary produces prolactin only if breasts are emptied
   b) posterior pituitary secretes oxytocin, causing "let-down" reflex, in which milk is ejected from ducts
      (1) oxytocin stimulated by sound of baby's cry or sucking
      (2) oxytocin inhibited by fright or stress
2. successful breast feeding depends on adequate production of prolactin and oxytocin
3. emotional factors significantly affect lactation by inhibiting hormone production

III. EFFECT OF LACTATION ON THE MOTHER

A. Physiological
1. increased stress on metabolic system
2. increased need for calcium and phosphate
   a) if intake is not adequate, calcium and phosphates will be drawn from mother's skeletal system, weakening her bones
   b) usually a large amount of calcium and phosphate is stored in mother's bones so only a poorly nourished mother will have difficulty
3. increase of dental cavities not related to calcium deficiency during lactation, but rather to enhanced bacterial growth in mouth

4. involution is assisted
5. decreased incidence of breast cancer
6. engorgement less painful
B. Psychological
1. number of mothers who breast feed is related to social and cultural factors
   a) success or failure in breast feeding is related to emotional factors and attitudes
   b) there has been a steady increase in the number of breast-feeding mothers since the middle 1960s
2. nursing is a pleasurable experience if the mother is ready and accepting
3. aversion to breast feeding can be caused by
   a) sexual inhibitions
   b) dislike of nudity
   c) fear of loss of figure
   d) unpleasant previous breast-feeding experiences
   e) difficult or unpleasant labor
   f) lack of support and instruction by health personnel
   g) leakage of breasts
   h) lack of freedom
4. advantages of breast feeding
   a) faster development of maternal feeling
   b) economical
   c) time-saving (no preparation of formula)
   d) feeling of fulfillment of completion of maternal cycle

IV. BENEFITS OF BREAST FEEDING TO THE NEWBORN
A. Each 100 ml of milk contains 75 kcal
1. fat makes up largest caloric component
2. lactose provides main CHO source; metabolizes to glucose and galactose for energy
   a) promotes growth of lactobacilli that act to control growth of harmful bacteria in intestine
   b) lactose enhances absorption of calcium needed to prevent rickets
3. protein: amino acids—cystine and taurine—found in high levels in human milk and low levels in cow's milk may stimulate tissue and brain growth
4. proteins found in abundance in human milk are more easily digested than casein proteins that are higher in cow's milk

- B. Renal solute load on kidney of breast-fed infant is much lower than in the formula-fed infant
- C. Breast milk contains many anti-infective ingredients, such as interferon, leukocytes, immunoglobulins
- D. Breast milk does not contain food antigens that are present in cow's milk, thereby minimizing potential allergies

V. IMPLICATIONS FOR NURSING PROCESS
- A. Need for instruction, support, and encouragement
- B. Nurses' attitudes may affect outcome
- C. Medications to assist lactation
    1. Syntocinon: synthetic oxytocin administered by nasal spray to activate let-down reflex
    2. any estrogen preparation is contraindicated
- D. Care of breasts
    1. support with bra
        a) nipple at midline
        b) no pressure exerted downward or upward
        c) garment should give good support, but not be too tight
    2. washing of breasts daily, no soap on nipples
    3. careful inspection of nipples for cracks or soreness
    4. observation of breasts for mastitis
    5. pads in bras to absorb leakage
    6. correct nipple position: the baby closes jaws on areola behind the nipple. Tongue must cup around nipple to cradle it. Tip of tongue should press up, causing nipple to be compressed against roof of baby's mouth and then a rippling action of tongue should occur followed by swallowing. Incorrect positioning and nipple confusion may cause problems in sucking
        a) correct positioning includes turning the whole baby toward mother's body with abdomen against mother's chest wall and head against the breast. Baby's head should be in crook of mother's elbow, with her hand holding bottom or legs of child. Grasp breast with other hand; take areola between thumb and forefinger and support rest of breast with other fingers. Do not depress breast tissue with thumb to free baby's nose because this may cause nipple to retract. There is new information that baby can free a breathing passage by itself. Slide thumb up breast to 2 inches above base of nipple and pull gently upward on skin, making the nipple easier for baby to grasp. To insert nipple, tickle baby's lower lip and insert nipple

as far as it will go into mouth when baby opens its lips in response to the tickling
7. prevention of nipple damage
   a) new research indicates that the practice of limiting nursing time during initial breast feedings does not prevent nipple soreness. Mothers should be instructed to use both breasts and to allow baby to feed until it is satisfied to stimulate the supply/demand response. The mother should be careful that pressure is not placed on one part of the areola and that as much of the areola as possible is placed into the baby's mouth
   b) baby should be put to breast immediately after delivery and at frequent intervals thereafter whenever the baby is hungry
   c) nipple damage may occur from the following conditions:
      (1) short frenulum may cause baby to retract tongue. To decrease nipple damage put downward pressure on baby's chin during nursing; will cause red lines on sides of nipple
      (2) if baby sucks too strongly the end of nipple may be very painful. To relieve pain, mother should pull down on baby's jaw with finger during sucking
      (3) chewed, macerated nipple may be caused by baby sucking its tongue, preventing nipple from entering mouth far enough. Suck training is done by inserting a finger (nail down) into baby's mouth, gently rubbing the hard palate, and then rubbing the soft palate with finger, pad down and nail up. Press down and forward with finger tip. Alternately, rub hard palate with down and forward pressure. Gums should be massaged from outside before inserting finger
      (4) cracked nipples may be caused by baby pulling up back portion of tongue. Suck training may be used to relieve condition
      (5) if nipple points down, baby will grasp it incorrectly; may cause horizontal red line on nipple. Mother should press down on top of breast with thumb to help nipple enter mouth straight
      (6) if mother presses with finger on top of areola she may cause a lateral laceration on top of nipple. Change in position of finger will prevent this laceration
      (7) nipple confusion occurs when a breast-fed baby has also been fed from a rubber nipple. Bottle-fed babies do not have to use their jaws to suck and may thrust their tongue forward to shut off the flow of milk from a rubber nipple

that drips milk even when they stop sucking. When these babies are placed back on the breast their tongue thrusting may push the mother's nipple out of their mouths and they will not nurse properly. This may cause the milk supply to decrease. To prevent this from occurring babies who must have a relief bottle should be fed with a special nipple (made by Nuk-Sauger) that simulates breast feeding, or the nipple should have holes in it that are small enough to prevent dripping when the baby is not actively sucking. A preemie nipple can be used or holes made with a needle in a blind nipple. When the bottle is held upside down milk should not leak out of it. It is best not to use any supplementary bottles for the first few months if possible. To break a baby of nipple confusion the baby can be fed with an eye-dropper until it responds to the breast again (usually within 24 hours)
- (8) the wearing of breast shields between feedings can help prevent nipple damage. The pressure on the nipples keeps them soft and protruberant, which helps mothers with inverted nipples and with engorgement. Nipple shields should not be used as they increase nipple soreness
- (9) babies who are lazy suckers should be switched from side to side and burped between switching of breasts (Scott, 1985)

8. prevention of engorgement
    a) if breast is not completely emptied, manual expression of remainder of milk should be used to relieve engorgement. It can also be used to provide a relief bottle for the nursing mother once the milk supply is well established
        - (1) after washing hands, mother cups breast in her hand, places thumb and forefinger together behind nipple, and applies pressure toward chest wall
        - (2) pressing and releasing should be done rhythmically to release milk flow
        - (3) milk should be directed into a container
9. when releasing infant from breast, break vacuum around nipple by insertion of finger between baby's mouth and breast
10. air drying after feeding
11. use of vitamin or lanolin ointment

E. Maintaining milk supply
   1. do not feed baby supplementary bottles during early period of lactation until milk is well established

2. alternate breasts for each feeding to allow complete emptying after milk supply is established
3. if baby fails to empty breast, teach mother manual expression of milk
4. feed baby on demand schedule
F. Mother assisted to find most comfortable feeding position
G. Nutrition
1. increase caloric intake calories daily according to individual need
2. protein increased to 20 g daily
3. increased intake of calcium, iron, and vitamins A, C, and D
4. increased fluid intake
5. foods to be avoided
   a) foods causing allergic reactions in infants, such as chocolate, etc.
   b) foods causing gaseous reactions in infants

VI. CONTRAINDICATIONS TO BREAST FEEDING
A. Chronic debilitating diseases
B. Communicable diseases

VII. BREAST FEEDING AND DRUGS
A. The following factors should be considered when women who are breastfeeding must take drugs
   1. although most drugs do appear in breast milk their levels are usually not over 1–2% of the maternal dose
   2. it is usually safe to breast feed if the milk/plasma ratio of drug and active metabolites is less than 1:1
   3. alkaline drugs pass more easily into breast milk than acidic drugs
   4. lipid drugs pass more readily into breast milk, especially during the first and second weeks postpartum
   5. infant drug plasma levels depend upon the ablty of the infant to absorb the drug from its GI tract and its ability to detoxify and excrete the drug
B. The following drugs are contraindicated during breastfeeding:
   1. anticholinergics
   2. chloramphenicol
   3. cytoxic drugs
   4. sex hormones
   5. diuretics
   6. ergot alkaloids

    7. gold salts
    8. immunosuppressives
    9. iodides
    10. stimulant laxatives
    11. radioactive drugs
    12. thioracil
    13. heroin
    14. marijuana
C. Drugs that may be contraindicated and need further research:
    1. benzodiazepines
    2. cimetidine
    3. long-term corticosteroids
    4. indomethacin
    5. lithium
    6. metronidazole
    7. oral contraceptives
D. With some of these drugs, temporary weaning and feeding of baby with frozen previously stored milk may be possible
E. In any case of drug taking the mother must ask if this drug is really necessary and whether another drug that is safer can be given instead (Nice, 1986)
F. Toxic substances from air and water pollution are found in breast milk. Dioxin, PCBs, and DDT are all found in human milk at rates higher than found in cow's milk. No clinical effects on infants have been found so far but long-term studies are needed. It is believed that infant fat stores dioxin and prevents it from reaching the organs where it can cause health problems. The dioxin is diluted in the baby's body as it grows rapidly in the early months. Dioxin causes cancer in laboratory animals, but its effects on humans are unknown

---

REFERENCES

Nice, F. J. (1986, April). Breastfeeding and medications: The pharmacist's role. *Pharmacy Times*, pp. 122–134.

Scott, J. (1985). Identifying and remediating sucking disorders in breastfeeding infants. In Happ, B., Odum, M., & Panke, C. (Eds.). *Breastfeeding and Women Today Conference Proceedings* (pp. 85–87). NCEMCH, Washington, D.C.

Chapter 18

Complications of the Postpartum Period

I. POSTPARTUM HEMORRHAGE
A. Definition
  1. bleeding from birth canal in excess of 500 ml
  2. delayed postpartum hemorrhage may occur up to 2 weeks after delivery
     a) breast feeding decreases incidence
B. Normal blood loss during and after delivery is 50–300 ml
C. Hemorrhaging occurs in 5% of deliveries
D. Etiology
  1. uterine atony (90% of cases)
  2. vaginal and cervical lacerations
  3. retention of placental fragments, clotting defects
  4. low or absent fibrinogen in blood
  5. distention of bladder
E. Predisposing factors
  1. controllable causes
     a) operative deliveries
        (1) forceps
        (2) injuries
     b) deep anesthesia
        (1) relaxation of abdominal muscles
     c) prolonged labor and maternal exhaustion

- d) mismanagement of third stage of labor
    - (1) kneading and squeezing of uterus may cause incomplete placental separation
- e) internal podalic version: changing the fetal position by manual manipulation through vagina (rarely utilized in modern obstetrics)
2. predetermined and uncontrollable causes
    - a) overdistention of uterus
        - (1) multiple pregnancy
        - (2) hydramnios
        - (3) large-sized baby
            - (a) if baby weighs 3200 g or more
            - (b) 4000 g or more weight: one in two chance of bleeding
    - b) abruptio placenta
    - c) placenta previa
    - d) history of previous postpartum hemorrhage
    - e) blood dyscrasias

F. Symptoms
1. bleeding may be moderate, continuous, and steady
    - a) extent of blood loss may not be realized
    - b) vital signs may not immediately indicate the seriousness of blood loss
2. bleeding may be massive and intense
    - a) vital signs reflect amount of blood loss
        - (1) rapid and thready pulse
        - (2) pallor
        - (3) falling blood pressure
        - (4) chilliness
        - (5) dyspnea and air hunger
    - b) restlessness
    - c) disturbed vision
    - d) unconsciousness

G. Diagnosis
1. condition of fundus
    - a) boggy fundus may be indication of uterine atony
    - b) firm and contracted fundus rules out uterine atony, but indicates need for search in vaginal and cervical area for lacerations
2. bright red blood is usually due to lacerations
3. venous blood is usually from the uterus

4. blood should be checked for fibrinogen levels
   a) afibrinogenemia may be cause of hemorrhage
   b) afibrinogenemia may result from hemorrhage

H. Prognosis
  1. depends upon mother's health status before and during labor; if following conditions exist, prognosis is not as favorable
    a) anemia
    b) exhaustion from prolonged labor
    c) poor uterine muscle tone
    d) poor nutritional status

I. Treatment
  1. during third stage of labor
    a) if severe blood loss occurs before placental delivery
      (1) fundal pressure
        (a) no squeezing or kneading
      (2) manual removal of placenta
        (a) if placenta accreta is present, attempts to remove placenta manually may cause massive hemorrhage
  2. after third stage of labor
    a) uterine atony
      (1) oxytocin administered
      (2) bimanual uterine compression
      (3) fluid, blood, and fibrinogen replacement
      (4) hysterectomy if all else fails
    b) lacerations of cervix and vagina
      (1) repair
      (2) sulcus tear even if repaired is prone to hemorrhage
      (3) packing of vagina

J. Nursing care
  1. assessment for prevention
    a) careful monitoring of
      (1) vital signs
      (2) uterine tone
      (3) amount and character of bleeding
  2. intervention for prevention
    a) correct technique in use of uterine massage
      (1) avoid overstimulation
    b) oxytocics given as ordered
  3. assessment during hemorrhage
    a) save blood-stained linen to aid in determining amount of blood loss

           b) monitor vital signs
           c) observe fluid and electrolyte balance
           d) check for transfusion reactions
        4. intervention during hemorrhage
           a) maintain bladder tone when vaginal packing is used
              (1) encourage voiding
              (2) increase fluid intake
              (3) catheterize if necessary
           b) maintain strict asepsis because resistance to infection is lower
           c) encourage nutrition: added protein, iron and vitamin C
           d) encourage careful and progressive ambulation to prevent recurrence
           e) provide emotional support: vital during the crisis period

II. PUERPERAL INFECTION
    A. Definition
       1. any temperature of 100.4°F occurring in any 2 successive days in first 10 postpartum days, except for first 24 hours
    B. Factors in control of incidence
       1. aseptic obstetrical technique
       2. increased prenatal care
       3. general improvement in health status and nutrition
       4. improved management of labor and delivery
       5. use of antibiotics
    C. Causative organisms
       1. most common: anaerobic streptococcus
          a) normal flora of vagina are usually nonpathogenic
       2. beta-hemolytic streptococcus
       3. staphylococcus
          a) may have become resistant to antibiotics
       4. E. coli
       5. gonococcus
       6. B. Welchi: rare, but occurs in criminal abortions
          a) associated with high mortality rate
    D. Predisposing factors
       1. hemorrhage and trauma during delivery
       2. exhaustion
       3. retention of placenta
       4. pre-existing condition can cause normal flora of vagina to become pathogenic
          a) anemia

Complications of the Postpartum Period

      b) malnutrition
      c) debilitation
E.   Modes of infection
    1. droplet
    2. poor asepsis
    3. poor personal hygiene
    4. sexual relations after membranes rupture
    5. during vaginal examination, normal flora may be carried to uterus where they are pathogenic
F.   Types of infection
    1. local lesion of perineum, vagina, cervix, and endometrium
    2. local infection may extend through venous circulation to cause
      a) infectious thrombophlebitis
      b) septicemia
    3. local infection may extend through lymphatics to cause
      a) peritonitis: inflammation of the peritoneum
      b) parametritis: inflammation of the connective tissue surrounding the uterus
      c) salpingitis: inflammation of the fallopian tubes
G.   Symptoms, treatment, and prognosis
    1. infections of perineum, vulva, vagina, and cervix
      a) symptoms
        (1) redness
        (2) swelling
        (3) pain
        (4) sensation of heat
        (5) serous and/or purulent discharge
        (6) burning during urination
        (7) temperature usually below 101°F
      b) treatment
        (1) opening and draining of wound
        (2) local application of antiseptic
        (3) antibiotic therapy
        (4) wet compresses
        (5) sitz baths
        (6) heat lamp
      c) prognosis
        (1) good if treatment begins before spread upward
    2. endometritis
      a) symptoms
        (1) discharge may either be foul smelling or profuse, or lochia may be retained and discharge scant

                (2) temperature range: 101°F to 105°F
                    (a) chilling may accompany temperature rise
                (3) rapid pulse and respiration
                (4) uterus usually enlarged
                    (a) disturbed involution
                (5) tenderness over uterus
                (6) severe and prolonged afterpains
                (7) headache
                (8) insomnia
                (9) anorexia
                (10) suppressed milk secretion
            b) treatment
                (1) antibiotics
                (2) bedrest: semi-Fowler's position
                (3) supportive therapy
                (4) increased fluid intake
                (5) aseptic precautions
            c) prognosis
                (1) if localized, usually recovers in 10 days
        3. infectious thrombophlebitis
            a) occurs in uterine, ovarian, hypogastric, femoral, popliteal, and saphenous veins
            b) symptoms
                (1) severe chills
                (2) swings in temperature: 96° to 105°F
                (3) pain, tenderness, redness, or blanching; skin temperature may be hotter or colder to the touch over the vein site
                (4) deep veins: pain may be only visible symptom
            c) treatment
                (1) bedrest
                (2) antibiotics
                (3) hot soaks
                (4) anticoagulant therapy: heparin infusion
                (5) observation for occurrence of embolism
            d) prognosis
                (1) good if no embolism occurs
                (2) embolism may cause death if it blocks a vital organ
                (3) recovery may be prolonged
        4. peritonitis
            a) symptoms
                (1) chill
                (2) fever: 103°–105°F

(3) pulse: very rapid, weak, compressible
(4) excruciating pain
(5) diarrhea and vomiting
(6) furred tongue
(7) restlessness
   b) treatment
      (1) antibiotics
      (2) supportive therapy
   c) prognosis
      (1) good to poor depending on early detection and treatment

H. Nursing care
1. assessment
   a) vital signs
   b) abnormal vaginal discharge (purulent)
      (1) foul odor
      (2) color
      (3) amount: scanty discharge may indicate an infectious process
   c) pain, redness, or swelling of the perineum
   d) sensation of heat
   e) discharge around suture line
   f) delayed involution
   g) pain and tenderness over uterus
   h) restlessness
   i) lethargy
   j) anorexia
2. intervention
   a) maintain asepsis to prevent infection
      (1) teach mother proper techniques for handwashing, breast care, and perineal care
   b) if infection occurs
      (1) continued and careful assessment
   c) institute isolation if necessary
      (1) if mother is isolated encouragement and support are essential
         (a) frequent reports on baby's condition
         (b) family should be taught aseptic techniques so they can visit
      (2) encourage mother to verbalize her feelings about her illness
      (3) maintain an increased fluid intake
      (4) encourage a high-protein diet

(5) provide frequent, uninterrupted rest periods
(6) give medication as ordered

III. NONINFECTIOUS THROMBOPHLEBITIS
A. Causes
  1. venous stasis
     a) early ambulation has led to a decrease in incidence
  2. clotting defects
  3. excess fibrinogen
B. Symptoms
  1. phlebothrombosis: spontaneous intravascular clotting with minimal inflammation
     a) may have no symptoms
     b) pain
     c) edema
     d) elevated TPR
     e) dorsiflexion of foot causes pain in calf: Homan's sign
     f) may lead to pulmonary embolism
  2. thrombophlebitis: inflammation of venous wall and clotting
     a) chill
     b) high fever
     c) pain
     d) edema
     e) bluish-white color
C. Treatment
  1. anticoagulants: may be continued at home for a period of time to prevent recurrence
  2. ace bandage to affected leg
  3. bedrest with leg elevated
  4. hot soaks
D. Prognosis
  1. good if no embolism occurs
  2. embolism may cause death
  3. recovery may be prolonged
E. Nursing care
  1. prevention
     a) early ambulation
     b) prevent stasis in leg circulation
        (1) proper use of stirrups
        (2) avoid prolonged sitting

2. assessment
    a) signs of inflammation and level of edema
    b) reaction to medication
        (1) evidence of increased bleeding
    c) reaction to immobility
    d) level of pain
    e) fear and anxiety level
3. intervention
    a) never massage as clot may become dislodged
    b) maintain bedrest with leg elevated
    c) maintain fluid intake
    d) apply hot soaks to affected leg as ordered
    e) encourage deep breathing exercise and frequent position change to prevent further complications
    f) provide encouragement and reassurance because hospitalization may be prolonged
    g) instruct to prevent recurrence
    h) allow verbalization of feelings

IV. BREAST DISORDERS

A. Mastitis: inflammation or infection of breast
    1. symptoms
        a) usually occurs between first to fourth week postpartum
        b) engorgement of breast
        c) chills
        d) rise in TPR
        e) breast: hard, red, and painful
    2. etiology
        a) infection through fissured nipples or organisms in lactiferous ducts
        b) most common organism: *Staphylococcus aureus*
        c) baby's throat source of infection
        d) may come from hospital personnel carriers
    3. prevention
        a) prevent cracked nipples through correct positioning of baby during feeding
        b) wash nipples with plain water to prevent milk encrustation
        c) do careful monitoring of hospital personnel for carriers
    4. treatment
        a) antibiotics
        b) hot soaks

5. prognosis
   a) usually good and clears rapidly
   b) may continue to breast feed during antibiotic treatment with synthetic penicillins or cephalosporins
B. Breast abscess: localized, walled off infection
   1. may need incision if no response to treatment
C. Nursing care
   1. assessment
      a) condition of breast
         (1) pain
         (2) redness
         (3) heat
         (4) engorgement
      b) condition of nipples
      c) vital signs
      d) nursing or nonnursing mother
   2. intervention
      a) support breast
      b) prevention and treatment of cracked nipples
      c) medications: antibiotics and analgesia as ordered
      d) hot soaks as ordered
      e) instruction regarding aseptic techniques to prevent spread of infection
      f) breast feeding may be continued with consent of physician
      g) additional support and reassurance will be necessary because breast feeding may be painful

V INFECTIONS COMMON DURING POSTPARTUM PERIOD

A. Urinary tract
   1. prevented by
      a) aseptic technique in catheterization
      b) not allowing bladder to become distended
      c) if retention occurs, urine is removed
      d) proper instruction regarding perineal care and handwashing
   2. dilation of ureters during pregnancy and trauma during delivery may predispose mother to urinary infections
   3. treated with antibiotics
B. Pneumonia
   1. incidence drastically lower since advent of early ambulation
   2. treated with antibiotics

Complications of the Postpartum Period

C. Prognosis of common infections depends on early detection and treatment and general health of mother; usually full recovery occurs
D. Isolation guidelines for postpartum patients who are infectious (Becker & Lagomarsino, 1987)
  1. all maternal and neonatal infectious conditions require careful handwashing by nurse and handwashing instructions for the parents
  2. AIDS
     a) gown and glove precautions advised
     b) breast feeding is contraindicated, but mother may visit nursery
     c) care should be taken by nurse to avoid puncture of skin with contaminated needles
     d) sodium hypochlorite solution used for any blood spills
     e) baby is bathed as soon after birth as possible
  3. chlamydia: genital, eyes of newborn, or pneumonia
     a) gloves should be worn when handling genital area or any secretions from infected areas
  4. diarrhea
     a) gown and gloves when handling feces
  5. gonorrhea
     a) gloves are used when in contact with any discharge from genitals
     b) may breast feed after 24 hours of antibiotic therapy
     c) baby is bathed as soon as possible after birth
  6. herpes simplex (active)
     a) gloves used when in contact with lesions
     b) if infant has signs of infection or a positive culture, gown and gloves used

VI HEMATOMAS

A. Symptoms
  1. severe local pain
  2. appearance of a tense, sensitive, and discolored tumor on the perineum
  3. if hematoma is in vagina and large, patient may not be able to void
B. Treatment
  1. ice packs as ordered
  2. small hematomas are left to be absorbed without treatment

296   QUICK REFERENCE TO MATERITY NURSING

        3. large hematomas may be incised and drained
           a) blood vessels are ligated if necessary
- C. Prognosis good; usually clears without sequelae if treated properly

VII POSTPARTUM ECLAMPSIA

- A. If patient has a prenatal history of pre-eclampsia
    1. careful observation of blood pressure and renal output
    2. immediate reporting of symptoms indicating increasing severity of condition
- B. Eclamptic convulsions may occur up to 1 week after delivery
    1. blood pressure should return to normal within 2 weeks
- C. Patient should be carefully followed for early detection of chronic hypertensive vascular disease

VIII. POSTPARTUM PSYCHOSIS

- A. Occurs early and may be seen immediately postpartum
- B. Any of the classified psychoses may occur during the postpartum period
- C. Theoretical causes
    1. involution of pituitary, which results in trophic hormone deficits: thyroid, adrenocortical, and gonadal
    2. childbirth may act as acute stressor that precipitates a psychosis in a person prone to mental illness
        a) unable to withstand stress of labor and delivery
        b) future fear of coping with baby or changing role
- D. Signs and symptoms
    1. insomnia
    2. confusion
    3. irritability
    4. apathy and depression
    5. delusions and hallucinations
    6. delirium
    7. inappropriate affect
- E. Nursing care
    1. assessment
        a) presence of any of the signs and symptoms of psychoses
        b) negative reaction to baby or father of child
- F. Implications for nursing process
    1. reduce stress of labor and delivery for all mothers
        a) instruction

b) natural childbirth if mother is adequately prepared and is capable
   c) father in labor room if prepared
   d) reassurance and emotional support
2. provide anticipatory guidance to aid in transition to new role
3. early detection of mothers who exhibit signs of problems with coping or adaptation to new role
4. assist mother in ventilation of feelings related to birth experience and reaction to infant
5. assist parents in development of a support system to assist new mother at home
6. provide care if symptoms occur
   a) observe carefully mothers who exhibit signs of disorder
   b) do not leave symptomatic patients alone or without careful supervision because of high incidence of suicide
   c) make immediate referral for psychiatric evaluation
   d) protect infant if safety is threatened
   e) give medication if ordered

REFERENCE

Becker, L., & Lagomarsino, W. (1987, November/December). Isolation guidelines for perinatal patients: Creating a new protocol. *Maternal Child Nursing,* pp. 400–404.

BIBLIOGRAPHY

Danner, S.C., & Cerutti, E.R. (1984). *Nursing your neurologically impaired baby.* Rochester, NY: Childbirth Graphics.

Danner, S.C. (1987, Fall). Teaching about breastfeeding. *Childbirth Educator,* pp. 26–33.

Jansson, P. (1985, May). Early postpartum discharge. *American Journal of Nursing,* pp. 547–550.

Johnson, J.M. (1972, September). Stillbirth—A personal experience. *American Journal of Nursing.*

Rubin, R. (1975). Maternity nursing stops too soon. *American Journal of Nursing.*

Sashara, A.A., et al. (1983). Pulmonary thromboembolism: Diagnosis and treatment. *Journal of the American Medical Association.*

Sumner, G., & Fritsch, J. (1977). Postnatal parental concerns: The first six weeks of life. *Journal of Obstetric and Gynecologic Nursing,* 6(3), 27–32.

Part V
Newborn

Chapter 19

Anatomy and Physiology of the Newborn

I. TRANSITION TO EXTRAUTERINE LIFE
   A. Predictable series of changes occurs in first 6 hours of life
      1. initial period of reactivity
         a) immediately after birth, lasts 15–30 minutes
         b) characterized by
            (1) rapid, fluctuating heartbeat
            (2) alertness
               (a) unmedicated normal newborn is highly responsive to stimuli
      2. period of relative inactivity
         a) from approximately 30 minutes to 2 hours after birth
            (1) thought to be a reaction to the extreme stimulation during labor, delivery, and birth
         b) heart and respiratory rates decrease
         c) spontaneous startles and twitches common
         d) infant responds to external stimuli with brief cry and goes back to sleep
      3. second period of reactivity
         a) from 2 to 6 hours after birth
            (1) may be brief or last several hours
         b) infant alert and responsive
         c) wide fluctuations in respiratory and cardiac rates recur
   B. Physiological and behavioral tasks that must be accomplished
      1. establish and maintain respiration, nutrition, and elimination, and temperature regulation
      2. establish patterns of arousal and sleep
      3. process, store and organize stimuli
      4. establish relationship to caregivers and environment

II. ANATOMY AND PHYSIOLOGY OF THE NEWBORN

A. Circulatory changes
1. oxygenation of blood; with first breath, pulmonary circulation changes
    a) pressure in right atrium increases because of respiratory circulation
    b) ductus arteriosus begins to close
        (1) if oxygenation not adequate, ductus has capacity to remain open or reopen
            (a) ductus arteriosus begins to atrophy and becomes ligamentum arteriosum; blood is pumped into pulmonary artery by right ventricle
                1. final closure: from 3 weeks to 4 months
    c) more blood is returned from lungs to left atrium, causing pressure to rise and foramen ovale to close
        (1) placental circulation ceases
        (2) ends of hypogastric arteries atrophy and become known as hypogastric ligaments
        (3) ductus venosus becomes occluded and becomes the ligamentum venosum
    d) umbilical vessels contract
        (1) umbilical vein becomes occluded and is known as ligamentum teres
2. heart rate
    a) tachycardia may be present during first 15–30 minutes of life
    b) between 120–140 bpm from 30 minutes to 2 hours
    c) stable from 2–6 hours
3. color
    a) acrocyanosis (cyanosis of extremities) may be present for first 24 hours
    b) circumoral pallor may be present during feeding or crying until foramen ovale is completely closed
    c) transition from brief cyanosis (15–30 minutes) to improved color and flush when crying (30 minutes—2 hours) to abrupt color changes (2–6 hours)

B. Initiation of respiration
1. pressure on the thorax during vertex delivery assists in expulsion of fluids from respiratory tract
    a) if baby delivered by cesarean section or is breech, fluid is not as readily expelled from lungs
        (1) the baby breathes rapidly; condition known as transient tachypnea

2. oxygen enters lungs and pulmonary alveoli expand
3. surfactant: lipid substance
   a) produced after the 24th week of gestation
   b) necessary to prevent alveolar collapse
4. infant is obligate nose breather
5. relatively large tongue
6. small glottis and trachea
7. lumen are narrower and can collapse easily
8. infant has increased amount of respiratory tract secretions
9. mucous membrane more susceptible to trauma
10. alveoli more sensitive to pressure changes
11. capillaries more friable and cannot expand and contract as easily as in adult
12. rib cage and respiratory muscles not well developed

C. Hematopoietic system
1. hemoglobin value higher than in adult
2. hypothrombinemia: prothrombin level is usually decreased after birth
   a) clotting time may be prolonged
   b) most acute between second and fifth day
   c) vitamin K is needed to produce prothrombin
      (1) spontaneous production of vitamin K is delayed until the normal flora of intestinal tract are established, usually within 1 week. Bacteria are needed to synthesize vitamin K in the intestine

D. Physiological resilience
1. neonate does not readily show overt signs and symptoms of abnormalities of body functioning, such as
   a) body temperature variations (high or low)
   b) blood chemistry changes, i.e., glucose
   c) changes in vital signs
2. disadvantages of physiological resilience
   a) conceals or minimizes physical signs of diagnostic value
   b) neonate does not react uniformly to drugs
3. advantages of physiological resilience
   a) when blood sugar drops for short periods the usual hypoglycemic reaction does not occur: can tolerate fluctuations in blood chemistry with less damage than adults
   b) can survive without breathing longer than an adult and with less brain damage

E. Negative balance
1. during first few days of life neonate is in state of negative balance
   a) postnatal weight loss

- b) loss of body fluids
- c) decreases in
  - (1) hemoglobin after second day
  - (2) nitrogen
  - (3) sodium
  - (4) chloride
2. positive balance is usually restored in 3–5 days

F. Heat regulation
1. unstable heat regulatory system due to immature hypothalamus
    - a) with exposure to cold, infant increases rate of metabolism without visible shivering
    - b) neonate uses a metabolic process called NST (nonshivering thermogenesis) to produce heat. This increased metabolism uses up energy and oxygen. The heat that the infant manufactures during NST comes from brown fat metabolism. Brown fat is found in infants, and when the available fat is used up the infant has difficulty maintaining body temperature when exposed to cold
2. body temperature greatly influenced by environmental temperature
    - a) when external factors cause the amount of heat lost to exceed the metabolic ability of the infant to maintain heat balance, body temperature drops
      - (1) factors contributing to imbalance in heat regulation
        - (a) air-conditioned delivery rooms
        - (b) immediate bathing of infant with prolonged and unnecessary body exposure
        - (c) exposure during newborn physical assessment
    - b) ability to maintain heat balance is also affected by the overheating of the environment
3. physiological basis for heat loss
    - a) less thermal insulation
    - b) blood vessels closer to surface
    - c) large body surface-to-weight ratio
    - d) immature vasomotor control
    - e) sweat glands do not function until about the fourth week of life
4. cold stress
    - a) imposes metabolic and physiological problems in all infants, regardless of gestational age or condition
      - (1) respiratory rate increased
      - (2) O_2 consumption and energy diverted from brain and cardiac function to thermogenesis
      - (3) increase in basal metabolic rate
        - (a) if protracted and severe, acidosis occurs

(4) if O_2 depleted, vasoconstriction occurs and jeopardizes pulmonary function
(5) increased levels of unbound bilirubin in circulation
G. Vital signs
1. temperature
a) axillary: 36.5–37°C (97.6°–98.6°F); should be taken until about 6 years of age
b) rectal: 35.5–37.5°C (96°–99.5°F)
(1) may be misleading; may not change with cold stress until metabolic activity decreases
c) becomes stable within 8–10 hours
(1) at birth slightly higher than mother's
(2) drops immediately after birth in adjustment to room temperature
(3) rises to normal in 8 hours
d) shivering mechanism undeveloped
e) between second and fourth day there may be a temperature rise due to dehydration
(1) any temperature of 100°F that persists for more than 24 hours must be checked
2. pulse
a) rapid
b) normal range: 120–150/min
c) irregular due to immature cardiac regulatory center in medulla
d) may be irregular for brief periods, especially after crying
3. respiration
a) irregular in depth, rate, and rhythm
b) normal range: 35–50/min
c) quiet
d) synchronous: diaphragm and abdominal muscles rise together
e) touching and stroking increase respiration and oxygen intake
f) too vigorous suctioning at birth may lead to secondary apnea
g) may appear to be Cheyne-Stokes with short periods of apnea with no evidence of distress
h) stabilized at 1–2 days at 30/min
i) respiration should be counted for full minute when baby is at rest
4. blood pressure
a) at birth: 60–80 mm Hg systolic and 40–50 mm Hg diastolic
b) at 10 days: 95–100 mm Hg systolic and slight increase in diastolic
c) varies with activity level
d) difficult to obtain accurate reading
e) 1-inch cuff is used

H. Skin
   1. usually dark pink but varies with ethnic origin
      a) pigmentation begins to deepen after birth
   2. soft
   3. may be covered with lanugo and vernix caseosa
      a) vernix caseosa dries spontaneously
      b) lanugo disappears during first week of life
      c) if absent may suggest postmaturity
      d) if abundant may suggest prematurity
   4. desquamation (peeling)
      a) occurs during first 2–4 weeks
   5. milia: tiny white papillae
      a) obstruction of sebaceous glands, particularly on nose and chin
   6. turgor
      a) elasticity and fullness of subcutaneous tissue indicate state of hydration
   7. physiological jaundice (third to fifth day)
      a) breakdown of excessive red blood cells no longer needed for oxygenation
      b) liver unable to break down bilirubin as quickly as necessary
      c) of no pathological significance; disappears between 7th and 14th day
      d) when bilirubin levels rise above 15 mg/100 ml, hyperbilirubinemia is present
I. Umbilical cord
   1. shrinks and darkens soon after birth
   2. turns black; complete necrosis occurs in 3–5 days
   3. falls off between 6–10 days
   4. heals completely within 2 weeks
J. Gastrointestinal system
   1. sucking pads in mouth and jaw disappear when infant no longer relies exclusively on sucking for food intake
   2. difficulty in moving solid food from lips to pharynx during first few months of life
   3. cardiac sphincter not fully developed at birth: may cause baby to swallow excess amount of air. Burping alleviates discomfort
   4. stomach empties in 2 or 3 hours
      a) slowed by foods high in protein and fat
      b) demand feeding patterns respond to individual differences in digestive patterns
      c) highly variable: may depend on time and amount of feeding, type and temperature of food, and the infant's state

5. stools
    a) meconium
        (1) first fecal material; sticky, odorless, greenish-black in color
        (2) passed in 8–24 hours
            (a) if no stool is passed within this time examination for obstruction is necessary
    b) transitional
        (1) 3–5 days
        (2) loose, greenish-yellow
        (3) contains mucus
    c) stools after fifth day depend on feeding method
        (1) breast fed: yellow, soft, pleasant sourish odor; two to four per day
        (2) formula: light yellow, firm, unpleasant odor; one to two per day
K. Anogenital area
    1. male
        a) penis and scrotum size varies
        b) testes descended in scrotal sacs
            (1) undescended testes may remain in abdomen or inguinal canal and may require hormonal therapy or surgical intervention to correct
        c) adhesions of foreskin (prepuce) common in newborn boys
            (1) adherence of the prepuce contraindicates any attempt at retraction
    2. female
        a) labia majora not well developed
        b) labia minora appear large and are exposed
        c) genital area may be swollen and have blood-tinged mucus discharge due to hormones transmitted by mother prenatally
            (1) condition disappears in second or third week
L. Breasts
    1. in both male and female, breasts may enlarge and secrete substance known as "witches milk"
        a) caused by hormones transferred by mother prenatally
        b) condition disappears in second or third week
M. Urinary system
    1. urine present in bladder at birth
        a) may void immediately or after several hours
            (1) first voiding may be dark amber and cloudy
            (2) urine becomes less concentrated as fluid intake increases
            (3) output may be scanty

(a) increases from 2 to 6 on first day up to 20 per day as intake increases
N. Skeletal system
 1. bones soft and flexible
 2. joints elastic
 3. muscles are not strong, coordinated, or controlled
  a) can raise head slightly in prone position but not in supine
  b) cannot support own head when held in upright position
O. Nervous system
 1. immature
  a) unstable
  b) poorly controlled
  c) sensitive to external stimuli
  d) brain; 25% of adult size
  e) incomplete myelinization of nerve fibers
 2. sufficient maturity to support adaptation to birth
  a) can coordinate respiratory and cardiac functions
  b) protective, feeding, and social reflexes present
 3. infant reflexes
  a) winking: occurs when something is brought near to eyes or eyes are exposed to bright light
  b) coughing and sneezing: protective, clears respiratory tract
  c) yawning: infant takes in increased amounts of oxygen
  d) rooting: when infant's cheek is stroked, the head will turn in that direction, assisting it in locating nipple for feeding
  e) sucking: anything touching lips initiates sucking reflex
  f) gagging: protective mechanism to prevent aspiration
  g) grasp: any object placed in hands will be grasped
   (1) grasping reflex fades with maturity and is replaced by conscious and purposeful movement
  h) walking reflex: when infant is held so that sole of foot touches a solid object, will make walking motions
  i) Moro (startle reflex): sudden stimulus causes infant to draw up legs, abduct and extend arms into embrace position
   (1) stimulus may be sudden noise, movement, or abrupt change in position
   (2) absence of a symmetrical Moro response usually indicates an abnormality
  j) Babinski reflex: when sole of foot is stroked, toes flair outward. This response to the Babinski reflex is normal only in the infant
  k) tonic neck: when infant lies on back, head will turn to one side

and arm and leg on that side are extended, opposite arm and leg are flexed
    l) there are other infant reflexes that may be checked by physician
P. Sensory abilities
  1. touch is most highly developed of all senses
    a) most acute on lips, tongue, ears, and forehead
    b) many reflexes are a reaction to tactile stimulation
  2. sight
    a) eyes: blue-gray at birth and attain permanent color between third and sixth month
    b) pupils react to light
    c) bright lights appear to be unpleasant
    d) discrimination and recognition of objects develop with maturity
    e) can usually follow bright object soon after birth
    f) can fixate and gaze intently at objects, especially human face
    g) strabismus and nystagmus may occur normally during first month
  3. hearing
    a) immediate response to sounds
    b) by fourth week may recognize mother's voice
    c) reacts with Moro reflex to loud or sudden noises
  4. taste
    a) more highly developed than sight or hearing
    b) has a preference for sweet taste
  5. smell
    a) some infants appear to smell breast milk
Q. Sleep
  1. neonate sleeps from 12–20 hours per day
  2. awakened by internal discomfort, such as pain and hunger
  3. Brazelton (1973) established six states of infant consciousness
    a) deep sleep
      (1) nearly still; occasional startle or twitch
      (2) no eye movement
      (3) occasional sucking movements
      (4) smooth and regular respirations
      (5) not easily aroused
    b) light sleep
      (1) some body movements
      (2) rapid eye movements (REM)
      (3) may smile or make sounds
      (4) irregular breathing patterns
      (5) response to stimuli

c) awake states:
   (1) drowsy
   (2) quiet alert
      (a) optimal state of arousal
      (b) attention focuses on stimuli
   (3) active alert
   (4) crying

R. Immune system
1. term and preterm newborn at increased risk for infection
   a) generalized immaturity of inflammatory and immune reactions (Medici, 1983)
   b) an increased number of portals of entry in the newborn, including
      (1) umbilical vessels
      (2) circumcision site
      (3) skin breaks: infant skin more delicate
2. cellular defenses
   a) polymorphonuclear leukocytes
      (1) ingest organisms
   b) monocytes
      (1) ingest organisms
      (2) play part in initiation of antibody formation
   c) lymphocytes
      (1) produce antibody if there has been previous contact with antigen
      (2) govern cell-mediated immunity
3. immunological factors
   a) immunoglobulins are synthesized by plasma cells
      (1) react specifically with the antigens that stimulate their formation
      (2) five groups
         (a) IgG
            1. cross placental barrier
            2. provide passive immunity
         (b) IgM
            1. first immunoglobulin made after birth
            2. if found in cord blood, infection suspected
         (c) IgA
            1. primary immunoglobulin of colostrum
               a. active against *E. coli*
         (d) IgD: little known

(e) IgE
1. involved in allergic reaction
2. significance in newborn period not established
4. other mechanisms to fight infection
a) gastric acid levels
b) development of intestinal flora
c) some antibodies pass through placenta, i.e., measles, mumps, smallpox
d) colostrum in breast-feeding mother supplies antibodies
e) antibodies supply passive immunity for limited period of time

III. BODY MEASUREMENTS
A. Gestational age
1. size and maturity in relation to gestational age are important to consider when determining condition of newborn
a) obstetrical data
b) birthweight, body length, and head circumference closely related to fetal growth
(1) below 10th percentile of measurements: small for gestational age (SGA)
(2) above 90th percentile of measurements: large for gestational age (LGA)
(3) between 10th and 90th percentile: appropriate for gestational age (AGA)
c) physical assessment
d) neurological assessment
B. Length
1. average: 20 inches (50 cm)
2. range: 18–22 inches (45–55 cm)
3. males usually longer than females
4. measurement should be made from top of head to heel
a) baby should be in recumbent position
C. Weight
1. average: 7–8 lbs
2. range: 6–8.5 lbs (2700–3850 g)
3. girls usually weigh less than boys
4. under 2500 g classified as premature and/or low birthweight
5. during first few days after birth, baby loses 6–10 oz (5–10% of birthweight) because of
a) withdrawal of maternal hormones

b) loss of fluid
c) loss of meconium and urine
d) usual NPO routine (12–24 hours)
e) regains birthweight within first 2 weeks
D. Head
1. large in proportion to rest of body
2. normal circumference: 13.2–14.8 inches (33–35.5 cm)
a) over 14.8 inches may be hydrocephalic
b) under 13.2 inches may be either microcephalic or premature
c) circumference of head and chest may be the same for the first day or two after birth
d) occipitofrontal circumference should be measured
(1) measurement should be retaken after resolution of molding or caput succedaneum
3. fontanels
a) openings at point of union of skull bones
b) anterior fontanel
(1) diamond shaped and located at juncture of two parietal bones and two frontal bones
(2) closes between 12–18 months
c) posterior fontanel
(1) triangularly shaped opening between occipital and parietal bone
(2) smaller than anterior fontanel
(3) closes by end of second month
d) fontanels bulge when baby cries or strains or if there is intercranial pressure
e) depression of fontanel may occur during dehydration
E. Chest
1. average size: 3/4 inches (2 cm) less than head
2. range: 12–13 inches (30–33 cm)
3. measure at nipple line
4. less than 12 inches (30 cm) may indicate preterm
5. at 2 years chest circumference should exceed that of head

REFERENCES

Brazelton, T. B. (1973). *Neonatal behavioral assessment scale.* Philadelphia: J. B. Lippincott.

Medici, M. (1983). The fight against infection: The neonate's defense mechanisms. *Journal of California Perinatal Association, 3*(2), 25.

Chapter 20

Nursing Care of the Newborn

I. ASSESSMENT

A. Immediate evaluation of the newborn
  1. Apgar done 1 minute after birth and repeated in 5 minutes
     a) any baby with an Apgar below 7 should be considered a high-risk infant
  2. gestational age assessment (Bash & Gold, 1981)
     a) important in differentiating between a premature baby and a baby who is small for gestational age (SGA) but is mature, and between the postmature baby and the baby who is large for gestational age (LGA)
     b) classification categories
        (1) neonate at term: 38–42 weeks gestation
        (2) neonate born before term: less than 38 weeks gestation
        (3) neonate born after term: after 42 weeks gestation
     c) assessment data used in determining gestational age
        (1) weight: neonate may be average, below average, or above average for gestational age based on weight percentile norms
        (2) measurements made during the pregnancy, such as ultrasound scanning
        (3) physical and neurological signs of maturity
  3. careful monitoring is needed during the transition period. During the second reactive phase suctioning of secretions may be necessary if they become profuse (Bash & Gold, 1981)
  4. body inspection
     a) head
        (1) size of head checked to evaluate proportion between head and chest

(a) circumference of head and chest recorded on newborn's chart

(2) abnormalities in shape
    (a) molding
        1. overlapping of cranial bones
        2. results in irregularity in shape and elongation of the head
        3. caused by forcing of head through birth canal
        4. most prevalent in first-borns and after a long, difficult labor
        5. molding may occur because of intrauterine pressure
        6. returns to normal in a few days
    (b) caput succedaneum
        1. swelling of soft tissues of presenting portion of scalp area that is encircled by cervix during labor
        2. apparent at birth
        3. subsides without treatment within 2 days
    (c) fontanels
        1. depression may indicate dehydration
        2. bulging may indicate hydrocephalus or neurological disorders
    (d) overriding of sutures
    (e) cephalohematoma
        1. collection of blood between cranial bone and periosteum
        2. caused by pressure of head against bony prominence of pelvis during labor
            a. capillaries rupture under periosteum
        3. may be apparent on delivery, but may form up to second day of life
        4. characteristics
            a. varying in size
            b. firm to touch
            c. increases in size for 1 or 2 days and then becomes softer
        5. regression of cephalohematoma usually occurs spontaneously during first 6 weeks of life
    (f) deviations in shape and position of head may occur because of position in utero
        1. are usually self-correcting in early infancy
        2. change of position prevents misshaping of head

Nursing Care of the Newborn 315

- b) skin color
    - (1) pallor may indicate shock or anemia
    - (2) jaundice in first 48 hours may indicate hemolytic disease, liver, or biliary abnormality
        - (a) early jaundice may be detected by placing several fingers on forehead or chest of baby and exerting gentle pressure; when fingers are suddenly removed, area will show a yellow tinge
    - (3) cyanosis
        - (a) acrocyanosis: normal phenomenon when rest of body is pink (first 24 hours)
        - (b) circumoral pallor may indicate respiratory, cardiac, or neurological disease
        - (c) when cyanosis decreases with crying, respiratory disorders should be suspected
        - (d) when cyanosis increases with crying, heart disease is suspected
    - (4) petechiae: pinpoint red spots due to ruptured capillaries; may indicate abnormality
    - (5) purpura: bluish-purplish discolorations caused by subdermal hemorrhage; may indicate abnormality or birth injury
- c) skin conditions to be noted
    - (1) Mongolian spots
        - (a) nonelevated bluish-gray areas of pigmentation
        - (b) seen most often in black, Asian, or Mediterranean infants
        - (c) fade in early childhood
    - (2) cutis marmorata
        - (a) pink or purplish capillary outlines on skin (mottling)
        - (b) seen most often over extremities
        - (c) thought to be vasomotor in origin
        - (d) disappears when circulation is increased; is transitory in nature
    - (3) nevus flammeus: port-wine stain
        - (a) flat, purple, or dark red lesion
        - (b) irregularly shaped
        - (c) if on bridge of nose, tends to fade; others do not
    - (4) nevus vasculosus: strawberry marks
        - (a) may be present at birth or appear during first 2 weeks
        - (b) may enlarge for 6 months to 1 year
        - (c) begins to regress at 1 year; most tend to disappear by age 10

(5) milia: small white papules found on nose, chin, and cheeks
    (a) formed by plugged sebaceous glands
(6) rashes
    (a) erythema toxicum: maculopapular rash
        1. may appear on any surface, except palms of hand and soles of feet
        2. occurs in 30–70% of babies
        3. resolves in 48–72 hours
        4. unknown cause
(7) areas of redness and scratch marks

d) eyes
    (1) almond shape may indicate Down syndrome
    (2) opacity may indicate congenital cataracts
    (3) discharges may indicate infection or injury
        (a) swelling and watery discharge may follow administration of silver nitrate
    (4) redness of conjunctiva may indicate injury or infection
        (a) isolation necessary if infection is present or suspected
    (5) gray-blue color
        (a) absence of pigmentation
        (b) eye color distinguishable by 3 months
    (6) small lacrimal gland but capable of producing tears

e) ears
    (1) low, abnormally shaped ears may indicate kidney malformation or chromosomal abnormality
    (2) the upper part of the ear lobe should be on same level as eye

f) mouth
    (1) asymmetry and abnormal contour may indicate paralysis
    (2) check for cleft palate and cleft lip
    (3) excessive salivation may indicate tracheo-esophageal fistula
    (4) check for tongue tie
    (5) check mucosa for abnormalities, i.e., white patches
    (6) any of these conditions may hinder feeding

g) umbilical stump
    (1) check for three vessels, two arteries, and one vein
    (2) if three vessels are not present it may indicate congenital abnormalities

h) abdomen
    (1) check for distention
    (2) check for umbilical or diaphragmatic hernia

Nursing Care of the Newborn   317

        (3) check for lack of synchrony between rise and fall of chest and abdomen during respirations. Movements should be synchronous
- i) genitals and anal region
  - (1) patency of anus may be tested by taking rectal temperature or by passage of meconium
  - (2) condition of genital area should be checked for
    - (a) swelling
      1. may be caused by pressure during labor and delivery
         a. usually breech delivery
      2. usually disappears within 2 weeks
    - (b) phimosis
    - (c) discharges
    - (d) descended testes
    - (e) presence of abnormalities
    - (f) fissures or sores
- j) skeletal system
  - (1) symmetry of movement of extremities
  - (2) check for dislocation of hip
    - (a) abduct hips to frog position
    - (b) check symmetry of buttock creases and length of legs
  - (3) check number of fingers and toes
  - (4) test for range of foot motion
    - (a) dorsiflexion
    - (b) dorsiflexion and inversion
    - (c) dorsiflexion and eversion
    - (d) plantar flexion and inversion
    - (e) plantar flexion and eversion
    - (f) plantar flexion
    - (g) limitations of any of these movements should be reported
- k) nervous system
  - (1) neurological reflexes should be elicited to rule out neurological disorders
  - (2) tremors and convulsions should be reported

5. vital signs
   a) respiration should be 40–60/min, synchronous, without retractions
   b) temperature should remain in range of 97.5–98°F (axillary)
   c) heart rate: normal range is 120–160 BPM; consistently slow or overly rapid rates may indicate circulatory problems. Rate rises during crying and drops during sleep

6. cry
    a) weak, shallow, high-pitched cry may indicate intracranial disorders
    b) grunting or moaning during breathing often accompanies respiratory distress
    c) stridor, a harsh, whistling sound, may indicate partial obstruction of respiratory tract
    d) wheezing may indicate abnormality
    e) cry resembling a cat's meow may indicate a mental retardation syndrome

B. Continuing observation of newborn
    1. color
        a) normal limits include
            (1) red skin color
            (2) acrocyanosis
            (3) jaundice after 48 hours
                (a) physiological in nature
                (b) bilirubin does not rise above 10–12 mg/100 ml
                (c) usually subsides within 1 week
    2. respiration
        a) excessive mucus may block respiratory passages
        b) breath sounds clear and equal bilaterally
    3. temperature
    4. elimination
        a) should void within 24 hours
        b) voiding should be frequent
        c) meconium should be passed within 24 hours
        d) stools should be checked for abnormalities
    5. sleeping
    6. activity level
    7. weight
    8. feeding behavior and patterns
    9. signs of infant distress
        a) increased rate and/or difficulty in respiration
        b) excessive mucus or drooling
        c) sternal retractions
        d) worried facial expressions
        e) cyanosis
        f) abdominal distention or mass
        g) inadequate voiding and/or expulsion of meconium
        h) vomiting of bile-stained fluid

i) jaundice 24–48 hours after birth
   j) convulsions
10. Brazelton neonatal assessment scale may be used to assess the behavioral characteristics and reflex patterns of the newborn (Brazelton, 1973)
   a) nursing care can be planned to meet the needs of the infant based on individual behavior patterns
   b) parents can be taught to respond to their infant's needs through mapping of the baby's usual behavioral patterns and responses
   c) Brazelton scale is used to assess the behavioral responses of the infant within six states of alertness
      (1) sleep states
         (a) deep sleep
         (b) light sleep
      (2) awake states
         (a) semiasleep, drowsy
         (b) quiet alert
         (c) active alert
         (d) crying
      (3) 17 reflex responses are also assessed, e.g., plantar grasp, hand grasp, Babinski, tonic neck, Moro, rooting, sucking, and others

II. INTERVENTION

A. Maintenance of adequate oxygenation
   1. airway of infant must remain patent
   2. mucus in nose and mouth should be gently suctioned with a bulb syringe or nasal catheter
   3. color and respirations must be carefully monitored. First 12 hours in newborn are particularly important for close observation
   4. infant placed on side to prevent aspiration
   5. care must be taken during feeding to prevent aspiration
   6. monitor for periods of apnea (Glista, 1978)
      a) apnea may be defined as cessation of respiration for 15 seconds when accompanied by cyanosis, or heart rate under 100/min and cessation of respiration for 20 seconds or more. Periodic breathing occurs commonly in newborns and is defined as respiratory pauses of 10–15 seconds without bradycardia or cyanosis
      b) severe or frequent periods of apnea are associated with morbidity and mortality

c) factors causing apnea include respiratory problems, deep suctioning and stimulation of the posterior pharynx, high environmental temperature, metabolic disorders, such as hypoglycemia, CNS disorders, sleep state, and abnormal positions
d) in uncomplicated apnea cutaneous stimulation, such as stroking the skin, will usually stimulate respirations
e) in apnea associated with pathology the underlying condition must be treated along with the apnea
7. controversy exists over use of baby powder, especially if baby is discharged with tracheotomy tube because there is a possibility of inhalation

B. Nutrition
1. newborn usually NPO for 6–12 hours
2. glucose or water usually given as first feeding
3. if sucking, swallowing, and retention are normal, formula is started
4. breast-fed babies need not be kept NPO because colostrum is nonirritating and easily swallowed even in the presence of excessive mucus; it also provides antibodies
5. formulas
    a) calculated according to age and body weight
    b) composition
        (1) protein: less in human milk than in any formula preparations
        (2) fat: more in human milk than in formula preparations
        (3) CHO: more in human milk than in most other preparations
        (4) such formulas as Similac and Enfamil more closely approximate human milk composition than does evaporated milk
6. preparation of formulas
    a) to prevent bacterial contamination sterilization by aseptic or terminal methods recommended when formula will be stored in refrigerator for 24 hours
7. feeding the formula-fed baby
    a) demand feeding schedule is preferred
    b) hospital nursery routine is often based on 3- to 4-hour schedule that may interfere with demand feeding
    c) temperature of formula may be warmed to room temperature or given directly from refrigerator
    d) the usual amount taken by baby during first initial feedings is 1–1.5 oz
    e) amount of intake gradually increases until full amount is taken (approximately 3–4 oz)
    f) amount of intake varies with metabolic rate of individual baby
        (1) an active baby will usually require more calories than a placid one

g) propping should be discouraged due to danger of aspiration and baby's need for close physical contact during feeding
h) bottle should be tilted so that excessive air is not ingested during feeding
i) nipple should be patent and openings small enough to permit slow feeding, which allows sucking needs to be fulfilled and helps prevent tongue thrust (abnormal forward thrust of tongue during swallowing) that can lead to speech and/or orthodontic problems
   (1) a special nipple is available that simulates the same sucking mechanism used in breast feeding and is preventive for tongue thrust (Nuk-Sauger nipple)
j) baby should be burped during and after the feeding to allow air that has been swallowed to be expelled
k) regurgitation and vomiting may occur due to
   (1) excessive mucus
   (2) improper feeding
   (3) abnormalities of GI tract
l) stomach of newborn empties in 1 1/2–4 hours or more
m) baby signals hunger through crying

C. Positioning
1. normal attitude of newborn is one of flexion
2. when on back, the thighs are externally rotated and knees are slightly flexed
3. when in prone position the baby has the ability to turn head to side
4. baby should not be placed on back because of danger of aspiration
5. position should be changed frequently, alternating between right and left side and prone position
6. hyperextension of neck should be prevented

D. Maintenance of body temperature
1. to protect from heat loss, baby should be carefully dried and wrapped in warm dry blankets
   a) direct skin-to-skin contact with mother is excellent way to prevent hypothermia
   b) radiant warmers may be used
      (1) careful monitoring of baby's temperature is essential
2. methods of maintaining normal temperature
   a) avoid exposure during bathing
   b) maintain warm room temperature
   c) avoid drafts
   d) wear adequate clothing
3. excessive heat should be avoided
   a) in warm weather baby should be clothed appropriately
   b) room temperature should not be excessively hot

E. Safety
   1. asepsis
      a) individual equipment
      b) adequate spacing of cribs; nursery should not be overcrowded
      c) rotation of nursery to which child is admitted
         (1) each unit is completely emptied and cleaned before another group is admitted
      d) nursery personnel limited in number
      e) medical asepsis is vital in nursery care of newborn
         (1) scrub gowns are worn by nursery personnel
         (2) handwashing
            (a) before entering nursery
            (b) between care of each baby
      f) cultures of various nursery areas taken at routine intervals
      g) dry dusting not utilized in terminal disinfection of equipment on discharge of baby
      h) immediate isolation when there is
         (1) any suspicion of illness in baby
         (2) an extramural birth
      i) if mother has a communicable disease, she should not feed baby
      j) diapers and waste should be placed in covered containers
      k) mothers should be taught aseptic practices
      l) personnel should not work in nursery when ill
   2. mechanical safety
      a) never leave baby on flat surface unattended
      b) baby should be held securely with adequate head support at all times
      c) care should be taken when safety pins are used
      d) when baby is weighed should be protected from falling
      e) thermometer should not be left in baby without supervision
F. Comfort measures
   1. bath
      a) frequency and value of sponge bathing in first week of life have been debated
      b) genital area must be cleansed with each diaper change
         (1) girls' genitalia cleansed from front to back
      c) nonirritating soap should be used
      d) cord area left exposed
      e) tub bath given when umbilicus is healed
   2. clothing should be loose and unrestrictive
   3. flat, firm mattress without a pillow is best
   4. diapers should be changed frequently

Nursing Care of the Newborn 323

G. Sleep and rest
  1. usually baby sleeps 12–20 hours daily
  2. sucking releases into sleep
  3. babies vary in sleep and activity patterns
  4. are usually awakened by hunger and/or discomfort
H. Circumcision
  1. removal of foreskin covering the glans penis
  2. indications
    a) phimosis: inability to retract foreskin
    b) done prophylactically to ensure genital cleanliness
      (1) if foreskin is not retracted frequently during personal hygiene, smegma builds up and may cause irritation
    c) ritual of Jewish religion
  3. timing of procedure is dependent upon
    a) condition of baby
      (1) delayed in babies with Rh factor, fetal distress, or other contraindications
    b) ritual or nonritual
      (1) ritual on eighth postpartum day
      (2) nonritual varies from time of birth to fourth day of life
  4. implications for nursing process
    a) dressing is not disturbed for 24 hours
    b) diaper area kept clean and dry
    c) watch for bleeding; report at once
    d) bathing delayed until area is healed
I. Emotional needs of newborn
  1. sensory stimulation
    a) tactile, visual, and auditory stimulation are necessary to enhance the emotional, mental, and physical development of the child
    b) sense of touch most developed sense at birth, making cuddling, holding, and stroking particularly valuable forms of stimulation
  2. mothering
    a) feeling of mothering transmitted to baby through its senses by the manner in which the baby is handled, spoken to, and played with
    b) sense of trust developed through the manner in which the mother meets the needs that are being expressed by baby. The primary needs of the baby are feeding, relief of discomfort and anxiety, and the need to be loved
      (1) in order to assist the mother in meeting the emotional needs of the infant an assessment of their interaction must be made
        (a) eye contact

  (b) the way baby is held
  (c) vocalization to child
  (d) touching and stroking behavior of mother
  (e) reaction of baby to mother
    1. appears relaxed in mother's arms
    2. stops crying when held by mother
    3. becomes rigid
    4. seems to cuddle into mother's arms
  (f) are there feeding problems?
  (g) is the mother anxious for baby to be returned to nursery?
  (h) verbal and nonverbal signs of mother when baby is present (e.g., anxiety, joy, fear, confidence)
  (i) mother's response to infant's crying
  (j) when father is present and is in contact with the infant similar assessment can be made
 3. intervention
  a) if there are disturbed interactions noted between parents and child
   (1) encourage verbalization of feelings of inadequacy, fear, and hostility related to infant care
   (2) maintain a nonjudgmental attitude
   (3) support the mother by reassurance and praise when indicated and teaching her aspects of child care of which she is unsure
   (4) enlist a support system of friends, others in similar situations, and relatives
   (5) refer for further supervision and assistance if necessary
   (6) assist mother in meeting her own dependency needs
J. Learning needs of the mother in relation to care of the newborn child
 1. for an adequate plan of teaching to be established it is necessary to assess the knowledge base and abilities of the new mother
  a) psychomotor skills of mother regarding feeding, handling, bathing, etc.
  b) knowledge of growth and development
  c) cultural practices and beliefs related to childrearing
  d) motivation for learning
  e) level of ability to understand instruction
 2. assessment must be made of mother's feelings toward the baby because anxiety and fear may interfere with learning
 3. depending on the assessment the following learning opportunities should be provided
  a) an opportunity to practice under supervision the psychomotor skills, such as feeding, bathing, dressing, and handling, etc.

b) preparation of the formula
c) the relationship between usual child care practices and cultural beliefs
d) nutrition for the developing infant
e) safety needs of the baby
f) importance of providing sensory stimulation to assist in development (all sensory modalities should be included)
g) importance of consistency in caring patterns so that the child will know what to expect
h) assistance in developing a flexible time framework within which the mother may work out a schedule that will meet family needs, self needs, and infant's needs
i) information about growth and development so that expectations of parents can be realistic
j) assistance in learning to respond to the new baby's communication efforts (crying, facial expression, body movements)
k) assistance in planning for continued health supervision of infant
l) community resources available to provide assistance to parents in fulfilling their parental role

REFERENCES

Bash, B.D., & Gold, A.W. (1981). *The nurse and the childbearing family.* New York: John Wiley.

Brazelton, T.B. (1973). *Neonatal behavioral assessment scale.* Philadelphia: J.B. Lippincott.

Glista, B. (1978). Problems of the very premature newborn. In Iffy, L., & Langer, A. (Eds). *Perinatalogy case studies* (pp. 541–543). Garden City, NY: Medical Examination Publishing Company.

Chapter 21
High-Risk Newborn

I. IDENTIFICATION OF RISK FACTORS
  A. Prenatal
    1. maternal
       a) age
       b) parity
       c) nutritional status
    2. previous pregnancy with complications
    3. maternal medical disorders
       a) central nervous system
       b) hematological or cardiovascular
       c) renal
       d) reproductive
       e) metabolic
          (1) diabetic
    4. complications in current pregnancy
  B. Intrapartal
    1. umbilical cord abnormality, i.e. prolapse
    2. rupture of membranes
       a) prematurity
       b) prolonged
    3. oligohydramnios or polyhydramnios
    4. amnionitis
    5. placenta previa or abruptio
    6. placental insufficiency
    7. abnormal fetal presentation
    8. dystocia of labor
    9. complication at delivery
    10. drug administration

C. Neonatal
   1. low Apgar score
   2. small or large for gestational age
   3. preterm birth
   4. born with birth defect

II. RESPIRATORY PROBLEMS
A. Causes
   1. fetal anoxia prior to delivery
      a) adequate supply of oxygen to fetus is dependent upon
         (1) normal oxygenation of maternal blood
         (2) normal maternal blood pressure
         (3) adequate relaxation of uterine musculature to permit placental filling
         (4) adequate attachment of the placenta to the uterine wall
         (5) free circulation of blood through placenta and umbilical cord
         (6) no fetal circulatory abnormalities
      b) fetal anoxia is caused by
         (1) maternal conditions
            (a) hypoxia secondary to cardiac failure
            (b) hypotension as a complication of spinal anesthesia
            (c) uterine tetany from Pituitrin or Pitocin administration
            (d) premature separation of placenta or other placental disturbances
            (e) placental dysfunction due to chronic hypertension or pregnancy-induced hypertension
            (f) renal disease
         (2) fetal conditions
            (a) prolapsed or knotted cord
            (b) premature rupture of membranes
            (c) fetal malpresentation
            (d) labor dystocia
            (e) drug administration
               1. leading to depression of neonate's CNS
            (f) rapid, precipitous, prolonged, or difficult delivery
            (g) injury to spinal cord or phrenic nerve, especially during breech delivery
            (h) aspiration of mucus, blood, amniotic fluid, or meconium
            (i) congenital malformations compatible with intrauterine life but not extrauterine life

High-Risk Newborn 329

   2. fetal anoxia at birth is caused by
      a) predelivery influences
      b) excessive analgesia or anesthesia leading to depression of fetal respiratory center
      c) rapid, precipitous, prolonged, or difficult delivery
      d) injury to spinal cord or phrenic nerve, especially during breech delivery
      e) aspiration of mucus, blood, amniotic fluid, or meconium
      f) congenital malformations compatible with intrauterine life but not extrauterine life
   3. neonatal anoxia is caused by
      a) obstruction of air passages
      b) congenital defects: cardiac and/or respiratory
      c) infections
         (1) bronchial pneumonia contracted in utero or shortly after birth, common in infants born after premature rupture of membranes or prolonged deliveries
      d) hemolytic diseases
      e) pre- or postmaturity
      f) respiratory distress syndrome (hyaline membrane disease)
      g) atelectasis of lungs
   4. types of anoxia
      a) anoxic anoxia: a deficit in arterial oxygen tension at which blood is delivered to cells
         (1) hemoglobin not completely saturated
         (2) occurs in hyaline membrane disease, aspiration, congenital cardiac problems, and cerebral defects
      b) anemic anoxia: occurs when hemoglobin levels are too low to carry adequate oxygen to cell and oxygen intake is normal
         (1) hemolytic disorders
      c) stagnant anoxia: occurs when circulation is inadequate so that oxygen transportation is retarded
         (1) shock or hemorrhage that causes circulatory collapse
      d) histotoxic anoxia: occurs when tissue cells are poisoned so that oxygen cannot be utilized
         (1) poisoning from chemical or drugs, e.g., ether, barbiturates
B. Classification of apnea
   1. primary
      a) infants who never breathe or those who gasp, or breathe irregularly or shallowly
   2. secondary
      a) vigorous hyper-respiratory effort in attempt to counteract hypoxia

C. Symptoms of respiratory complications
   1. tachypnea (over 60 respirations per minute)
      a) one of earliest signs
      b) common indicator
   2. nasal flaring
      a) infant is obligate nose breather
         (1) nares dilate in attempt to increase air flow with inspiration
   3. chest retractions
      a) soft tissues of thorax and intercostal muscles pulled in on inspiration with rib cage expansion
      b) difficult and labored breathing
   4. asynchronous (seesaw) respirations
      a) chest flattens and abdomen expands on inspiration
      b) appears with more severe distress
   5. expiratory grunting
D. Major syndromes causing respiratory distress
   1. atelectasis
      a) primary: nonexpansion of alveoli
         (1) causes
            (a) underdevelopment of respiratory saccules
            (b) immaturity of diaphragm and other respiratory muscles
            (c) hypermobility of thoracic cage
            (d) defects in peripheral respiratory mechanism
            (e) illness
            (f) brain injury with damage to respiratory center
            (g) maternal oversedation prior to delivery
            (h) premature birth
      b) secondary: collapse occurs after initial expansion of alveoli
         (1) causes
            (a) pulmonary disease
            (b) abnormality in thoracic cavity, such as
               1. enlarged heart
               2. tumors or cysts
      c) may be complete or partial
      d) symptoms
         (1) irregular, rapid respirations
         (2) respiratory grunts, retractions, and flaring of nostrils with inspiration
         (3) chest rales
         (4) mottled skin
         (5) intermittent or constant cyanosis, decreases during crying or oxygen therapy

High-Risk Newborn 331

    e) diagnosed by x-ray
    f) treatment
       (1) bronchoscopy may be done
       (2) oxygen with high humidity administered
       (3) respiratory stimulants may be ordered
       (4) position changed frequently to allow expansion of lungs
       (5) skin stimulated to induce increased respiration
       (6) antibiotics to prevent secondary infection
       (7) aspiration prevented by careful feeding
2. pneumonia
    a) important cause of neonatal morbidity and mortality
    b) may be acquired
       (1) transplacentally by generalized intrauterine infection
       (2) transplacental or pneumonia acquired perinatally is often called congenital pneumonia; associated with
         (a) prolonged rupture of membranes
         (b) chorioamnionitis
         (c) prolonged labor
         (d) premature labor and birth
         (e) fetal distress
       (3) during birth
         (a) aspiration of infected amniotic fluid or secretions from birth canal
           1. onset during first several days of life
       (4) postnatally
         (a) aspiration pneumonia
           1. first symptom is attack of coughing or choking
           2. subsequent symptoms are similar to infectious pneumonia
           3. prevention
             a. careful feeding
             b. does not usually occur in breast-fed babies
             c. nipple openings should not be free flowing
             d. position baby on abdomen or side after eating
             e. if infant chokes, it should be held upside down and back gently stroked to drain aspirated fluid from lung
         (b) infectious pneumonia
           1. causes
             a. aspiration of infected amniotic fluid or vaginal secretions
             b. contact with someone who harbors organisms

  c. causative organisms
   (1.) *E. coli*
   (2.) enterococci
   (3.) klebsiella
   (4.) staphylococcus
   (5.) streptococcus
 2. signs
  a. rapid respiration
  b. flaring of nares
  c. respiratory grunt, retraction
  d. temperature rises or may be subnormal
  e. listless, pale, cyanotic
  f. abdominal distention
  g. refuses feeding
  h. diagnosed by x-ray
 (c) causative organisms: respiratory viruses
3. neonatal respiratory distress syndrome: hyaline membrane disease
 a) incidence (Behrman et al., 1983)
  (1) major cause of death in newborn period
  (2) the shorter the gestation period and lower the weight, the greater the incidence
   (a) 60% of infants less than 28 weeks gestation
   (b) 15–20% of infants between 32–36 weeks
   (c) 5% of infants after 34 weeks
   (d) rare at term
  (3) occurs more frequently in
   (a) babies of diabetic mothers delivered before 34 weeks
   (b) Cesarean section delivery
   (c) precipitious delivery after antepartal hemorrhage
   (d) asphyxia
   (e) prior history of affected infant
  (4) caused by lack of adequate alveolar surfactant production (antiatelectasis factor) in infant lungs
   (a) lung compliance decreases and breathing becomes difficult. Alveoli collapse after each respiration. Hyperventilation and hypoperfusion of the alveoli; asphyxia may result
 b) prevention
  (1) prevent premature birth
  (2) avoid unnecessary or untimely Cesarean section
   (a) ultrasound measurements
   (b) ascertain L/S ratio

(3) use antenatal steroid therapy
c) signs
  (1) increase in respiratory rate
  (2) sternal retractions
  (3) expiratory grunt
  (4) flaring of nares
  (5) cyanosis not always apparent or may be confined to extremities
    (a) if severe, then skin appears pale and dusky
  (6) apnea spells
  (7) gradual CNS depression with increasing flaccidity of musculature
d) intervention: aimed at respiratory support
  (1) provide oxygen
    (a) in combination with humidity and with warmth
    (b) mechanisms
      1. by hood
        a. does not correct CO_2 level
        b. does not assist ventilation
      2. continuous positive airway pressure (CPAP)
        a. prevents alveolar collapse
        b. does not correct CO_2 levels
      3. positive end-expiratory pressure (PEEP)
      4. bag and mask: used intermittently
      5. extracorporeal membrane oxygenation (ECMO)
        a. new theory using a modified heart-lung machine
          (1.) provides temporary cardiopulmonary support
          (2.) one study demonstrated the treatment was tolerated and baby's lungs healed without pulmonary fibrosis (Bartlett, 1985)
  (2) control temperature of environment
  (3) maintain nutrition by IV administration
  (4) monitor blood gas levels, BP, and respiration
  (5) maintain appropriate pH levels
  (6) use human surfactant immediately after birth; appears to reduce the symptoms of RDS
e) complications
  (1) retrolental fibroplasia: caused by high concentrations of oxygen
  (2) pulmonary hemorrhage
  (3) pneumothorax

             (4) atelectasis
             (5) sepsia
             (6) bronchopulmonary dysplasia: possible sequela to positive pressure ventilation (Jensen, 1985)
                 (a) change in lungs results in focal areas of emphysema
                 (b) difficulty in weaning infant from ventilator may be first symptom
                 (c) recovery may take months
                 (d) mortality between 30–50%
        4. meconium aspiration syndrome
           a) may require resuscitation at birth
           b) signs: chest retractions, tachypnea, and cyanosis
           c) diagnosed by x-ray

   E. Nursing care of infants with respiratory distress
      1. assessment
         a) heart rate may be increased (over 150)
         b) temperature and skin color: cyanosis or pallor may occur; temperature may rise or fall
         c) activity and muscle tone: infant may show signs of hyperactivity or flaccidity
         d) cry: moaning or whining indicates problem
         e) appetite may decrease or infant may have difficulty in feeding
         f) respiration
            (1) rate
                (a) above 60/min or rapid rise indicates danger
                (b) increase and then decrease below 30 with periods of apnea indicates extreme danger
            (2) rhythm
                (a) prolonged irregularity is a danger signal
            (3) retractions
                (a) simple: abdomen and chest rise together with slight indentation over sternal area; flaring of nares occurs
                (b) paradoxical: abdomen rises and chest sinks during inspiration, reversed during expiration; marked intercostal and xiphoid retraction, chin lag, respiratory grunt, and severe respiratory distress
         g) blood chemistry for signs of acidosis
         h) nasopharyngeal passages for presence of mucus
      2. intervention
         a) maintain adequate oxygenation
         b) maintain humidity
         c) give medications as ordered

d) change position frequently: cutaneous stimulation may assist in restoring respiratory pattern in apneic periods
e) feed carefully
f) do gentle suction when indicated
g) prevent hypothermia by maintaining the temperature of the environment and by limiting infant exposure
h) monitor vital signs frequently
i) prevent fatigue and exhaustion
  (1) avoid prolonged feedings
  (2) gavage may be necessary
j) be prepared for periods of apnea by having oxygen apparatus ready
k) monitor fluid intake and output
  (1) rate of infusions carefully controlled
l) use respiratory monitor until infant weighs 1800 g (4 lbs) and condition is stabilized
  (1) check monitor
m) monitor blood gas levels

III. BIRTH INJURIES

A. Classification
  1. soft tissue
    a) cephalohematoma
    b) caput succedaneum
    c) subcutaneous fat necrosis
      (1) caused by pressure against pelvis or from forceps
      (2) lesion resolves in few days without treatment
    d) cyanosis, ecchymosis, petechiae, and edema
      (1) usually occur on buttocks or extremities
      (2) may be sign of more severe illness
    e) hemorrhage into abdominal wall
      (1) may cause liver damage
B. Skeletal injuries
  1. molding
  2. fractures
    a) most commonly seen in version or breech deliveries
    b) common in long bones, clavicle, or jaw
    c) heal rapidly but need immobilization
    d) dislocations must be reduced immediately
    e) skull fracture
      (1) location of fracture determines severity
      (2) subdural hemorrhage may occur if blood vessel injured

C. Nervous system injuries
  1. paralysis
     a) facial
        (1) caused by pressure on facial nerve by forceps
        (2) prognosis: condition transitory and usually disappears in a few days
     b) arm
        (1) brachial palsy or Erb's palsy, common terms for arm paralysis
        (2) caused by pressure on brachial plexus in breech extraction
        (3) prognosis: recovery spontaneous within weeks or months; surgery may be needed for those few cases that do not heal spontaneously
     c) nursing intervention
        (1) careful observation
        (2) careful handling to minimize trauma and discomfort
        (3) for facial paralysis, careful feeding due to sucking defects
        (4) parental support
        (5) maintenance of proper position
  2. intracranial hemorrhage
     a) caused by brain trauma leading to bleeding into cerebellum, pons, and medulla oblongata
     b) symptoms
        (1) cyanosis
        (2) abnormal respirations
        (3) sharp, shrill, weak cry
        (4) flaccidity
        (5) convulsions
        (6) tense fontanel
        (7) increased intracranial pressure
        (8) shock
        (9) acidosis
     c) in full-term large infants, occurs more often in
        (1) prolonged labors
        (2) forceps delivery
        (3) version and extraction
        (4) precipitate deliveries
     d) intracranial hemorrhage due to hypoxia and hypovolemia is seen more often in preterm infant; not related to trauma
     e) nursing intervention
        (1) rest with minimum handling
            (a) feeding with minimum effort of infant
                1. gavage or IV

(2) vitamins C and K to control hemorrhage as ordered
(3) head of infant kept above level of hips
(4) careful and continued observation for changes in symptoms
(5) maintenance of body temperature
(6) oxygen as necessary
  f) prognosis: depends on extent of damage
 3. phrenic nerve injury
  a) results in diaphragmatic paralysis
  b) symptoms
   (1) cyanosis
   (2) irregular thoracic respirations without abdominal movement on inspiration
  c) infant may require mechanical ventilation

IV. HEMOLYTIC DISEASE OF NEWBORN
A. ABO incompatibility
 1. mild hemolytic disease
 2. father's blood type is A or B, mother's blood type is O, baby will therefore be type A or B
 3. baby produces A or B antigens that enter mother's bloodstream, causing mother to produce A or B antibodies. These antibodies cross back into baby's bloodstream and cause hemolysis of baby's red blood cells
 4. symptoms
  a) jaundice occurring within 48 hours
  b) mild anemia
  c) negative or low Coombs' test
 5. treatment
  a) light therapy
   (1) undressed baby is exposed to fluorescent daylight bulbs; eyes are covered
   (2) bilirubin is decomposed by photo-oxidation in the skin
  b) exchange transfusion if bilirubin rises above 20 mg/100 ml of blood
 6. prognosis: usually recovers spontaneously
B. Rh incompatibility
 1. when mother is Rh-negative and father is Rh-positive, the mother's blood does not contain the Rh factor whereas it is present in the father's. Because the Rh factor is a dominant gene there is a high probability that the baby will be Rh-positive. At the birth of the first Rh-positive baby, the Rh factor may enter the mother's bloodstream, causing her to form antibodies to this factor. In subsequent

pregnancies these maternal antibodies may cross the placental barrier and enter the fetal bloodstream. This may cause hemolysis of the red blood cells if the baby is Rh-positive. Sensitization of the mother may also occur if she has received a Rh-positive blood transfusion
2. RhoGam is a vaccine that must be used within 72 hours after delivery to prevent sensitization of mother to the Rh-positive factor
3. erythroblastosis fetalis: the condition of the infant that occurs because of Rh incompatibility: incidence has greatly diminished because of use of Rhogam
    a) signs and symptoms
        (1) anemia present at birth or soon after, varies in severity
        (2) yellow vernix caseosa
        (3) jaundice occurring within 24 hours
        (4) enlarged liver and spleen
        (5) positive Coombs' test
        (6) elevated serum bilirubin
    b) hydrops fetalis
        (1) most severe form of erythroblastosis fetalis
        (2) symptoms
            (a) generalized edema of the infant beginning in utero
            (b) marked anemia
            (c) severe jaundice
            (d) enlarged liver and spleen
        (3) prognosis
            (a) infant usually stillborn
            (b) if born alive invariably dies within short period
    c) kernicterus
        (1) occurs when CNS becomes involved due to persistent high bilirubin levels (20 mg/100 ml of blood)
        (2) symptoms
            (a) anorexia
            (b) lethargy
            (c) abnormal Moro reflex
            (d) opisthotonos
            (e) convulsions
            (f) spasticity
        (3) prognosis
            (a) high death rate
            (b) mental retardation
4. treatment of Rh incompatibility
    a) prevented by use of RhoGam

b) careful check of antibody titer levels in mother during pregnancy
c) if titer levels are high or increase rapidly, intrauterine exchange transfusion may be done
d) fresh Rh-negative blood is used for transfusion
e) Coombs' test done at birth from cord blood
f) careful monitoring of bilirubin level
g) exchange transfusion if bilirubin level remains high
h) light therapy
i) research team is attempting to use synthetic protein to bind with enzyme that converts hemoglobin to bilirubin
    (1) excess hemoglobin excreted without being converted to bilirubin (*Science News*, 1988)

C. Implications for nursing process
  1. assessment
     a) check for early signs and symptoms relating to the manifestations of hemolytic disease
     b) do continuing assessment for any worsening of symptoms
     c) observe for reactions to phototherapy
     d) check for changes in feeding and/or sleeping patterns
     e) monitor color of urine and stools
  2. intervention
     a) phototherapy
        (1) protect eyes during therapy
        (2) remove eye protection during feeding and bathing to provide sensory stimulation

V. INFECTIONS

A. Neonate has lower resistance to pathogens because antibodies are not developed
  1. most common bacterial and viral pathogens causing infection
     a) *Staphylococcus aureus*
        (1) causes respiratory infection and impetigo
     b) staphylococcus coagulase positive (hospital staph) is resistant to most antibiotics; causing impetigo and infection in any open skin tissue
     c) streptococcus causes skin and respiratory infections
     d) *E. coli* causes respiratory and gastrointestinal infections
     e) salmonella causes respiratory and gastrointestinal infections
     f) shigella causes respiratory and gastrointestinal infections
     g) viruses cause gastrointestinal and respiratory infections

2. modes of transmission
    a) through nose and throat secretions of nursery personnel and mother
    b) skin infection of personnel and mother
    c) poor handwashing technique
    d) fomite contamination
        (1) humidifiers
        (2) faucets
        (3) sinks
        (4) articles of infant care
3. disease manifestations of pathogens
    a) impetigo
    b) respiratory infections
    c) cord infections
    d) circumcision infections
    e) gastrointestinal disturbance
        (1) diarrhea
        (2) vomiting
    f) eye infections
    g) septicemia
B. Ophthalmia neonatorum
    1. infection of eye caused by gonococcus and chlamydial organisms
    2. acquired during delivery from mother's vaginal canal
    3. may result in blindness if not treated
    4. state law requires preventive treatment
        a) silver nitrate 1% (effective only for GC)
        b) antibiotic eye ointment (effective for both organisms)
C. Thrush: an infectious disease of the newborn caused by *Candida albicans,* which is a fungus
    1. transmission
        a) acquired during delivery if mother has a monilia infection
        b) acquired from infected personnel who use poor asepsis
    2. symptoms include mucus white patches on mucosa of mouth that cannot be removed
    3. treatment
        a) antibiotics
        b) gentian violet 1% applied to lesion
D. TORCH: acronym for *T*oxoplasmosis, *O*ther (syphilis, varicella, chlamydia, B. hemolytic strep), *R*ubella, *C*ytomegalovirus, *H*erpes simplex
    1. toxoplasmosis

a) follows hand-to-mouth contact with contaminated cat litter or ingestion of infected rare meat
b) associated with severe defects in infant
c) can be diagnosed by Sabin-Feldman dye test or indirect immunofluorescent test
  (1) cannot distinguish chronic from acute infection
d) treatment: drugs may be teratogenic
2. syphilis
  a) preventable by treatment in early pregnancy
  b) symptoms may be present at birth or may occur up to 4 months of age
    (1) highly infectious skin lesions found primarily on
      (a) face
      (b) buttocks
      (c) palms
      (d) soles of feet
    (2) mucus patches
      (a) mouth
      (b) anus
    (3) rhinitis (snuffles)
    (4) hoarseness
    (5) deformity of nails
    (6) alopecia
    (7) enlargement of lymph nodes
    (8) enlargement of liver and spleen
    (9) osteochondritis of long bones
    (10) CNS involvement
  c) diagnosis made from symptoms with a positive serology
  d) treatment
    (1) isolation
    (2) antibiotics
3. chlamydia
  a) causes neonatal conjunctivitis or pneumonia
  b) treatment of mother delayed until after delivery because of possible teratogenic effects of therapy
  c) prognosis: good if diagnosed and treated as early as possible
4. rubella
  a) maternal infection early in pregnancy frequently leads to congenital defects
  b) if acquired later in pregnancy, may lead to
    (1) intrauterine growth retardation

(2) premature delivery
(3) live birth with active infection
5. cytomegalovirus
    a) infection during pregnancy may result in abortion, stillbirth or neonatal disease (CMID)
    b) symptoms
        (1) infant is small and has microcephaly
        (2) anemia
        (3) thrombocytopenia
        (4) hyperbilirubinemia
6. herpes virus (Type II)
    a) usually acquired during delivery
    b) may be acquired
        (1) transplacentally
        (2) ascending infection
        (3) direct transmission from another person
    c) delivery by cesarean section if mother actively infected is advised
E. Hepatitis B (Larson, 1987)
    1. transplacental infection rare
    2. if fetus exposed during birth process, high probability of acquiring infection
        a) may become a chronic carrier. About 25% develop cirrhosis, liver carcinoma, or chronic disease, which can be transmitted to others
            (1) risk of chronicity can be reduced by administration of hepatitis B immune globulin
F. Group B streptococcus (GBS) (Larson, 1987)
    1. common cause of neonatal sepsis in Western hemisphere
    2. neonates at greater risk
        a) premature
        b) prolonged or premature rupture of membranes
        c) mother of lower socioeconomic status
    3. forms of GBS
        a) occurs during first few days of life and accompanied by respiratory distress, fulminant sepsis, and shock
            (1) high mortality even with antibiotics
        b) occurs about 5 to 7 days and often associated with meningitis
G. Gonorrhea
    1. infrequent infection except for ophthalmia neonatorum
H. AIDS (acquired immune deficiency syndrome)
    1. neonates exposed to the virus by transplacental infection or ingestion of breast milk

2. etiology
    a) causative agent: type C retrovirus (HTLV-III)
        (1) proliferates with helper T-lymphocytes
            (a) decreases number
            (b) interferes with function
            (c) causes a cellular immunodeficiency
        (2) antibody to virus develops
            (a) does not seem to protect against disease
            (b) presence of antibody is a diagnostic criteria of the disease or of the carrier
3. symptoms
    a) failure to thrive
    b) recurrent bacterial infection
    c) persistent oral candidiasis
    d) chronic diarrhea
    e) hepatosplenomegaly
    f) lymphadenopathy
    g) parotitis
    h) interstitial pneumonitis
4. prognosis
    a) presently no cure for disease
        (1) symptoms usually appear at 6 to 8 months
        (2) usual age when diagnosis is made: 18 months
    b) life is prolonged by supportive therapy
        (1) overall 60% of those diagnosed have died
5. prevention
    a) presently the only prevention is to reduce risk of becoming infected or infecting someone else
    b) estimated that in 1991 between 10,000–20,000 children in U.S. will be infected (Pollack, 1988)
6. psychosocial issues
    a) associated with guilt
        (1) sexually transmitted
        (2) spread by use of infected needles (drug abusers)
    b) patients and parents faced with fear, hopelessness, and prejudice
    c) congenital AIDS indicated maternal infection
        (1) 25% of women find out about their illness after having a baby with positive test for HIV
        (2) some mothers become sick and die before their child
    d) principles of HIV-antibody testing
        (1) informed consent
        (2) counseling at time of testing

                (3) confidentiality
            e) impact on nurse of caring for AIDS patient
                (1) face fear of contracting disease
                    (a) may be pressured by family to leave employment
                    (b) extremely low rate of infection
                (2) frustration
                    (a) hopelessness of disease
                (3) burnout
                (4) feelings of loss
                (5) support essential to those caring for patients
I. Epidemic diarrhea
    1. causes
        a) staphylococcus
        b) *E. coli* most common organism
        c) predisposing factors
            (1) overcrowding in nursery
            (2) poor personal hygiene of personnel and mothers
            (3) poor aseptic nursery technique
    2. symptoms: sudden onset of profuse watery stools
    3. treatment
        a) immediate isolation
        b) antibiotics
        c) prevention of dehydration through use of IV feeding
    4. prognosis: high mortality rate
J. Implications of infections of newborn for nursing process
    1. assessment
        a) monitor vital signs
            (1) in many cases during an infectious process there may not be a rise in temperature
        b) observe for signs of infection
            (1) lethargy
            (2) anorexia
            (3) irritability
            (4) abnormal discharge from body orifices
            (5) skin eruptions or inflammation
            (6) abnormal bowel or bladder manifestations
            (7) respiratory irregularities
            (8) changes in skin color
            (9) mucous membrane lesions
    2. intervention
        a) immediate isolation of infected baby and personnel
        b) aseptic technique carefully followed

c) treatment of infection with appropriate drugs
d) prevention of complications, e.g., dehydration
e) support, information, and reassurance to parents

REFERENCES

Bartlett, R., et al. (1985, October). Extracorporeal circulation in neonatal respiratory failure: A prospective randomized study. *Pediatrics,* pp. 478–487.

Behrman, R., & Vaughan, V. (1983). *Textbook of pediatrics.* Philadelphia: W.B. Saunders.

Jensen, M., & Bobak, I. (1985). *Maternity and Gynecologic Care* (3rd ed.). St. Louis: C.V. Mosby.

Larson, E. (1987, November/December). Trends in neonatal infection. *Journal of Obstetric and Gynecologic Nursing,* pp. 404–416.

New therapy blocks newborn jaundice. (1988, April 16). *Science News,* p. 247.

Pollack, H., et al. (1988). *Feelings and their medical significance.* Columbus, OH: Ross Laboratories.

Chapter 22

Birth Defects (Congenital Anomalies) and Other Complications

I. DEFINITION OF BIRTH DEFECT

A. A structural or functional variant from the normal range that is inherited by any Mendelian mode of transmission or caused by a mutation, infection, and/or chemical or physical insult to embryo or fetus.
   1. over 3000 defects have been identified

II. CLASSIFICATION

A. Anomalies compatible with intrauterine life only, e.g., anencephaly
B. Anomalies compatible with extrauterine life, only with immediate surgical intervention, e.g., imperforate anus
C. Anomalies compatible with extrauterine life, e.g., umbilical hernia

III. NEURAL TUBE DEFECTS

A. Anencephaly: a malformation of the brain and/or cerebral hemispheres. Scalp and cranium may be missing
   1. prognosis: no chance of survival
B. Congenital hydrocephalus
   1. occurs in about 1 in 2000 fetuses
   2. caused by abnormal enlargement of cerebral ventricles and skull because of increased intraventricular pressure
      a) normal circulation of fluid disturbed
      b) may have obstruction, excess secretion of fluid, or problem in absorption
   3. surgery usually performed soon after birth (shunts)
      a) complications: septicemia and pulmonary thrombosis

4. serious developmental delay and neurological damage are common
- C. Meningomyelocele (spina bifida)
    1. defect in closure of spinal column. Membranes surrounding the spinal cord and/or the spinal cord may protrude from opening. Often accompanied by hydrocephalus
    2. child is usually paraplegic
    3. treatment
        a) closure of spinal column
        b) rehabilitative treatment
        c) Cesarean section, if defect is identified before birth, appears to lessen effects of the condition
- D. Microcephaly
    1. well-formed but small head
    2. incidence related to prenatal X-ray exposure or some infectious disease

IV. NEUROLOGICAL DISORDERS

- A. Wide range of defects can affect the neurological system
    1. chromosomal abnormality
    2. infection
    3. drug withdrawal
    4. neoplasm
- B. Implications for nursing process
    1. assessment
        a) abnormalities in reflex reactions
        b) accurate measurements of head
        c) signs of irritability, lethargy, twitching, and tremors
        d) frequency and length of convulsions
        e) skin condition around myomeningocele
        f) feeding behavior
        g) skin breakdown in case of hydrocephalus
        h) changes in vital signs
        i) careful assessment of nonspecific clues is essential
            (1) high-pitched cry
            (2) low-set ears
            (3) jitteriness
    2. intervention
        a) change position frequently
        b) protect baby from injury during convulsions
        c) reduce irritating stimuli, such as noise or sudden movements, to decrease incidence of convulsions

d) engage in careful feeding practices
e) use padding to prevent pressure near and around abnormalities

V. CONGENITAL HEART DISEASE
A. Incidence
1. occur in 3 of every 1000 births
2. account for about 50% of deaths from malformations in first year of life
B. Unclear etiology
1. in some cases a family tendency can be noted
C. Types of defects
1. patent ductus, the fetal opening between pulmonary artery and aorta, fails to close at birth
a) corrected by surgery with good prognosis
2. patent foramen ovale, a fetal opening between right and left atrium, fails to close at birth
a) corrected by surgery with good results
3. ventricular septal defects
a) vary in size
b) blood shunts from right to left ventricle
c) if defect is small, no treatment is necessary and may close normally. Large defects require surgery
4. coarctation of the aorta (stenosis)
a) narrowing of aorta
b) may be corrected by surgery with good prognosis
5. tetralogy of Fallot
a) combination of four defects
(1) pulmonary stenosis
(2) ventricular septal defect
(3) overriding aorta
(4) hypertrophy of right ventricle
b) corrected by surgery with a high mortality rate
6. transposition of the great vessels
a) vessels arise out of the wrong ventricles
b) corrected by surgery with a high mortality rate
7. other defects occur rarely
D. Symptoms of newborns with congenital heart disease
1. cyanosis
2. dyspnea
3. tachycardia
4. difficulty with feeding

5. failure to thrive
6. heart murmurs
7. stridor or choking spells
8. anoxic attacks
E. Surgery usually performed as early as possible

VI. RESPIRATORY SYSTEM
   A. Congenital laryngeal stridor
      1. abnormality in or around larynx
      2. symptoms
         a) noisy respiration
         b) crowing sound in inspiration
      3. surgery indicated if condition is severe
   B. Occlusion of nasal passage
      1. may be either unilateral or bilateral
      2. usually obstructed at junction of nasopharynx by membrane or bony growth
      3. symptoms
         a) dyspnea
         b) difficulty in feeding
         c) mouth breathing
      4. treated by surgical intervention
   C. Diaphragmatic hernia
      1. herniation of abdominal viscera into thoracic cavity
         a) extent varies from minimal herniation to herniation so severe during the prenatal period that lung development is hampered
      2. prompt surgical repair after stabilization of infant is necessary
      3. prognosis dependent on extent and success of surgery
   D. Nursing assessment
      1. vital signs
      2. color
      3. feeding behavior
      4. activity
      5. cry
         a) effect on physiological state
      6. intake and output
      7. nutritional status
   E. Intervention
      1. maintain cardiovascular and respiratory function: maintain patent airway
         a) O_2 as appropriate
         b) suction as necessary

Birth Defects and Other Complications 351

        c) position
- 2. record findings carefully
- 3. maintain body temperature
- 4. minimize stress and fatigue
- 5. medicate as ordered
- 6. provide parental support
- 7. do slow, careful feeding
- 8. observe for respiratory difficulty or periods of apnea

VII. GASTROINTESTINAL MALFORMATIONS
- A. Tongue tie: frenum linguae
    1. vertical fold of mucous membrane under tongue sometimes interferes with sucking and speech
    2. can be corrected surgically
- B. Cleft lip and cleft palate
    1. failure of maxillary and palatal processes to close
    2. leads to problems in feeding and speech and danger of infection
    3. corrected surgically
    4. speech therapy when older
- C. Esophageal atresia: esophagus is not closed
    1. during feeding, infant chokes and turns blue: infant should not be fed
    2. excessive drooling and mucus secretion
    3. corrected by surgery
    4. place infant in semi-Fowler's position with head raised
    5. notify physician immediately
- D. Tracheoesophageal fistula
    1. opening between trachea and esophagus
    2. symptoms and treatment same as esophageal atresia
- E. Pyloric stenosis
    1. hypertrophy of pyloric muscles interferes with ability to empty contents of stomach
    2. symptoms include projectile vomiting after feeding
    3. corrected by surgery with good prognosis
- F. Intestinal obstructions
    1. complete or partial by stenosis or atresia at any level of intestinal tract
    2. primary symptoms: vomiting and no stools
    3. corrected by surgery
- G. Imperforate anus
    1. membrane over anal opening or absence of anus
    2. no stools

3. corrected by surgery
- H. Biliary tract obstruction
    1. flow of bile into intestine is blocked
    2. symptoms include clay color or white stools, jaundice, bile-stained urine
    3. corrected by surgery
- I. Omphalocele
    1. intestine protrudes out of umbilicus without skin covering
    2. must be protected with wet dressing until surgery
    3. corrected by surgery
- J. Umbilical hernia
    1. protrusion of intestine with skin covering at umbilicus
    2. may reduce spontaneously without surgery
- K. Implications for nursing process
    1. assessment
        a) feeding behavior
        b) presence, time of occurrence, frequency, and character of vomiting
        c) bowel function: character and frequency of stools
        d) excess salivation and drooling
        e) nutritional status
        f) structure of mouth
        g) patency of rectum
        h) condition of umbilical cord stump
    2. intervention
        a) careful and appropriate feeding to prevent aspiration
        b) maintenance of fluid intake
        c) feeding to be withheld if tracheo-esophageal fistula or esophageal atresia is suspected.

VIII. GENITOURINARY SYSTEM

- A. Hypospadias: urethra opens on lower surface of penis, can be corrected by surgery
- B. Agenesis of kidneys or ureters: incompatible with extrauterine life
- C. Cystic or polycystic kidneys can in later life interfere with urine production
- D. Sexual ambiguity
    1. cause may be genetic or iatrogenic
    2. important to establish genetic sex and sex of rearing immediately to permit corrective surgery
    3. parents need support

E. Extrophy of bladder
   1. cause unknown
   2. separation of symphysis and abdominal wall results in an external bladder with mucosa
   3. nursing intervention
      a) prevent infection
      b) provide good skin care to area
      c) meet psychosocial needs of parents and infant
      d) provide adequate parental education

IX. MUSCULOSKELETAL SYSTEM
A. Clubfoot: talipes equinovarus
   1. adduction and supination of forefoot
   2. may be casted or placed in Dennis and Brown splint
B. Congenital dislocation of hip
   1. head of femur not in acetabulum
   2. placed in cast
C. Torticollis (wryneck)
   1. head in downward position on one side with chin rotated to the other side
   2. corrected by exercise
   3. two-thirds disappear with little or no treatment
   4. if persistent or recurrent, resection of muscles is necessary

X. INBORN ERRORS OF METABOLISM
A. Large group of disorders
   1. result from a defect of gene action
      a) protein (usually an enzyme) can be absent or altered
      b) metabolism of a carbohydrate, a protein, or a fat may be affected
   2. recessive inherited disorder
B. Disorders
   1. PKU
      a) enzyme necessary to break down phenylalanine is absent
      b) phenylalanine builds up in brain, causing mental retardation
      c) early detection is possible because of mandatory blood testing of newborns in many states
      d) mental retardation can be prevented by a diet that excludes phenylalanine

354   Quick Reference to Maternity Nursing

        e) adult women with PKU need nutritional counseling when considering pregnancy
   2. albinism
      a) melanin is not synthesized
      b) skin, hair, and eyes are not pigmented
   3. Tay-Sachs disease
      a) synthesis of gangliosides affected
      b) infant at about 14 months has progressive neurological involvement that eventually leads to blindness and death

XI CHROMOSOMAL ABERRATIONS

A. Structure or number of chromosomes is altered: can be either autosome or sex chromosome
   1. loss of chromosome
      a) cri-du-chat syndrome
        (1) deletion of short arm of B-group chromosome
        (2) cry resembles that of a kitten
        (3) affected individual is mentally retarded
      b) Turner's syndrome (XO)
        (1) female has only one X chromosome
        (2) characteristics include short stature and webbed neck
        (3) individual is sterile
   2. breakage of chromosomes
   3. extra chromosome
      a) Down syndrome (trisomy 21)
        (1) positive correlation with maternal age
          (a) influence of paternal age being investigated
        (2) child has 47 chromosomes
        (3) characteristics
          (a) slanting eyes
          (b) flat nose
          (c) simian palm crease
          (d) wide space between second and third toes
          (e) protruding tongue
          (f) broad, pudgy neck
          (g) flaccid muscles
        (4) mental retardation may range from moderate to profound
        (5) very often other congenital defects are also present
      b) Klinefelter's syndrome (XXY)
        (1) male has extra X chromosome

(2) characteristics include a tendency to be tall with long legs
(3) may have aberrant behavior
(4) individual is sterile

XII BABY OF A DIABETIC MOTHER
A. Effect of diabetes in mother on fetus
 1. glucose crosses placenta and insulin does not, causing increased blood sugar levels in fetus
 2. fetus reacts by increasing output of insulin
 3. increased insulin production may lead to hypertrophy of pancreas
 4. increased danger of stillbirth
B. Effect of diabetic mother on infant
 1. hyperinsulin production may occur, leading to hypoglycemia
 2. oversized baby who may be immature
 3. increased incidence of respiratory distress syndrome
 4. increased incidence of congenital malformations
 5. hypocalcemia or hypomagnesemia may occur
 6. hyperbilirubinemia during first 42–72 hours of life may occur
C. Infant of diabetic mother is at increased risk for congenital malformation
 1. no one specific phenotype or malformation
  a) cause of teratogenic mechanism is being investigated
   (1) control of disease seems to be a factor (Gabbe & Oh, 1987)
D. Clincial manifestations
 1. infant is larger than average
 2. infant has enlarged viscera
 3. hypoglycemia and hypocalcemia may occur
 4. infant is at great risk for RDS
E. Treatment
 1. careful control of mother's diabetic status through insulin, diet, and activity regulation
 2. early delivery through induction or cesarean section
 3. maintenance of infant's fluid and electrolyte balance to prevent acidosis
 4. hourly blood glucose monitoring for 4–6 hours after birth. If hypoglycemia occurs, IV glucose is given
 5. phototherapy may be needed in high bilirubin levels
F. Implications for nursing process
 1. assessment of infant

a) irritability, tremors, twitches, and convulsions may indicate hypocalcemia
b) blood chemistry deviations
c) neurological assessment
d) vital signs
e) intake and output
f) vomiting or diarrhea, which may influence fluid and electrolyte balance
g) feeding behavior
h) nutritional status
2. intervention
a) monitor parenteral therapy to prevent injury and rapid overhydration
b) report any significant changes in fluid and electrolyte balance and neurological status
c) careful positioning to decrease respiratory difficulties
d) careful feeding
e) treat as if premature

XIII. POSTMATURITY

A. Pregnancy that exceeds 42 or 43 weeks
B. Oversized fetus may cause problems in labor and delivery
C. Not all prolonged pregnancies are postmature as the EDC is not always accurate
  1. postmaturity implies progressive placental insufficiency
D. Accurate gestational age must be determined through sonogram and fundal measurements
E. Fetal status is monitored through 24-hour urinary estriol, maternal plasma HCS levels, and oxytocin challenge tests
F. If fetal state is normal, pregnancy is allowed to go to term
G. If fetal distress or dysmaturity is found, labor is induced
H. Physical signs of postterm infants
  1. desquamation of skin
  2. long fingernails
  3. meconium staining of skin
I. Implications for nursing process
  1. assessment
    a) physiological status
    b) maternal-infant interaction
    c) birth injuries

XIV. PARENTAL REACTION TO THE NEWBORN WITH COMPLICATIONS

A. Parents go through grieving process that may include
   1. hostility to staff
   2. guilt feelings about their responsibility for defect
   3. denial
   4. rejection of child
B. Should be educated to understand causes of defects during prenatal period
C. Should be offered opportunity after delivery to ventilate feelings and grief
D. Need early contact with and responsibility for care of child
E. Need continuous support and understanding by health professional
F. If the infant dies (*Briefs,* 1982)
   1. the parents go through the grieving process, which is complicated by
      a) not "knowing the baby"
      b) society that does not always acknowledge the loss
      c) feelings of inadequacy or guilt
         (1) woman may feel like a failure
   2. grieving parents
      a) need an opportunity to verbalize feelings
      b) help in recognizing the reality and individuality of the baby
         (1) parents benefit from contact with infant so they have some memories of it
      c) help in dealing with feelings
   3. needs of other family members who are grieving need to be recognized
   4. some families may be assisted by participation in a support group or by a grief counseling program

---

REFERENCES

Coping with perinatal loss. (1982, February). *Briefs,* pp. 10-12.

Gabbe, S., and Oh, W. (eds). (1987). *Infant of the diabetic mother.* Columbus, OH: Ross Laboratories.

Chapter 23

Low Birthweight Infant

I. DEFINITION: ANY INFANT WEIGHING LESS THAN 2500 GRAMS
 A. Classifications
   1. preterm: born before the 37th week of gestation
      a) accounts for two-thirds of low birthweight (LBW) infants
   2. Small for gestational age
      a) accounts for about one-third of LBW infants
      b) weight below the 10th percentile
         (1) growth retarded in utero
   3. small for gestational age and premature
      a) a baby may be born before term and be small for gestational age
 B. Implications
   1. 5–7% of births are LBW
      a) approximately 1% are under 1500 g
   2. LBW babies are almost 40 times more likely to die in neonatal period
      a) survival rates at lower birthweights improving with increased technological equipment and skilled care
   3. LBW babies are at increased risk for morbidity
      a) CNS handicaps
      b) respiratory complications

II. ETIOLOGY OF PRETERM LABOR AND IUGR
 A. Causes are not known and are difficult to separate (Herron & Dulock, 1987)

B. Socioeconomic/demographic factors
   1. more than two children at home without domestic help
   2. low income or unskilled work
   3. single parent
   4. inadequate support systems
   5. maternal age less than 18 years or greater than 35
   6. no prenatal care
   7. lack of education
   8. lack of childbirth experience, which deters women from recognizing contractions
   9. poor nutrition
   10. race
C. Medical/obstetrical history
   1. previous preterm labor
   2. previous preterm delivery
   3. spontaneous or induced abortions
   4. a period of less than 1 year between the last birth and the conception of the present pregnancy
   5. any uterine anomaly that prevents expansion: hypoplastic uterus, septate or bicornuate uterus, intrauterine synechiae, leiomyomas
   6. previous DES exposure in utero
   7. incompetent cervix
   8. prepregnancy maternal weight lower than 100 lb (45.5 kg)
   9. maternal height less than 5 ft (152.4 cm)
D. Current pregnancy
   1. uterine overdistention
      a) multiple pregnancy
      b) polyhydramnios
   2. bleeding
      a) placenta previa
      b) abruptio placentae
      c) vasa previa
   3. malformations of the fetus or of the placenta and severe intrauterine growth retardation (IUGR)
   4. weight gain of less than 10 lbs (4.5 kg) by 26 weeks gestation
   5. weight loss of 5 lbs (2.25 kg) at any time during pregnancy
   6. maternal illness or disease
      a) high maternal fever
      b) acute pyelonephritis
      c) hypertension and pre-eclampsia
      d) cardiac, renal, and bowel disease

        e) diabetes mellitus
        f) bacteriuria, albuminuria, generalized peritonitis
        g) acute systemic bacterial or viral infections
     7. retained IUD
     8. premature rupture of the membranes
     9. stress
E.   Behavioral/lifestyle
     1. smoking more than 10 cigarettes per day, alcoholism, and drug usage
     2. factors that can cause excessive fatigue and may trigger uterine contractions, such as strenuous work or activities, climbing more than three flights of stairs on a routine daily basis to reach living quarters, and commuting more than 1½ hours each day
     3. any event or series of events precipitating unusual anxiety, such as death of a family member or close friend, loss of employment by either the expectant father or the pregnant woman, or separation of the pregnant woman from the expectant father through a dissolved relationship or divorce

III. PREVENTION OF LOW BIRTHWEIGHT
A.   Prepregnancy risk identification
     1. when risk is recognized counseling and patient education can begin
B.   Health education related to reproduction (before pregnancy if possible)
     1. knowledge of risk factors related to poor outcomes
     2. importance of immunization against rubella
     3. impact of environmental teratogen in the early weeks of pregnancy
     4. importance of early, regular prenatal care
     5. knowledge of relationship between smoking, drinking, drug use, and poor nutrition on pregnancy outcome
C.   During pregnancy women should be taught
     1. symptoms of preterm labor
     2. method for feeling and timing uterine contractions
     3. to notify physician if she has signs of labor of
        a) rupture of membranes
        b) leaking of fluid
        c) vaginal bleeding
        d) change in vaginal discharge

Exhibit 23-1 Physical Maturity Chart

External Sign	0	1	2	3	4
Edema	Obvious edema of hands and feet; pitting over tibia	No obvious edema of hands and feet; pitting over tibia	No edema		
Skin texture	Very thin, gelatinous	Thin and smooth	Smooth; medium thickness. Rash or superficial peeling	Slight thickening. Superficial cracking and peeling especially of hands and feet	Thick and parchment-like; superficial or deep cracking
Skin color	Dark red	Uniformly pink	Pale pink; variable over body	Pale; only pink over ears, lips, palms, or soles	
Skin opacity (trunk)	Numerous veins and venules clearly seen, especially over abdomen	Veins and tributaries seen	A few large vessels clearly seen over abdomen	A few large vessels seen indistinctly over abdomen	No blood vessels seen
Lanugo (over back)	No lanugo	Abundant; long and thick over whole back	Hair thinning especially over lower back	Small amount of lanugo and bald areas	At least ½ of back devoid of lanugo
Plantar creases	No skin creases	Faint red marks over anterior half of sole	Definite red marks over >anterior ½; indentations over < anterior ⅓	Indentations over >anterior ⅓	Definite deep indentations over >anterior ⅓

Nipple formation	Nipple barely visible; no areola	Nipple well defined; areola smooth and flat, diameter <0.75 cm	Areola stippled, edge not raised, diameter <0.75 cm	Areola stippled, edge raised, diameter >0.75 cm
Breast size	No breast tissue palpable	Breast tissue on one or both sides, <0.5 cm diameter	Breast tissue both sides; one or both 0.5–1.0 cm	Breast tissue both sides; one or both >1 cm
Ear form	Pinna flat and shapeless, little or no incurving of edge	Incurving of part of edge of pinna	Partial incurving whole of upper pinna	Well-defined incurving whole of upper pinna
Ear firmness	Pinna soft, easily folded, no recoil	Pinna soft, easily folded, slow recoil	Cartilage to edge of pinna, but soft in places, ready recoil	Pinna firm, cartilage to edge; instant recoil
Genitals Male	Neither testis in scrotum	At least one testis high in scrotum	At least one testis right down	
Female (with hips half abducted)	Labia majora widely separated, labia minora protruding	Labia majora almost cover labia minora	Labia majora completely cover labia minora	

*If score differs on two sides, take the mean.

Source: From *Developmental Medicine and Child Neurology*, 8, p. 507. Copyright 1966 by Blackwell Scientific Publications, Ltd. Adapted by permission.

Exhibit 23-2 Neurological Maturity Chart

NEUROLOGICAL SIGN	SCORE					
	0	1	2	3	4	5
POSTURE						
SQUARE WINDOW	90°	60°	45°	30°	0°	
ANKLE DORSIFLEXION	90°	75°	45°	20°	0°	
ARM RECOIL	180°	90–180°	<90°			
LEG RECOIL	180°	90–180°	<90°			
POPLITEAL ANGLE	180°	160°	130°	110°	90°	<90°
HEEL TO EAR						
SCARF SIGN						
HEAD LAG						
VENTRAL SUSPENSION						

Source: From "Clinical Assessment of Gestational Age in the Newborn Infant" by L.M.S. Dubowitz, V. Dubowitz, and C. Goldberg, 1970, *Journal of Pediatrics,* 77 (1). Copyright 1970 by The C.V. Mosby Company. Reprinted by permission.

           4. methods for decreasing stress and anxiety
           5. change behaviors that increase risk
              a) if possible prior to pregnancy
           6. reduce fatigue
D.   Treatment or prevention of associated causes

IV.   ASSESSMENT
A.   Manifestations of IUGR after birth
       1. widely spaced skull sutures
       2. low weight-to-length ratio
       3. little subcutaneous fat and muscle mass
       4. dry, peeling, and/or cracked skin
B.   Gestational age
       1. use of Dubowitz scales (Exhibits 23-1 and 23-2)

V.   PHYSICAL CHARACTERISTICS OF PRETERM INFANT
A.   The characteristics will vary with gestational age and weight
       1. when determining whether the newborn is preterm or SGA, the following physical screening devices are useful
          a) sole creases
             (1) preterm infant: has few or no sole creases
             (2) full-term infant: has more and deeper creases
          b) ears
             (1) preterm: flat and shapeless
             (2) mature infant: incurving of two-thirds of pinna
          c) breast
             (1) preterm: the nipples are hard to detect and there is no breast tissue
             (2) mature infant: has a raised areola and a small amount of breast tissue
          d) genitals
             (1) male
                (a) preterm: testes are high in canal, few rugae are present in scrotum
                (b) full term: testes are lower, many rugae are present
             (2) female
                (a) preterm: clitoris prominent and labia majora are small
                (b) full term: labia majora cover the clitoris
       2. additional observations of physical and neurological signs may also be done

B. Color
   1. pink or dark red
   2. acrocyanosis
   3. cyanotic
   4. jaundiced
C. Cry
   1. feeble
   2. cries infrequently
D. Activity
   1. usually reduced
   2. poor muscle tone
E. Reflexes
   1. sucking, gagging, and swallowing may be absent or feeble
   2. tonic neck and Moro may be present or ill-defined
F. Skin
   1. small amount of vernix caseosa
   2. ecchymotic areas common
   3. large amounts of lanugo
      a) lanugo may be absent in a baby who was delivered extremely early, may be abundant if baby delivers later
   4. little if any subcutaneous fat
   5. transparent or thin and smooth
   6. veins can be seen
G. Head and face
   1. large in proportion to body size
   2. small fontanels
   3. round or ovoid head with little molding
   4. sharp and angular features
   5. the earlier the date of delivery, the less cartilage is present in the ear
H. Chest
   1. thoracic rib cage weak due to immature bone calcification
I. Genitalia
   1. enlarged labia minora and clitoris
   2. testes may be undescended

VI. PROBLEMS OF PRETERM INFANTS

A. Respiratory problems
   1. caused by
      a) immature chest, muscular, and skeletal development

        b) weak gag and cough reflexes
        c) decrease in number of functional alveoli
     2. lead to danger of
        a) atelectasis
        b) apnea
        c) respiratory infections
        d) respiratory distress syndrome (RDS)
B. Feeding problems
     1. caused by
        a) weak sucking and swallowing reflexes
        b) small stomach capacity
        c) weak gag and cough reflex
        d) immature sphincter
        e) weak abdominal muscles
     2. may lead to
        a) aspiration
        b) inadequate intake
        c) abdominal distention
        d) vomiting
        e) problems in assimilation and absorption
        f) inadequate nutrient storage
        g) problem in metabolizing nutrients
C. Problem of maintaining body temperature
     1. caused by
        a) excessive loss of heat by radiation
        b) lack of heat production due to inactivity
        c) small amount of subcutaneous fat
        d) skin capillaries not well controlled
        e) relation of surface area to mass
           (1) surface area is larger in relation to total baby weight
     2. may lead to
        a) dehydration
        b) hypoxemia
        c) metabolic acidosis
        d) depletion of glycogen storage
        e) reduction of blood glucose levels
D. Unstable acid-base and electrolytic balance
     1. caused by
        a) immature kidneys
        b) dehydration or overhydration
        c) RDS
        d) diarrhea

2. may lead to
   a) edema
   b) acidosis
   c) dehydration
   d) oliguria
   e) death
E. Hemolytic immaturity
   1. caused by
      a) capillary fragility and permeability
      b) inability to synthesize vitamin K
      c) immature liver functioning
   2. may lead to
      a) jaundice
      b) petechiae
      c) ecchymosis
      d) hemorrhage
      e) anemia
F. Lowered resistance to infection
   1. caused by
      a) lack of maternal antibodies
         (1) placental transmission occurs in last trimester
      b) immature neonatal immune system
   2. can lead to a variety of infections
      a) bacterial
         (1) pneumonia
         (2) septicemia
         (3) meningitis
         (4) group B streptoccocal disease
         (5) diarrhea
         (6) urinary tract infection
         (7) conjunctivitis
         (8) omphalitis: infection of the umbilical stump
         (9) necrotizing enterocolitis
            (a) bacterial infection plays role; however, no evidence that it initiates disease process (Korones, 1986)
            (b) necrosis of small or large intestine
               1. disease can involve small patch or can extend over entire length of intestine
            (c) can lead to perforation
            (d) occurs in 1–3% of infants admitted to ICUs (3500–5000 babies)
               1. range of mortality reported from less than 10% to 55%

2. smaller the baby, the greater the chance of occurrence
- (e) occurs between 5 to 10 days, usually after feedings are begun
- (f) predisposing factors include prematurity, RDA, apneic spells, or other severe perinatal stessors
- (g) symptoms
  1. vomiting (bile and blood)
  2. lethargic, poor appetite
  3. abdominal distention
- (h) other causes include early feeding of premature infants with formula, and injury to intestinal mucosa
- (i) condition may be mild or severe. In severe cases there is a high mortality rate
- (j) treatment
  1. antibiotics
  2. NPO even if illness is only suspected
  3. IV fluids
- (k) human breast milk may play an important role in preventing this condition
  - b) viral infections
    - (1) congenital rubella syndrome
    - (2) cytomegalovirus
    - (3) herpes virus infection
    - (4) AIDS
  - c) protozoan infection
    - (1) toxoplasmosis

G. Central nervous system problems
  1. caused by
     a) immaturity of CNS
     b) anoxia
     c) prolonged prothrombin time leading to intracranial hemorrhage
     d) hydrocephalus
  2. problem can arise anytime during perinatal period
     a) prenatally
        (1) chronic fetal distress
        (2) severe postmaturity
     b) during labor and delivery
        (1) placenta previa
        (2) prolapsed cord
     c) during the postnatal period
        (1) congenital malformation

            (2) hypoglycemia
            (3) infection
        3. may lead to
            a) seizures
            b) motor deficits
            c) cerebral palsy
            d) mental retardation

VII. PROBLEMS OF SMALL FOR GESTATIONAL AGE (SGA) BABIES
   A. Preterm
      1. as described in Section VI
   B. Term or postterm
      1. usually have been exposed to chronic hypoxia
         a) may have respiratory depression
         b) may have meconium aspiration syndrome
      2. hypoglycemia
      3. increased chance of heat loss because of small amount of subcutaneous fat

VIII. IMPLICATIONS FOR NURSING PROCESS
   A. Assessment
      1. respirations
         a) rate and quality
         b) dyspnea, apnea, or tachypnea
            (1) tachypnea: respirations over 60/min
            (2) may be a sign of complication, such as anemia, CNS problem, RDS
            (3) may be due to high environmental temperature or transitory tachypnea of the newborn that disappears spontaneously in 2–3 days
         c) sternal and costal retractions
         d) nasal flaring
         e) cyanosis
         f) seesaw respirations
         g) expiratory grunting
      2. temperature
      3. heart rate
      4. reflexes

5. neurological symptoms: tremors, twitching, convulsions, irritability, lethargy
6. intake and output
    a) check for signs of dehydration, including poor skin turgor, lethargy, lowered urinary output, loss of weight, dry skin
    b) diarrhea
7. skin: turgor, color, and condition
8. edema
9. change in activity
10. blood gases
11. blood chemistries
12. sucking ability
13. feeding behavior
    a) suck, swallow, gag, and cough reflexes
    b) time and effort needed to feed
    c) fatigability
    d) weight gain or loss
    e) vomiting or regurgitation
14. cry
15. muscle tone
16. reaction to stimuli
17. presence of petechiae, ecchymosis
18. abdominal distention
19. frequency, amount, and character of stools and urine
20. vomiting
21. weight gain
22. injuries
    a) molding of head
    b) asymmetry of body
    c) unnatural rotation or extension of joints

B. Intervention
1. maintain body temperature
    a) neonatal heat loss occurs through radiation, conduction, convection, and evaporation. After birth the neonate loses heat by radiation to cold wall of delivery room or isolette or if placed on a metal table or through moving air currents
    b) the mature infant can increase heat production through nonshivering thermogenesis. The premature infant has less ability to do this
    c) the premature infant who suffers heat loss may develop acidosis, hypoxia, and hypoglycemia
    d) newborn should be dried immediately, placed under radiant

heat, wrapped in warm blankets, or placed in warm incubator. Oxygen should be warmed and humidified
   e) abdominal skin temperature should be kept at 97–98°F
   f) hyperthermia should be avoided
   g) energy should be conserved
      (1) handle as gently and as little as possible
2. maintain oxygen and humidity in isolette
   a) oxygen tension of arterial blood should not exceed 100 mm Hg and should be maintained between 60–80 mm Hg
   b) if child develops cyanosis at the maximum level of oxygen intake prescribed to prevent retrolental fibroplasia (40% concentration), then a higher concentration of oxygen may be necessary. This can only be administered under conditions where continuous monitoring of blood gases is possible
   c) concentration of oxygen must be analyzed every 2 hours with an oxygen analyzer. Performance of analyzer must be checked daily
   d) neonate must be observed for periods of dyspnea and apnea. Apnea is particularly likely to occur during REM sleep. Management of apnea includes treating underlying cause if there is one and also the apnea itself. Stroking of the skin is helpful; bag and mask resuscitation may be needed
3. feeding: intake should be 100/200 cal/kg of body weight
   a) if sucking reflex is absent, gavage or parenteral feeding may be administered
      (1) if gavage is necessary, always lubricate tube with water, rather than oil
      (2) chill tube to facilitate insertion
      (3) check placement of tube in stomach through aspiration of stomach contents by negative pressure from a syringe
      (4) do slow feeding with constant observation
   b) gavage and IV fluids are also used if the sucking reflex is intermittent
   c) do not use nipple if respiratory rate is ≥60/min
   d) start oral feedings with sterile water
   e) complications of gavage include vagal stimulation with apnea and bradycardia
   f) check for regurgitation, cyanosis, respiratory problems, and abdominal distention when using intermittent gavage or indwelling nasal catheter
   g) do slow, small frequent feedings if sucking reflex is present
   h) place on side after feeding to prevent aspiration

            i) if parenteral fluid is administered, monitor drip rate carefully to prevent overhydration
            j) assure adequate intake of nutrients
        4. positioning
            a) change position frequently
            b) handle gently and carefully to prevent injury
            c) maintain normal body alignment
        5. use aseptic technique to prevent infections
        6. provide sensory stimulation
            a) recent research indicates that premature infants may benefit from increased and early auditory, visual, tactile, and kinesthetic stimulation

IX. PARENTAL REACTION
A. May be afraid to touch or handle child
B. Grief reaction is normal and has a predictable pattern
        a) denial
            (1) cushions impact
        b) gradual awareness of reality
            (1) feelings of anger, guilt, shame and helplessness
                (a) mourn loss of "perfect" child
                (b) may be afraid to handle the baby
                (c) may have
                    1. sleep disturbances
                    2. periods of crying
                    3. loss of interest in daily activities
                    4. depression
                        a. may signal a need for verbalization
                (d) attempt to make sense of loss
                    1. raise question: Why me? What did I do wrong?, etc.
        c) acceptance
            (1) may take months to reach this stage
B. Implications for nursing process
    1. assessment
        a) parental reaction and behavior patterns
        b) interaction of parents with
            (1) baby
            (2) other family members
            (3) staff

             c) coping mechanisms
             d) support systems
        2. intervention
             a) provide an atmosphere that encourages open communication and verbalization of feelings
             b) share information with parents
                  (1) use terminology they can understand
                  (2) answer all questions
             c) provide appropriate reassurance and support
             d) provide opportunity for parents to interact with baby
                  (1) helps foster attachment
                  (2) helps diminish feelings of inadequacy
             e) make referral
                  (1) to parent support groups
                  (2) for counseling if necessary
             f) teach parents to care for baby
                  (1) allow them to assume as much responsibility as they can as early as possible

REFERENCES

Herron, M., & Dulock, H. (1987). *Preterm labor* (2nd ed.). Series 2, Module 5. White Plains, NY: March of Dimes.

Korones, S.B. (1986). *High risk newborn infants.* St. Louis: C.V. Mosby.

BIBLIOGRAPHY

Bobak, H., & Jensen, M. (1987). *Essentials of maternity nursing.* St. Louis: C.V. Mosby.

Church, J., et. al. (1986). New scarlet letter(s): Pediatric AIDS *Pediatrics, 77* (3), 423–427.

Dubowitz, L.M.S., et. al. (1970). Clinical assessment of gestational age in the newborn infant. *Journal of Pediatrics, 77* (1).

Edwards, L., et. al. (1988, April). Nursing management of the human response to the premature birth experience. *Neonatal Network*, pp. 82–86.

Few, B. (1987, March/April). Neonatal update: Surfactant replacement therapy. *Maternal Child Nursing*, p. 129.

Flook, M.H. (1982). *Assessment of risk in the newborn: Neonatal growth and maturity.* White Plains, NY: March of Dimes.

Hynan, M. (1988, Spring). What high-risk parents need from educators. *Childbirth Educator*, pp. 26–31.

Lawhon, G. (1988, Spring). The growth and development of preterm babies. *Childbirth Educator*, pp. 36–39.

Lewis, M. & Zarin-Ackerman, J. (1977). Early infant development. In Behrman, R.E., et al. (Eds.). *Neonatal-perinatal medicine: Diseases of the fetus and infant* (2nd ed.). St. Louis: C.V. Mosby.

Moore, M. (1983). *Realities in childbearing* (2nd ed.). Philadelphia: W.B. Saunders.

Neeson, J., & May, K. (1986). *Comprehensive maternity nursing.* Philadelphia: J.B. Lippincott.

Robertson, P., & Berlin, P. *The premature labor handbook.* New York: Doubleday and Company.

Subramanian, K.N., et. al. (1987). ECMO for severe neonatal respiratory failure. *Contemporary OB/GYN,* pp. 21–37.

Appendix A

Laboratory Tests Used During Pregnancy

I. HCG (HUMAN CHORIONIC GONADOTROPIN) IS THE BASIS FOR MODERN PREGNANCY TESTS

A. Agglutination: inhibition test consists of a two-step process that may be done with a slide or a tube
 1. the woman's urine is mixed with serum containing antibodies to HCG. A carrier coated with HCG is then added.
 2. if the test is positive the HCG in the woman's urine will bind with the serum antibodies and will *not* agglutinate with the carrier antigen. In a negative test clumping or agglutination *will* occur
 3. test that uses slide takes 2 minutes. Tube test takes 2 hours and is more sensitive
 4. to reduce the chance of a false-negative result test is usually done 6 weeks after last menstrual period. Urine is collected in a clean specimen bottle
B. Radioreceptor assay (RRA): highly sensitive and accurate
 1. measures the competition of HCG for receptor sites on the cell membrane
 2. can be done 2 weeks after conception: takes 1 hour
C. Radioimmunoassay: measures the B-subunit of HCG. Can be used 8–9 days after conception
 1. takes 1 to 3 hours and is very accurate
D. New tests that are simpler and highly sensitive will soon be available
E. Home pregnancy tests: claim to be 95% reliable if used correctly. Used 15 days after a missed period. Urine must be clear and uncontaminated by dirt or particles. No vibrations should be near the testing area
F. False negative test results may be caused by
 1. errors in reading
 2. too much dilution of urine

3. urine stored too long at room temperature
4. use of certain drugs
G. False-positive results may be caused by
1. errors in reading
2. use of certain drugs
3. detergent on glassware
4. HCG from other sources, such as malignant tumor or molar pregnancy

II. ULTRASOUND DIAGNOSIS OF PREGNANCY

A. Used to observe the fetus within the uterus within 5 weeks after last menstrual period
B. Real-time ultrasound: used most frequently as it is fast and inexpensive. Used to determine fetal presentation, fetal measurements, signs of fetal life, diagnosis of multiple gestation, location of the placenta, fetal anomalies, and when used prior to amniocentesis, fetal age
C. When real-time ultrasound is not available the gray scale (B-scan) may be used. It is also used in placental problems and to observe the gestational sac
D. Woman should have a full bladder and is asked to drink several glasses of water before the test
E. Women report many positive feelings toward the baby when they can see it moving on the oscilloscope
F. In 1984 NIH held a conference to assess the safety of ultrasound in pregnancy. It was determined at that time that, although there was no evidence that ultrasound was harmful to mother or fetus, it was desirable that the procedure not be used on a routine basis. Further studies on safety were recommended

III. ASSESSMENT OF FETAL STATUS

A. Amniocentesis
1. 10 to 20 cc of amniotic fluid is removed from the amniotic sac by a needle inserted through the abdominal wall. The site for the procedure is selected after localization of the placenta by ultrasonography and palpation of the fetus
2. a relatively safe procedure if performed properly by skilled physicians. Such complications as maternal hemorrhage, infection, puncture of the fetus, or miscarriage (1.3% miscarriage rate) may occur

3. sterile technique must be used. Prior to procedure patient must void and fetal heart rate (FHR) is checked. FHR rate is checked immediately after withdrawal of fluid and every 15 minutes for 1 hour after procedure
4. careful preparation of the woman for the procedure is important to allay any anxiety or fear
5. usually performed after the 14th week of pregnancy when there is sufficient amniotic fluid formed to allow removal of needed amount without affecting the fetus. Under study is the performance of amniocentesis earlier than 14 weeks
6. used to diagnose genetic defects of the fetus due to chromosomal abnormalities, inborn errors of metabolism, neural tube defects, sex-linked defects, bilirubin, levels in Rh problems, and L/S ratio, which measures surfactant in fetal lung
7. in cases where a genetic defect is discovered the patient may choose to have an abortion. Because of the delay in performing amniocentesis some women choose to have chorionic villus sampling, which can be done earlier (results of amniocentesis may take 2–3 weeks)
8. a local anesthetic is used and some discomfort may occur from the injection. Abdominal cramps may occur for a few hours immediately following the procedure
9. to avoid the possibility of Rh sensitization of the mother when the mother is Rh negative, RhoGam is usually given after the procedure

B. Chorionic villus sampling: can be used to detect genetic defects instead of amniocentesis
1. plastic catheter is inserted vaginally into the uterus where a sample of the villi is obtained through aspiration. Ultrasound is used to guide the instrument; may also be done transabdominally
2. can be done 8 to 10 weeks after last menstrual period and results are obtained in 2–4 days. If abortion is chosen when a congenital defect, such as Down syndrome, is detected an earlier-stage abortion can be performed
3. neural tube defects cannot be detected
4. risks are under study and may include septic shock and miscarriage (2% miscarriage rate)

C. Fetoscopy: an experimental technique that introduces a fetoscope into the amniotic cavity through the abdomen
1. ultrasound is used to locate fetus and placenta
2. used for direct visualization of fetus and fetal blood, and skin sampling
3. performed at the 17th week

      4. difficult procedure that must be performed by experts
      5. complications include miscarriage and infection. Antibiotics may be given to prevent infection
- D. A newer technique is the insertion of a needle into the umbilical cord using ultrasound to view the fetus. This technique allows fetal blood sampling to assess blood counts, liver function, blood gases, and acid-base balance
      1. in Rh babies blood transfusions may be given through this technique
      2. extreme skill is needed and complications include bleeding from the cord, premature labor, and infection
- E. Estriol determinations from maternal urine or blood
      1. estriol is the predominant estrogen produced during pregnancy
      2. serial determinations can assist in assessing fetal status in hypertension, diabetes, placental insufficiency states, and other conditions
      3. significant fall in urinary estriol: 35%
      4. significant fall in plasma estriol: 50%
      5. signs of fetal distress include a downward trend or precipitous fall
      6. false-negative results are rare
      7. false-positive results occur about one-third of cases
      8. in interpreting estriol values, such factors as maternal renal disease, drugs, multiple pregnancies, bedrest, and other conditions that may increase or decrease estriol levels must be considered
      9. values for estriol should be taken serially and compared to earlier values because of the wide range of normal values
- F. Human placental lactogen (hPL) is found in serum by the 28th day of pregnancy
      1. low levels of hPL may indicate fetal distress, threatened abortion, toxemia, and IUGR
      2. estriol levels must be examined when hPL levels indicate a possible problem
      3. hPL levels may be high in multiple gestation and certain maternal conditions or diseases
- G. Assessment of fetal movement
      1. fetal movements increase in normal pregnancies as the pregnancies progress
      2. a sudden decrease in fetal movements may indicate fetal problems. The degree of change in the number of movements is very important
      3. at 30 weeks women are asked to count the number of fetal movements in a 12-hour period. If less than ten fetal movements are felt for a 2-day period woman is asked to report this to the physician for further study

H. Fetal heart rate monitoring: used in hypertension, IUGR, diabetes, postmaturity and other conditions
   1. nonstress test (NST)
      a) evaluates the FHR in relation to fetal movement
      b) FHR should accelerate in response to fetal movement
      c) the recording is carried out until two accelerations are observed within any 10-minute period. There is no minimal time limit
      d) a reactive pattern requires two accelerations of at least 15 BPM in amplitude and 15 seconds in duration associated with fetal movement. If a reactive pattern is not observed in 40 minutes the test is classified as nonreactive. Glucose may be given to the mother or sound used to stimulate a reactive pattern
      e) a sinusoidal pattern has absent accelerations with baseline repetitive oscillations. This may indicate a problem. This pattern may be followed up by a reactive pattern
      f) nonreactive and sinusoidal patterns should be followed by CST (contraction stress test)
      g) in both NST and CST the preparation of the mother is similar. The mother will usually be anxious because the test indicates that the physician suspects a problem. The mother will need careful explanations and preparation for the test. Mother lies in a semi-Fowler's position or in a lateral tilt with right hip elevated. The fetal heart monitor should be applied carefully and maternal blood pressure taken at the beginning and during the procedure
   2. contraction stress test (CST): provides information on fetal reserve oxygen
      a) measures FHR in response to uterine contractions
      b) uterine contractions are stimulated by IV oxytocin infusion or breast massage. Oxytocin administration usually takes 90 minutes, whereas breast massage can usually elicit a CST within 40 minutes without the trauma of an IV. In breast stimulation the nipple is rolled or tugged for 10 minutes to stimulate contractions. A warm moist compress is sometimes placed on the breast before the stimulation is done
      c) if oxytocin administration is used, careful supervision of the infusion and the length of the contraction is needed
      d) oxytocin is contraindicated in threatened preterm labor, hydramnios, placenta previa, multiple fetuses, rupture of membranes, and previous cesarean section
      e) CST is indicated when fetus is in danger in third trimester. If negative it is usually repeated weekly

        f) positive test: consistent late deceleration of FHR after onset of uterine contraction
        g) negative test: at least three contractions within 10 minutes lasting 40 seconds without late FHR decelerations
        h) suspicious test: occasional late decelerations that do not repeat with each contraction
        i) unsatisfactory test: poor tracing or lack of sufficient contractions
        j) there have been both false-positive and false-negative CST results so tests must be interpreted carefully
I. Serum alphafetoprotein (AFP) maternal blood test: screens for neural tube defects (NTD) at 16–18 weeks gestation
    1. elevated AFP may indicate neural tube defect, abortion, fetal death, multiple pregnancy. False-positive results are common and test should be confirmed by amniocentesis
    2. a low serum AFP may indicate possible Down syndrome and should be followed by sonogram and amniocentesis for further clarification
J. Lecithin/sphingomyelin ratio
    1. measures surfactant activity of fetal lung by assessing amniotic fluid
    2. value of 1.5-1 indicates an immature lung with a risk of RDS
    3. value of 2.0 indicates a mature lung with low risk of RDS, except for an infant of a diabetic mother
K. New frontiers in fetal testing undergoing research
    1. earlier amniocentesis and later chorionic villus sampling currently being tested for safety and accuracy
    2. trans-abdominal chorionic villus sampling uses a small amount of placental tissue drawn out through a needle inserted in the abdomen
    3. ultrasound vaginal probe
    4. ultrasound tests during second trimester can spot fetuses at risk for Down syndrome; signs are shorter thigh bones and extra roll of skin at back of neck

Index

A

Abdomen
  newborn, 316-317
  postpartum period, 269
Abdominal pregnancy, 132
Abdominal wall, postpartum period, 256
ABO incompatibility, 136-137
  newborn, 337
Abortion, 51
  dangers of, 129
  methods of
    dilation and curettage (D&C), 128
    dilation and evacuation (D&E), 128
    hysterotomy, 129
    prostaglandin E_2 infusion, 128
    RU 486, 128
    saline induction, 128-129
  nursing process and, 129
  reasons for, 127
  spontaneous abortion
    etiology of causation, 130
    psychological factors, 131
    symptoms, 130
    treatment, 130-131
  types of, 127
Abruptio placentae, 126-127
Abscess, breast, 294

Acrocyanosis, 302
Acute fatty liver, in pregnancy, 156-157
Adherent placenta, 234
Adjustment, postpartum, stages of, 259-260
African natives, maternal care, 3
Afterpains, assessment of, 264
Age, high-risk pregnancy, 124
Agenesis of kidneys/ureter, 352
Agglutination, pregnancy test, 377
AIDS
  newborn, 342-344
  postpartum period, 295
Albinism, 82, 354
Alcohol abuse
  fetal alcohol syndrome, 84-85
  in pregnancy, 158
Aldomet, in pregnancy, 168
Allergy, to sperm, 44, 47, 48-49
Alphafetoprotein test, 91-92, 382
America, colonial, maternal care, 5-6
American Indians, maternal care, 3
Amnesiacs, use during labor, 214-215
Amniocentesis, 90, 378-379
  and maternal age, 124
Amniotic fluid, 77-78
Amniotomy, 240

Analgesics
  postpartum period, 275
  in pregnancy, 166
  use during labor, 213-214
Anemic anoxia, 329
Anencephaly, 233, 347
Anesthesia
  cesarean section, 219
  general anesthesia, 215-216
  during labor, 187
  nursing process and, 216, 220
  regional anesthesia, 216-218
  spinal anesthesia, 218-219
Anogenital area, newborn, 307
Anovulation, treatment, 48
Anoxia, 328-329
  causes of, 328-329
  types of, 329
Anoxic anoxia, 329
Antacids, in pregnancy, 165-166
Antibiotics
  postpartum period, 276
  in pregnancy, 167
Anticonvulsants, in pregnancy, 169
Antiemetics, in pregnancy, 166
Antihypertensives, in pregnancy, 168
Antiprostaglandins, in pregnancy, 171
Apgar, 199, 200, 207 313
Apnea
  newborn, 319-320
  types of, 329
Apresoline, in pregnancy, 168
Arm paralysis, newborn, 336
Artificial insemination, 49
Asepsis, newborn, 322
Aspiration pneumonia, 331
ASPO (American Society for Prophylaxis in Obstetrics), 97
Asynchronous (seesaw) respirations, 330
Atelectasis, 330-331
  causes of, 330
  symptoms, 330
  treatment, 331
Autosomal defects, 80-81
Autosomal recessive conditions, 81-82
Awake states, newborn, 310

B

Babinski reflex, 308
Backache, in pregnancy, 108-109
Back labor, 223
Bandl's ring, 228
Baptism, newborn, 208
Barbiturates
  in pregnancy, 163-164
  use during labor, 212
Bartholin's gland, 39
Basal body temperature (BBT), 47-48, 56-57
Bath, newborn, 322
Battered women, pregnancy risks, 157-158
Beta-adrenergic receptor stimulants in pregnancy, 171
Beta thalassemia, 92
Biliary tract obstruction, 352
Birth control. *See* Contraception
Birth defects
  chromosomal abnormalities, 354-355
  classification of, 347
  congenital heart disease, 349-350
  gastrointestinal defects, 351-352
  genitourinary system defects, 352-353
  musculoskeletal system defects, 353
  neural tube defects, 347-348
  neurological disorders, 348-349
  parental reactions to, 357
  postmaturity, 356
  respiratory defects, 350-351
  See also Fetal abnormalities; High-risk newborns; specific defects.
Birthing alternatives, 188-189
Birthing rooms, 188-189
Bladder
  extrophy of, 353
  postpartum period, 267-268
Blastocyst, 76
Blood, postpartum period, 257
Blood incompatibilities, in pregnancies, 135-137
Blood pressure, in pregnancy, 105
Blood sample, fetus, 200-201
Body temperature, newborn, 305
  maintenance of, 321

Bonding, parent-child, 261, 272-273
Bowel function, postpartum period, 268
Brachial palsy, 336
Bradycardia, fetus, 197, 198
Braxton-Hicks contractions, 184
Brazelton scale, 319
Breast feeding
　benefits to newborn, 279-280
　care of breasts, 280
　as contraception, 53-54
　contraindications to, 283
　drugs and, 283-284
　drug stimulation of lactation, 280
　effects on mother, 278-279
　engorgement, prevention of, 282
　establishment of lactation, 278
　mechanisms of, 278
　milk supply, maintenance of, 282-283
　nipple damage, prevention of, 281-282
　nursing process and, 280-283
　nutritional factors, 279-280, 283
Breasts, 40
　anatomy of, 277-278
　care during pregnancy, 108
　change in pregnancy, 104
　newborn, 307
　postpartum disorders
　　breast abscess, 294
　　mastitis, 293-294
　postpartum period, 257, 268-269
Breathing techniques, prepared childbirth, 222, 223
Breech presentation, 232-233
　etiology, 232-233
　management, 233
　prognosis, 233
　types of, 180-181 232
Bronchopulmonary dysplasia, 334
Bulbo-urethral glands, 34
Butorphanol, use during labor, 213

C

Calcium, in pregnancy, 114
Candida albicans, 340
Caput succedaneum, newborn, 314
Cardiac glycosides, in pregnancy, 168

Cardiovascular system, change during pregnancy, 105, 148
Cephalocaudal growth, 76
Cephalohematoma, newborn, 314
Cervical cap, 65
Cervix
　and complications of labor/delivery, 235
　incompetent, treatment for, 130-131
　in labor, 184-185
　postpartum infection, 289
　postpartum period, 256
Cesarean section
　anesthesia, 219
　court-ordered 158
　increasing incidence of, 235-236
　indications for, 236
　patient management, 236-237
　psychological factors, 237
Chemicals/gases, and fetus, 86
Child abusers, at-risk women, 159
Chills, postpartum period, 266
Chlamydia
　newborn, 341
　postpartum period, 295
Chloasma (mask of pregnancy), 106
Choriocarcinoma, 133
Chorionic villi sampling, 91, 379
Chorioretinitus, 154
Chromosomal abnormalities
　cri-du-chat syndrome, 354
　Down syndrome, 354
　infertility and, 45
　Klinefelter's syndrome, 354-355
Circulatory system
　fetal, 74, 76
　newborn, 302
Circumcision, 323
Circumoral pallor, 302
Classes for expectant parents, 96
Cleft lip, 351
Cleft palate, 80, 86, 351
Clomid, 48
Clubfoot, 353
Coarctation of the aorta, 349
Cocaine, in pregnancy, 163-164

Coitus interruptus, as contraception, 53
Color-blindness, 82
Complete breech, 232
Complications of labor/delivery
  accident/injuries, 249-250
    inversion of uterus, 250
    rupture of uterus, 249
    sudden death, 250
  breech presentation, 232-233
  face-brow presentation, 231
  fetal abnormalities related to, 233-234
  meconium aspiration syndrome, 229-230
  occiput posterior presentation, 230-231
  operative interventions
    Cesarean section, 235-238
    episiotomy, 239
    forceps delivery, 237-238
    vacuum extraction, 238-239
  passage-related abnormalities, 234-235
  pathological retraction ring, 228
  placental abnormalities, 234
  precipitate delivery, 228-229
  premature rupture of membranes (PROM), 229
  prolapsed cord, 231-232
  shoulder-traverse lie presentation, 231
  uterine dysfunction, 227-228
Conception
  fertilization, 69
  implantation, 69-70
Condom, as contraception, 55
Congenital dislocation of hip, 353
Congenital heart disease, 86
  coarctation of the aorta, 349
  patent ductus, 349
  patent foramen ovale, 349
  stenosis, 349
  tetralogy of Fallot, 349
  transposition of the great vessels, 349
  ventricular septal defects, 349
Congenital hydrocephalus, 347
Congenital laryngeal stridor, 350
Constipation, in pregnancy, 104, 107
Continuous caudal block, 217-218

Contraception, 51
  breast feeding as, 53-54
  coitus interruptus, 53
  condom, 55
  diaphragm, 54-55
  douche, 54
  future methods, 65-66
  IUD (intrauterine device), 58-60
  morning-after pill, 65
  nursing process and, 68
  oral contraceptives, 60-64
  rhythm method, 56-58
  spermicides, 55-56
  sterilization, 64-65
  vaginal sponge, 56
Contractions
  assessment, 194
  fetal monitoring, 195-200
  intervention, 194-195
  true vs. false labor, 184
Contraction stress test, 381-382
Cooley's anemia, 82, 92
Coombs' test, 339
Coumarin derivatives, in pregnancy, 167
Court-ordered obstetrical procedures, 158
Couvade, 3
Credé method, 6
Cri-du-chat syndrome, 354
Cry, newborn, 318
Curtis marmorata, 315
Cyanosis, 302, 315, 337
Cyclopropane with oxygen, general anesthesia, 215
Cystic/polycystic kidneys, 352
Cystitis, in pregnancy, 154
Cytomegalovirus, 85
  newborn, 342
  in pregnancy, 154

D

Darvon, postpartum period, 275
Deceleration, fetus, 198
Decidua, 70
Deladumone, postpartum period, 275
Demerol, use during labor, 213
Depression, postpartum blues, 262, 274

Descent, mechanism of labor, 182
Detoxification program, 165
Diabetes
　newborn of diabetic mother, 355-356
　in pregnancy, 142-147
　　at-risk women, 143
　　classes of, 143
　　effects of, 144-145
　　management, 145-147
Diaphragm, as contraception, 54-55
Diaphragmatic hernia, 350
Diaphragmatic paralysis, 337
Diarrhea, epidemic, newborn, 344
Diethylstilbestrol, postpartum period, 275
Dilation and curettage (D&C), abortion, 128
Dilation and evacuation (D&E), abortion, 128
Dioxin, in breast milk, 283
Diuretics, in pregnancy, 169
Diuril, in pregnancy, 169
Doptone/Doppler, fetal heart rate, 193
Douche, as contraception, 54
Down syndrome, 80, 316, 354
Drug dependence and pregnancy, 158-159, 164-165
　heroin/cocaine/barbiturates, 163-164
Drugs and breast feeding, 283-284
Drugs and labor
　amnesiacs, 214-215
　analgesics, 213-214
　narcotic antagonists, 214
　sedatives, 212-213
　tranquilizers, 214
Drugs and pregnancy
　categorization of, 161-162
　effects on fetus, 162-163, 172-174
　high-risk pregnancy, 167-171
　and maternal physiological changes, 162
　over-the-counter drugs, 165-167
　placenta, role in, 162, 211-212
　self-medication, 163
Duncan mechanism, 185
Dyspnea, in pregnancy, 105, 109
Dystocia, 227

E

Ears, newborn, 316
Eclampsia, 140-142
　management of, 140-141
　postpartum period, 296
　symptoms, 140
Ectopic pregnancy, 131-132
Edema, in pregnancy, 109
Egyptians (ancient), maternal care, 3-4
Eighteenth century, maternal care, 5
Ejaculation, physiology of, 35
Electrical field method, birth control, 66
Embryo, period of, 78
Emotional care, newborn, 323-324
Endocrine abnormalities, infertility, 45, 46, 47-48
Endocrine system, change in pregnancy, 106
Endometriosis, 46, 47
Endometritis, 46
　postpartum period, 289-290
Enemas, during labor, 186
Engagement, mechanism of labor, 182
Epidemic diarrhea, newborn, 344
Epididymis, 33
Epidural anesthesia, 216-217, 219
Episiotomy, 205
　types of, 239
Epispadias, 44
Erb's palsy, 336
Ergotrate, postpartum period, 275
Erythema toxicum, 316
Erythroblastosis fetalis, 338
Esidrix, in pregnancy, 169
Esophageal atresia, 351
Estrogen, 40-42
Ethanol
　in pregnancy, 170
　for preterm labor, 244
Exercise, during pregnancy, 108-109, 116-117
Extension, mechanism of labor, 182
External rotation, mechanism of labor, 183
Extrauterine pregnancy, 132
Extrophy of bladder, 353
Eyes, newborn, 309, 316
　care of, 207

F

Face-brow presentation, 231
Facial paralysis, newborn, 336
Faintness, in pregnancy, 111
Fallopian tubes, 39
False labor, signs of, 184
False-negative, pregnancy test, 377
False-positive, pregnancy test, 378
Family planning
  barriers to, 51-52
  needs in, 52-53
  nursing process and, 67-68
  reasons for, 51
  services for, 52
  See also Contraception.
Father-child interaction, postpartum period, 261
Female reproductive physiology, 35-42
Fenoterel, in pregnancy, 171
Fertility workup
  female, 45-46
  male, 46-47
Fertilization, 69, 76
Fetal abnormalities
  genetic factors, 80-82
  multifactoral inheritance, 86
  pre-natal screening tests, 90-92
  prevention, nursing process in, 86-92
  teratogens, 82-86
  "TORCH" complex of infections, 85-86
  See also specific topics.
Fetal alcohol syndrome, 84-85, 158
Fetal blood sampling, 200-201
Fetal development
  amniotic fluid, 77-78
  anatomical development, 76-77
  embryo, period of, 78
  fetal membranes, 77
  fetus, period of, 78-79
  ovum, period of, 76-77
  principals of, 76
  processes in, 76
  sex determination, 79
Fetal heart rate (FHR), 99
  assessment, 192-193
  factors causing changes, 199-200
  intervention, 193-194
  methods for determining FHR, 189-190, 193
Fetal monitoring, electronic
  abnormal patterns, 189-190
  and contractions, 195-200
  data, significance of, 198
  data interpretation, 197-198
  external monitoring, 195-196
  factors causing changes, 199-200
  internal monitoring, 196-197
  nursing assessment, 192-193
  risks, 189
Fetal physiology
  circulatory system, 74, 76
  placental development, 71
  placental function, 74, 76
Fetal stethoscope, 193
Fetoscopy, 90-91, 379-380
Flatulence, 104, 108
Flexion, mechanism of labor, 182
Folic acid, in pregnancy, 115-116
Follicle-stimulating hormone (FSH), 35, 40, 41, 46
Fontanels, 312, 314
Footling, 232
Footling breech, 181
Forceps delivery, 237-238
  dangers, 238
  indications for, 237
  types of forceps, 237-238
Formula feeding, newborn, 320-321
Fractures, newborn, 335
Frank breech, 180, 232
Frenum linguae, 351
Full breech, 181
Fundal height, measuring, 99
Furosemide, in pregnancy, 169

G

Gagging reflex, 308
Gamete intra-fallopian tube transfer (GIFT), 49-50
Gastrointestinal defects
  biliary tract obstruction, 352
  cleft lip, 351

Index 389

cleft palate, 351
esophageal atresia, 351
imperforate anus, 351
intestinal obstructions, 351
omphalocele, 352
pyloric stenosis, 351
tongue tie, 351
tracheoesophageal fistula, 351
umbilical hernia, 352
Gastrointestinal system
  change in pregnancy, 104
  newborn, 306-307
General anesthesia
  contraindications, 215
  disadvantages, 215
  types, 215
Genetic factors in birth defects
  autosomal defects, 80-81
  autosomal recessive conditions, 81-82
  sex chromosome abnormalities, 82
Genital herpes, in pregnancy, 153
Genitals, newborn, 307, 317
Genital tract abnormalities, infertility, 43-44, 47
Genitourinary system defects
  agenesis of kidneys/ureters, 352
  cystic/polycystic kidneys, 352
  extrophy of bladder, 353
  hypospadias, 352
  sexual ambiguity, 352
Glucocorticoids, in pregnancy, 170
Gonadotropin-releasing hormone (GnRH), 41
Gonorrhea
  newborn, 342
  postpartum period, 295
  in pregnancy, 152
Government programs, maternal/child care, 8-10
Gravida, definition of, 177
Greeks (ancient), maternal care, 4
Group B streptococcus, newborn, 342

H

Harvey, William, 5
Head, newborn, 312, 313-314

Hearing, newborn, 309
Heartburn, 104
  in pregnancy, 107
Heart disease
  congenital, newborn, 349-350
  in pregnancy, 147-150
    classes of, 147
    diagnosis, 148
    management, 149
    risks, 148
Heart rate, newborn, 302
Heat, and fetus, 86
Heat regulation, newborn, 304-305
Hebrews, maternal care, 4
HELLP syndrome, 142
Hematomas, postpartum period, 295-296
Hematopoietic system, newborn, 303
Hemophilia, 82
Hemorrhage
  postpartum period
    diagnosis, 286-287
    etiology, 285
    predisposing factors, 285-286
    prognosis, 287
    symptoms, 286
    treatment, 287-288
  in pregnancy, 125-127
Hemorrhoids, in pregnancy, 104, 107
Heparin, in pregnancy, 167
Hepatitis B, 85-86
  newborn, 342
Heroin, in pregnancy, 163-164
Herpes virus, 85
  newborn, 342
  postpartum period, 295
  in pregnancy, 153
Heterozygote screening, 92
Heterozygous state (Dd), 80-81
High-forceps, 238
High-risk newborns
  birth injuries
    intracranial hemorrhage, 336-337
    paralysis, 336
    phrenic nerve injury, 337
    skeletal injuries, 335
    soft tissue, 335

hemolytic disease
   ABO incompatibility, 337
   nursing process and, 339
   Rh incompatibility, 337-339
infections
   AIDS, 342-344
   chlamydia, 341
   cytomegalovirus, 342
   epidemic diarrhea, 344
   gonorrhea, 342
   Group B streptococcus, 342
   hepatitis B, 342
   herpes virus, 342
   most common pathogens, 339
   nursing process and, 344-345
   ophthalmia neonatorum, 340
   rubella, 341-342
   syphilis, 341
   thrush, 340-341
   TORCH syndrome, 340-341
respiratory problems
   anoxia, 328-329
   apnea, 329
   atelectasis, 330-331
   hyaline membrane disease, 332-334
   meconium aspiration syndrome, 334
   nursing process and, 334-335
   pneumonia, 331-332
   symptoms of, 330
risk factors, identification of, 327-328
High-risk pregnancy
   ABO incompatibility, 136-137
   abortions, 127-131
   abruptio placentae, 126-127
   acute fatty liver, 156-157
   age, 124
   alcohol abuse, 158
   and battered women, 157-158
   cytomegalovirus, 154
   diabetes, 142-147
   drug abuse, 158-159
   drugs used, 167-171
   eclampsia, 140-142
   ectopic pregnancy, 131-132
   extrauterine pregnancy, 132
   genital herpes, 153
   heart disease, 147-150

HELLP syndrome, 142
hydramnios, 134-135
hyperemesis gravidarum, 135
hypertension, 150-151
maternal PKU, 156
molar pregnancy, 132-133
monilia, 153
out-of-wedlock pregnancy, 124-125
parity, 125
placenta previa, 125-126
pre-eclampsia, 137-140
psychosocial problems of
   mother-to-be, 159-161
puerperal pulmonary embolus, 157
respiratory disease, 151-152
Rh factor, 135-136
rubella, 155
socioeconomic factors, 123
special needs of mother-to-be, 123
toxoplasmosis, 154-155
urinary infections, 153-154
varicella, 155-156
venereal disease, 152
Hindus, maternal care, 4
Hippocrates, 4
Histogenesis, 76
Histotoxic anoxia, 329
Home pregnancy tests, 377
Hormones
   female, 40-42
   male, 35
   and onset of labor, 181-182
   postpartum period, 258
   in pregnancy, 73-74
   and preterm labor, 242
Human chorionic gonadotropin (HCG), 133
Human placental lactogen (hPL), 106, 133
Hyaline membrane disease, 332-334
   complications, 333-334
   incidence of, 332
   intervention, 333
   prevention, 332
   signs of, 333
Hydatidiform mole, 132-133
Hydralazine, in pregnancy, 169

Hydramnios, 134-135
Hydremia, 257
Hydrocephalus, 233
Hydrodiuril, in pregnancy, 169
Hydrops fetalis, 338
Hydrotubation, 46, 47
Hyperactive labor, 194
Hyperemesis gravidarum, 135
Hyperprolactinemia, 48
Hypertension
   antihypertensive drugs, 168-169
   diuretics, 169
   in pregnancy, 150-151
      eclampsia, 140-141
      pre-eclampsia, 137-139, 150
      types of, 150
Hyperthyroidism, 48
Hypertonic uterine dysfunction, 227
Hypertonus, 194
Hypoactive labor, 194
Hypospadias, 44, 352
Hypothrombinemia, 207
Hypotonic uterine dysfunction, 227-228
Hysterosalpingogram, 46
Hysterotomy, abortion, 129

I

Immune system, newborn, 310-311
Imperforate anus, 351
Implantation, 69-70, 76
Incompetent cervix, treatment, 130-131
Induction of labor
   amniotomy, 240
   contraindications for, 240
   drugs used, 240-241
      oxytocin, 240-241
      prostaglandin E_2 gel, 241
      indications for, 239
Infections
   female, 44, 47
   newborn, 339-345
   postpartum period, 294-295
Infectious thrombophlebitis, postpartum period, 290
Infertility
   causes of, 43-45

fertility workup, 45-47
psychological factors, 51
treatment methods, 47
   female, 47-48
   gamete intra-fallopian tube transfer (GIFT), 49-50
   in vitro fertilization, 49
   male, 48-49
   ovum transfer, 49
   for sexual dysfunction, 50-51
   surrogate motherhood, 50
   types of, 43
Informed consent, women in labor, 190
Inhalation analgesia, use during labor, 213-214
Insulin management, diabetic pregnancy, 145-146
Intracranial hemorrhage, newborn, 336-337
Internal monitoring, fetus, 196-197
Internal rotation, mechanism of labor, 182
Intestinal obstructions, 351
Intrauterine growth retardation (IUGR), 99
In vitro fertilization, 49
Involution, uterus, 255-256, 265
Iron, in pregnancy, 114
Isoniazid, 151
Isoxsuprine, in pregnancy, 171
IUD (intrauterine device)
   as contraception, 58-60
   contraindications, 59
   side effects, 60
   types of, 58-59

J

Jaundice, newborn, 306, 315

K

Kernicterus, 338
Kidneys, cystic, 352
Klinefelter's syndrome, 82, 354-355
Kneeling, 232

L

Labor
  birthing alternatives, 188-189
  causes of
    hormonal, 181-182
    placental aging, 182
    uterine distension, 182
  comfort factors, 202-203
  contractions, 184, 194-195
  fetal blood sampling, 200-201
  fetal monitoring, 189-190, 192, 195-200
  informed consent and, 190
  lacerations, 205-206
  mechanisms of, 182-183
  nursing process and, 190-209
  onset of, signs of, 183-184
  pain, causes of, 221
  parental decision-making areas, 186-190
  placenta, delivery of, 185, 206
  position of fetus, 179-180
  positions during, 187, 204-205
  post-labor reactions, 185-186
  presentations of fetus, types of, 180-181
  psychological factors, 203-204, 224
  stages of, 184-186
  transition, 204
  true vs. false labor, 184
  vaginal discharge, 201-202
  vital signs, 201
  See also Anesthesia and labor; Complications of labor/delivery; Drugs and labor; Induction of labor; Prepared childbirth.
Lacerations, during labor, 205-206
Lactation. *See* Breast feeding
Lactation supressants, postpartum period, 275
La Leche League, 96
Lamaze method, 222
Laparscopy, 46
Lasix, in pregnancy, 169
Laxatives, in pregnancy, 166
Left mentum anterior (LMA), 180

Leg cramps
  in labor, 205
  in pregnancy, 106, 111
Legislation, maternal/child care, 8-10
Leopold's maneuvers, 99
Lightening (engagement), 183
Linea nigra, 106
Lochia
  assessment of, 264, 265-266
  postpartum period, 256
Longitudinal lie, 179
Lorfan, use during labor, 214
Low birthweight infants
  assessment of, 365
  causes of, 359-361
  definition of, 359
  implications of, 359
  nursing process and, 370-372
  parental reaction to, 373-374
  physical characteristics of, 365-366
  physical maturity chart, 362-363
  prevention of, 361, 365
  problems of, 366-370
Low forceps, 237
Luteal phase defect, 45, 130
Luteinizing hormone (LH), 35, 41

M

Maculopapular rash, 316
Magnesium sulfate
  eclampsia, 140
  in pregnancy, 170
  for preterm labor, 245
Male reproductive physiology, 33-35
Maple syrup urine disease (MSUD), 82
Massage
  in labor, 224
  uterus, postpartum 265
Mastitis, postpartum period, 293-294
Maternal/child care
  changing concepts in, 23-24, 28
  government programs, 8-10
  historical view, 3-10
  modern problems, 21-23
  modern trends, 11-21

needs for, 23
Standard of Practice, nursing, 24-28
Maternal PKU, in pregnancy, 156
Meconium, 307, 317
Meconium aspiration syndrome, 229-230, 334
Medieval era, maternal care, 5
Medrol, 49
Membranes
   fetal, 77
   premature rupture of membranes (PROM), 229
   rupture of, 183
Meningomyelocele, 348
Metabolic disorders
   albinism, 354
   PKU, 81 353-354
   Tay-Sachs disease, 82 354
Metabolism, change in pregnancy, 105
Methadone maintenance, 165
Methergine, postpartum period, 275
Methoxyflurane, general anesthesia, 215
Microcephaly, 348
Mid-forceps, 238
Milia, 316
Minerals, supplementation in pregnancy, 114, 167
Miscarriage. See Spontaneous abortion
Molar pregnancy, 132-133
Molding of head, newborn, 314
Mongolian spots, 315
Monilia, in pregnancy, 153
Monilia infection, 340
Morning-after pill, as contraception, 65
Morning sickness, 107
Moro reflex, 308
Morphogenesis, 76
Moschion, 4
Mother-child interaction
   bonding, 261, 272-273
   intervention, 324
   learning needs of mother, 324-325
   mothering, 323-324
   nursing intervention, 271-274, 324
   postpartum period, 261
Mouth, newborn, 316

Multipara, 184
   definition of, 177
Multiple pregnancy, and complications of labor/delivery, 234
Muscular dystrophy, 82
Musculoskeletal system, change in pregnancy, 106
Musculoskeletal system defects
   clubfoot, 353
   congenital dislocation of hip, 353
   torticollis, 353
   wryneck, 353

N

Nalbuphine, use during labor, 213
Nalline, use during labor, 214
Narcan, use during labor, 214
Narcotic antagonists, use during labor, 214
Nasal passage, occlusion of, 350
Nausea (morning sickness), in pregnancy, 107
Necrotizing enterocolitis, 368
Negative balance, newborn, 303-304
Nembutal, use during labor, 212
Neonatal respiratory distress syndrome. See Hyaline membrane disease
Nervous system, newborn, 308-309, 317
Neural tube defects, 86
   anencephaly, 347
   congenital hydrocephalus, 347
   meningomyelocele, 348
   microcephaly, 348
   spina bifida, 348
Neurological disorders, birth defects, 348-349
Neurological maturity chart, 364
Nevus Flammeus, 315
Nevus vasculosus, 315
Newborn
   anogenital area, 307
   body measurements, 311-312
   breasts, 307
   circulatory system, 302
   first hours of life, 301
   gastrointestinal system, 306-307

heat regulation, 304-305
hematopoietic system, 303
immediate care of, 207-208
immune system, 310-311
negative balance, 303-304
nervous system, 308-309
physiological resilience, 303
respiration, 302, 305
sensory system, 309
skeletal system, 308
skin, 306
sleep states, 309-310, 319
umbilical cord, 306
urinary system, 307-308
vital signs, 305
See also Birth defects; High-risk newborn; Low birthweight infant.
Newborn assessment
abdomen, 316-317
Apgar, 313
Brazelton scale, 319
cry, 318
ears, 316
eyes, 316
genitals, 317
gestational age assessment, 313
head, 313-314
infant distress, signs of, 318-319
mouth, 316
nervous system, 317
skeletal system, 317
skin color, 315, 318
skin conditions, 315-316
umbilical stump, 316
vital signs, 317
Newborn care
body temperature, maintenance of, 321
circumcision, 323
comfort measures, 322
emotional care, 323-324
nutrition/feeding, 320-321
oxygenation, maintenance of, 319-320
positioning, 321
safety guidelines, 322
sleep, 323
Nitrous oxide with oxygen, general anesthesia, 215

Noninfectious thrombophlebitis, postpartum period, 292-293
Norplant, 66
NST (nonshivering thermogenesis), 304
Nutrition
breast feeding, 279-280, 283
newborn, 320-321
postpartum period, 270-271

O

Obstetrical history, recording of, 177
Occiput posterior presentation, 230-231
Oligohydramnios, 135
Omphalocele, 352
Ompholites, 368
Ophthalmia neonatorum, 340
Oral contraceptives
as contraception, 60-64
contraindications, 64
dangers of, 63
side effects, 62-63
types of, 61-62
Out-of-wedlock pregnancy, high-risk pregnancy, 124-125
Ovarian pregnancy, 132
Ovaries, 38-39
Over-the-counter drug and pregnancy, 165-167
Ovum, period of, 76-77
Ovum transfer, 49
Oxygen
in hyaline membrane disease, 333
maintenance of, newborn, 319-320
Oxytocin/oxytocic drugs
administration of, 240-241
after delivery, 206, 275
and labor, 181

P

Pain, labor, causes of, 221
Pain management, during pregnancy, 118
Para, definition of, 177
Paracervical block, 216
Paralysis, newborn, 335
Pare, Ambrose, 5

Parenthood, preparation for, 95-96
Paresthesias, 111
Parity, high-risk pregnancy, 125
Patent ductus, 349
Patent foramen ovale, 349
Pathological retraction ring, 228
Pelvic inflammatory disease (PID), 44
Pelvis, 35-38
   and complications of labor/delivery, 235
   regions of, 179
Penis, 34
Penthane, general anesthesia, 215
Perganol, 48
Peridural anesthesia, 216-217
Perineum
   healing, postpartum period, 266-267
   postpartum infection, 289
   postpartum period, 256
Peritonitis, postpartum period, 290-291
Pernicious vomiting, 135
Petechiae, 315
Phenobarbital
   in pregnancy, 170
   use during labor, 212
Phenylketonuria (PKU), 81, 353-354
   maternal PKU, 156
Phenytoin, 139
Phrenic nerve injury, newborn, 337
Physiological resilience, newborn, 303
Pica, 116
Pink show, 183
Pitocin, 240
PKU. See Phenylketonuria
Placenta
   abnormalities
      adherent placenta, 234
      in pregnancy, 125-127
      placenta accreta, 234
      retained placenta, 234
   development of, 71
   drug transfer, 162, 211-212
   functions of, 71, 73-74
   hormones of, 106
   and onset of labor, 182
   separation/expulsion in labor, 185, 206

Placenta previa, 125-126
Pneumonia
   newborn, 331-332
      aspiration pneumonia, 331
      causes of, 331
      infectious pneumonia, 331-332
      symptoms, 332
   postpartum period, 294
Pneumothorax, 333
Polydactylia, 80
Polyhydramnios, 134
Port-wine stain, 315
Postcoital test, 46
Postmaturity, 356
   induction of labor, 239
Postpartum complications
   breast disorders, 293-294
      breast abscess, 294
      mastitis, 293-294
   eclampsia, 296
   hematomas, 295-296
   hemorrhage, 285-288
   infections, 294-295
   noninfectious thrombophlebitis, 292-293
   psychosis, 296-297
   puerperal infection, 288-292
Postpartum period
   drugs used, 275-276
   nursing assessment/intervention, 263-275
   nursing goals, 263
   physiological changes
      abdominal wall, 256
      blood, 257
      breasts, 257
      cervix, 256
      hormones, 258
      lochia, 256
      perineum, 256
      skin, 257
      urinary tract, 256-257
      uterus, 255-256
      weight loss, 257
   psychological factors
      adjustment, stages of, 259-260
      parent-child bonding, 261, 272-273

postpartum blues, 262, 274
sexuality, 275
Precipitate delivery, 228-229
Pre-eclampsia, 137-140
    symptoms, 137-138
    treatment, 138-139
Pregnancy
    community resources, 96-97
    examinations
        initial visit, 98-99
        throughout pregnancy, 99-102
    exercise, 108-109, 116-117
    learning needs of parents to be, 96-97, 121-122
    nutrition, 101, 112-116
        minerals, 114
        protein, 114-115
        recommended changes, 113-114
        vitamins, 115-116
    pain management, 118
    physiological changes, 102-106
        breasts, 104
        cardiovascular system, 105
        endocrine system, 106
        gastrointestinal system, 104
        metabolism, 105
        musculoskeletal system, 106
        nursing care related to, 106-118
        reproductive system, 102-103
        respiratory system, 105
        skin, 105-106
        urinary system, 105
    prenatal maternal care, 97-102
    problems, warning signs, 101
    psychological factors, 118-121
    sex, 118
    signs of, 97
    tests for, 377-378
    weight, 100
    working, 117
    See also High-risk pregnancy.
Premature rupture of membranes (PROM), 229
Prenatal screening
    alphafetoprotein test, 91-92, 382
    amniocentesis, 90, 378-379
    chorionic villi sampling, 91, 379

contraction stress test, 381-382
fetal heart monitoring, 380
fetal movement, assessment, 380
fetoscopy, 90-91, 379-380
future tests, 382
heterozygote screening, 92
for human placental lactogen, 380
lecithin-sphingomyelin ratio, 382
necessity for, 91
ultrasonography, 91, 378
Prepared childbirth
    advantages of, 225
    breathing techniques, 222, 223
    eclectic approaches, 223-224
    hypnosis, 224
    Lamaze method, 222
    nursing process and, 224-225
    positions used, 223, 224, 225
    Read method, 222
Preterm infants. *See* Low birthweight infants
Preterm labor
    at-risk mothers, test for, 247-249
    categories of, 243-244
    causes, 241-242
    definition, 241
    drugs used, 170, 244-247
    management, 243
    nursing process and, 242-243
Primary uterine inertia, 227
Primigravida, 184
    definition of, 177
Primipara, definition of, 177
Progesterone, 41
    and labor, 181
Progestin, birth control, 66
Prolactin, 257
Prolapsed cord, 231-232
    management, 232
    predisposing factors, 231
Propranolol, in pregnancy, 168
Prostaglandin E_2
    inducing labor, 241
    infusion for abortion, 128
Prostaglandins, and labor, 181-182
Prostate gland, 33
Protein, in pregnancy, 114-115

Protein disorders, 81
Proximidistal growth, 76
Psychological factors
  Cesarean section, 237
  infertility, 51
  labor, 203-204, 224
  parental reactions
    birth defects, 357
    low birthweight infants, 373-374
  postpartum period
    adjustment, stages of, 259-260
    postpartum blues, 262, 274
    psychosis, 296-297
  pregnancy, 118-121
  psychosocial problems and mother-to-be, 159-161
  spontaneous abortion, 131
Psychosis, postpartum period, 296-297
Pubic areas, shaving, 186
Pudendal block, 216
Puerperal infection
  causes of, 288, 289
  endometritis, 289-290
  infectious thrombophlebitis, 290
  nursing process and, 291-292
  peritonitis, 290-291
  predisposing factors, 288
  types of, 289
Puerperal pulmonary embolus, 157
Puerperium
  definition of, 255
  See also Postpartum period.
Pulmonary aspiration, 215
Pulmonary hemorrhage, 333
Pulse, newborn, 305
Purpura, 315
Pyelonephritis, in pregnancy, 153-154
Pyloric stenosis, 351

R

Radioimmunoassay, pregnancy tests, 377
Radioreceptor assay (RRA), pregnancy tests, 377
Rashes, newborn, 316
Read method, 222
Reflexes, newborn, 308-309

Regional anesthesia
  continuous caudal block, 217-218
  paracervical block, 216
  peridural anesthesia, 216-217
  pudendal block, 216
Renaissance, maternal care, 5
Reproductive system
  change in pregnancy, 102-103
  female, 35-42
  male, 33-35
Reserpine, in pregnancy, 168
Respiration, newborn, 302, 305
Respiratory defects
  congenital laryngeal stridor, 350
  diaphragmatic hernia, 350
  nasal passage, occlusion of, 350
Respiratory disease, in pregnancy, 151-152
Respiratory system, change in pregnancy, 105
Restitution, mechanism of labor, 183
Retained placenta, 234
Retrograde ejaculation, 47
Retrolental fibroplasia, 333
Rh incompatibility
  newborn, 337-339
    erythroblastosis fetalis, 338
    treatment, 339
  and pregnancy, 135-136
Rhogam, 338
Rhythm method, as contraception, 56-58
Right occiput anterior (ROA), 180
Right sacroposterior (RSP), 181
Ritodrine, 245-246
  in pregnancy, 171
Romans (ancient), maternal care, 4
Rooting reflex, 308
Rotation, fetal, 230
RU 486, abortion, 128
Rubella, 85
  newborn, 341-342
  in pregnancy, 155
Rueff, Jakob, 5

S

Sabin-Feldman dye test, 155
Salbutomol, in pregnancy, 171

Saline induction, abortion, 128-129
Schultze mechanism, 185
Scopolamine, use during labor, 214
Seconal, use during labor, 212
Sedatives
  postpartum period, 275
  in pregnancy, 167, 170
  use during labor, 212-213
Semen analysis, 46-47
Seminal vesicles, 33
Sensory stimulation, newborn, 323
Sensory system, newborn, 309
Seventeenth century, maternal care, 5
Sex, during pregnancy, 118
Sex chromosome abnormalities, 82
Sex determination, fetus, 79
Sexual ambiguity, 352
Sexual dysfunction, infertility, 45, 50-51
Sexuality, postpartum period, 275
Shoulder-traverse lie presentation, 231
Sickle cell disease, 92
Sight, newborn, 309
Silver nitrate, 207, 340
Sims-Huhner test, 46
Skeletal injuries, newborn, 335
Skeletal system, newborn, 308, 317
Skin
  change in pregnancy, 105-106
  newborn, 306
  postpartum period, 257
Skin color, newborn, 302, 315, 318
Skin conditions, newborn, 315-316
Sleep
  newborn needs, 323
  postpartum period, 266
  sleep state of newborn, 309-310, 319
Smell, newborn, 309
Smoking, in pregnancy, 85, 163
Socioeconomic factors, high-risk pregnancy, 123
Sodium amytal, in pregnancy, 170
Soranus of Ephesus, 4
Sperm, 34-35
Spermicides, as contraception, 55-56
Spina bifida, 348
Spiramycin, 155

Spontaneous abortion
  etiology of causation, 130
  psychological factors, 131
  symptoms, 130
  treatment, 130-131
  types of, 127
Stagnant anoxia, 329
Standard of Practice, nursing, 24-28
Startle reflex, 308
Statistical terms, definitions, 11
Stenosis, 349
Sterilization
  as contraception, 64-65
  tubal ligation, 64-65
  vasectomy, 64-65
Stilbestrol, postpartum period, 275
Stimulants, in pregnancy, 163
Stools, newborn, 307
Strawberry marks, 315
Subarachnoid anesthesia, 218-219
Sucking reflex, 308
Superantagonist, birth control, 66
Supine hypotensive syndrome, in pregnancy, 105
Surrogate motherhood, 50
Susrata, 4
Synthroid, 48
Syntocin, 240
  and lactation, 280
Syphilis, 86
  newborn, 341
  in pregnancy, 152
Systemic abnormalities, infertility, 45, 48-49

T

Tachycardia, fetus, 197-198, 199
Tachypnea, 330
Tachysystole, 194
Taste, newborn, 309
Tay-Sachs disease, 82, 92, 354
Teratogens and birth defects
  alcohol, 84-85
  drugs, 84
  effects of, 82-83
  principles of teratogenesis, 83

research conditions, 83-84
smoking, 85
Terbutaline sulfate, 171, 246
Testes, 33
Testosterone, 35
Tetonic contractions, 194
Tetralogy of Fallot, 349
Thiazides, in pregnancy, 169
Thrush, 340-341
T. mycoplasma infection, 44, 47
Tocolytic agents, in pregnancy, 170
Tongue thrust, 321
Tongue tie, 351
Tonic neck reflex, 308
"TORCH" complex of infections, 85-86, 340-341
Torticollis, 353
Toxoplasmosis, 85
  in pregnancy, 154-155
Tracheoesophageal fistula, 351
Tranquilizers, use during labor, 214
Transition, labor, 204
Transposition of the great vessels, 349
Transverse lie, 181
Trends, statistical, modern, 11-21
Trisomy 13-15/trisomy 17-18, 81
Trophoblastic disease, 132-133
Tubal ligation, 64-65
Tubal pregnancy. See Ectopic pregnancy
Tuberculosis (TB), in pregnancy, 151-152
Turner's syndrome, 82
Twentieth century, maternal care, 6-10

U

Ultrasonic monitoring device, fetal heart rate, 193
Ultrasonography, 91, 378
Umbilical cord
  care of, 207
  newborn, 306
Umbilical hernia, 352
Umbilical stump, assessment of, 316
Urethra, 33
Urinary infections, in pregnancy, 153-154

Urinary system
  change in pregnancy, 105
  newborn, 307-308
Urinary tract, postpartum period, 256-257, 294
Uterine distension, and labor, 182
Uterine dysfunction, 227-228
Uterine wall, 39
Uterus, 39
  and complications of labor/delivery, 234-235
  inversion of, 250
  and onset of labor, 182
  postpartum assessment, 264
  postpartum period, 255-256
  rupture of, 249

V

Vaccine, birth control, 66
Vacuum extraction, fetus, 238-239
Vagina, 40
  and complications of labor/delivery, 235
  postpartum infection, 289
Vaginal discharge
  labor, 201-202
  in pregnancy, 110
Vaginal ring, birth control, 66
Vaginal sponge, as contraception, 56
Valium
  in pregnancy, 169
  use during labor, 214
Varicella, in pregnancy, 155-156
Varicosites, in pregnancy, 105, 109
Vas deferens, 33
Vasectomy, 64-65
Vasodilator, in pregnancy, 169
Vegetarianism, in pregnancy, 116
Venereal disease, in pregnancy, 152
Ventricular septal defects, 349
Vistaril, use during labor, 214
Vital signs
  newborn, 305, 317
  postpartum period, 269-270
Vitamin K, newborn, 207
Vitamins, in pregnancy, 115-116, 167

Vomiting, pernicious, 135
Vulva
   and complications of labor/delivery, 235
   postpartum infection, 289

W

Walking reflex, 308
Weight
   loss, postpartum period, 257
   pregnancy, 100
White classification system, 143
WHO, definition of maternity care, 6-7
Winking reflex, 308
Witches milk, 307
Working, during pregnancy, 117
Wryneck, 353

Y

Yawning reflex, 308

Z

Zona drilling, 49
Zoster immune globulin, 156
Zoster immune plasma, 156
Zygote, 76

About the Authors

Beverly Raff, RN, PhD, is vice president for professional services at the March of Dimes Birth Defects Foundation headquarters in White Plains, New York. She was formerly associate professor of maternity nursing at Adelphi University. In 1986 she was named Perinatal Nurse of the Year by the American Nurses Association.

Arlyne Friesner, RN, EdD, former dean of the College of New Rochelle School of Nursing, is currently working as a consultant and writer.